HUMAN DEVELOPMENT
An Interactional Perspective

DEVELOPMENTAL PSYCHOLOGY SERIES

SERIES EDITOR
Harry Beilin

Developmental Psychology Program
City University of New York Graduate School
New York, New York

In Preparation

EUGENE S. GOLLIN. (Editor). *Malformations of Development:*
Biological and Psychological Sources and Consequences

ALLEN W. GOTTFRIED. (Editor). *Home Environment and Early*
Cognitive Development: Longitudinal Research

Published

DAVID MAGNUSSON AND VERNON L. ALLEN. (Editors). *Human*
Development: An Interactional Perspective

DIANE L. BRIDGEMAN. (Editor). *The Nature of Prosocial Development:*
Interdisciplinary Theories and Strategies

ROBERT L. LEAHY. (Editor). *The Child's Construction of Social Inequality*

RICHARD LESH and MARSHA LANDAU. (Editors). *Acquisition of*
Mathematics Concepts and Processes

MARSHA B. LISS. (Editor). *Social and Cognitive Skills:*
Sex Roles and Children's Play

DAVID F. LANCY. *Cross-Cultural Studies in Cognition and Mathematics*

HERBERT P. GINSBURG. (Editor). *The Development of*
Mathematical Thinking

MICHAEL POTEGAL. (Editor). *Spatial Abilities: Development and*
Physiological Foundations

NANCY EISENBERG. (Editor). *The Development of Prosocial Behavior*

WILLIAM J. FRIEDMAN. (Editor). *The Developmental Psychology of Time*

SIDNEY STRAUSS. (Editor). *U-Shaped Behavioral Growth*

The list of titles in this series continues on the last page of this volume.

HUMAN DEVELOPMENT
An Interactional Perspective

Edited by

DAVID MAGNUSSON
Department of Psychology
University of Stockholm
Stockholm, Sweden

VERNON L. ALLEN
Department of Psychology
University of Wisconsin—Madison
Madison, Wisconsin

1983

ACADEMIC PRESS
A Subsidiary of Harcourt Brace Jovanovich, Publishers
New York   London
Paris   San Diego   San Francisco   São Paulo   Sidney   Tokyo   Toronto

155
H918

ACADEMIC PRESS, INC.
111 Fifth Avenue, New York, New York 10003

United Kingdom Edition published by
ACADEMIC PRESS, INC. (LONDON) LTD.
24/28 Oval Road, London NW1   7DX

Library of Congress Cataloging in Publication Data
Main entry under title:

Human development: an interactional perspective.

    Bibliography: p.
    Includes indexes.
    1. Developmental psychology--Addresses, essays,
lectures. 2. Personality and situation--Addresses,
essays, lectures. I. Magnusson, David. II. Allen,
Vernon L., Date
BF713.5.H78 1983   155   83-7077
ISBN 0-12-465480-0

Contents

Contributors   xiii

Preface   xvii

I
INTRODUCTION

1
An Interactional Perspective for Human Development   3

DAVID MAGNUSSON and VERNON L. ALLEN

Contemporaneous and Developmental Perspectives   3
A Mechanistic versus a Dynamic Model of Man   6
An Interactional Position   7
The Environment   9
The Person   18
The Developing Person in the Environment   22
Summary and Conclusions   26
References   27

II
THE ENVIRONMENT: ITS ROLE IN HUMAN DEVELOPMENT

2
Patterns of Infant–Mother Attachment as Related to Maternal Care: Their Early History and Their Contribution to Continuity   35

MARY D. SALTER AINSWORTH

Description of the Ainsworth Longitudinal Project   35
Patterns of Attachment as Assessed in the Strange Situation   36
Attachment, Stability, and Continuity   44
Direction of Effects in Mother–Infant Interaction   46
Attachment Research and the Person–Environment Interaction Perspective   50
References   53

3
Conceptions of Environment in Childrearing Interactions   57

MARIAN RADKE-YARROW and LEON KUCZYNSKI

A History of Orientations   58
Concepts of Interaction   60
Concepts and Contents of Rearing Environments   62
Rearing Studies of Normal and Depressed Mothers   66
Conclusions and Prospects   71
References   74

4
The "Person" Characteristics of Children and the Family as Environment   75

ELEANOR E. MACCOBY and CAROL NAGY JACKLIN

Interactions of Child and Parent Characteristics   76
The "Effective" Environment of Parent and Child   79
Mutual Influence: The Changing Interpersonal Environment   82
Longer-Term Interactions   85
Conclusions   89
References   90

5
The Person–Environment Relationship: Lessons from Families with Preterm Infants   93

BARBARA R. TINSLEY and ROSS D. PARKE

The Impact of Children on Families: Some Recent Research Trends   93
The Impact of the Premature Infant on the Caregiver–Infant Relationship   95

Beyond the Mother–Infant Dyad: The Father–Infant Dyad and the Family Triad as
  Contexts for Development of the Preterm Infant   97
Community Support Systems and Preterm Infants   100
Conclusion   106
References   106

6

Physical and Social Environment as Factors in Development   111

JOACHIM F. WOHLWILL

From the Social to the Physical Environment—and Back   111
Physical and Social Environment Compared   114
Developmentally Relevant Forms of the Environment–Behavior Relationship   117
Developmental Changes in the Role of Environmental Modes   120
Evidence Concerning the Environment–Development Interaction   123
Conclusion   125
References   127

III
THE PERSON: COGNITIVE PROCESSES

7

The Development of Personal Theories of Reality from an Interactional Perspective   133

SEYMOUR EPSTEIN and NANCY ERSKINE

The Nature of Personal Theories of Reality   133
The Progress of Scientific and Personal Theories   137
Precursors to a Theory of Reality   140
Development of a Personal Theory of Reality during Adolescence   144
Development of a Personal Theory of Reality during Adulthood   145
References   146

8

Delay of Gratification as Process and as Person Variable in Development   149

WALTER MISCHEL

Combining Experimental and Correlational Strategies   149
Processes Underlying Effective Delay: Situational and Cognitive Determinants 152
Delay Ability as a Person Variable   157
Long-Term Correlates of Early Waiting Behavior   159
Conclusions   163
References   164

9
Concern with One's Competence: Developmental Shifts in Person–Environment Interaction   167
HEINZ HECKHAUSEN

The Developing Self as an Agent of Change in Coping with Interactions	168
A Developmental Step Reversing the Implications of Being Praised or Blamed	173
A Midlife Trap for Achievement-Motivated Executives at the Top Level	177
Conclusions	182
References	183

10
Person–Situation Interactions in Human Development: Cognitive Factors and Coping Strategies   187
IRWIN G. SARASON and BARBARA R. SARASON

Person–Situation Interactions	187
Interactions and Continuity versus Change	188
Intervention and Person–Situation Interaction Systems	189
Summary and Conclusions	195
References	197

IV
THE PERSON: BIOLOGICAL PROCESSES

11
The Role of Genes as Determinants of Behavior   201
MARIANNE RASMUSON

Genes and Development	201
Sex Determination	203
Single Genes Can Affect Behavior	204
Multifactorial Background and Threshold Traits	205
Quantitative Traits	206
Gene–Environment Interaction	209
An Evolutionary Perspective	210
Conclusions	211
References	212

12
Endocrinology and Behavior   213
PETER ENEROTH

Receptors	214
Cyclicity	216
Conclusions	218
References	219

13

The Inheritance of Human Deviance   221

SARNOFF A. MEDNICK, TERRIE E. MOFFITT, VICKI POLLOCK, SHARON TALOVIC,
WILLIAM F. GABRIELLI, JR., and KATHERINE T. VAN DUSEN

Genetics in the Etiology of Schizophrenia	222
Genetics in the Etiology of Alcoholism	225
Genetics in the Etiology of Criminal Behavior	229
What Is Inherited in Deviance?	237
Conclusion	239
References	240

14

Biological and Psychosocial Risk Factors and Development during Childhood   243

BERNHARD MEYER-PROBST, HANS-DIETER RÖSLER, and HELFRIED TEICHMANN

The Rostock Longitudinal Study on Two-Year-Olds	244
The Rostock Longitudinal Study on Six-Year-Olds	252
References	258

15

From Emotional State to Emotional Expression: Emotional Development from the Perspective of Person–Environment Interaction   261

MICHAEL LEWIS and LINDA MICHALSON

The Noninteractive, Biological Approach to Emotional Development	264
An Interactive, Socialization Model of Emotional Development	265
Socialization Rules	268
Implications for Personality Development and Psychopathology	272
References	274

V

SOCIAL ADAPTATION: THE PERSON IN THE ENVIRONMENT

16

A "Goodness of Fit" Model of Person–Context Interaction   279

RICHARD M. LERNER

The "Goodness of Fit" Model	280
Empirical Support for the Goodness of Fit Model	282
Enhancing Goodness of Fit	290
References	292

17

Statistical and Personal Interactions: Facets and Perspectives 295

MICHAEL RUTTER

Additive Co-action	296
Synergistic Interaction	297
Buffering Effects	300
Ordinal and Disordinal Interactions	301
Transactional Effects	305
Ecological Considerations	307
Personal Interactions as Descriptors of the Environment	309
Interactions as Selectors of Environments	310
Interactions in Terms of Opportunities	313
Conclusions	314
References	315

18

The Stability of Change:
Psychosocial Development from Adolescence to Young Adulthood 321

RICHARD JESSOR

A Prospective Study of Problem Behavior and Psychosocial Development	322
Psychosocial Change from Adolescence to Young Adulthood	324
The Temporal Stability of Changing Psychosocial Attributes	330
The Prediction of Differential Psychosocial Change	333
Predicting the Timing of Transition Behavior	338
Conclusions	340
References	341

19

Childhood Environment and Maturity of Defense Mechanisms 343

GEORGE E. VAILLANT

Ego Mechanisms of Defense: A Definition	344
Empirical Validation	346
The Failure of Childhood Environment to Predict Adult Mechanisms of Defense	350
Premorbid Predictors of Maturity of Defenses	350
Conclusion	352
References	352

20

Low School Achievement and Aggressive Behavior in
Adolescent Boys 353

DAN OLWEUS

Basic Variables	354
Possible Hypotheses	354

Methods   356
Results   357
Discussion   362
References   365

VI
USES OF INTERACTIONAL PERSPECTIVE:
CONCEPTUAL AND METHODOLOGICAL ISSUES

21
Implications and Applications of an Interactional Perspective for Human Development   369

DAVID MAGNUSSON and VERNON L. ALLEN

General Implications   370
Units of Analysis   371
Person versus Variable Approaches to Developmental Research   372
Prediction of Behavior versus Lawfulness of Processes   374
Stability Coefficients as Indicators of Temporal Consistency   375
Limitations of Cross-Sectional Research   378
A Plea for Longitudinal Research   378
Data Collection and Treatment   379
Analysis of Environments   381
An Interactional Model of Maladaptation, Stress, and Behavioral Disorders   382
A Final Comment   385
References   386

Subject Index   *389*

Contributors

Numbers in parentheses indicate the pages on which the authors' contributions begin.

Mary D. Salter Ainsworth (35), Department of Psychology, University of Virginia, Charlottesville, Virginia 22901

Vernon L. Allen (3, 369), Department of Psychology, University of Wisconsin—Madison, Madison, Wisconsin 53706

Peter Eneroth (213), Research and Development Laboratory, Department of Obstetrics and Gynecology, Karolinska Hospital, Stockholm, Sweden

Seymour Epstein (133), Department of Psychology, University of Massachusetts, Amherst, Massachusetts 01003

Nancy Erskine (133), Department of Psychology, University of Massachusetts, Amherst, Massachusetts 01003

William F. Gabrielli, Jr.[1] (221), Social Science Research Institute, University of Southern California, University Park, Los Angeles, California 90089

Heinz Heckhausen[2] (167), Psychologisches Institut, Ruhr Universität, Bochum, Federal Republic of Germany

Carol Nagy Jacklin (75), Department of Psychology, Stanford University, Stanford, California 94305

Richard Jessor (321), Institute of Behavioral Science, University of Colorado, Boulder, Colorado 80309

[1]Present address: Institute for Behavioral Genetics, University of Colorado, Boulder, Colorado 80309.

[2]Present address: Max-Planck-Institut für Psychologische Forschung, Munich, Federal Republic of Germany.

Leon Kuczynski (57), Department of Health and Human Services, National Institutes of Health, Bethesda, Maryland 20205

Richard M. Lerner (279), Department of Individual and Family Studies, College of Human Development, The Pennsylvania State University, University Park, Pennsylvania 16802

Michael Lewis (261), Institute for the Study of Child Development, Department of Pediatrics, Rutgers Medical School, University of Medicine and Dentistry of New Jersey, New Brunswick, New Jersey 08903

Eleanor E. Maccoby (75), Department of Psychology, Stanford University, Stanford, California 94305

David Magnusson (3, 369), Department of Psychology, University of Stockholm, Stockholm, Sweden

Sarnoff A. Mednick (221), Social Science Research Institute, University of Southern California, University Park, Los Angeles, California 90089

Bernhard Meyer-Probst (243), Kinderneuropsychiatrische Abt der Nervenklinik, Wilhelm Pieck Universität, Rostock 9, German Democratic Republic

Linda Michalson (261), Institute for the Study of Child Development, Department of Pediatrics, Rutgers Medical School, University of Medicine and Dentistry of New Jersey, New Brunswick, New Jersey 08903

Walter Mischel (149), Department of Psychology, Stanford University, Stanford, California 94305

Terrie E. Moffitt (221), Social Science Research Institute, University of Southern California, University Park, Los Angeles, California 90089

Dan Olweus (353), Department of Personality Psychology, University of Bergen, Bergen, Norway

Ross D. Parke (93), Department of Psychology, University of Illinois at Urbana-Champaign, Champaign, Illinois 61820

Vicki Pollock (221), Social Science Research Institute, University of Southern California, University Park, Los Angeles, California 90089

Marian Radke-Yarrow (57), Department of Health and Human Services, National Institutes of Health, Bethesda, Maryland 20205

Marianne Rasmuson (201), Department of Genetics, University of Umeå, Umeå, Sweden

Hans-Dieter Rösler (243), Kinderneuropsychiatrische Abt der Nervenklinik, Wilhelm Pieck Universität, Rostock 9, German Democratic Republic

Michael Rutter (295), Department of Child and Adolescent Psychiatry, Institute of Psychiatry, De Crespigny Park, Denmark Hill, London, SE5 8AF, Great Britain

Barbara R. Sarason (187), Department of Psychology NI-25, University of Washington, Seattle, Washington 98195

Irwin G. Sarason (187), Department of Psychology NI-25, University of Washington, Seattle, Washington 98195

Sharon Talovic (221), Social Science Research Institute, University of Southern California, University Park, Los Angeles, California 90089

Helfried Teichmann (243), Kinderneuropsychiatrische Abt der Nervenklinik, Wilhelm Pieck Universität, Rostock 9, German Democratic Republic

Barbara R. Tinsley[3] (93), Department of Psychology, Wesleyan University, Middletown, Connecticut 06457

George E. Vaillant (343), Massachusetts Mental Health Center, Boston, Massachusetts 02115

Katherine T. Van Dusen (221), Social Science Research Institute, University of Southern California, University Park, Los Angeles, California 90089

Joachim F. Wohlwill (111), Division of Individual and Family Studies, College of Human Development, The Pennsylvania State University, University Park, Pennsylvania 16802

[3]Present address: Department of Psychology, University of Illinois at Urbana-Champaign, Champaign, Illinois 61820.

Preface

In this book, individual development from infancy to adulthood is presented as a process of continuous reciprocal interaction between the individual and the environment. More specifically, the volume focuses on (a) development of behavior as viewed from the perspective of person–environment interaction and (b) consequences of the interactional framework for further theory construction, empirical research, and methodological problems in developmental psychology.

An interactional approach to the analysis of human functioning has important theoretical and methodological consequences for psychological research and application. Two Stockholm conferences, in 1975 and 1979, were devoted to the analysis of behavior in a contemporaneous perspective. A natural next step was to consider human development from the perspective of person–environment interaction; this was the focus of interest for the third Stockholm conference, which was held from June 27 to July 2, 1982.

This book is based on that conference. It consists of six parts. The first and last parts are chapters written by the editors of this volume, and Parts II–V consist of the papers presented at the symposium.

The introductory chapter is an attempt by the editors to describe the present status of interactional psychology, with particular reference to the developmental perspective of human functioning, and to discuss certain conceptual distinctions that we believe are essential for the analysis of human development.

The papers from the symposium have been grouped into four categories, each prefaced by an introduction and commentary. Given the diversity of the issues dealt with, the grouping of the papers was not self-evident. Several of the papers could have referred to more than one of the categories. Finally, the papers were grouped under the following main themes:

Part II: The social and physical environments (Chapters 2–6)
Part III: Cognitions and competence (Chapters 7–10)
Part IV: Biological factors (Chapters 11–15)
Part V: Social adaptation and maladaptation (Chapters 16–20)

The total pattern of chapters reflects one goal we had when planning the book, namely, to cover different aspects of the person–environment interaction process. On the person side the chapters deal with both biological and psychological factors, and on the environment side both the physical and social environments are discussed. Both normal and deviant patterns of development are dealt with by the contributors, who represent the different viewpoints on human development and different research traditions adhered to and practiced in Europe and in the United States.

The publication of a book with this particular theme was based on the conviction that if the consequences of an interactional approach to the study of human development are made explicit and taken more seriously in empirical research, not only will we have a more effective psychological theory, but we will also be able to contribute more effectively to the formation of physical and social environments that are adapted to the needs and potentialities of individuals and groups. The last chapter of the book is an attempt by the editors to discuss and draw attention to implications that we believe are particularly important for further research on human development.

Several people contributed to making the conference successful and to the production of this book. First of all we want to express our gratitude to the participants for their contribution to the symposium and to this volume. Their scientific attitudes and knowledge led to fruitful, stimulating, and exciting discussions during the symposium.

The symposium was made possible by grants from the Swedish Tercentenary Fund and the Swedish Council for Research Planning. It was also supported by funds from IBM, the University of Stockholm, and the Department of Psychology of Stockholm University.

We are grateful to Patricia Allen, Lars R. Bergman, Urie Bronfenbrenner, J. Mc V. Hunt, Saul B. Sells, and Håkan Stattin for their valuable comments and suggestions on the first and final chapters. We also thank Ola Andersson, Gunnel Backenroth, Boel Bissmarck, and Bertil Törestad for their effectiveness in the preparation and carrying through of the symposium, and Boel Bissmarck, Ingrid Goobar, and Bertil Törestad for their editorial contributions to the manuscript.

I

Introduction

In the first chapter of this book we attempt to present the basic concepts of a person–environment interactional perspective on human development. It is not the purpose of this introductory chapter to provide a comprehensive review of theories and empirical research on individual development; it is, rather, to discuss and draw attention to what we regard as main aspects of the process of person–environment interaction during the course of individual development. To achieve these goals, we briefly discuss the basic systems in individuals and in the environment that are operating in the interaction process and how they operate together in the course of development.

At a very general level the main ideas behind what has been designated an interactional view here are not new. However obvious they may appear when they have been formulated—and they have been formulated in general terms for decades—they have had surprisingly little impact until recently on sophisticated theorizing and empirical research. It is the aim of this chapter to explicate the basic principles that comprise an interactional perspective and to emphasize the importance of taking them seriously in the area of human development.

HUMAN DEVELOPMENT:
AN INTERACTIONAL PERSPECTIVE

1

An Interactional Perspective for Human Development

DAVID MAGNUSSON   VERNON L. ALLEN

It seems self-evident that we need systematic research on human development. However, it might be worthwhile to make explicit the primary purposes and uses of developmental research:

1. Knowledge about the developmental processes of maturation and learning contributes to a deeper understanding of contemporaneous behavior at each stage of development.
2. An understanding of the process of individual development—the nature of the many complex factors and how they operate together—is of intellectual interest in itself.
3. Understanding the factors that underlie development makes it possible to create environments that are better suited to the needs and potentialities of individuals and groups, and this understanding thereby helps to promote better psychological and physical health over the life span.
4. An understanding of individual development may provide us with the basis for developing more effective intervention techniques designed to prevent maladaptive and antisocial behavior.

It is our firm belief that these goals can be better and more efficaciously pursued if developmental research is performed in the perspective of person–environment interaction as briefly summarized in the following sections.

Contemporaneous and Developmental Perspectives

Human behavior can be analyzed and discussed from either a contemporaneous (synchronic) or a developmental (diachronic) perspective. It is indeed

3

HUMAN DEVELOPMENT:
AN INTERACTIONAL PERSPECTIVE

possible and scientifically defensible to study behavior from a contemporaneous perspective, without giving any attention to the individual's past developmental history (as, for example, advocated by Kurt Lewin, 1948). Yet, an understanding of an individual's previous experiences can also contribute significantly to a better interpretation of his or her present behavior, just as a knowledge of the history of a society can help make its present condition more explicable. In this section we will first offer some comments on the contemporaneous and developmental approaches before moving on to a consideration of the interactional position.

THE CONTEMPORANEOUS PERSPECTIVE

In very general terms, it is possible to distinguish three main approaches to contemporaneous explanations for behavior. One approach gives primary emphasis to explanatory concepts based on characteristics of the *person*. Though different in many important respects, classic trait theory and psychodynamic theories are proponents of this approach.

In contrast to the person-oriented approach, other researchers have placed primary emphasis on the *environment* (particularly that part of it that can be delineated as the momentary situation) when explaining behavior contemporaneously. In this approach, the aim of research has been to find and define general laws of behavior as a function of the kind and intensity of external stimuli. Proponents of this approach can be found in stimulus–response (S–R) psychology, reinforcement theory, certain forms of field theory, and among social psychologists, for example.

In contrast to the approaches taken in traditional personality psychology, a third approach, *interactionism,* has been formulated on the basis of early theoretical formulations by researchers representing very different perspectives (behaviorists, trait psychologists, psychodynamicists, personologists, social psychologists, etc.) and on findings of empirical research during the last two decades concerning personality consistency and person–situation interaction (Endler & Magnusson, 1976; Magnusson & Endler, 1977). According to the interactional view, behavior is part of the continuously ongoing, bidirectional person–situation interaction in which the person is the intentional active agent (Magnusson, 1980a). It is fair to say that the interactional approach to the study of contemporaneous behavior has stimulated a considerable amount of research and that it is now widely accepted as a general framework for understanding behavior contemporaneously (see, e.g., Rutter, Chapter 17).

THE DEVELOPMENTAL PERSPECTIVE

In traditional research on behavior from a developmental perspective, a polarization between a person-oriented and an environment-oriented approach can also be discerned. The *person-oriented* approach is similar to but broader than the analogous approach in research on contemporaneous behavior. Advocates of this approach to development focus on the important role played by genetic and biological factors as determinants of individual development and emphasize the role of early experience. Much of the research in this tradition has dealt with the development of intelligence and personality traits and has been based on the general assumptions of "fixed intelligence" and "predetermined development," to use the terminology employed by Hunt (1961) in his classic book on the nature–nurture problem. This terminology reflects a strong emphasis on stability rather than change in the course of individual development, which is typical for this approach. The person-oriented approach, which emphasizes heredity and stability, has had advocates over the years, and this position is still alive and active (see, e.g., Eysenck & Eysenck, 1981).

The *environment-oriented* approach to the study of development emphasizes factors in the environment as the main determinants of individual development. Proponents of this approach stress the wide possibilities for change in the course of development owing to environmental conditions (see, e.g., Brim & Kagan, 1980). Though much of the research reflecting this approach has been concerned with intelligence, more interest has been devoted to social development than in the person-oriented approach. The environment-oriented approach has had many strong and influential proponents. Early behaviorism championed the view that conditions in the environment are strong determinants of development, as likewise do (though to a less extreme degree) present-day adherents of social learning theories, and a more current example of this orientation is found in the life-span development movement (Baltes, Reese, & Nesselroade, 1977).

The nature–nurture debate is concerned with issues that have strong societal implications. During the 1920s and 1930s eugenic ideas were influential in many countries. Eugenicists argued for such things as "sterilizing 'inferior' individuals, preserving 'racial purity', and restricting immigration of 'less developed' ethnic and racial groups [Rensberger, 1983, p. 30]." The argument that environmental conditions determine human development and that major changes in the course of development can be achieved by changing the environment has had a strong impact in Western countries, particularly after World War II. This influence is reflected not only in educational policies (e.g., enrichment and compensatory programs) and child-upbringing philosophy, but also in societal policies concerning the creation of physical and social environments.

The contrasting views espoused by supporters of the person- and environment-oriented positions often have been discussed in terms of the nature–nurture issue. These theories differ in the degree of emphasis placed on the view that human functioning is the result of the "unfolding" of predetermined tendencies, as opposed to the view that behavior is elicited and shaped by environmental stimuli. The two perspectives on the developmental process can be considered, respectively, as "push" (internal) versus "pull" (external) models for the development of individuals from childhood to maturity.

The early formulations of the problem in terms of hereditary *or* environmental factors as determinants of development were soon replaced by formulations in terms of "how much" influence can be attributed to nature and nurture. That this position is still of current interest is documented in a recent book by Eysenck and Eysenck (1981), in which the authors conclude, on the basis of a review of empirical research, that 70–75% of interindividual differences in major personality characteristics can be attributed to hereditary factors. The Jensen debate at the beginning of the 1970s, which stirred up so much emotional controversy (Jensen, 1969), was mainly concerned with the nature–nurture issue in terms of the question, "How much?" The reason for the elicitation of deep emotional reactions to this question was undoubtedly the strong political–societal implications of the different answers.

A third position on the nature–nurture issue was formulated by Anastasi (1958). She proposed that the basic scientific problem is not if one *or* the other of two main sources determines development or *how much* each of them contributes, but rather *how* hereditary and environmental factors, independently and in interaction, influence human development (cf. the discussion on the person–situation issue by Endler, 1973). Anastasi's position on the nature–nurture problem is consistent with the interactional approach to development, which is the perspective emphasized in this book. In developmental research this perspective has been emphasized by Hunt (1981), Lerner (1978), Sameroff (1975), and Ulvund (1980), among others.

A Mechanistic versus a Dynamic Model of Man

Among the basic models of man, two can be distinguished as having special importance for the present discussion: mechanistic and dynamic (Reese & Overton, 1970; Sarbin, 1977; Tyler, 1981). These two models use different root metaphors as concepts for explaining human behavior (Pepper, 1942).

The *mechanistic* model takes the machine as the basic metaphor. In this representation of psychological functioning, the individual is seen as passive and reactive rather than as an active agent. Complex psychological phenomena are regarded as being reducible to simpler elements or operations and, analogously, qualitative changes are reducible to quantitative changes. Laws remain constant and invariant over time, and strict determinism is assumed. Thus, independent and dependent variables can be clearly specified. Even though a mechanistic model of man may no longer be accepted explicitly by psychologists as a basic metaphor, it still exerts a strong influence on psychological theory and research.

The *dynamic* model is the converse of the mechanistic model because it views man as being inherently active and as acting upon the environment rather than as being only a passive recipient of external stimuli. The model emphasizes that all parts of an ongoing system are interrelated in a complex way, therefore it is not always meaningful to maintain the distinction between dependent and independent variables, since an element may be related to other elements in the process both as a cause and as an effect. Moreover, the individual is an organized configuration of parts, with the whole being greater than the sum of the parts and giving meaning to the constituent parts. What will be discussed in the next section as an interactional position is based upon the dynamic model of man.

An Interactional Position

As shown earlier, the historical process in research both on contemporaneous behavior and on development has led investigators to adopt an interactionistic position. Before discussing more extensively the components that are involved in person–environment interaction, we shall provide a brief overview.

Basic to an interactional view of individual functioning—in both a contemporaneous and a developmental perspective—is a focus on the continuously ongoing, bidirectional interaction between an individual and his or her environment (especially the situation in which the individual appears). In the interaction process, person and environment are regarded as indispensably linked to one another (see Lerner, Chapter 16, and Olweus, Chapter 20, in this volume). The individual and his or her environment(s) form, in Bell's (1979) words, "a moving, bidirectional system [p. 822]." Individual functioning in the process is not determined by person factors or situation factors in isolation, but by inseparable person and situation interactions. Thus, this view leads to the conclusion that models for individual functioning should focus simultaneously on person factors, environment factors, and the interaction between them. From a developmental point of view, the person–environment interaction is regarded as a continuously emerging and ever-changing process over time—as symbolized not by a circle but by a helix or spiral.

In all formulations of an interactional position the reciprocal character of the person–environment interaction is emphasized (Ittelson & Cantril, 1954). Reciprocity implies that the individual is influenced by his environment at each stage of development, and at the same time that he influences the environment. Thus, the individual is not a passive receiver of external stimulation from the outer world; rather, he is an active and intentional actor who interprets the information about environmental conditions and events and acts upon the environment in the frame of reference of his own mediating system and with his own plans, motives, goals, and so forth. He seeks some environments and avoids others, and he can change his environment by acting directly upon it. For example, his own behavior will determine to some extent the behavior of other family members who form an important aspect of his own environment (see, e.g., Davis & Hathaway, 1982). Examples of this aspect of the person–environment interaction and its implications for development can be found in the research on parent–child relationships (see Bell, 1968). The child is both the creation of and a creator of his or her environment (Kessen, 1979).

It should be emphasized that when we discuss development in terms of an interaction between an individual and his environment, we do not assume two separate parts of equal importance acting upon each other in a mechanistic way. The primary goal for psychology can be formulated as understanding and explaining why individuals feel, think, react, and act as they do in real-life situations—the main object of interest is the person. It is the task for research on development to contribute to that goal. However, it is a basic assumption of the interactional paradigm that individual functioning cannot be understood in isolation from the environmental context in which the individual develops and is functioning. Therefore, we are interested in the environment in order to understand the person.

A SYSTEM VIEW OF PERSON–ENVIRONMENT INTERACTION

As emphasized earlier, in an interactional framework the person and the environment are not viewed as discrete units, but as being interconnected in a dynamic process of mutual influence and change. From his specific perspective Lewin (1948) formulated this view: "The development of experimental psychology shows more and more definitely that a person and what might be called his psychological environment cannot be treated as separate entities but are dynamically one field [p. 174]."

Person–environment interaction can be conceptualized as being an open system—as one special instance of the concept of a living system that has been discussed by, for example, Bertalanffy (1968) and J. G. Miller (1978). (See also Bronfenbrenner, 1979a, who applies the system approach to development.) In addition to reciprocal influence among elements, open systems also are characterized by complexity, organization among subunits, the existence of feedback mechanisms, and accessibility to inputs from other systems (e.g., DeGreene, 1978).

Within the person–environment system itself the person is, of course, one system. The person is also composed of a set of subsystems that operate at another level of organization, that is: (*a*) a mediating system (including world conceptions and self-conception systems); (*b*) a biological–physiological system; and (*c*) an action–reaction system. We discuss these subsystems of the person in a later section.

Beyond the level of the person–environment interaction are other larger and more encompassing systems as well, such as the family, the small group, the community, and so on. Thus, other open systems exist both above and below the level of the person–environment interaction. A complete understanding of the process involved in the person–environment interaction requires giving attention to the fact that it is only one of many systems that are embedded within a more general hierarchical arrangement, and this hierarchy is characteristic of all living systems.

For our present purposes, some of the characteristics of a hierarchical model of systems have especially important implications, namely, that phenomena at a given level rely on all the lower levels, that phenomena at a given level may be controlled by higher levels, and that new properties emerge at each successively higher level.

Viewed in the broad perspective of levels of systems, it becomes clear that any attempt to explain the process by which the person–environment interaction occurs may be greatly enriched by (or may even require) information taken from systems operating at higher and lower levels also. For example, the nature of processes occurring in a system at a higher level may strongly influence (and set limits on) the processes and outcomes that occur at the level of the person–environment interaction. Bronfenbrenner's (1977a,b, 1979b) insightful and stimulating analysis of organizational levels in the ecology demonstrates that this approach has great potential for contributing to the understanding of developmental processes. In this book, the importance of this view is emphasized by Tinsley and Parke (Chapter 5).

In sum, then, we conceptualize person–environment interaction as an open system, and as being only one of many systems existing within a hierarchical arrangement of systems that extend from the micro-level (e.g., physiological processes) to the macro-level (society and culture). A more satisfactory knowledge about this total hierarchy of systems, and their interactions over time, should contribute to better understanding of human development. The precise nature of the processes underlying development in a person–environment system (whether continuous or discontinuous) will depend upon a variety of factors present in the person and the environment.

In the next two major sections we shall discuss the environment and person components involved in the interactional process. Within the limited space available, we can only point to some of the most important elements of these very complex systems.

The Environment

That behavior cannot be understood contemporaneously without considering the environmental context in which it occurs has been emphasized for decades, not only by psychologists, but also by anthropologists, by sociologists, and by those having an ethological view, among others (see Magnusson, 1982). Though most of the discussion about the environment has concentrated on contemporaneous view of behavior, it is obvious that the points made are equally important for analysis and discussion of individual functioning from a developmental perspective (see Bloom, 1964; Bronfenbrenner, 1979b; Hautamäki, 1982; Vygotsky, 1929, 1963, 1974; Wasserman & Lewis, 1982). This is certainly true when the issue under consideration is human development from the perspective of person–environment interaction.

The role of the situations that individuals encounter during the course of development was stressed as early as the 1920s by Thomas (1927, 1928). At that early time, Thomas also discussed many of the problems that are the focus of attention in discussions and research on environments today. He noted the distinction between actual and perceived environments and situations (an issue that will be touched upon later in this section); he discussed the problems connected with defining and demarcating a situation; and he argued that situational conditions must be incorporated in models of behavior.

In spite of the theoretical formulations about the importance of considering the environmental context in models of human behavior, surprisingly little theoretical and empirical research has been done that aims to conceptualize and categorize environments and situations so as to make it possible to treat the environmental side of the person–environment interaction in a systematic, scientific way (see, e.g., Barker, 1968; Bloom, 1964; Sells, 1963). However, during the 1970s, mainly as a result of the intense debate on personality consistency and the theory and empirical research in an interactional framework, theoretical and empirical work on environments and situations has grown and become an important and interesting field of research in personality (see, e.g., Magnusson, 1978, 1981a). Another line of research developed under the heading of environmental psychology has become a strong and important field with contributions of great importance also for behavior in a developmental perspective, particularly with respect to person–environment interactions (see Russell & Ward, 1982, for a recent review).

Systematic analysis of environments and situations imply many difficult theoretical and methodological problems. They have been dealt with in more detail in other connections (see, e.g., Magnusson, 1978, 1981a,b,c; Pervin, 1978). Here a few aspects of direct importance for the issue under consideration will be briefly touched upon.

LEVELS OF OPERATING FACTORS

The total environment in which individuals develop forms a complex system of physical–geographical, social, and cultural factors that interact with each other and with the individuals living and acting in it (Bloom, 1964). Directly and indirectly the environment influences an individual's behavior at many levels of generality. Of course, there does not exist any given set of boundaries demarcating in an obvious way different levels in the hierarchical system of operating factors. However, as a basis for systematic analysis and discussion of the role of environmental factors in the person–environment interaction process, the environment can be broken down into levels of analysis along a continuum ranging from a macro-level to a micro-level (see Bronfenbrenner, 1977a, 1979a; Craik & Zube, 1976; Magnusson, Dunér, & Zetterblom, 1975; Moos, 1973; Stokols, 1977) or ordered along a dimension of proximity to the individuals who are perceiving and acting in it (Jessor, 1981; Jessor & Jessor, 1973; Pervin, 1978).

The authors referred to earlier (and others) have presented different demarcation points with respect to levels of analysis of the environment. For simplicity of discussion we will distinguish three levels, namely, momentary situations, micro-environments, and macro-environments. As stated above, the demarcations between levels are to some extent arbitrary, and the concepts are fuzzy. Each subsidiary level is embedded in the higher levels, upon which its functioning depends.

The *actual situation* (as distinguished from the perceived situation) can be defined as that part of the environment that is accessible to sensory perception on a certain occasion (Magnusson, 1981b). The *perceived momentary situation* is an actual situation that is interpreted and to which meaning is attributed in the frame of the micro- and macro-environments in which it is embedded.

In a developmental perspective, situations play an important role because it is in actual situations that we encounter and form our conceptions about the world and develop specific kinds of behavior for dealing with it. Situations present (at different levels of specification) the information that we process, and they offer the feedback necessary for building valid conceptions of the outer world. Knowledge about the kinds of actual situations that an individual has encountered, along with the accompanying physical, social, and cultural micro-environments, will help us understand behavior at different stages of development.

The *micro-level* of the environment may be defined as that part of the total physical and social environment that an individual is in contact with and can interact with directly in daily life during a certain period of time (in the family, at school, at work, during leisure time, etc.). The micro-environment is, to some extent, specific to individuals even within the same family. This is important from a developmental perspective because the micro-environment determines the types of situations an individual will encounter.

The *macro-level* of the environment is that part of the total environment that in some way or another influences and determines the character and functioning of the micro-environment. For the social environment this involves the physical, social, cultural, economic, and political structure of the society in which individuals grow up, including technology, language, housing, laws and regulations, customs, etc. At this level the environment is common to most members of groups living in it.

Before leaving the discussion of levels of environmental influence on development, comments should be made about the role of these levels in person–environment interaction. Models for the view of contemporaneous behavior have mainly been concerned with the individual's interaction with the environment at the level of situations, that is, with person–situation interactions (see, e.g., Magnusson & Endler, 1977). However, for an understanding of many important aspects of development it is essential to incorporate different levels of the total environment in the paradigm of developmental research. This is the reason that this book is devoted to the broader perspective of person–environment interaction, of which person–situation interaction is a subsystem.

CHARACTERISTICS OF THE ENVIRONMENT

Within each of the vertical levels (macro-level, micro-level, and situation) environments differ with respect to factors that are important to human development. A distinction has been made between *structural* characteristics (such as complexity, clarity, strength, promotive versus restrictive) and *content* characteristics (such as tasks, goals, paths, rules, roles, expectancies, and norms) that are offered by the social environment (Magnusson, 1978). One of the most important environmental factors for human development operates at all levels of environment: the extent to which the environment promotes or restricts various kinds of behaviors in the social and physical environments (both man-made and natural). At a very general level environments differ, for example, with respect to the paths they allow and demand for reaching individual goals (Arsenian & Arsenian, 1948). In the area of cognitive development, factors in the micro-environment have been discussed by, among others, Elardo, Bradley, and Caldwell (1975), who dealt with *complexity;* by Yarrow, Rubenstein, Pedersen, and Jankowski (1972), who dealt with *responsiveness;* by Yarrow, Rubenstein, and Pedersen (1975), who dealt with *variety* in the micro-environment; and by Wachs (1979), who investigated environmental *specificity.*

FUNCTIONS OF THE ENVIRONMENT

The environment serves two important functions: It is a source of *active stimulation,* and it provides a *general context* within which specific behaviors occur (see Wohlwill, 1973).

In discussing the environment as a source of stimulation and the role of such stimulation for individual development, a central concept is *optimal stimulation* (Hebb, 1955; Leuba, 1955), with its subconcepts *preference* (the preferred level of stimulation) and *enhancement* (the developmentally optimal level of stimulation) (see Wachs, 1977). Optimal stimulation must be discussed with regard to time and age of the individual. As pointed out by Wohlwill (1973), much research on the role of environmental stimulation in individual development seems to imply a monotonic relation between amount or diversity of external stimulation and optimal development. However, there is enough empirical evidence to suggest that there is an optimal level of stimulation with respect to both preference and enhancement. Either too little or too much stimulation will result in less satisfaction and less adequate development than occurs with intermediate stimulation. A good example can be found in empirical research on stress, in which too high and too low demands on activity both lead to the same kind and amount of physiological and psychological stress reactions.

What constitutes optimal environmental stimulation varies among individuals and with time and age for an individual, and it varies between the sexes (see Uzgiris, 1977; Wachs, 1979). A certain level of stimulation does not have the same effect on an individual at all points in time and at all ages. The extent to which changes in optimal stimulation take place depends, among other things, on the type of person and kinds of environmental factors that are involved. The optimal level of stimulation will vary depending upon each individual's own adaptation level, which is based on prior experience, learning, and maturational factors.

Optimal stimulation can be particularly critical during specific periods of age. This is the case when the organism is prepared for and responsive to stimulation that will not have the same effect at other stages of development (see the discussion on readiness, p. 25, 26). The crucial role of optimal stimulation at a critical period of development is demonstrated in the findings by Hubel and Wiesel (1970), who showed that the ocular system of kittens does not develop adequately, and will not be able to recover later, if the necessary patterned stimulation is not available during the first period of life.

In addition to the important function of providing stimulation through the discrete factors that reside in the environment and actively impinge on the organism, another function performed by the environment is to provide a *context*, or frame of reference, for ongoing behavior. As a general context for behavior, the external environment is not a direct source of stimulation but is primarily a stage upon which a wide range of behaviors can be manifested.

THE ENVIRONMENT AS A CARRIER OF INFORMATION

When discussing the environment in terms of optimal stimulation and context for behavior, an important distinction between the environment as a releaser of responses and the environment as a carrier of information must be maintained. These different views can refer to classical learning theory and modern social learning theories. In classical learning theory emphasis is placed on the establishment of S–R contingencies in which responses are "stamped in" as reactions to preceding stimuli and events. In contrast, modern social learning theories assume that behavior develops in a learning process in which two types of perceived contingencies are formed, (*a*) situation outcome contingencies (implying that certain situational conditions will lead to certain outcomes); and (*b*) behavior outcome contingencies (implying that certain actions from the individual himself will have certain predictable consequences). According to this view the environment not only serves as a complex of stimuli to which an individual reacts. It also offers the information that makes it possible to make valid predictions about the outer world, that is, to exert *predictive control*. And it makes it possible to foresee the outcomes of different lines of action as a basis for effective purposive action, that is, to exert *action control*. For development, Aronfreed (1968) summarizes the position:

> One of the points of agreement among contemporary versions of general behavior theory is on the requirement that direct stimulus control must be subordinated to representational cognition. . . . The mediational power of cognitive representation therefore allows the child's conduct to be governed with a certain amount of consistency that could not be produced, if his actions were closely bound to immediate situations [pp. 68–69].

Using this perspective, optimal stimulation for development presupposes two conditions in the actual environment: (*a*) consistent patterning; and (*b*) influencability (Magnusson, 1980b; Mineka & Kihlström, 1978).

The first requirement for optimal stimulation is that the environment is patterned and consistent. Only under these conditions can the individual make valid predictions about aspects of the external world. This is a prerequisite for the individual's assigning meaning to the environment, and for his building valid conceptions about situation–outcome contingencies and behavior–outcome contingencies in the environment. The better the environment is patterned in a way that can be perceived by our senses and interpreted in a meaningful way, the more it will function optimally both as a source of stimulation and as a context for behavior during the course of development.

The second requirement that must be fulfilled for optimal stimulation is that the environment can be influenced by the individual's action and that this can be done in a predictable way. That is, the individual must be able to exert active control of his or her environment. This is a prerequisite for a satisfactory development of self-identity, of cognitive and social competence, and of feelings of control.

Both these conditions in the actual environment are needed as a basis for purposive behavior and thus for healthy development. It is not enough that the environment be predictable; it must also be controllable. The external world is certainly highly predictable for a slave, but it is nonetheless not a condition we would recommend as being conducive to healthy development because the environment cannot be affected at all by the individual's own actions.

Physical environments differ with respect to breadth and diversity of objects and events; but within the limits of available objects and events they are generally structured and function in a consistent way. The patterning is available to be understood by the child to the extent that he or she has the perceptual–cognitive and intellectual resources and is given the opportunity to observe and deal with it. In contrast to physical environments, *social* environments are not patterned in and of themselves. Rather, the patterning is created by other people for the individual at an early age—mostly by caretakers. It is the patterning and consistency in other people's behaviors, their demands, their rewards and punishments, and so forth, that determine if there is a consistent pattern of "lawfulness" in the social environment that can be used for assigning meaning to the environment and for making valid predictions about situation–outcome contingencies and behavior–outcome contingencies in the external world. In this book the role of caretakers in structuring the child's social environment is dealt with by Radke-Yarrow and Kuczynski in Chapter 3.

ACTUAL VERSUS PERCEIVED ENVIRONMENTS

An old philosophical distinction frequently referred to in analyses of the environment is that between (*a*) the environment "as it is" (e.g., described in terms of physical and sociocultural properties) and (*b*) the environment as it is perceived and interpreted by a person experiencing it. These two conceptions may be designated the *actual* and the *perceived* environments, respectively (see Magnusson, 1981b).

THE ACTUAL ENVIRONMENT

The Social Environment.   Among researchers in development most of the interest in the environment has been devoted to its social and cultural aspects. Both cognitive and social development are strongly dependent upon the character of the social environment. It affects these aspects of individual development at all levels of generalization from the laws and customs that are characteristic for the culture down to the family, the habits, norms, rules, and relationships that are specific to, for example, a family or a small group. Recently special attention has been given to those aspects of the social environment called "social support." Social support has been investigated in connection with many aspects of the life of adults; it is likely to be particularly important for positive psychological development (Sarason & Sarason, 1980).

For a long time developmental research dealt mainly with contextual aspects of the social environment expressed in rather gross, general measures such as social class, socioeconomic status, parents' educational level, and the like. However, the strong tendency to investigate more specific aspects of the environment for human development is obvious, and these aspects are discussed in this book by Ainsworth (Chapter 2) and Maccoby and Jacklin (Chapter 4).

The Physical Environment.   If research on social environment and development was mainly devoted to gross, overall aspects for a long time the reverse is true for the physical aspects of the environment and their role in development. The importance for individual development of the amount and diversity of stimulation from the environment at a very specific level of objects and situations has been demonstrated empirically and discussed theoretically. For example, White (1959) emphasized the role of the child's interaction with the inanimate environment in his discussion of competence as an important factor in motivation, and Hunt (1961, 1966) underlined the importance of the physical patterning of stimulation when he treated development of intelligence and intrinsic motivation. In his discussion of cognitive development, Piaget (1964) stated: "Experience of objects, of physical reality is obviously a basic factor in the development of cognitive structures [p. 178]." The recent research by Hubel and Wiesel (1970) illustrates the crucial role of patterned stimulation for the development of a perceptual system. Special attention is given to the role of the physical environment by Wohlwill in Chapter 6 of this book.

Both the character of the natural environment and the character of the man-made environment as a context for behavior play an important role in individual development by setting the limits and offering opportunities for physical activity that is a prerequisite for physical, cognitive, and social development. Many of the problems that have become so difficult in our societies are obviously due to the fact that the physical environments in which we grow up, live and work, and spend our leisure time have not been constructed with due consideration given to human potentialities and needs. By forming the physical environment in a certain way, we promote some types of behaviors and prohibit others—bad or good. This implies a challenge to psychology. Effective research on the physical environment might contribute knowledge that could form the basis for the construction of physical environments that are better adapted to the needs and potentialities of individuals and groups and thus promote physical and mental health.

THE PERCEIVED ENVIRONMENT

The actual environment influences an individual's behavior directly to some extent. However, most of the influence is exerted via the individual's perceptions and interpretations of the environment. It is the environment as it is perceived, interpreted, and given meaning to by the individual, that is, the cognitive representation of the external world, that is acted upon in most cases.

In theories of behavior, the importance of considering environments and situations as they are perceived has been underlined for decades not only by psychologists (see, e.g., Allport, 1937; Angyal, 1941; Bowers, 1973; Cattell, 1963; Endler, 1975; Jessor, 1956; Rotter, 1954; Schneider, 1973; Stagner, 1976) but also by sociologists and anthropologists (see, e.g., Berger & Luckman, 1966; Goffman, 1964; Mead, 1934; Thomas, 1927, 1928). Obviously the "real world" in which we experience, feel, think, and act is the world as we perceive it, or as formulated by Thomas (1928) in what Merton (1957) has called the Thomas theorem: "If men define situations as real, they are real in their consequences."

The perceived environment forms the stage for the individual's planning and pursuit of long- and short-term goals. Thus, the validity of our cognitive representations of the outer world determines the efficacy with which we can deal with our physical and social environments. The extent to which it is a valid cognitive representation of the outer world depends upon factors in the environment (degree of patterning in a way that is meaningful and observable) and upon factors in the individual (his capacity to interpret information from the environment and use it for assimilation and accommodation in relation to existing cognitive representations). It should be strongly emphasized, however, that the perceived environment is not merely a cognitive, emotionally neutral picture of the physical and social environments: Emotions and values are associated (sometimes very strongly) with objects, persons, places, situations, and events.

The preceding discussion leads to the conclusion that, in order to understand why an individual feels, thinks, and acts as he does in a specific situation, it is necessary to determine his conceptions and cognitive representations of the world and his perceptions and interpretation of the situation in which he finds himself. This is a basic assumption underlying the formulations of an interactional psychology, which asserts that the individual's pattern of stable and changing behaviors across situations is typical for him and can be explained in terms of his characteristic way of perceiving and interpreting situations and situational cues. (World conceptions and situation perception will be dealt with further in a later section on person factors in the person–environment process.)

ENVIRONMENTAL CHANGE

Individuals change during their lifetimes, and the environments that confront and influence their courses of development change as well. Changes that are important to individual development take place both in the macro- and in the micro-environment. The existence of environmental changes at different levels of the environment has serious consequences for both cross-sectional and longitudinal research on development. It means that factors in the individual that determine maturation and learning in the course of development are nested within factors in the environment that are changing at the same time. This line of reasoning raises the issue of separating age effects from generation effects in empirical research (Baltes, 1968).

Changes in the Macro-environment. The macro-environment undergoes constant change. Technical innovations have drastically changed our physical macro-environment. Compare, for example, the situation today with the situation only 50 years ago with respect to our possibilities for travel, for communication and exchange of information, and for industrial production. Ideological and political movements influence and change educational opportunities, educational systems, and societal norms, rules, and roles. The implication is that a person growing up and staying in the same environment may die in quite another macro-environment than the one into which he was born. Constant change also means that different generations are born into different environments with different norms, value systems, and demands (see Elder, 1977).

Changes in the Micro-environment.   Changes in macro-environments also lead, of course, to changes in the micro-environments that are embedded in them. In addition, there are various categories of changes that occur in an individual's micro-environment, for example:

1. The individual changes his environment by direct action. A baby who is crying night after night and does not eat regularly influences the behavior of its parents, and a rebelling teenager may affect the emotional climate of the family (see, e.g., Davis & Hathaway, 1982).
2. The individual may actively seek new situations to appear in and avoid earlier ones. The reason for this may be, for example, psychological and biological maturation that leads to new interests. Sometimes actively seeking new situations may imply moving to totally new micro-environments.
3. Role transitions often lead to new kinds of situations. This is the case, for example, when advancing to new job positions, marrying, or becoming a mother. Many of these role transitions are normative and common to most people in a society, whereas others are specific to groups or to individuals (Featherman, 1980; Sarason & Sarason, Chapter 10 of this volume).
4. Specific occurrences (for example, birth of a child, change in father's income, family moving to a new apartment) may change the character of the micro-environment for an individual.
5. A different social environment for a person may be caused by biological (or sometimes psychological) changes in him or her. For example, it is reasonable to assume that the social environment reacts differently to a girl after physical maturation than before, and that aging leads to other reactions from the environment.

The Person

As emphasized earlier in this chapter, the individual is the intentional, active agent in person–environment interactions. For a discussion of the person side of that process, a distinction can be made between three aspects of an individual's functioning, each of which can be discussed in terms of a subsystem of phenomena and a subdomain of variables that are of special interest for psychological theory and research. The three subsystems are (*a*) the mediating perceptual–cognitive system with its affective tones; (*b*) the biological system; and (*c*) manifest behavior. The distinctions do not mean that these subsystems are distinct with given, self-evident boundaries; to some extent the concepts are fuzzy and the domains are arbitrarily delineated.

This is not the place to attempt a comprehensive presentation of all the important person-centered factors that are involved in the person–environment interaction process. To do so would be tantamount to summarizing a large portion of the current knowledge in the field of psychology. For those interested in such a summary, the recent contribution by Brim and Kagan (1980), which presents a comprehensive discussion of many aspects of these issues in development, and the reviews of their book by Block (1981) and Yarrow (1981) are recommended. We shall only sketch briefly here a few of the most essential aspects of individual functioning that deserve attention in a discussion of person–environment interaction.

THE MEDIATING SYSTEM

A crucial role in an individual's interaction with his environment is played by his mediating system of *organized contents* with associated *affective tones* and *coping strategies* (Magnusson, 1980a; see also Sarason & Sarason, Chapter 10, and Vaillant, Chapter 19, in this volume). The existing mediating system determines the way information about the external world is selected, interpreted, and used, and it forms the stage for dealing with problems and plans of action by means of cognitive activity. Which factors are involved and how they function are the interests of researchers in the fields of perception, cognition, information processing, and decision making. Various models for dealing with problems in these areas from a contemporaneous perspective have been suggested, and they include such different concepts as categories, dimensions, schemata, plans, programs, semantic networks, and coping strategies (see, e.g., Miller, Galanter, & Pribram, 1960; Neisser, 1976; Piaget, 1952; Rummelhart & Ortony, 1977; Shank & Abelson, 1977).

From an interactional perspective it is important to observe that, with few exceptions, these models have concentrated on the organization and functioning of the cognitive system as it deals with information, to the neglect of other significant aspects such as emotions, values, and goals (see, e.g., Kunst-Wilson & Zajonc, 1980, who discussed the role of affect in cognition). Piaget's model of cognition is an illustrative case. The limitations of a pure informational approach cannot be emphasized too strongly. The neglect of emotions, values, and goals as important aspects of the process by which an individual deals with his environment and with his inner problems may be one of the main reasons that research on cognitive processes, information processing, and decision making has not contributed more to interesting and relevant questions about how individuals function in real-life situations.

The emotions and values which are associated with specific aspects of the physical and social environments (see p. 17), and which are bound to specific cognitive contents, play a crucial role in determining how an individual selects, interprets, and treats external information with regard to his expectations, decisions, plans, and actions. The central role of goals in the mediating system and in the individual's dealing with internal and external problems has recently been discussed and elaborated by Pervin (1983), and Bower (1981) has presented research showing the importance of emotions for cognitive processes.

The importance of a child's active interaction with his physical and social environments in the development of optimal mediating systems has been particularly emphasized by researchers concerned with cognitive–intellectual development. To give a few prominent examples among the most influential researchers in this field, Hunt (1961), Piaget (1964), and Vygotsky (1929, 1963, 1974) all very clearly represent interactional positions. A recent contribution to the discussion of development of competence in an interactional perspective has been given by Ulvund (1981), and Heckhausen (Chapter 9) in this book deals with the same topic. Modern theories of motivation are clearly interactionistic (see, e.g., Hunt, 1961, 1965, 1966; Nygård, 1981; Ulvund, 1980).

World Conceptions.   Important aspects of the mediating system that functions at each stage of development are the conceptualizations and cognitive representations of the outer world (see Chapter 7 in this volume, by Epstein and Erskine, on individuals' theories of reality). At each stage of development the total system of conceptions about the outer world plays a crucial role in a person's inner thoughts as well as in his actual behavior. To a considerable degree one's conceptions of the world determine which kinds of environments and situations one seeks and avoids, which situational cues and events one attends to, and how one interprets them. These interpretations form the main basis for a person's actual manifest behavior and also contribute to producing changes in the mediating system.

Self-conception.   Finally, any discussion of person factors must give some attention to that subcomponent of world conceptions that has been referred to as the self-concept. The person's perceptions or conceptions about self refer to cognitions and affective responses about self in relation to the physical, social, and psychological environments (Bandura, 1977). The self-concept system can be described by structural characteristics (complex, differentiated, etc.) and by affective or evaluative loadings (good–bad, like–dislike). Most important of these, however, are the evaluative and cognitive dimensions as they are perceived by the person. The evaluative dimension concerns the positive or negative affect that is associated with the conception of one's self, as conveyed by terms such as self-esteem, self-confidence, and the like (to use positive ends of the dimension). As for the cognitive dimension, the perception by an individual of the degree of his or her competence and of the ability to control outcomes in the physical and social environments plays a crucial role in influencing many aspects of one's behavior, as attested to by the extensive body of research now available on the topic of control and helplessness (Abramson, Seligman, & Teasdale, 1978; Bandura, 1978; Seligman, 1975).

THE BIOLOGICAL SUBSYSTEM

The biological aspects of the individual play an important role (too often overlooked in psychology) in individual functioning, in both a contemporaneous and a developmental perspective. Findings in recent physiological research have opened up interesting possibilities for the understanding not only of physiological processes themselves but also of other aspects of individual functioning (Dunn, 1980; McGeer, 1980).

The physiological system is in a continuous, reciprocal interaction with the mediating system and with behavior; it is influenced by and influences both. Recent physiological research has shown that role of hormones and neurotransmitters is crucial for cognitive and emotional functioning, as manifested, for example, in anxiety and depression. A person's physical equipment determines to some extent his behavior by setting the limits and offering the possibilities for various kinds of behaviors, and its fitness determines to a great extent his satisfaction and well-being.

The role of the biological side of the individual is clearly demonstrated in the strong determination of behavior by maturational factors during development in infancy and childhood, but biological factors continue to exert a powerful influence on behavior throughout the life span. At the most basic level, the onset and course of certain developmental sequences are determined genetically in a normative way and are common to all normally developing individuals. In other instances biological development takes place in a process of maturation and learning in interaction with the environment on the basis of and within the limits set by inherited factors. In this book special consideration is given to biological factors for development by Rasmuson (Chapter 11), who deals with genetic factors in development in general, by Eneroth (Chapter 12), who deals with endocrinological factors in development, by Mednick *et al.* (Chapter 13), who discuss the inheritance of human deviance, and by Meyer-Probst and his associates (Chapter 14), who deal with factors operating at birth as determinants of biological vulnerability during childhood.

MANIFEST BEHAVIOR

This subsystem consists of the *actions* and *reactions* that are exhibited by an individual. It refers to the behaviors that are initiated by the individual when acting as an intentional agent and to the responses that are made as reactions to external stimuli. Sometimes the behavior involves the person as a whole; at other times only discrete and fragmentary portions of the total individual will be involved. Finally, an individual's actions and reactions may be expressive and/or instrumental.

Most personality theories have concentrated mainly on the lawfulness of mediating processes, using different intervening variables and hypothetical constructs to explain manifest behavior (Magnusson, 1981a). Less interest has been devoted to the lawfulness of actual behavior and to the explicit formulations of models of behavior as distinct from models in terms of mediating processes and for personality traits. For efficacious research on behavior in itself and its relation to mediating processes, the need for models of lawfulness of manifest behavior is just as obvious as it is for models of lawfulness of mediating processes. Whether it is clear to the researcher or not, a model of behavior is implicitly assumed when studying behavior per se and the relation between factors in the mediating system of perceptions and cognitions on the one hand and behavioral aspects on the other.

An interactional model of actual behavior in a contemporaneous perspective assumes that what is characteristic of an individual is his or her typical pattern of changing and stable behaviors across situations, which reflects his or her typical way of adjusting and reacting to different situational conditions. In terms of data for a certain behavior, this implies that a person is best described for each kind of behavior by a cross-situational profile that is typical for him or her.

Thus, we need two parameters to distinguish among individuals and to study interindividual differences with respect to a certain type of behavior, namely: (a) the mean level of intensity (reflected in the main variance due to persons in a Person × Situation matrix of data) and (b) the specific pattern of the cross-situational profile (reflected in the interaction variance of a Person × Situation matrix of data for a sample of individuals for a certain type of behavior).

THE INTERPLAY OF SUBSYSTEMS

All of the types of factors that we have distinguished in this section are in a process of continuous interaction with each other; this includes the factors within each of the systems and the factors from different systems. For example, thoughts evoke physiological reactions (interpreting a situation as threatening causes excretion of adrenalin in the medulla), physiological reactions are accompanied by emotions, thoughts and physiological processes influence actions, and one's own actions influence self-conceptions and later behavior.

The Developing Person in the Environment

DEVELOPMENT OF MEDIATING SYSTEMS

The way an individual's mediating system functions at a certain stage of development is the result of previous developmental processes of learning and maturation that take place within the limits of his or her inherited dispositions in a constant process of interaction with the environment. By *assimilating* new knowledge and experience into existing categories and by *accommodating* old categories and forming new ones, the individual develops a total system of structured contents in a continuous interaction with his physical, social, and cultural environments (Flavell, 1972). As emphasized earlier, in this process, emotions play an important role. In the learning process, affective tones become bound to specific contents and actions, and coping strategies develop for dealing with different environments and situations.

It follows that the characteristics of the mediating system in a person (the specific categories built up, the specific contents of the categories, the affective tones bound to the categories' contents, and the coping strategies) will depend to some extent on the character of the environment that the individual encounters in the developmental learning process. To the extent that environments in which we are reared are similar, the main characteristics of our world conceptions will share common characteristics. When the environments in which we develop differ markedly (between cultures, for example) the total mediating system will also differ. To the extent that our interpretation of the outer world determines our behavior, great cross-cultural differences in actual behavior can be explained even in situations that are similar in some objective sense.

Physical and social environments are never identical for children even if they are reared in the same family. Among other things, this contributes to interindividual differences in conceptions of the outer world and thus to differences in the interpretation of single situations even among individuals who have grown up in the same general environment.

STRUCTURES AND PROCESSES

The total system of person factors discussed above is in a state of constant transition. These transitions mean successive changes both in the structure of the factors underlying the dynamic process of interaction and in the character of the process itself. In a discussion of these transitions the concepts of *structures* and *processes* are central in both contemporary and developmental approaches to behavior.

Structures are the result of processes, and processes take place within existing structures. Research on behavior in the contemporaneous perspective is mainly concerned with processes within given structures. The functioning of structures at a certain stage of development cannot be explained satisfactorily without understanding the processes that have led to such structures. For a full understanding of the processes in development we need to understand the structures and their interplay at successive stages of development. Development, in an interactional perspective, is a matter of how structures develop as a result of the processes in which existing structures in the individual and the environment are in continuous interaction, and how these structures operate in interaction with the physical and social environments at successive stages of development.

That structures operating at a certain stage of development are the result of processes is valid not only for the mental structures but also for biological structures, as discussed by Eneroth in Chapter 12 of this book (see, e.g., Kolata, 1977). This underlines again the spiral character of the person— environment interaction in development.

CONSISTENCY

A central issue in the person–situation debate in the field of personality during the 1970s was the stability and consistency of individual functioning. Much confusion in the debate was (and still is) caused by failure to maintain some basic conceptual distinctions (*a*) between consistency of manifest behavior in terms of stable rank-orders (i.e., relative stability) and consistency in terms of cohesive, predictable patterns; (*b*) between consistency of behavior and consistency of mediating processes; and (*c*) between cross-situational and temporal consistency. The importance of maintaining these distinctions for research in personality on contemporaneous behavior has been underlined elsewhere (see Magnusson & Endler, 1977). However, these distinctions are equally important in theoretical and empirical research on development.

Relative Consistency–Coherence.   Lawfulness of manifest behavior can be discussed in two contrasting models of consistency (Magnusson, 1976): (*a*) the relative stability model and (*b*) the coherence model.

The relative stability model assumes that consistency is reflected by the stable rank-orders of individuals for a certain type of behavior (e.g., aggression) across situations. High stability is then expressed in high coefficients for agreement between the rank-order of individuals in different situations.

The coherence model, which reflects an interactional view implies that consistency of behavior is sought in consistent, lawful patterns of behavior across situations. These patterns may be partly specific to individuals, as reflected in partly specific cross-situational profiles for each type of behavior. The more specific to individuals is such a profile, the lower will be the coefficients for stability of rank-orders of individuals across situations.

During recent decades a vast amount of research has been performed to test the two models. Here it is enough to conclude that the results clearly show that the relative stability model is not sufficient to explain interindividual cross-situational differences in behavior. Though most of the variance in a Person × Situation matrix of data is usually due to the main effect of persons, enough variance is left that can be explained by interindividual differences in patterns of cross-situational profiles to support the coherence model.

In a developmental perspective the pattern of manifest behavior that is characteristic of a person changes with time. During some periods changes may be stronger than normally; sometimes they are restricted to specific behaviors, and sometimes they cover broader aspects of behavior. Changes in manifest behavior due to biological changes in the individual during puberty and aging, for example, are easily recognizable. Such changes also take place as a result of development of the perceptual–cognitive interpretations of the external world (see p. 17). Changes in patterns of manifest behavior often result from changes in the environment caused by the individual's active choice of new environments or by changes in his existing environment (see p. 7).

Consistency of Behaviors–Consistency of Mediating Processes. A distinction between consistency of individual functioning at the level of manifest behavior and at the level of the mediating system is necessary. There is not a one-to-one relation between the two levels. Behavior may be totally lacking in relative stability across situations and across time, while the mediating process functions in a totally lawful and consistent way in selecting, interpreting, and transforming information into actions. One and the same motive in the mediating system may be expressed by very different behaviors in different situations, and the same behavior in different situations may be caused by very different motives in the mediating system (see the discussion about equifinality and equipotentiality by Hammond, 1955). In a developmental perspective, this distinction becomes obvious. For example, the same goal may be expressed by an individual in very different kinds of behaviors at different ages, and the same kind of behavior may reflect very different motives at different ages.

Cross-situational–Temporal Consistency. Research on contemporaneous behavior in personality has been mostly concerned with cross-situational consistency (Mischel, 1973, 1977). For research on development the main interest is in consistency across time and age, without neglecting cross-situational consistency. In analyses of temporal consistency the distinctions made earlier in this section are important. From an interactional view, the main interest is in consistency over time in cross-situational patterns rather than in the relative stability for each variable.

The degree of temporal consistency in individual functioning will depend upon several factors, including the types of responses under observation (e.g., biological, cognitive, or social) and the age period under consideration, including the beginning and the total length of time. In any event, stability or instability of behavior is a matter of degree. Furthermore, there are serious problems surrounding issues of measurement and statistics in this area (see, e.g., Ragosa, Brandt, & Zimowski, 1982).

READINESS

In developmental research, the organism's readiness to respond to an external stimulus in the environment is a concept of central importance. It is well known from research using a number of species that a given stimulus in the environment may have a very strong effect at one age, but will be ineffective (or show a marked attenuation of impact) if presented either prior to or subsequent to this particular time period (see Chapter 11 in this volume by Rasmuson). The concept of "readiness" to respond, then, refers to the condition of the organism at a particular age period with respect to optimal responsiveness to a certain element in the environment. Perhaps the best-known example of readiness can be found in the phenomenon of "imprinting" in certain bird species, as demonstrated by Lorenz (1965) and others. It is doubtful that analogous "critical" periods (in the strong sense of the concept) exist with regard to the effect of environmental stimuli at the human level, but it is clear that at particular age periods during development the individual has a greater sensitivity and responsiveness to *some* aspects of the environment than to others.

An example of the importance of person–environment interaction in development is the fact that readiness for a certain type of change is not enough for development to take place. Optimal development also presupposes the occurrence of the appropriate environmental stimulation at a certain level. Thus, the concept of readiness implies that development is selective, that is, restricted to a particular subcategory of stimuli occurring in the environment. Optimal development is produced by the conjoint occurrence of the appropriate readiness in the person system and the appropriate stimulus category in the environment system.

Subsystems within the person are constantly changing during developmental phases from infancy to adulthood. And changes occurring in either the biological system or the perceptual–cognitive system (including the individual's world conceptions and self-conceptions) may be responsible for creating a state of heightened readiness to respond to a stimulus in the environment that did not previously exist. As an example, consider changes in the biological (hormonal) and self subsystems during the teenage years and their contribution to the increased readiness of such individuals to attend to appropriate cues and to respond to members of the opposite sex.

Summary and Conclusions

The basic components of the person–environment interaction perspective were presented and discussed in this chapter. The general framework for the analysis of behavior makes the basic assumption that the thoughts, feelings, and actions of a person cannot be explained by taking into account person factors or situation factors alone; instead, operation of the person and the environment as a system must be considered to gain an adequate understanding of a person's functioning. Different subsystems exist within the general environment system (actual and perceived environments) and within the general person system (e.g., mediating, biological, and action–reaction). Moreover, interaction takes place both within and across these systems.

It was stressed throughout this chapter that person–environment interaction is a continuous and reciprocal (bidirectional) process in which the environment influences the person and at the same time the person influences the environment. Thus, interaction is a dynamic process that should be conceived of as a continuous spiral in which both the person and the environment are being changed as a consequence of the interaction. Attention was also devoted to selected specific issues in human development that may be clarified by using the interaction perspective.

For a long time, psychology has suffered severely from fragmentation and separation of different areas of theorizing and research. One major consequence has been that results from research in different areas cannot be discussed and related to each other in a common frame of reference. This is most probably a primary reason why we have so little real accumulation of systematic knowledge in psychology—which is a prerequisite for, and an indication of, a maturing science in progress. We believe that an interactional perspective as outlined in this chapter offers a psychologically realistic framework for further theorizing and research on development that will enable us to overcome the deficiencies of the present situation.

References

Abramson, L. Y., Seligman, E. P., & Teasdale, J. D. Learned helplessness in humans. *Journal of Abnormal and Social Psychology,* 1978, *87,* 49–74.

Allport, G. W. *Personality.* New York: Holt, 1937.

Anastasi, A. Hereditary, environment and the question "How?" *Psychological Review,* 1958, *65,* 197–208.

Angyal, A. *Foundations for a science of personality.* Cambridge, Mass.: Harvard University Press, 1941.

Aronfreed, J. *Conduct and conscience: The socialization of internalized control over behavior.* New York: Academic Press, 1968.

Arsenian, J., & Arsenian, J. M. Tough and easy cultures: A conceptual analysis. *Psychiatry,* 1948, *11,* 377–385.

Baltes, P. B. Longitudinal and cross-sectional sequences in the study of age and generation effects. *Human Development,* 1968 *11,* 145–171.

Baltes, P. B., Reese, H. W., & Nesselroade, J. R. *Life-span developmental psychology.* Monterey, Calif.: Brooks/Cole, 1977.

Bandura, A. Self-efficacy: Toward a unifying theory of behavior change. *Psychological Review,* 1977, *84,* 191–215.

Bandura, A. The self-system in reciprocal determinism. *American Psychologist,* 1978, *33,* 344–358.

Barker, R. G. *Ecological psychology: Concepts and methods for studying the environment of human behavior.* Stanford, Calif.: Stanford University Press, 1968.

Bell, R. Q. Reinterpretation of the direction of effects in studies of socialization. *Psychological Review,* 1968, *75,* 81–95.

Bell, R. Q. Parent, child, and reciprocal influences. *American Psychologist,* 1979, *34,* 821–826.

Berger, P., & Luckman, T. *The social construction of reality.* Garden City, N.J.: Doubleday, 1966.

Bertalanffy, L. von. *General system theory.* New York: Braziller, 1968.

Block, J. The many faces of continuity. *Contemporary Psychology,* 1981, *26,* 746–750.

Bloom, B. S. *Stability and change in human characteristics.* New York: Wiley, 1964.

Bower, G. H. Mood and memory. *American Psychologist,* 1981, *36,* 129–148.

Bowers, K. S. Situationism in psychology: An analysis and a critique. *Psychological Review,* 1973, *80,* 307–336.

Brim, O. G., & Kagan, J. *Constancy and change in human development.* Cambridge, Mass.: Harvard University Press, 1980.

Bronfenbrenner, U. Toward an experimental ecology of human development. *American Psychologist,* 1977, *32,* 513–531. (a)

Bronfenbrenner, U. Lewinian space and ecological substance. *Journal of Social Issues,* 1977, *33,* 199–213. (b)

Bronfenbrenner, U. *The ecology of human development.* Cambridge, Mass.: Harvard University Press, 1979. (a)

Bronfenbrenner, U. Contexts of child rearing: Problems and prospects. *American Psychologist,* 1979, *34,* 844–850. (b)

Cattell, R. B. Personality, role, mood, and situation perception: A unifying theory of modulators. *Psychological Review,* 1963, *70,* 1–18.

Craik, K. H., & Zube, E. H. (Eds.), *Perceiving environmental quality: Research and applications.* New York: Plenum, 1976.

Davis, A. J., & Hathaway, B. K. Reciprocity in parent–child verbal interactions. *Journal of Genetic Psychology,* 1982, *140,* 169–183.

DeGreene, D. B. Force fields and emergent phenomena in sociotechnical macrosystems: Theories and models. *Behavioral Sciences,* 1978, *23,* 1–14.

Dunn, A. J. Neurochemistry of learning and memory: An evaluation of recent data. *Annual Review of Psychology,* 1980, *31,* 343–350.

Elardo, R., Bradley, R. H., & Caldwell, B. M. The relation of infants' home environments to mental test performance from six to 36 months: A longitudinal analysis. *Child Development,* 1975, *46,* 71–76.

Elder, G. H. Family history and the life course. *Journal of Family History,* 1977, *2,* 279–304.

Endler, N. S. The person versus the situation—A pseudo issue? A response to Alker. *Journal of Personality,* 1973, *41,* 287–303.

Endler, N. S. A person–situation interaction model for anxiety. In C. D. Spielberger & I. G. Sarason (Eds.), *Stress and anxiety.* Washington, D.C.: Hemisphere, 1975.

Endler, N. S., & Magnusson, D. Toward an interactional psychology of personality. *Psychological Bulletin,* 1976, *83,* 956–974.

Eysenck, H., & Eysenck, M. *Mindwatching.* London: Michael Joseph, 1981.

Featherman, D. L. Schooling and occupational careers: Constancy and change in wordly success. In O. G. Brim, Jr., & J. Kagan (Eds.), *Constancy and change in human development.* Cambridge, Mass.: University Harvard Press, 1980. Pp. 675–738.

Flavell, J. H. An analysis of cognitive developmental sequences. *Genetic Psychology Monographs,* 1972, *86,* 279–350.

Goffman, E. The neglected situation. *American Anthropologist,* 1964, *66,* 133–136.

Hammond, K. R. Probabilistic functioning and the clinical method. *Psychological Review,* 1955, *62,* 255–262.

Hautamäki, A. Activity environment, social class and voluntary leaving: An interpretation and application of Vygotsky's concept. *Publications of the University of Joensu* (Joensu, Finalnd), Series A, No. 22, 1982.

Hebb, D. O. Drives and the CNS (conceptual nervous system). *Psychological Review,* 1955, *62,* 243–254.

Hubel, D. H., & Wiesel, T. N. The period of susceptibility to the physiological effects of unilateral eye closure in kittens. *Journal of Physiology,* 1970, *206,* 419–436.

Hunt, J. McV. *Intelligence and experience.* New York: Ronald, 1961.

Hunt, J. McV. Intrinsic motivation and its role in psychological development. In D. Levine (Ed.), *Nebraska Symposium on Motivation*. Lincoln, Neb.: University of Nebraska Press, 1965. Pp. 189–282.

Hunt, J. McV. The epigenesis of intrinsic motivation and early cognitive learning. In R. N. Hober (Ed.), *Current research in motivation*. New York: Holt, 1966. Pp. 355–370.

Hunt, J. McV. The role of situations in early psychological development. In D. Magnusson (Ed.), *Toward a psychology of situations: An interactional perspective*. Hillsdale, N.J.: Erlbaum, 1981. Pp. 323–342.

Ittelson, W. H., & Cantril, H. *Perception: A transactional approach*. Garden City, N.Y.: Doubleday, 1954.

Jensen, A. R. How much can we boost IQ and scholastic achievement? *Harvard Educational Review*, 1969, *39*, 1–117.

Jessor, R. Phenomenological personality theories and the data language of psychology. *Psychological Review*, 1956, *63*, 173–180.

Jessor, R. The perceived environment in psychological theory and research. In D. Magnusson (Ed.), *Toward a psychology of situations: An interactional perspective*. Hillsdale, N.J.: Erlbaum, 1981. Pp. 297–322.

Jessor, R., & Jessor, S. L. The perceived environment in behavioral science: Some conceptual issues and some illustrative data. *American Behavioral Scientist*, 1973, *16*, 801–828.

Kessen, W. The American child and other cultural inventions. *American Psychologist*, 1979, *34*, 815–820.

Kolata, G. B. Hormone receptors: How are they regulated? *Science*, 1977, *186*, 747–748, 800.

Kunst-Wilson, W. R., & Zajonc, R. B. Affective discrimination of stimuli that cannot be recognized. *Science*, 1980, *207*, 557–558.

Lerner, R. M. Nature, nurture, and dynamic interactionism. *Human Development*, 1978, *21*, 1–20.

Leuba, C. Toward some integration of learning theories: The concept of optimal stimulation. *Psychological Reports*, 1955, *1*, 27–33.

Lewin, K. *Resolving social conflicts*. New York: Harper, 1948.

Lorenz, K. *Evolution and the modification of behavior*. Chicago: University of Chicago Press, 1965.

McGeer, P. L., & McGeer, E. G. Chemistry of mood and emotion. *Annual Review of Psychology*, 1980, *31*, 273–307.

Magnusson, D. The person and the situation in an interactional model of behavior. *Scandinavian Journal of Psychology*, 1976, *17*, 253–271.

Magnusson, D. On the psychological situation. Reports from the Department of Psychology, the University of Stockholm, 1978, No. 544.

Magnusson, D. Personality in an interactional paradigm of research. *Zeitschrift für Differentielle und Diagnostische Psychologie*, 1980, *1*, 17–34. (a)

Magnusson, D. Learned helplessness—Welfare for good or bad. *Skandinaviska Enskilda Banken: Quarterly Review*, 1980, 3–4. (b)

Magnusson, D. *Toward a psychology of situations: An interactional perspective*. Hillsdale, N. J.: Erlbaum, 1981. (a)

Magnusson, D. Problems in environmental analyses—An introduction. In D. Magnusson (Ed.), *Toward a psychology of situations: An interactional perspective*. Hillsdale, N. J.: Erlbaum, 1981. Pp. 3–7. (b)

Magnusson, D. Wanted: A psychology of situations. In D. Magnusson (Ed.), *Toward a psychology of situations: An interactional perspective*. Hillsdale, N. J.: Erlbaum, 1981. Pp. 9–32. (c)

Magnusson, D. *Persons in situations: Some comments on a current issue*. Invited address at the First European Conference on Personality, Tilburg, Holland, May, 1982.

Magnusson, D., Dunér, A., & Zetterblom, G. *Adjustment: A longitudinal study*. Stockholm: Almqvist & Wiksell, 1975.

Magnusson, D., & Endler, N. S. Interactional psychology: Present status and future prospects. In D. Magnusson & N. S. Endler (Eds.), *Personality at the crossroads: Current issues in interactional psychology.* Hillsdale, N. J.: Erlbaum, 1977.

Mead, G. H. *Mind, self, and society.* Chicago: University of Chicago Press, 1934.

Merton, R. K. *Social theory and social structure.* Glencoe, Ill.: The Free Press, 1957.

Miller, G. A., Galanter, E., & Pribram, K. H. *Plans and the structures of behavior.* New York: Holt, 1960.

Miller, J. G. *Living systems.* New York: McGraw-Hill, 1978.

Mineka, S., & Kihlström, J. F. Unpredictable and uncontrollable events: A new perspective on experimental neurosis. *Journal of Abnormal Psychology,* 1978, *87,* 256–271.

Mischel, W. Toward a cognitive social learning reconceptualization of personality. *Psychological Review,* 1973, *80,* 252–283.

Mischel, W. On the future of personality measurement. *American Psychologist,* 1977, *32,* 246–254.

Moos, R. Conceptualizations of human environments. *American Psychologist,* 1973, *28,* 612–665.

Neisser, U. *Cognition and reality: Principles and implications of cognitive psychology.* San Francisco: Freeman, 1976.

Nygård, R. Toward an interactional psychology: Models from achievement motivations research. *Journal of Personality,* 1981, *49,* 363–387.

Pepper, S. C. *World hypotheses: A study in evidence.* Berkeley: University of California Press, 1942.

Pervin, L. A. Definitions, measurements, and classifications of stimuli, situations, and environments. *Human Ecology,* 1978, *6,* 71–105.

Pervin, L. A. The stasis and flow of behavior: Toward a theory of goals. In M. M. Page (Ed.), *Personality: Current theory and reearch.* Lincoln, Neb.: University of Nebraska Press, 1983. Pp. 1–53.

Piaget, J. *The origins of intelligence in children.* New York: International Universities Press, 1952.

Piaget, J. Development and learning. *Journal of Research in Science Teaching,* 1964, *2,* 176–186.

Ragosa, D., Brandt, D., & Zimowski, M. A growth curve approach to the measurement of change. *Psychological Bulletin,* 1982, *92,* 726–746.

Reese, H., & Overton, W. Models of development and theories of development. In L. R. Goulet & P. B. Baltes (Eds.), *Life-span developmental psychology: Research and theory.* New York: Academic Press, 1970.

Rensberger, B. Margaret Mead. *Science 83,4(3),* 1983, 28–37.

Rotter, J. B. *Social learning and clinical psychology.* New York: Prentice-Hall, 1954.

Rummelhart, D. E., & Ortony, A. The representation of knowledge in memory. In R. C. Anderson, R. J. Spiro, and W. E. Montague (Eds.), *Schooling and the acquisition of knowledge.* Hillsdale, N. J.: Erlbaum, 1977.

Russell, J. A., & Ward, L. M. Environmental psychology. *Annual Review of Psychology,* 1982, *33,* 651–688.

Sameroff, A. L. Transactional models in early social relations. *Human Development,* 1975, *18,* 65–79.

Sarason, J., & Sarason, B. *Abnormal psychology: The problem of maladaptive behavior.* Englewood Cliffs, N. J.: Prentice Hall, 1980.

Sarbin, T. R. Contextualism: A world view for modern psychology. In J. K. Cole (Ed.), *Nebraska symposium on motivation, 1976.* Lincoln, Neb.: University of Nebraska Press, 1977.

Schneider, D. J. Implicit personality theory: A review. *Psychological Bulletin,* 1973, *79,* 294–309.

Seligman, M. E. P. *Helplessness: On depression, development, and death.* San Francisco, Calif.: Freeman, 1975.

Sells, S. B. An interactionist looks at the environment. *American Psychologist,* 1963, *18,* 696–702.

Shank, R., & Abelson, R. *Scripts, plans, goals, and understanding.* Hillsdale, N. J.: Erlbaum, 1977.

Stagner, R. Traits are relevant: Theoretical analysis and empirical evidence. In N. S. Endler & D. Magnusson (Eds.), *Interactional psychology and personality*. New York: Wiley, 1976.

Stokols, D. Origins and directions of environment–behavioral research. In D. Stokols (Ed.), *Perspectives on environment and behavior*. New York: Plenum, 1977.

Thomas, W. I. The behavior pattern and the situation. *Publications of the American Sociological Society: Papers and Proceedings*, 1927, *22*, 1–13.

Thomas, W. I. *The child in America*. New York: Knopf, 1928.

Tyler, L. E. More stately mansions—Psychology extends its boundaries. *Annual Review of Psychology*, 1981, *32*, 1–20.

Ulvund, S. E. Cognition and motivation in early infancy: An interactionistic approach. *Human Development*, 1980, *23*, 17–32.

Ulvund, S. E. The physical basis for the identification of physical environmental parameters in the development of early cognitive competence. *Scandinavian Journal of Education Research*, 1981, *25*, 125–140.

Uzgiris, I. C. Plasticity and structure. The role of experience in infancy. In I. C. Uzgiris & F. Weizmann (Eds.), *The structuring of experience*. New York: Plenum, 1977. Pp. 153–178.

Vygotsky, L. S. The problem of the cultural development of the child. *Journal of Genetic Psychology*, 1929, *3*, 415–432.

Vygotsky, L. S. Learning and mental development at school age. In B. Simon & J. Simon (Eds.), *Educational psychology in the USSR*. London: Routledge & Kegan Paul, 1963.

Vygotsky, L. S. *Denken und Sprechen*. Berlin, 1974.

Wachs, T. D. The optimal stimulation hypothesis and early development: Anybody got a match? In I. C. Uzgiris & F. Weizmann (Eds.), *The structuring of experience*. New York: Plenum, 1977. Pp. 153–178.

Wachs, T. D. Proximal experience and early cognitive-intellectual development: The physical environment. *Merrill-Palmer Quarterly*, 1979, *25*, 3–41.

Wasserman, G. A., & Lewis, M. The effects of situations and situation transitions on maternal and infant behavior. *The Journal of Genetic Psychology*, 1982, *140*, 19–31.

White, R. W. Motivation reconsidered: The concept of competence. *Psychological Review*, 1959, *66*, 297–333.

Wohlwill, J. F. The concept of experience: S or R? *Human Development*, 1973, *16*, 90–107.

Yarrow, L. J. The many faces of continuity. *Contemporary Psychology*, 1981, *26*, 746–750.

Yarrow, L. J., Rubenstein, J. L., & Pedersen, F. A. *Infant and environment: Early cognitive and motivation development*. New York: Wiley, 1975.

Yarrow, L. J., Rubenstein, J. L., Pedersen, F. A., & Jankowski, J. J. Dimensions of early stimulation and their differential effects on infant development. *Merrill-Palmer Quarterly*, 1972, *18*, 205–218.

II

The Environment:
Its Role in Human
Development

Chapters in this section are organized around the theme of the role of the social and physical environments in development. The first chapter, written by Ainsworth, reviews and integrates the substantial body of research that has accumulated on the topic of attachment of the infant to its caregiver. From an intensive analysis of infants, Ainsworth has identified three different patterns of infant–mother attachment. Research has shown that the patterns of infants' attachments show a considerable amount of stability across time. Ainsworth notes that research on attachment can be seen as being highly congruent with the general concepts of person–interaction theory.

Radke-Yarrow and Kuczynski focus on interaction in childrearing. The family constitutes the principal social environment for the child during the period of social and personal development. The childrearing patterns of parents are certainly an important context in which person–environment interaction takes place. What do parents actually do? To answer this question, the authors describe a research strategy that stresses systematic observation over time of behaviors pertinent to childrearing in a naturalistic (but controlled) setting.

In Chapter 4, Maccoby and Jacklin discuss in some detail several specific instances of parent–child interaction. Data from a longitudinal study by the authors permitted an examination of the effect of characteristics of the child (such as sex, activity level, and "difficultness") on the behavior exhibited in interaction with a parent. Characteristics of the child were found to influence the type of behavior shown by the parents; hence, the child helps create his or her own social environment.

33

HUMAN DEVELOPMENT:
AN INTERACTIONAL PERSPECTIVE

Tinsley and Parke, in Chapter 5, look at the social environment in a much broader perspective, and with reference to the problem of premature (preterm) infants. The authors extend the conceptualization of the environment beyond the mother–child dyad to include the father–child relationship and the entire family in its ecological setting. This consideration leads the authors to focus on the role of formal and informal social support systems in assisting families experiencing a stressful event.

A detailed conceptual analysis of the role of the environment during a child's development is provided by Wohlwill in Chapter 6. Distinguishing between the physical and social environments Wohlwill calls attention to important differences and similarities between these two aspects of the total environment. A classificatory scheme is proposed that makes distinctions among the different modes of operation of the environment in relation to the development of behavior.

2

Patterns of Infant–Mother Attachment as Related to Maternal Care: Their Early History and Their Contribution to Continuity

MARY D. SALTER AINSWORTH

The data upon which this paper is based stem from two sources. The primary relationship between patterns of infant–mother attachment and maternal care practices has been elucidated in my longitudinal, naturalistic study of mother–infant interaction throughout the first year of life. The data that support a claim for a contribution of these patterns of attachment to continuity of development stem from the work of a number of other researchers. Although both sets of data have already been variously published, they will be reviewed here in summary form, as a basis for a discussion of personality development from the perspective of person–environment interaction.

Description of the Ainsworth Longitudinal Project

Much rests upon the Ainsworth longitudinal study of mother–infant interaction and the development of patterns of infant–mother attachment in the first year of life. So far it is the most comprehensive and intensive study of its kind. The sample consisted of 26 white, middle-class mother–infant pairs in the Baltimore area who had been contacted through pediatricians in private practice before the infant's birth. Both pediatricians and families were told that we were interested in studying the social development of normal babies in normal, intact homes. Six of the infants were firstborn, 20 were not; 16 were boys, and 10 were girls. All but 4 were bottle-fed from the beginning. Only 4 of the mothers had any employment outside the home for any part of the baby's first year.

HUMAN DEVELOPMENT:
AN INTERACTIONAL PERSPECTIVE

Visits were made to the home at 3-week intervals from 3 to 54 weeks after the baby's birth, each visit lasting approximately 4 hours so there were approximately 72 hours of observation of each dyad. Each visitor–observer had his or her own families to follow through, with occasional joint visits as reliability checks. The observers were instructed to observe and to record as much as possible of what the baby did, especially in interaction with other people, what the mother did and said, and what all other persons present did and said relevant to the baby. The raw data consisted of typed transcripts of coherent narratives dictated by the observer from his/her notes after the visit. In addition, at 51 weeks mother and baby were brought to the university for a controlled laboratory situation that we called "the strange situation," meaning strange in the sense of unfamiliar.

Although the data collection was onerous, it paled in comparison with the task of analyzing the narrative accounts of the home visits. This task took years and resulted in a series of reports of separate data analyses that will be drawn together and summarized here. However, it is convenient to begin with the patterns of infant–mother attachment as they emerged in terms of behavior in the strange situation.

Patterns of Attachment as Assessed in the Strange Situation

Originally designed by Ainsworth and Wittig (1969) to investigate normative behavior in an unfamiliar situation, the main yield of the strange situation was to highlight individual differences in the qualitative nature of the infant's attachment to his mother (Ainsworth, Blehar, Waters, & Wall, 1978).

The situation was composed of eight episodes. The first was a brief introductory episode, followed by two pre-separation episodes; one with mother and baby alone in a room that contained a massive array of toys designed to elicit exploratory behavior, and another following it in which a stranger was present also. Then came a separation episode in which the baby and the stranger were alone together; followed by an episode of reunion with the mother. Then came another separation, in which the baby was first left entirely alone, and then the stranger returned. Finally, the mother returned a second time. It was the baby's behavior in the two reunion episodes that contributed most as an indication of the nature of infant–mother attachment.

Three main patterns of attachment were identified. These were at first labeled Patterns A, B, and C, before the differences between them could be interpreted. These labels have stuck throughout a large number of replications of this procedure by others.

In white, middle-class American samples, Pattern B babies are most numerous, accounting for roughly two-thirds (e.g., Ainsworth *et al.*, 1978; Main & Weston, 1981; Matas, Arend, & Sroufe, 1978; Waters, 1978). These babies may be characterized as *securely attached* to their mothers. In the reunion episodes they behaved as 1-year-olds might be expected to behave. Although they explored freely in the first pre-separation episode, when their mothers returned from brief separations in the unfamiliar environment they sought to be close, and if picked up they tended to resist being put down again too soon.

Babies displaying Patterns A and C were identified as being *anxiously attached* to their mothers. Pattern C babies tended to behave anxiously throughout the strange situation, even in the pre-separation episodes. They tended to be acutely distressed in the separation episodes. In the reunion episodes they obviously wanted to be close to their mothers, but their reactions to her were ambivalent, indeed often angry. Hence, they were identified as *anxious and ambivalent* in their attachment to the mother. They were least numerous in all middle-class samples so far studied, accounting for approximately one-tenth.

Babies displaying Pattern A behavior were somewhat more numerous, accounting for about one-quarter of the samples. They did not behave according to expectations. They seemed not to be disturbed by separation from the mother, and when she returned they tended to avoid her, either steadfastly ignoring her or mingling avoidance with proximity-seeking behavior. Because of this reunion behavior they have been labeled as *anxious and avoidant* in their attachment to the mother. They did not appear to be anxious in the strange situation, however; they were judged to be anxiously attached because of their behavior at home.

MATERNAL BEHAVIOR AS RELATED TO INFANT BEHAVIOR AND INFANT ATTACHMENT PATTERN

Maternal Behavior Relevant to Feeding.   The first analysis of the home-visit data dealt with maternal behavior relevant to the feeding situation (Ainsworth & Bell, 1969). Four main dimensions were identified: who determined when the baby was to be fed—baby or mother; who determined when the feeding was to be terminated; how solid foods were introduced; and to what extent the baby's rate of intake governed the mother in her pacing of feeding. For each of these dimensions rating scales were developed, each scale stressing the extent to which the mother showed sensitive responsiveness to the baby's rhythms, signals, pacing, and preferences—either gearing her behavior to his, thus making him an active partner in the feeding interaction, or herself dominating their transactions (Ainsworth & Tracy, 1973).

The mothers whose ratings were low for responsiveness on these four scales in the first quarter of the first year had babies whose feedings could only be characterized as unhappy, not only in the first quarter but in the fourth quarter as well. With respect to attachment, the babies classified as securely attached to their mothers on the basis of their behavior in the strange situation at 12 months had mothers who had been significantly more sensitive to infant signals relevant to feeding during the first quarter of the year (Ainsworth *et al.,* 1978).

Maternal Responsiveness to Infant Crying.   Every instance of infant crying, including fussing, that occurred during home visits throughout the first
year was coded. Two main measures of maternal unresponsiveness to crying
were derived: how many crying episodes were totally ignored by the mother,
and the duration of her unresponsiveness, measured in minutes per hour during which the baby cried and mother either ignored the cry or delayed in
responding. Similarly, two chief measures of infant crying were derived from
the coding: frequency of crying episodes per hour, and duration of crying in
minutes per hour (Bell & Ainsworth, 1972).

The amount that an infant cried during the first quarter of his first year was
found to have no correlation whatsoever with how much he cried in later
quarters. However, the degree of maternal responsiveness to infant crying
tended to be consistent throughout the first year. The most interesting finding
was that mothers who were relatively responsive to crying in any one quarter
had babies who cried relatively *more* in later quarters. There was no support
whatsoever for the proposition that maternal responsiveness to crying results
in the baby learning to cry more. Furthermore, the appropriateness of the
intervention a mother made in response to crying was found to be unrelated to
the amount of later crying. To respond and to respond promptly seemed to be
more effective in long-term reduction of crying than responding appropriately.

If a baby does not learn to cry more when his mother responds promptly to
his cries, what *does* he learn? It seemed likely that he might well learn to trust
his mother, and expect her to be responsive to him. Thus, he should become
secure in his attachment to her, and indeed this proved to be the case. Mothers
of Pattern B babies showed significantly less delay in responding to their crying
than did the mothers of the anxiously attached babies of Patterns A and C
(Ainsworth *et al.,* 1978). Furthermore, babies whose mothers responded
promptly to their signals—both crying and other signals—learned more varied
and clearer modes of non-crying communication than did the babies of mothers who were relatively unresponsive to crying (Bell & Ainsworth, 1972).

Maternal Behavior in Face-to-Face Situations.   Blehar, Lieberman, and
Ainsworth (1977) reported an analysis of face-to-face interactions during the
period when the babies of the longitudinal sample were from 6 to 15 weeks of
age. Positive infant behaviors such as vocalizing, smiling, and bouncing were
found to be associated both with playful maternal behavior and with maternal
behavior that was paced so as to mesh contingently with infant behavior. On
the other hand, mothers who initiated interactions silently and with an unexpressive face, or who sustained a matter-of-fact "routine" expression while
face to face, had babies who tended merely to look at them, and mothers who
lacked contingent responsiveness tended to have infants who relatively often
terminated the interaction before it really got started—perhaps by crying.

Babies who were anxiously attached to their mothers by the end of the first
year, more than those who were securely attached, had tended in the first

quarter to fail to respond to maternal initiations of face-to-face interaction and/or to terminate it once it had begun. Their mothers tended to be those who maintained an unexpressive manner when face-to-face with the baby, whereas the mothers whose babies became securely attached to them were conspicuous for contingent pacing of their behavior in face-to-face situations (Ainsworth *et al.* 1978).

Behavior in Everyday Separation and Reunion Situations.   Every instance of the mother leaving the room was coded, and every instance of her return. The babies in this sample did not consistently protest mother's departure; on the average they did so in only about one-quarter of the episodes at most. Once locomotion emerged, following was a more frequent response than crying when mother left the room (Stayton, Ainsworth, & Main, 1973). The measures of maternal behavior found to be associated with relatively frequent separation protest were unresponsiveness to crying and general insensitivity to infant signals (Stayton & Ainsworth, 1973).

Once separation protest became consolidated, it seemed to be *the* cardinal sign of anxiety in a baby's attachment to his mother. Even those babies who avoided their mothers in the reunion episodes of the strange situation were significantly more likely than the securely attached babies to show separation protest at home, even though they did *not* do so in the strange situation (Ainsworth *et al.,* 1978).

In reunion episodes in the home environment, mothers differed in the consistency with which they acknowledged the baby upon entering the room. Mothers whose babies were anxiously attached to them did so significantly less often than did mothers whose babies were securely attached—another manifestation of response to infant signals being related to the security of infant–mother attachment. Mothers who were promptly responsive to infant crying, and who had been rated as accepting, cooperative, and generally responsive to infant signals, tended to have babies who responded to their return after a brief absence with a positive greeting—smiling, vocalizing, reaching, approaching, and the like—rather than greeting her with a cry. As might be expected, such positive greetings also served to distinguish infants who were securely attached from those who were anxiously attached to their mothers.

Maternal Behavior Relevant to Infant Obedience.   For the last quarter of the first year, after locomotion had been achieved, every instance was coded of the mother issuing commands such as "No! No!" "Don't touch!" "Come!" "Sit!" "Give it to me!" and the like, whether or not she reinforced such commands with physical interventions. Infant response was coded as compliance or noncompliance with the command. Three maternal variables were positively and strongly related to infant compliance. Disobedient infants tended to have mothers who had been rated as insensitive to infant signals and communications, rejecting, and interfering, whereas infants who were cooperative, complying with commands, tended to have mothers rated as sensitive, accepting, and cooperative. Maternal efforts toward discipline, as reflected by frequency of issuing commands or frequency of physical interventions to back them up, were essentially uncorrelated with infant obedience. Furthermore, infants identified as securely attached showed significantly more frequent cooperation with maternal commands than either of the groups who were anxiously attached to their mothers (Stayton, Hogan, & Ainsworth, 1971).

Maternal Behavior Relevant to Close Bodily Contact.   Every instance was coded in which a baby was picked up and then perhaps held, and every instance in which he was put down afterward (Blehar, Ainsworth, & Main, in preparation). From this coding a number of maternal variables were derived. Three of these dealt with the amount of holding: how often the mother picked the baby up, the total duration of holding time in minutes per waking hour, and the mean duration of a pickup episode. Other measures referred to qualitative features of maternal behavior: the proportion of holding that was either tender and careful or inept, and the percentage of pickup episodes in which the mother displayed affectionate, or playful, or abrupt and interfering behavior. The infant measures consisted of positive and negative responses to being picked up and put down.

The way a baby responded to close bodily contact with his mother in the first quarter gave no basis for prediction of how he would behave in later quarters. However, maternal behavior relevant to contact tended to be consistent throughout the baby's first year.

A series of factor analyses were undertaken to clarify the relationships among maternal behaviors and between them and infant behaviors in each quarter. Two main dimensions of maternal behavior were found, one dealing with the amount the mother held the baby and the other with qualitative differences. Tender/careful, affectionate, and playful maternal behaviors were toward one end of the qualitative dimension and inept holding and interfering pickups toward the other. Of all the behaviors, tender/careful holding emerged as the most definitive of the qualitative dimension—at least throughout the first three quarters.

Although in the first two quarters there was some association between relatively long holding and the positive qualitative variables, this disappeared by the third quarter. Thus, early on, mothers who held their babies for relatively long times tended to be more tender, affectionate, and playful, but this was not necessarily the case in the second half of the first year.

More striking was the fact that in each quarter positive infant responses both to being picked up and to being put down were associated with not how long they were held but with *how* the mother held them, whereas negative responses to being picked up and put down were associated with inept holding and later with interfering pickups.

Of course, these within-quarter factor analyses gave no clear indication of whether it was the mother's behavior that influenced the baby's behavior or vice versa, or whether the influence was quite reciprocal. Further cross-quarter correlational analyses were undertaken to examine direction of effects. Tender/careful holding in any one quarter seemed significantly to influence positive infant response to being held in later quarters, whereas the reverse was not the case. On the other hand, from the second quarter on, positive infant response to being held seemed to influence the mother toward more frequent affectionate behavior later on, whereas the reverse was not the case. These two findings together suggest a "virtuous spiral." Mothers who are tender and careful early on, gearing their behavior to the baby's behavioral cues, tend to evoke a positive response in the baby, which carries over into later quarters; this positive response tends to evoke affectionate maternal behavior, which probably in turn reinforces positive infant response, and so on. Relationships across time between inept maternal holding and infant negative response to being held were also examined. First-quarter maternal ineptness seemed to begin a vicious spiral; it was associated with infant negative response to holding in later quarters, but from the second quarter on there was as much evidence for infant negative response being the cause of maternal ineptness as for its being the effect.

Infant responses to close bodily contact were significantly related to patterns of infant–mother attachment. The securely attached, Pattern B babies were not only distinguished from the anxiously attached, Pattern A and C babies by all the indicators of security versus anxiety already mentioned, but also by the fact that they responded more positively both to close bodily contact with their mothers and to its cessation. In particular, during the fourth quarter, the Pattern A babies differed from both B and C babies: These anxious–avoidant infants almost never "sank in," molding their bodies to the mother's body when held.

Maternal behavior relevant to close bodily contact was even more significantly related to quality of infant–mother attachment. Mothers who in the first quarter were relatively tender/careful and affectionate when holding their babies had babies who were securely attached to them by the end of the first year, whereas those who handled the baby ineptly tended to have anxiously attached babies later on. A more striking finding was that mothers of the anxious–avoidant, Pattern A infants *all* showed a marked aversion to close bodily contact, whereas none of the mothers of the Pattern C or B babies did. Thus, although they did not hold their babies for significantly less time, somehow they must often enough have expressed rebuff when their babies sought close contact that this had profound influence on the infants.

Mothers of the anxious–avoidant, Pattern A babies also differed from the other two groups of mothers in that they tended to be unexpressive emotionally when dealing with their babies, and to be rigid and perfectionistic. Indeed, some of them could be identified as classically obsessive–compulsive characters. Furthermore, they had previously been found to be more rejecting than other mothers in the sample, having their positive feelings for their infants more frequently overwhelmed by irritation, resentment, or downright anger.

Finally, the anxious–ambivalent, Pattern C babies were found to be more often angry than the securely attached, Pattern B babies—but the anxious–avoidant, Pattern A babies were significantly more angry than either of the other two groups.

INTERPRETATION OF FINDINGS

There seems no doubt that the main feature of a mother's behavior that is associated with her baby's secure attachment to her is her sensitive responsiveness to his signals and communications—across all important contexts of their interaction. The second main facet of maternal behavior that is highlighted in the Ainsworth longitudinal sample is attitude toward and behavior relevant to close bodily contact with the baby, and this seemed particularly significant in distinguishing between the two patterns of anxious infant attachment to the mother. Although an infant's demands for close bodily contact become less frequent and less urgent as time goes on, even within the first year, there is reason to believe that early interaction relevant to contact may shape patterns of relationship between child and mother that persist long after contact itself has become less frequently important to the baby than it is in the first few months. According to Bowlby's (1969) attachment theory, it makes sense that a mother's response to a demand for contact is so important, because when attachment behavior is activated at high intensity more proximity is not enough; only close contact will do.

The ambivalence of Pattern C babies, both at home and in the strange situation, is easily understood. Their mothers, who were very inconsistent in their responsiveness to signals, often failed to pick the baby up when he most wanted contact, and often put him down again long before he was ready to be put down. Consequently, when attachment behavior is intensely activated the baby has no confident expectation that his mother will respond to his need for close contact. Having been frustrated in such situations often enough in the past, his desire for close contact is intermingled with anger, because he rather expects his mother to be unresponsive. He wants contact and is angry if his mother does not respond, or if she tries some other mode of interaction, and yet he is still angry if she picks him up and is difficult to soothe; indeed he may struggle to be put down only to protest and seek to be picked up again.

The dynamics of mother–infant interaction associated with the anxious–avoidant Pattern A are more complex, as Main (e.g., 1977) has argued. While the mother of a Pattern C baby is likely to enjoy contact with him, even though she is often imperceptive of his need for it, the mother of a Pattern A baby tends to find such contact aversive. Despite her efforts to hide this aversion, it must come across to the baby in tense and reluctant behavior in close contact, and at least occasionally as active rebuff. It is assumed that the baby picks this up, and that it is especially significant to him because it is when he is most stressed that he most urgently seeks contact. Even a few rebuffs when his attachment behavior has been activated at high intensity would tend to lead him to expect painful rebuff whenever he especially wants to be close. There- fore, whenever stress leads him to want contact urgently, it also activates an expectation of rebuff and associated anger. He is caught in a severe and recur- rent approach–avoidance conflict. He wants contact and dares not seek it for fear of rebuff.

Such a conflict in relation to the mother figure is very threatening. Hence, the Pattern A baby resorts to a defensive maneuver. In a stressful situation, such as the strange situation, he defensively excludes from perception environ- mental clues that otherwise might activate both attachment behavior and an- ger at high intensity, so it is as though he does not register the fact that his mother has left the room or that she has returned after an absence. Instead he resorts to a diversionary activity, which in this situation is to handle the toys in the room, behaving much as though nothing had happened—although, ac- cording to Sroufe and Waters (1977), his heartbeat betrays that he was indeed affected at some level by the stressful events.[1] To view avoidance of his mother as a defensive process makes sense of the otherwise paradoxical fact that the Pattern A baby behaves quite differently in equally brief separation situations in the familiar home environment—where he is likely to protest mother's departure and to follow her, showing more separation distress than a securely attached infant.

USE OF THE MOTHER AS A SECURE BASE FROM
WHICH TO EXPLORE

Ainsworth (e.g., 1967, 1972; Ainsworth & Bell, 1970) reported on the phenomenon of the infant, having acquired locomotion, cheerfully moving away from his mother in order to explore interesting features of his world. During such exploration he seems aware of his mother's whereabouts, for he keeps visual tabs on her, and may occasionally smile or vocalize to her across a distance. Every now and then he tends to return to her, perhaps achieving contact with her for a moment, but then moves off again to continue his exploratory play. This voluntary distancing of himself from her in the interests of exploration is in striking contrast to the distress that may be occasioned if she unexpectedly distances herself from him, in which case the infant's attach- ment behavior may be activated at high intensity and his exploration aban- doned. Even in the strange situation babies tend to use their mothers as a

---

[1]Sroufe and Waters found that Pattern A babies showed much the same pattern of acceleration of heart rate as did the babies of other patterns upon the mother's departure from and return to the room, even though their behavior suggested indifference to such events. Furthermore, during the separation and reunion episodes when they were ostensibly busy in exploratory play the episodic deceleration of heart rate implying attentive interest was conspicuously lacking.

secure base from which to explore in the first pre-separation episode when mother and infant are alone together.

In the familiar home environment the mother's mere presence may offer some security even to an anxious baby. Indeed, so strong is the tendency, at least toward the end of the first year, to explore the environment that babies who are securely attached to their mothers cannot be distinguished from those who are anxiously attached in terms of time spent away from the mother in exploratory play. Ainsworth, Bell, and Stayton (1971) found that to differentiate securely from anxiously attached infants in terms of the balance between attachment and exploratory behavior at home it was necessary to examine the degree of "smoothness" in transition from attachment to exploratory behavior and also the extent to which positive rather than negative affect was manifested in conjunction with attachment behavior. However, once these were taken into account, the attachment–exploration balance in home behavior was found to be significantly related to the patterns of attachment highlighted in the strange situation.

Attachment, Stability, and Continuity

Stability of infant–mother attachment patterns has been examined by re-testing the dyad in the strange situation after a lapse of time long enough to prevent carry-over of anxiety induced by the situation from one testing to the next. In three middle-class American samples, infants, accompanied by their mothers to the strange situation, were observed first at 12 months and later at 18 months of age. Waters (1978) found remarkable stability; 96% of the sample were classified in the same A/B/C groups at both testings. Connell (1976) and Main and Weston (1981) found 80% and 81% to be identically classified. Such findings suggest that the way a baby organizes his behavior toward an attachment figure—in this case his mother—tends toward stability. However, it is not clear whether the persistence of this organization is because the infant's internal organization resists change despite changing circumstances or because the nature of his interaction with his mother remains stable. It seems likely that both factors play a part.

Working with a large sample of mother–infant dyads of low socioeconomic status Vaughn, Egeland, Sroufe, and Waters (1979) threw some light on this issue. They found substantially less stability of attachment pattern, 62%, between 12 and 18 months. The shifts from secure to anxious attachment were associated with more stress impinging on the mother, whereas the shifts from anxious to secure were associated with a decrease in stress. Assuming that increases or decreases in experienced stress in her life circumstances would lead a mother to alter her behavior in interaction with the baby, this finding suggests that quality of infant–mother attachment is indeed geared to quality of interaction. However, one might well expect that changes in the infant's organization of his behavior toward his mother would lag somewhat behind the changes in her behavior.

Beyond approximately 18 months of age, the strange-situation procedure as currently formulated no longer provides a valid assessment of the quality of a child's attachment to a specific figure. The strange situation becomes increasingly less stressful, and less likely to activate attachment behavior at high intensity. Brief separation is less distressing and proximity- and contact-seeking behavior is less strongly activated (Maccoby & Feldman, 1972; Marvin, 1977). During this period, as Sroufe (1979) emphasized, the major developmental issues faced by a child shift substantially, and hence the contextual significance of a given behavior also shifts. However, when toddlers and older preschoolers are observed in contexts that highlight appropriate developmental issues, substantial coherence in development has been found by a number of investigators (Arend, Gove, & Sroufe, 1979; Londerville & Main, 1981; Main, 1973; Matas et al., 1978; Waters, Wippman, & Sroufe, 1979).

At 22 months toddlers who had been judged securely attached to their mothers at 12 months of age, in comparison with those judged nonsecure, were superior in exploratory play and language acquisition (Main, 1973). They were more cooperative with both relatively familiar adults and mothers, less likely to show active disobedience, and more capable of "internalized control" (Londerville & Main, 1981). At 24 months toddlers who had been identified as securely attached at 12 or 18 months were affectively positive and persistent in solving difficult problems, and able to seek and/or to accept help from their mothers when needed. In contrast, anxious–avoidant toddlers were conspicuously noncompliant and aggressive with their mothers, and more likely to seek help from the unfamiliar experimenter, whereas the anxious– ambivalent children relied on their mothers excessively, gave up readily on the most difficult problems, and exhibited frustration behavior (Matas et al., 1978). At 24 months toddlers previously identified as securely attached showed more "affective sharing" with their mothers than those previously identified as anxiously attached (Waters et al., 1979).

At $3\frac{1}{2}$ years children who at 15 months had been assessed as securely attached to their mothers were clearly more socially competent in their behavior with age peers in a preschool setting (Waters, et al., 1979). Lieberman (1977) also found a positive relationship between secure attachment to mother in 3-year-olds (assessed concurrently in the home) and social competence with age peers. With their sample of $3\frac{1}{2}$ year-olds Waters and his associates (1979) found that those previously identified as securely attached scored higher on a measure of ego strength and effectance.

At 5 years, in a kindergarten setting, children who had been securely attached to their mothers at 18 months were found to be more ego resilient and more moderately controlled than others.[2] Anxious–avoidant children had emerged as overcontrolled, and anxious–ambivalent children as undercontrolled, and both groups were less ego resilient (Arend et al., 1979).

---

[2]The concepts and measures of ego resilience and ego control were adapted from the work of Block and Block (e.g., 1978).

These findings are congruent with Bowlby's (1973) conceptualization of pathways of development. Not only the tendency toward stability of the family environment in which a child is reared, but also "homeorhetic" processes within the individual himself tend to keep development in the same pathway in which it began early on. These homeorhetic processes would include the way an individual organizes his experience within himself—the representational models he constructs of his environment, himself, and the significant persons in his life. As time goes on the homeorhetic processes become increasingly more resistant to change than they were in the earliest years, and play an increasingly potent role in contributing to continuity of development.

Direction of Effects in Mother–Infant Interaction

Implicit in the concept of person–environment interaction is that both person and environment contribute to the interaction between them. Yet, much more evidence has been presented here of the mother's contribution to the interaction and her influence on the child's behavior and development than of the infant's contribution to it and thus his influence on her behavior. There are two chief reasons for this.

First, the infants in the Baltimore sample represented a relatively narrow range of constitutional differences, in that (possibly with one exception) they were normal, healthy, full-term babies born into relatively advantaged intact families. None suffered from organic damage, significant physical handicap, or chronic illness. The appearance or behavior of none presented any of the major challenges to parents that have drawn attention to child effects on adult behavior. On the other hand, the personalities of the mothers covered a very wide range, from stable and healthy to very disturbed. Had the sample included more infants with anomalies or fewer mothers with personality disorders more evidence of infant effects on maternal behavior might well have emerged.

Second, the major dimension of maternal behavior found related to the later security or insecurity of infant–mother attachment was sensitive responsiveness to infant signals and other behavioral cues. Such responsiveness tends to mask infant effects on the mother, because the sensitive mother gears her behavior to the cues of this particular infant. And, although all the mothers in the sample adjusted their behavior more or less appropriately to developmental changes in infant behavior, this too was masked by the way in which the measures of maternal responsiveness were defined.

Despite a search in our observational records for significant behavioral differences among the neonates of the Baltimore sample that might be related to later qualitative differences in infant–mother attachment, we found none. Such qualitative differences were so consistently related to differences in maternal behavior that we could only conclude that in this sample, at least, it was the mother's contribution to the interaction that was more powerful than the effect of inherent individual differences among infants upon maternal behaviors.

Let us consider, however, the findings of other studies of infant–mother attachment in order to arrive at a more balanced picture of direction of effects. Two bodies of literature seem especially relevant: those dealing with neonatal differences and/or differences in infant temperament and their relationship to later quality of attachment, and cross-cultural studies.

NEONATAL DIFFERENCES AND INFANT TEMPERAMENT

So far, two studies have reported relationships between neonatal measures and later infant–mother attachment patterns. Lower birthweight and lower APGAR[3] scores were found to be related to later Pattern C, anxious–ambivalent attachment by Connell (1974). In samples of families of low socioeconomic level, Waters, Vaughn, and Egeland (1980) found that Pattern C babies had differed from Pattern A and B babies on a number of items of Brazelton's (1973) Neonatal Behavioral Assessment Scale, administered when they were 1 week old. Specifically, they were lower on items reflecting orientation, motor maturity, and regulation. These initial difficulties were transient, for no significant relationship was found between items of a second testing a few days later and subsequent quality of attachment.

It seems that neonatal differences assessed by the Brazelton scale do not necessarily reflect lasting individual differences in temperament, even though they may well highlight important differences in neonatal condition—related to prenatal or perinatal factors that may in some instances be rectified within a few days by adequate mothering. Thus, Woodson, Reader, Shephard, and Chamberlain (1981) found that amount of neonatal crying was significantly associated with an acidemic condition (low blood pH), which in turn was associated with even subclinical differences in degree of perinatal anoxia. Within a few days, however, the effect "washed out." The studies of both Woodson's and Waters's teams suggest that neonatal assessments, however accurately they may reflect neonatal condition, cannot be taken as assessments of lasting individual differences. How could it be, therefore, that they could be associated with assessments of quality of infant–mother attachment a year later? It seems likely that if an infant whose neonatal condition is anomalous is paired with a mother insensitive to infant cues, interaction might well begin in an anxious way and continue thus even though the initial condition of the infant improved rapidly.

It is usually assumed that temperamental differences refer to characteristics that are lasting because they stem from differences in genetic constitution, or possibly to lasting effects of prenatal or perinatal insults. However, Thomas, Chess, Birch, Hertzig, and Korn (1963) made their initial assessment of infant

[3]The APGAR scoring procedure provides an overall assessment of the infant's physical condition immediately after birth.

temperament at 3 months of age, by which time the babies in the Baltimore sample were already showing the effects of previous interaction with their mothers. Such assessments therefore may, on the whole, reflect lasting characteristics, but do not distinguish between those stemming from early person–environment interaction and those inherent in the newborn. Furthermore, their assessments of temperament—as well as the assessment procedures devised by others following their lead—have so far been dependent on maternal report, so that it is difficult to know how much of the apparent stability of child behavior over time is due to stability of maternal perception of the child. More relevant to the attachment issue, however, are several pieces of evidence that make it seem very unlikely that temperamental differences among infants are related to the nature of the attachment relationships they form with parent figures or to the stability of patterns of attachment over time.

Vaughn, Taraldson, Crichton, and Egeland (1981) found that the only significant relationships between scores on the Carey Infant Temperament Questionnaire (Carey, 1970) and other maternal and infant measures in their study were with maternal characteristics and attitudes assessed when the infant was 3 months of age, and not with any measures of infant behavior including the assessment of later attachment pattern. Both Lamb (1978) and Main and Weston (1981) reported no significant relationship between infant patterns of attachment to mother and to father. Presumably, the organization of the attachment to each figure reflects the infant's history of interaction with that figure rather than a temperamental trait predisposing the child to be generally secure or insecure in his or her relationships. Similarly, Crittenden (1983) found that infants who are "difficult" in interaction with an abusive mother tend to be "cooperative" when interacting with another familiar person who is sensitive to infant cues, which suggests that they were not temperamentally difficult.

On the other hand, there is evidence that patterns of attachment to parent figures may affect subsequent interaction with new figures. Thus, Main and Weston (1981) found that babies who were securely attached to both parents showed readiness to establish a positive social relationship with an unfamiliar adult and to respond affectively to his changing moods, whereas babies who were nonsecure with both parents were not at all ready to do so, and babies secure with one parent but not with the other fell in between. It seemed that the way the infant had centrally organized his behavior toward parents determined his reaction to a new person with whom he had had only a short time to become familiar. Crittenden (1983) suggested that infant ability to respond directly to the behavior of a new partner without being influenced by the inner organization built up in the course of long-term interaction with parent figures may diminish in the course of development. Thus, in the second year of life the abused child may respond to another interactional partner as he ordinarily responds to his abusive mother, even though the new partner behaves very differently than the mother does. This suggestion fits the findings of George and Main (1979) that abused toddlers showed more avoidance and aggression both to day caregivers and to age peers than did a matched control group of nonabused toddlers from disturbed families. Indeed, as Bowlby (1973) suggested, environmental changes (including changes in quality of interaction with key figures) early in life may make it possible for an individual to shift from one pathway of development to another fairly readily, but as the "home-orhetic" processes within the individual himself become further consolidated change becomes increasingly more difficult. Thus, in a sense, the persistent characteristics that have been attributed to temperament may well become more conspicuous as development proceeds, and more and more a result of "person–environment" interaction in distinction to the genetic and other "organic" influences presumably influencing the newborn.

CROSS-CULTURAL STUDIES OF
INFANT–PARENT ATTACHMENT

Insofar as attachment behavior and complementary parental (caregiving) behavior have a species-characteristic genetic basis, as Bowlby (1969) proposed, a basic core of similarities should be found across different cultures. Ainsworth (1977), comparing the findings of her Baltimore and Ganda studies, reported much similarity in the development of infant attachment behavior, in the distinction between secure and anxious patterns of attachment, and in the ways maternal attitudes and behavior were related to differences in attachment patterns. Nevertheless, to the extent that maternal caregiving behavior is "environmentally labile" and responsive to cultural influences, some cross-cultural differences could be expected, and indeed were found in regard to three important facets of infant behavior: frequency and intensity of separation anxiety, intensity of fear of strangers, and the use of the mother as a secure base from which to explore.

Unfortunately, the strange-situation procedure that has proved useful as the basis for assessment of quality of infant–parent attachment in white, middle-class American samples may not be relevant elsewhere. In societies in which infants rarely encounter strangers and rarely if ever are left with them or alone the strange-situation procedure might well be so alien to their experience to make it both unduly stressful and quite inapplicable.

Nevertheless, there have been useful investigations in various cultures and subcultures in Western societies using our strange-situation assessments of quality of attachment. Bell (in preparation) replicated most of the findings of our Baltimore study with a sample of black, disadvantaged mother–infant dyads in Baltimore. She found a higher incidence of anxious attachment in the black sample, which seemed obviously related to the higher incidence of disorganization in these very disadvantaged homes and to inconsistent, ad hoc substitute-care arrangements. But the relationships between mother–infant interaction variables and infant attachment patterns were entirely congruent with the findings for the white, middle-class Baltimore sample. Furthermore, the findings for the low SES Minnesota sample studied by Sroufe, Vaughn, Waters, Egeland, and their associates seem also to be essentially congruent, to judge from findings both published and not yet published.

Grossmann and Grossmann (1982) undertook a replication of the general outlines of our Baltimore study in two samples, the first in North Germany and the second in South Germany. In conjunction with the South German study there was also a replication of the study by Main and Weston (1981). The findings of the South German study to date are essentially congruent with our findings and those of Main and Weston. There was, however, a striking discrepancy in the case of the North German study; nearly half of the infants were identified as anxious–avoidant in their attachment to their mothers, whereas only one-third were identified as securely attached—a near-reversal of the distribution of the patterns usually found in American middle-class samples.

The Grossmanns suggest that cultural pressures led the North German mothers to emphasize training toward obedience and independence, beginning approximately with the emergence of locomotion in the middle of the baby's first year. Regardless of their previous sensitivity to infant behavioral cues, they tended increasingly to withhold themselves from close bodily contact with the infants and from expressing tenderness or affection in the context of contact; specifically, they tended to respond to crying by trying to divert the babies or by scolding them rather than by picking the babies up as the Baltimore mothers still tended to do. Perhaps the most interesting implication of this study is that, regardless of the mother's "reasons" for responding insensitively to infant cues and for withholding bodily contact, the outcome was the same as found in the Baltimore study, namely, making more likely the development by the infant of an anxious–avoidant pattern of attachment to his mother. Whether the prediction from such a pattern toward later development is the same in both cases, however, can only be ascertained by follow-up research.

Attachment Research and the Person–Environment Interaction Perspective

In my view, attachment theory (e.g., Bowlby, 1969) has inspired research wholly congruent with the person–environment interaction perspective as outlined by Magnusson and Allen in this volume (Chapters 1 and 21). Lest this congruency be not clearly self-evident, it may be useful here to point to some of the ways in which the research reported in this chapter represents an interactional perspective.

In my own longitudinal study of the development of infant attachment to mother throughout the first year, the obvious focus was on the baby as "person" and on maternal behavior as the most salient feature of "environment." In regard to the biological substrate of the person, the baby, attachment theory led us to emphasize the commonalities in our sample of healthy, normal neonates, in particular the system of proximity-promoting behaviors (the attachment system) believed to have evolved because of the survival advantage afforded by maintenance of proximity to a caregiving figure, which was expected to result in the baby becoming attached to the mother as principal caregiver. Among other commonalities to which attention was paid were other behavioral systems, such as the exploratory, fear, and food-seeking systems, and their interplay with attachment behavior.

In the earliest weeks after birth an infant's chief mode of promoting and maintaining proximity to and contact with his mother is through the fact that his behavior, and in particular his attachment behavior, has signal value to his caregiver, activating a complementary system of caregiving behavior, which is also presumed to have a genetically based, species-characteristic, ground plan. In the case of both infant and mother, individual differences could be expected, especially in the case of the mother, who had become much more complexly organized than the infant in the course of her interactions with her environment over her lifetime.

As might have been expected on the basis of attachment theory, differences among mothers in the extent to which they, for whatever reasons, were available to the infant and responsive to the infant's behavioral cues emerged as crucial factors in determining the security versus insecurity of the infant's attachment to her. However, before a clear-cut attachment to a specific figure is formed, other important developmental changes intervene: regulation of basic rhythms of hunger, activity, and sleep–wake cycles, differentiation among the persons that constitute the social environment, and at least the beginnings of the concept of the continuing existence of persons when they are not present to perception. Although this chapter's report of research findings has not focused on them, concepts of mediating processes are essential to our view. Indeed, the "environmental situation" becomes increasingly defined as the "perceived situation" in terms of these mediating processes.

Since rhythms become regulated more or less in harmony with the behavior of the caregiver, we must infer that from the very earliest days of life a baby begins to form some kind of primitive expectations about the behavior of his caregiver(s) and its relation to his own primitive awareness of needs, wishes, and feelings. Although an active participant in interaction with his environment from the beginning, the baby only gradually becomes capable of intentional behaviour, of envisaging goals, of formulating plans, and of choosing ways to implement plans. However, by approximately the middle of the first year of life, at about the same time that locomotion first appears, intentional behavior emerges. From this point on, according to Bowlby (1969), the infant's interaction with its environment is best viewed in terms of control-systems theory, and his behavior interpreted as "goal-corrected." Once goal-corrected behavior emerges it becomes increasingly less useful to view infant behavior in terms of discrete variables and more essential to consider behaviors related to the same system as having functional equivalence.

Also about the middle of the baby's first year, it becomes necessary to infer that the baby has made a start in building up representational models of the significant features of his environment, based on but supplanting the more primitive expectations he has been building up all along. The representational model he has formed of his mother, as accessible and responsive or inaccessible and unresponsive, is the basis of the security versus insecurity of his attachment to her. In any given situation what he expects of her as a product of his previous experience in interaction with her is brought by him as a "person" into the present situation and is a factor in determining his behavior as well as her own actual behavior in that situation.

Eventually, a young child builds a representational model of self, on the basis of his experience of interaction with his environment including the significant other persons in it, perhaps especially his mother. Throughout all or most of the first year it seems likely that the model of self is primitive, but it seems altogether likely that the baby has to some extent organized his sense of competence—his confidence in being able to affect what happens to him—both as a result of his interactions with his physical environment and as a result of his experience of being able to influence the behavior of other people, especially his mother.

Although the attachment research reported in this chapter has seemed to focus on outcome—quality of the infant–mother attachment relationship—the implicit emphasis has been on understanding the processes underlying the outcome. It must be clear that a chief theme has been patterning and organization of behavior rather than continuity of discrete behavioral variables. This, of course, leads us to the issue of consistency or stability across situations and over time. The research of others who have dealt with consistency of infant–mother attachment patterns across time and their coherence with later patterns of behavior has strongly suggested stability and coherence. I view these findings not so much as an indication that early experience has lasting effects on development but as a demonstration of the lawfulness and continuity of processes of person–environment interaction. Of equal importance are the instances of instability and lack of coherence; presumably these too may be understood in terms of lawful processes. The findings of Vaughn and his associates (1979), that shifts of attachment pattern could be related to increases or decreases of stress impinging on the mother and hence presumably affecting her interaction with the child, suggest that a lawful process is involved. At this stage in research into infant–mother attachment, there has been so much congruity of findings that reports that imply failures to replicate seem without value unless supported by evidence showing how lawful processes account for the discrepancies.

This brings us to the importance of observations of the behavioral phenomena in the natural environment. The validity of the strange-situation procedure as a basis for assessing attachment originally rested on the congruency of patterns of strange-situation behavior with patterns of mother–infant interaction at home throughout the first year. There has been a tendency in research dealing with later preschool years to rely heavily upon this laboratory procedure or laboratory supplements with little or no effort to examine the congruency between behavior in the controlled laboratory situation and behavior in the natural environment.

In regard to stability of attachment patterns and their influence on subsequent development, however, attachment research has clearly been in line with the perspective characterizing this volume. The emphasis has been on consistency of lawful processes and structures rather than on consistency of specific behavior, and upon coherence of patterns of behavior both across situations and across time.

Finally, let us return to the "environment" side of the child's interaction with his mother. Obviously, one could focus attention on the mother as a person and the baby as an important part of the environment with which she is interacting. Her behavior is much more directly affected by the wider environmental context than that of the baby, who tends to be affected indirectly through the effect of such context on his mother and other significant figures in his life. Furthermore, the mother as "person" brings to her interaction with a wider and more complex environment a "structure" and pattern of processes that is the product of a long history of person–environment interaction. To gain an understanding of how it is that mothers, fathers, and other caregivers behave the way they do in interaction with an infant in their care clearly constitutes a significant research enterprise, and one that should contribute importantly to the success of intervention efforts intended to improve an infant's prospects of optimal development. Nevertheless, research tends to progress through a succession of small projects of limited scope. No one project can take into account more than part of the complexity implicit in person–environment interaction. In evaluating a project one should focus more on the issue of how its findings dovetail with or fill in the gaps left by previous projects rather than upon the issue of what that specific project has failed to illuminate. Proceeding from a person–environment interaction perspective should facilitate the process of linking the findings of separate investigations together in a coherent way rather than viewing them as conflicting or controversial.

References

Ainsworth, M. D. S. *Infancy in Uganda: Infant care and the growth of love.* Baltimore: Johns Hopkins University Press, 1967.

Ainsworth, M. D. S. Attachment and dependency: A comparison. In J. L. Gewirtz (Ed.), *Attachment and dependency.* Washington, D.C.: V. H. Winston & Sons, 1972.

Ainsworth, M. D. S. Infant development and mother–infant interaction among Ganda and American families. In P. H. Leiderman, S. R. Tulkin, & A. Rosenfeld (Eds.), *Culture and infancy: Variations in the human experience.* New York: Academic Press, 1977.

Ainsworth, M. D. S., & Bell, S. M. Some contemporary patterns of mother–infant interaction in the feeding situation. In A. Ambrose (Ed.), *Stimulation in early infancy*. New York: Academic Press, 1969.

Ainsworth, M. D. S., & Bell, S. M. Attachment, exploration, and separation: Illustrated by the behavior of one-year-olds in a strange situation. *Child Development*, 1970, *41*, 49–67.

Ainsworth, M. D. S., Bell, S. M., & Stayton, D. J. Individual differences in strange-situation behavior of one-year-olds. In H. R. Schaffer (Ed.), *The origins of human social relations*. New York: Academic Press, 1971.

Ainsworth, M. D. S., Blehar, M. C., Waters, E., & Wall, S. *Patterns of attachment: A psychological study of the strange situation*. Hillsdale, N.J.: Erlbaum, 1978.

Ainsworth, M. D. S., & Tracy, R. L. *Infant feeding and attachment*. Paper presented at the meeting of the American Psychological Association, 1973.

Ainsworth, M. D. S., & Wittig, B. A. Attachment and exploratory behavior of one-year-olds in a strange situation. In B. M. Foss (Ed.), *Determinants of infant behavior* (Vol. 4). London: Methuen, 1969.

Arend, R., Gove, F., & Sroufe, L. A. Continuity of individual adaptation from infancy to kindergarten: A predictive study of ego-resiliency and curiosity in preschoolers. *Child Development*, 1979, *50*, 950–959.

Bell, S. M., & Ainsworth, M. D. A. Infant crying and maternal responsiveness. *Child Development*, 1972, *43*, 1171–1190.

Bell, S. M. *Cognitive development and mother–child interaction in the first three years of life*. Monograph in preparation.

Blehar, M. C., Ainsworth, M. D. S., & Main, M. *A monograph on mother–infant interaction relevant to close bodily contact*. In preparation.

Blehar, M. C., Lieberman, A. F., & Ainsworth, M. D. S. Early face-to-face interaction and its relation to later infant–mother attachment. *Child Development*, 1977, *48*, 182–194.

Block, J. H., & Block, J. The role of ego-control and ego-resiliency in the organization of behavior. In W. A. Collins (Ed.), *Minnesota symposium on child psychology* (Vol. 13). Hillsdale, N. J.: Erlbaum, 1978.

Bowlby, J. *Attachment and loss* (Vol. 1): *Attachment*. New York: Basic Books, 1969.

Bowlby, J. *Attachment and loss* (Vol. 2): *Separation: Anxiety and anger*. New York: Basic Books, 1973.

Brazelton, T. B. *Neonatal Behavioral Assessment Scale*. Philadelphia: Lippincott, 1973.

Carey, W. B. A simplified method for measuring infant temperament. *Journal of Pediatrics*, 1970, *77*, 188–194.

Connell, D. B. *Individual differences in infant attachment related to habituation as a redundant stimulus*. Unpublished master's thesis, Syracuse University, 1974.

Connell, D. B. *Individual differences in attachment: An investigation into stability, implications, and relationships to structure of early language development*. Unpublished doctoral dissertation, Syracuse University, 1976.

Crittenden, P. M. *Mother and infant patterns of interaction: Developmental relationships*. Unpublished doctoral dissertation, University of Virginia, May 1983.

George, C., & Main, M. Social interactions of young abused children: Approach, avoidance, and aggression. *Child Development*, 1979, *50*, 306–318.

Grossmann, K., & Grossmann, K. E. *Maternal sensitivity to infants' signals during the first year as related to the year-olds' behavior in Ainsworth's strange situation in a sample of North German families*. Paper presented at the International Conference on Infant Studies, Austin, Texas, March 1982.

Lamb, M. E. Qualitative aspects of mother and father infant attachments. *Infant Behavior and Development*, 1978, *1*, 265–275.

Lieberman, A. F. Preschoolers' competence with a peer: Relations with attachment and peer experience. *Child Development*, 1977, *23*, 3–27.

Londerville, S., & Main, M. Security, compliance, and maternal training methods in the second year of life. *Developmental Psychology,* 1981, *17,* 289–299.

Maccoby, E. E., & Feldman, S. S. Mother-attachment and stranger-reactions in the third year of life. *Monographs of the Society for Research in Child Development,* 1972, *37* (Serial No. 146).

Main, M. *Exploration, play, and level of cognitive functioning as related to child–mother attachment.* Unpublished doctoral dissertation, Johns Hopkins University, 1973.

Main, M. Analysis of a peculiar form of reunion behavior seen in some daycare children: Its history and sequelae in children who are home-reared. In R. Webb (Ed.), *Social development in daycare.* Baltimore: Johns Hopkins University Press, 1977.

Main, M., & Weston, D. R. The quality of the toddler's relationship to mother and to father: Related to conflict behavior and the readiness to establish new relationships. *Child Development,* 1981, *52,* 932–940.

Marvin, R. S. An ethological–cognitive model for the attenuation of mother–child attachment behavior. In T. M. Alloway, L. Krames, & P. Pliner (Eds.), *Advances in the study of communication and affect* (Vol. 3): *The development of social attachments.* New York: Plenum, 1977.

Matas, L., Arend, R. A., & Sroufe, L. A. Continuity of adaptation in the second year: The relationship between quality of attachment and later competence. *Child Development,* 1978, *49,* 547–556.

Sroufe, L. A. The coherence of individual development. *American Psychologist,* 1979, *34,* 834–841.

Sroufe, L. A., & Waters, E. Heart rate as a convergent measure in clinical and developmental research. *Merrill-Palmer Quarterly,* 1977, *23,* 3–28.

Stayton, D. J., & Ainsworth, M. D. S. Individual differences in infant responses to brief, everyday separations as related to other infant and maternal behaviors. *Developmental Psychology,* 1973, *9,* 226–235.

Stayton, D. J., Ainsworth, M. D. S., & Main, M. B. The development of separation behavior in the first year of life: Protest, following, and greeting. *Developmental Psychology,* 1973, *9,* 213–225.

Stayton, D. J., Hogan, R., & Ainsworth, M. D. S. Infant obedience and maternal behavior: The origins of socialization reconsidered. *Child Development,* 1971, *42,* 1057–1069.

Thomas, A., Chess, S., Birch, H., Hertzig, M., & Korn, S. *Behavioral individuality in early childhood.* New York: New York University Press, 1963.

Vaughn, B., Egeland, B., Sroufe, L. A., & Waters, E. Individual differences in infant–mother attachment at twelve and eighteeen months: Stability and change in families under stress. *Child Development,* 1979, *50,* 971–975.

Vaughn, B. E., Taraldson, B. J., Crichton, L., & Egeland, B. The assessment of infant temperament: A critique of the Carey Infant Temperament Questionnaire. *Infant Behavior and Development,* 1981, *4,* 41–46.

Waters, E. The reliability and stability of individual differences in infant–mother attachment. *Child Development,* 1978, *49,* 483–494.

Waters, E., Vaughn, B., & Egeland, B. Individual differences in infant–mother attachment relationships at age one: Antecedents in neonatal behavior in an urban, economically disadvantaged sample. *Child Development,* 1980, *51,* 208–216.

Waters, E., Wippman, J., & Sroufe, L. A. Attachment, positive affect, and competence in the peer group: Two studies in construct validation. *Child Development,* 1979, *50,* 821–829.

Woodson, R., Reader, F., Shephard, J., & Chamberlin, G. Blood pH and crying in the newborn infant. *Infant Behavior and Development,* 1981, *4,* 41–46.

3

Conceptions of Environment in Childrearing Interactions

MARIAN RADKE-YARROW   LEON KUCZYNSKI

The interaction of person and environment is a perspective in most theories of development and behavior. It is a formulation that sets very difficult challenges, however, when one turns seriously in research to the work of identifying, measuring, and interpreting the interdependencies between person and environment. In this paper, childrearing is the context for examining issues of person–environment interaction. Since biological inheritance, a history of experience and learning, and a continuing interpersonal environment are brought together in the family, one should expect interactional processes and influences at many levels. We focus on the generally extended period of intimate interdependencies of parents and children, and the effects of this component of life experience upon the behavior of the participants.

The intensity of research on rearing reflects the importance of this subject and the degree to which it stubbornly resists efforts to understand its operations and outcomes. Research information about how the infant evolves into the child and the child into the adult has come from many sources. At times, the stimulus to scientific interest has been the scientist–parent who has found in his/her child the wonder and puzzlement of development and parenting. At other times, clinicians have sought explanations for adult psychopathology in the individual's childhood history. Over the years, doubts about societal practices of institutionalizing children have raised questions and instigated investigations concerning the effects on children of living in environments without parents. From the perspective of learning theories, psychologists have attempted to pinpoint the effects on children of specific techniques of control and discipline by simulating these dimensions of parenting in the laboratory.

57

HUMAN DEVELOPMENT:
AN INTERACTIONAL PERSPECTIVE

ISBN 0-12-465480-0

The natural interplay of parents and children has also been systematically recorded, although usually under very limited circumstances. Descriptions of rearing in other cultures have added to knowledge concerning the influence of rearing environments. Experimental and naturalistic data from research with animals, too, have provided broadened perspectives. Still another layer of variables concerns the genetic and neurobiological determinants of behavior. Despite this rich accumulation of perspectives and of investigative efforts, inconclusive evidence, conflicting findings, and major gaps in knowledge concerning the processes and outcomes of rearing leave much to be investigated. A general question that hovers over this domain of study is how directly have interactional processes been studied.

We begin with a brief review of theoretical orientations regarding determinants of individual development, and the roles given to person and environment in research on childrearing. Next we consider the concept of interaction with its various meanings in childrearing research. We then focus on the "environmental" component of intrafamilial influences, examining the conceptualization and content of rearing environment and research strategies for studying it. By way of example, a program of ongoing studies is used to provide concreteness to the issues presented. These studies reflect the collaborative work of Leon Kuczynski, Carolyn Zahn-Waxler, Mark Cummings, Ronald Iannotti, Leon Cytryn, Donald McKnew, and Marian Radke-Yarrow at the National Institute of Mental Health. We end this chapter with suggestions and questions for research.

A History of Orientations

How has individual development been explained? What importance has been ascribed to the various components of person (biological and psychological) and environment (familial and extrafamilial) in the developing child? Biology and environment have been variously emphasized in attempting to understand child development. A belief in a parental influence on the child's outcome is neither novel nor modern: "Honour thy father and thy mother that thy days may be long upon the land"; "As the twig is bent, the tree inclines"; and "Spare the rod and spoil the child" express the idea of parental influence. But, when human development became the object of scientific interest, the complexities of these influences became apparent, and a diversity of theories evolved.

In theories of infant development it is not surprising that a strong biological orientation was blended with environmental (mothering) influences. Early clinical reports by Spitz (1965) and others dramatized the devastating effects of separation from mother on the infant's physical and psychological development and pointed to the inherent needs of the young organism. Theories about "critical periods" made biological–experiential interdependencies most explicit with regard to the infant's biological clock and the appropriate timing of crucial experience. In a similar vein, Bowlby's (1951) "tie to the mother" formulation of built-in biological needs and essential mothering detailed the origins of psychological well-being for the infant. The essential union of biological infant needs and readiness to respond to specific environmental conditions was no more clearly demonstrated than in Harlow and Harlow's (1969) work, in which infant rhesus monkeys experimentally deprived of mothering succumbed to serious pathologies in behavioral development. Panksepp, Herman, Conner, Bishop, and Scott (1978), working with infant guinea pigs, experimentally demonstrated the role of brain opiate systems in establishing and modulating infant attachment and separation responses; these behaviors were altered biochemically, demonstrating again the biobehavioral interactions present in early development.

In the preceding examples of psychobiological orientations, infancy has been the common thread; rearing variables have had critical roles within capabilities specifically set by biological development. Past the infancy period, biobehavioral orientations have not been influential in childrearing research. The stage theories of Piaget, the psychologist, Freud, the psychiatrist, and Gesell, the pediatrician, come closest to such formulations. Each assumes a changing maturational readiness of the organism for given kinds of experience and also a constraining effect of the maturational stage on any environmental influence. However, in none of these formulations is there any specificity with respect to stage–environment interaction. In Piaget's developmental theory, for example, the interaction of the child's cognitive structures with the environment lies at the heart of development. Yet in focusing on the nature of the cognitive structures the theory has neglected delineating the role of the environment and has played down the influence of parents. In Kohlberg's (1969) cognitive developmental formulation of socialization, parents are portrayed as having a minimal or even negative influence on moral development.

For whatever reason, there is a sharp discontinuity between the psychobiological orientation found in infant research and the wholly environmental orientation that has predominated in the vast socialization research with older children that began in the 1950s. Guided by conceptualizations from psychoanalytic, Hullian, and social learning traditions, researchers investigated the effects of parental practices on child behavior, generally in the sense of contemporaneous "antecedents" and "consequences." Very little of this research has been developmental in formulation. A few experimental studies (Cheyne, 1972; Grusec & Redler, 1980; LaVoie, 1974; Parke, 1974) have interpreted the effects of various adult-influence techniques in terms of age of child, and other studies (Clifford, 1959; Newson & Newson, 1963, 1968, 1976) have described socialization and rearing environments of children of different ages, but none has articulated a biological–environmental theory. In general, research into socialization has not dealt systematically with how children of different developmental levels process rearing experiences, what experiences

they require, and what experiences are provided in a developmentally se-
quenced manner by parents. Basically, childrearing research, for a period of
years, dropped the *person* and concentrated on the *environment,* that is, parental behavior, in explaining child behavior.

A challenge to the prevailing formulation came in the writings of Sears
(1951) and Bell (1968) in which dyadic, reciprocal processes between parent
and child were emphasized. This perspective called for methodology that was
little developed—mainly one in which the ongoing effects of child and parent
on each other could be observed. To some degree, this changed conceptualization contributed to the revival of interest in observational methods for investigating social interchange, opening possibilities, theoretically at least, for studying feedback effects of parent and child on each other. However, the core
orientation was one of dyadic interchange in an environmental sense, that is,
how child and parent become the environmental stimuli for response from the
other. This has not been entirely the case. Especially in Bell's writings, inherent
biological characteristics of the child (such as temperament) have been stressed
as modifiers of parental behavior and influence. Again, it has often been the
temperament of infants that has interested investigators, with little research
consideration given to parallel qualities of older children and parents as modifiers of the effects of the parent–child interaction. The need for a view of
development in which the inputs of biology and environment are considered in
a sophisticated manner is being increasingly appreciated. Maccoby (1980), for
example, has stressed the need for an orientation that links developmental–biological factors with rearing influences. In her words, research has not
been sufficiently aimed at comprehending the dynamics of development as they
"intersect with the inputs from environment."

In summary, research on child development is beginning to rediscover person variables in interaction with environmental variables. As these formulations take shape, they appear to be conceived at new levels of complexity, in
regard to both persons (child and parent) and environments. In the following
discussion, we are primarily concerned with one dimension of complexity—the
environments in which parents and children interact with one another.

Concepts of Interaction

Since the concept of interaction has been dealt with extensively in other
chapters in this book, it is surveyed briefly here only in terms of the methods of
this field and what they achieve with regard to the assessment of interactive
influences between parent and child.

In a considerable portion of childrearing studies, a history of interaction is
implied, rather than studied directly. Such is the case in correlational research,
in which data on rearing behavior are obtained by interviewing mothers about
their usual practices in caring for and regulating their children. These variables

are then correlated with characteristics of the children. While serving to point out the existence of relationships, findings from these studies leave open to dispute the nature of the processes of influence.

In other research on rearing, either parent effects or child effects are emphasized. The experimental analogs of specific parental behaviors fall into this classification. In highly controlled settings, the effects of adult acts of reinforcement, punishment, reasoning, modeling, nurturance, etc., on child behavior are measured. Although this approach is useful in identifying variables that may operate in child–adult interactions, extrapolations to childrearing interactions of real families must be made cautiously. Aside from concerns about the validity of unfamiliar socializing agents, and of contrived situations that use novel games and tasks as the setting of interaction, these studies provide information about only a one-sided segment of an interaction. In another respect, the laboratory provides a faulty analog of socialization processes. Usually, the influence of a single administration of an adult technique is assessed in terms of an act of immediate or delayed compliance. In the home, using as an example a child's oppositional behavior and a parent's efforts to change it, one would expect the child to commit the same transgression repeatedly over time, on each occasion eliciting different reactions from the parent, before the behavior is finally brought under control (Yarrow, Campbell, & Burton, 1968). The impact of such cumulative influences on the same behavior cannot be assessed with one-time observations.

In recent years, interactive approaches to childrearing have focused on *direct behavioral interchanges* between parent and child. Cairns (1979) describes this interchange as a feedback process by which organisms influence each other by acting and reacting. Studies using these methods have been carried out most vigorously and rigorously with infants and toddlers, who are the researcher's ideal subjects in many ways. Compared with older children, the infant's life situations are relatively limited, and are more "public" and more accessible to the scientist. Many (if not most) critical situations in the infant–mother interaction can be observed, and they can be observed over a period of time. The same cannot be so easily accomplished with older children.

That direct observation is a viable research strategy with school-aged children has been demonstrated in the work of Patterson and his associates (1980, 1981), who studied families with seriously aggressive children as well as matched families with normal children. By investigating the serial dependence of behaviors between parents and children, these researchers show how patterns of techniques and responses evolve from immediate interactions and create spirals of aversive interchange. To verify their coercion theory of interaction in disturbed family systems, parents and children are studied in both controller and recipient roles, as architects and products.

An obvious advantage of direct observations of behavioral exchanges is the validity derived from the fact that parent and child are the actors. Much of the value of this approach depends, however, upon the adequacy of the sampling of behavior and upon the appropriateness of the analytic procedures employed. When short samples of time or limited sampling of settings are used, in laboratory or field, problems occur in extrapolating the data to rearing processes. Decisions governing the segmenting of behavior into units are especially critical for determining the kinds of interpretations of interaction that can be made. The consequences of various unit systems are not well understood.

Probably the most important kind of childrearing interaction, that between parent and child *from a longitudinal or life-history perspective,* is least understood and least often investigated directly. The reciprocal influences of parents' behaviors and children's behaviors continue over time, but undoubtedly change not only as a function of developmental events but of many non-normative events as well. How the patterns of behaviors evolve and become established and the long-term impacts of specific interactions are not explained in research focused on immediate interactions. An understanding of parent–child interactions from a longitudinal perspective is ultimately required for convincing explanations concerning the environmental transmission of behavior patterns.

From this survey of approaches, it becomes clear that, generally speaking, the field has depended heavily on inferring processes of interactive effects and upon measuring immediate adult influences on immediate child responses. There has been less work through which we can trace the cumulative influences of rearing variables.

Concepts and Contents of Rearing Environments

It is easy to speak theoretically about interactive processes in the rearing environments created by parent and child, but it is quite a different matter to specify the significant components of behavior by parent and child that critically affect the development of each participant. It seems reasonable to begin the process by examining parental behaviors, which, especially for young children, are likely to control the greater amount of environmental variance.

There is an extensive research literature on parental rearing variables. Among the earlier formulations of the rearing environment is Schaefer's (1959) circumplex model in which parent–child relationships are characterized by dimensions of control–autonomy and love–hostility. Other investigators (such as Baumrind, 1978; Block, 1965; Hoffman & Saltzstein, 1967; Lytton, 1980; Sears, Maccoby, & Levin, 1957; and many others) have distinguished within these broad dimensions and have also added other variables. From an overall view of these studies, certain conceptualizations of rearing dominate: the dimensions of control (authoritarian, authoritative, permissive, love-oriented, inductive, and power-assertive disciplinary styles) and maternal love or rejection. Although the importance of these variables should not be minimized, it is more than likely that parents and children experience rearing in terms of a far richer organization of relationships. All who have engaged in research on rearing would probably agree that the field labors under a weight of tradition in its variables and that research paradigms have been seriously limited. In the remainder of this chapter we will suggest directions for investigating the rearing environment.

We can begin to formulate a more adequate representation of rearing by identifying the range of functions that parents perform in relation to their children.

1. Parents provide physical care and physical and psychological protection. Apart from an early focus on physical care by Freudian researchers who drew implications for character formation from feeding and toileting experiences, rearing variables in this aspect of parenting have not been at the forefront of conceptualizations of childrearing environments, and certainly do not apply past infancy. While there have been few insights regarding parental styles of physical care, it is increasingly clear from research stemming from a biological perspective that variables of physical care, such as nutrition, are important determinants of psychological outcomes in children. Recently, Barrett, Yarrow, and Klein (1982) reported that early malnutrition was associated with a variety of deficits in social and emotional functioning including affective expression, social involvement, and activity level.

In ethological perspectives the protection of the young has been a central function of parent behavior. A constellation of attachment behaviors is viewed to be instinctive responses for protection against predators (Bowlby, 1969). However, past infancy, parental monitoring and protection have been neglected in psychological conceptualizations of the childrearing environment. We define monitoring as the function by which parents inform themselves of their children's behavior and needs in order to decide whether or how to intervene on behalf of their children. Patterson and Cobb (1981) have suggested that a lack of monitoring, in the sense of keeping track of children's whereabouts, is an antecedent of problem behaviors in children. In our own observations of mother–toddler interaction we have noted that mothers frequently question their children about their internal states: their physical needs, emotional states, knowledge, desires. Since childrens' internal states are unobservable or often difficult to infer from their behavior, verbal monitoring has implications for the parents' ability to intervene in a way that is appropriate to the needs of their children. Related to monitoring is the actual provision of protection not only from physical danger, but also from experiences that may be psychologically harmful. Experiences from which children are shielded (strong negative emotions in parents, aggression, sexual experiences, information of many kinds) may be as important to their development as experiences to which they are exposed. One may also wonder whether, throughout childhood, in the normal range of rearing, the intensities and qualities of care and protection may not have considerable psychological significance for the child's concept of self (e.g., health, vulnerability, mastery) and the parent–child relationship. Interactions involving care and protection may also be avenues for other parental functions, such as nurturance, teaching, and regulation.

2. Parents regulate, control, and motivate their children's behavior. As already noted, there is an extensive literature on parental control and discipline; however, conceptualizations of control variables such as reasoning and punishment need to be differentiated further (Grusec & Redler, 1980; Henry, 1980; Kuczynski, 1983). From the perspective of what is missing, two points are relevant. First, researchers have dealt mainly with reactive control measures by the adult, that is, the adult's response to the child's transgressions or accomplishments. Conceptualizations of control techniques need to be extended to include anticipatory methods by the parent, namely, methods by which the parent programs the environment and provides rules and moral lessons, not in response to the child but in order to avoid problematic behavior. Second, it is striking that the literature on regulation is almost totally concerned with technique, not content. The focus has been on the methods used by parents rather than on the kinds of behaviors that parents are trying to control, and the research has generally skipped over how the parent administers any given control technique (e.g., amount and quality of sensitivity to the child's state, specific emotional settings, and purpose of the control).

3. Parents teach and provide knowledge and skills. *Teaching* covers a vast terrain in the parent–child interaction: motor skills, language, problem-solving strategies, strategies for self-control, coping with emotions, knowledge of the social and physical environments, moral and conventional values, and conceptions of self and others. Variations in the content of teaching in children's rearing environments are, of course, immense. As in the literature on regulation, research has emphasized variations in the methods of teaching; rarely has the cognitive content of the rearing environment been assessed (e.g., Watts & Barnett, 1973). So few studies have dealt with the following: What do parents talk about with their children? What is explained, argued, valued? To what ideas are children exposed concerning the behavioral and physical environments? How does the cognitive content of rearing change in the course of children's development?

4. Parents provide an affective environment. *Affects* belong in the conceptualizations of the rearing environment—as components of the parent–child interaction, as regulators of behavior, and as avenues of communication. In the literature on childrearing, affective variables have been represented mainly in the framework of love and rejection. Maternal love was the supreme variable in early infancy research (e.g., Bowlby, 1951; Spitz, 1965). Love, like rejection, has often been treated as an enveloping climate in which the infant or child is reared. Axes of affection–hostility (acceptance–rejection) have long been global descriptors of parent–child relationships and, in many ways, have been cited as important causative factors in good and not-so-good developmental outcomes (e.g., Olweus, 1980). Findings in the clinical literature link anger and

tension between parents and affective disturbance in children (Anthony, 1975). In the socialization literature, withdrawal of love and induction of guilt have been studied as parents' manipulations of affect (Hoffman, 1970) in order to gain control over the child's behavior. Social learning experiments have had difficulty in dealing with parental love or nurturance. It is not readily operationalized and manipulated experimentally and therefore has had relatively little impact on laboratory studies of behavior (for discussion, see Radke-Yarrow, Zahn-Waxler, & Chapman, in press).

We propose a research approach to the affective dimensions of rearing that would include the range of emotions (anger, sadness, love, joy, fear, contentment) as they occur in momentary and in persistent senses in family experiences. These emotions may be directed to the child and conveyed in interactions with the child. They may also be conveyed in the family environment although not directed to the child. The role of parental emotions as influences on children's behavior and as potential determinants of children's own affective characteristics has been relatively neglected in developmental studies.

5. Parents invest in and identify with their child. *Investment* is an admittedly vague but not pale dimension in the life experiences of child and parent. A pervasive difference among parent–child pairs is the kind and amount of shared experience and the investment or identification with each other. While it is considered seriously in clinical work, there has been a lack of attention to this aspect of parent–child interaction in systematic research.

6. Parents facilitate their children's interaction with the physical and interpersonal environments. The parents' role in *facilitating* or encouraging the child's *autonomous* interaction with the physical and interpersonal environments is not neatly conceptualized. This important dimension has appeared in the earlier literature as encouragement of independence in the child (e.g., Sears *et al.*, 1957) and more recently, in work with infants, as encouraging mastery (Yarrow, McQuiston, MacTurk, McCarthy, Klein, & Vietze, in press). Research perspectives have tended to concentrate on the child's interaction with the parent, not on factors that direct children toward other aspects of the social and physical environments. The idea of the mother as a "secure base" from which the child explores his or her physical and social environments is one perspective of the mother's facilitative role (e.g., Ainsworth, Blehar, Waters, & Walls; 1978). Less studied are the more active features of parents' facilitative behaviors toward their children at various developmental stages, for example, offering choices, providing materials, making suggestions for exploration, and facilitating interactions between peers and in other social relationships beyond the parent–child dyad.

We have been building a case for a broadened conceptualization of interactional processes in childrearing, focusing on the range of functions involved in parenting. By considering behaviors in terms of the functions in which the parent is engaged, it becomes evident that different functions are likely to involve very different kinds of interactions with the child and are likely to occur in very different situations and under very different circumstances. It follows that the sampling of rearing interactions is of critical importance.

In the childrearing literature, the gathering of data tends to be done in single, standard settings. Thus, the parent–child interaction in the laboratory is typically assessed in "free-play" situations. Observations in the home usually occur in group settings, such as mealtime with everyone at the table or during a period before dinner in the living room. The "strange" situation (Ainsworth *et al.*, 1978) is widely used to assess the early mother–child relationship. We do not know how adequately these settings sample or represent the typical or critical interactions of the participants. Investigations of rearing that take into account intersetting and interfunction consistency and variability would differentiate environments in important ways and provide clues to adaptive and deviant functioning. The inflexibility of some rearing patterns across situations could be as much a marker of certain maladaptive functioning as consistency in other dimensions is a sign of adaptive functioning.

In this chapter we have elaborated a number of conceptual and methodological issues in the investigation of person–environment interactions in the context of childrearing. We have proposed that, by sampling parent and child behaviors in ways that guarantee situational and contextual representativeness and that have some depth in time, reasonably sound assessments of rearing environments can be reached. In the following section we illustrate, using studies from our laboratory, some attempts to address the kinds of issues that have been discussed.

Rearing Studies of Normal and Depressed Mothers

The implementation of research ideals is a long, hard step and is always an approximation. As such an approximation, we developed two research strategies that make it possible to examine patterns of parent and child behaviors and interactions, taking into account the range of functions and situations that comprise rearing and that permit sampling over considerable periods of time. We present these strategies in some detail because they are departures from traditional approaches. One uses the mother as a trained research observer, and the other uses a naturalistic laboratory paradigm to permit the direct observation of a programmed diversity of rearing circumstances. From each strategy we believe it is possible to obtain a more systematic and detailed assessment of critical environmental factors than is available with more usual approaches.

In Strategy A mothers are trained as research assistants to observe systematically and to report on specified events in their children's lives (most of which are inaccessible to an outside observer and many of which are rare and "unscheduled"). For example, mothers have been asked to focus on incidents in which they have disciplined the child, in which the child has observed emotional distress in someone, or in which he or she has hurt someone.

Mothers' observations and reporting are done according to a prescribed format. Basically, they provide a narrative account of an event; in terms of our example, this would be an episode in which the child has caused an emotional distress in someone. Mothers dictate their observations into a tape recorder as soon after the event as possible. The report requires sequencing of behavior and specificity of behavior and affect, covering the child's, the victim's, and the mother's responses. (For details of the techniques, the training of the mothers, and the findings, see Zahn-Waxler & Radke-Yarrow, 1981.) Reporting is a long continuing process over a period of months, across situations and participants. These data are obtained along with those gathered by researchers at repeated home visits and those from laboratory sessions in which the child is observed with mother and peers.

Strategy A is being used in a series of studies, which have as their objectives investigation of the role of emotional events in the child's immediate environment. In one study with normal families and their 1-year-old children (Zahn-Waxler & Radke-Yarrow, 1981), the research questions were concerned with development, How do the child's patterns of emotional responsiveness emerge and change during the second and third years of life? and with socialization (Zahn-Waxler, Radke-Yarrow, & King, 1979), How does the mother enter into the child's emotional development? Trickett and Kuczynski (1983) investigated patterns of discipline in families with child-abusing and non-child-abusing parents. By obtaining data on children's misbehaviors, parental discipline, and affective reactions during naturally occurring incidents of serious parent–child conflict, this study offers samples of the relatively infrequent kinds of interaction that may set the occasion for child abuse.

In Strategy B rearing is sampled broadly, as naturally as possible, and over time. To achieve a reasonable representation of rearing, the research families (mothers with two children, 2 and 5 years of age) spend three half-days (morning, afternoon, and morning or afternoon), spaced over 2 weeks, in an informal laboratory setting that is a small apartment: a suite of rooms plus a kitchen and bathroom. The mother's understanding is that she will "take care of" her children pretty much "as usual," but she knows that some special things will be asked of them. Their time in the apartment at each visit is long, so that natural interaction eventually returns to the mother–children triad. The total time involved and the times of day guarantee the sampling of many natural rearing activities (physical care, meals, opportunity for play, work, loafing, watching TV, being bored, being tired, encountering new persons, being in family groups with changing compositions, meeting crises, having new experiences, being free not to interact). All sessions are video-recorded. The framework of the external environment is standard for the families; the structure and use of the environment is very much their contribution. In addition to the natural flow of events, standard events are woven into the visits. These are plausible events in daily experience, chosen to sample specific kinds of responses: Mother is called out of the room; mother is "burdened" by multiple tasks or by having to keep the children from using tempting but forbidden objects; teaching tasks and introduced frustrations are imposed, and so on. Mothers are selected on the basis of psychiatric screening; they have diagnoses of depression or are without psychiatric diagnosis.

Additional kinds of information are gathered in each set of visits. Mother's perceptions and goals concerning her own rearing behavior and her child's behavior and an account of the family's current life are obtained. Each child is seen for psychiatric assessment. The study is designed with return visits spaced over several years.

Mother's behavior and children's behavior create the psychological environment of rearing. Maternal environment is conceptualized in terms of the rearing functions described earlier. In addition to the mother's behaviors specifically directed to the child, her indirect influences—those aspects of the stimulation such as energy level, content of mother's activities, affective expression are also considered. A primary category of indirect environmental influences considered in this study is the mother's affective state. Parental behavior and interventions and child behavior are analyzed in detailed categories.

The research strategy is being used to investigate the environmental transmission of behavior patterns in families with and without maternal psychopathology. The research objectives are multilayered: There is strong evidence of genetic influences in affective disorders (Nurnberger & Gershon, in press). Therefore, observations of depressed mothers involve the researcher in the intricate questions of how this disorder is manifested in the maternal role and how it thereby experientially affects her offspring. Much of the symptomatology of depression (apathy, irritability, sadness, self-preoccupation, and, in bipolar depression, extreme fluctuations between mania and depression) has significant implications for how rearing functions are performed. The direct documentation of parent–child interaction at successive ages in early childhood will substitute for the "implied interaction" approach that customarily links early experience with later pathology. By sampling at successive periods, it is possible in this study to examine the emergence and transformation of children's behavior patterns, adaptive and pathological, in the context of maternal behavior. In both the normal and pathological families, a primary objective is to obtain information on specific influences of the parent–child interaction with respect to affective dimensions of rearing and child personality.

By being less constricted in psychological contexts and settings these strategies have yielded a richer data base than do the typical laboratory and naturalistic strategies that we have used in the past. Such data present advantages and problems. Among the advantages of Strategy A, are that we have successfully elicited the large number of childrearing functions that we have discussed in a preceding section. The data permit the tracking of interactional processes at several levels from immediate, minute sequences to larger units of behavior such as episodes and contexts.

The frustrations of such a data base arise from our realization that the conceptualizations and constructs that can be derived from the childrearing literature are too few and too global to describe the interactions that we observe. Mothers and children spend long periods of time in conversation. What is known about the content and significance of conversation for development? Mothers and children exchange affectionate behaviors. Is there any significance to specific patterns and functions of affection? Mothers and children watch television. What is the role of the television set in interaction? Conceptualizations of good parenting in childrearing measures seem to be excessively child-oriented. Presumably, the more protection, affection, responsiveness, and stimulation, the better. One is struck by the possibility that these functions can be overdone. One senses that some mothers should leave their children alone more often. Others have difficulty in defending their own time from the demands of their children. We are still in the process of data gathering and since it is clear that conceptualization will provide the principal challenge of our work, we will convey some of the qualitative features of parent–child interaction with which we are grappling.

First is the issue of rearing functions, and what has been accomplished by the sampling designed in Strategy A. Three variables emerge that distinguish the environments in important ways: (a) in their structures; (b) in the complexity of the behavioral settings; and (c) in the variability of mothers' behaviors within and across activities. It is apparent that mothers balance rearing functions very differently. They differ in the total amount of time spent interacting with the child versus time occupied by leisure activities or chores. They differ also in the weightings they give to the various rearing activities: While regulation seldom occurs in some families, it is a steady presence in others. Teaching and caretaking are equally variable. In other words, socialization in different families takes place along quite different channels.

Environments also differ in the dimension of complexity—in terms of the number and levels of activities that mothers carry on simultaneously. A complex environment is created by mothers who, while providing physical care, at the same time teach, nurture, and facilitate the child's experimentation with the environment. Environments created by other mothers consist of a series of single, punctuated behaviors directed to the child.

An example in more detail may be illuminating. On each day of the study, mothers must prepare and serve a meal. Consider the mother who begins by telling her child that she is going to prepare lunch and describing to him what is available in the cupboard. After asking his preferences, she expresses reservations about the nutritional value of his first choice, engages his help in getting the table readied, and keeps up a relaxed but steady flow of conversation and teaching that extends throughout their meal together. By contrast, mealtime for others is the mother putting the food in front of her child and then sitting down opposite the child with a magazine propped up beside her plate. In still another family, mealtime is an unregulated opening of the refrigerator door as each takes his or her own choices. In standard, constrained mealtime paradigms in which families have for the research purposes gathered together with the expectation that they are to interact, such variations would be less likely to be found.

A second measurement objective that these data meet is that of supplying details of behavior and sequences of interaction within different rearing activities. In observing mothers' teaching and conversations with children, much can be learned from the content of the information and expectations that mothers communicate. Again by way of example, some mothers continuously inform the child about future events and changes that will take place in his environment, preparing the child for upcoming stresses and pleasures (e.g., "We will have a nap after lunch." "A doctor is coming for a visit.") and giving the child an idea of what the future holds in store (e.g., "We're going to see daddy after we leave here." "It's going to be cold walking to the car."). For other children what happens next can only be a series of unpredictable surprises.

The function of regulation also appears in new lights when one examines the content of what is being regulated. For some, regulation appears almost entirely to occur in reaction to a transgression of the child, either low-level breaches of social conventional standards (e.g., "Keep your feet off the chair." "I told you to put away your toys.") or high-intensity aversive or oppositional behaviors of the child that inherently demand intervention. For other mothers such reactive discipline rarely occurs. Occasions for discipline are averted by anticipatory means (prior statement of rules, prompts, cautions, lessons). The single and ubiquitous technique of commands is used in reactive and anticipatory ways, not only restricting and prohibiting the child's initiations, but also in serving to teach and motivate the child to develop instrumental skills or to set the child up for reinforcing acts of competence.

The need for further refinement in assessments of disciplinary methods becomes evident in observing in these mothers the variable forms of their reasoning and power-assertive techniques. Variations in the content of these techniques, we assume, have different effects on children of different ages and in different situations. Besides *which* techniques are employed, one learns for what provocations and *how* the mother administers discipline—reflexively, angrily, or with careful calculation—and whether discipline is confined to the situation of transgression, with a good relationship then being reestablished, or is prolonged into subsequent interactions. An account of one mother's reactions to her 6-year-old's minor transgression illustrates the unrelenting aspects of some disciplinary interactions: The child is spanked, given explanations of why his behavior is bad, and sent to be by himself. The child, with hostile protests, submits at each stage and finally asks forgiveness, with a series of offered gifts. Each of these is refused by the mother, who continues her scolding.

The affective dimensions of rearing have a high priority in our research interests. As in the case of the other functions, moods and emotions are investigated both as they enter into specific interactions and as they are represented in the rearing environment considered as a whole. In one of our analyses, the emotional expressions of mother and child are assessed on a minute-by-minute basis, yielding affective profiles of the participants. Screening out the content of all other behaviors, one is struck by differences in the emotional climates of rearing environments. Happy, pleasant, and humorous interactions punctuated by occasional stresses represent some of the environments. The affective bleakness of other environments, in which codes of neutral, apathy, and sadness predominate, is as oppressive to the observer as it must be for the participants. It is not unusual in these settings for the parent or child to flick on the television to game shows and soap operas gushing with emotion. Often no one watches, but it may serve its purpose by providing a source of affective stimulation.

We have presented no comparisons between normal and depressed mothers and their children, since our sample has not yet built to an adequate number in the several categories of diagnoses. However, we have noted a preliminary developmental finding that, on psychiatric assessment, the older children (5–7 years) of depressed mothers (unipolar and bipolar are combined) are showing a pattern that is different from their younger siblings and from the children of normal parents, namely, a higher frequency of clearly depression-related problems. The intervening processes and transformations will be tracked by seeing these children in successive visits to the apartment.

Conclusions and Prospects

Looking at childrearing at a new level of detail, one cannot escape a realization of its complexity. Over the years research in this field has proceeded with two quite different objectives and strategies. One is to break into the complexity by trying to extract specific influence processes that hold regardless of circumstance and behavior. The other is an attempt to deal with the intact system of relationships and with a search for patterned processes and interactions. Each strategy, when it has "gone it alone," has come to an impasse that has then resulted in accommodations in research formulations, methods, or both.

We have taken the route of investigating rearing in its natural complexity. In our opinion, this approach can enrich the field at this state of knowledge by providing firsthand documentation of rearing, with the validity that comes with parent (as opposed to experimenter) and child as participants. This will add to the relatively scant knowledge we have about what parents do with their children. One of the benefits of good raw data is the new variables that are forced upon us, and the new questions that are raised. In this way, it is the stimulus for stretching research minds to develop necessary concepts and tools.

A conceptualization of rearing as an organized system of parents and children interacting in multiple settings requires the development of new or adapted methods. Designing research so as to obtain rich exposure to ongoing rearing does not preclude the examination of specific processes within rearing, and under controlled conditions, because experiments in the context of "live" rearing interactions can be carried out. In this way some of the best of naturalistic and experimental methodology can be utilized. However, the basic source of material for a developmental theory of socialization must certainly come from extensive naturalistic data obtained over time.

A sophisticated conception and assessment of rearing environments is especially timely in this period in science when we are witnessing great advances in the neurosciences and in the biology of the developing child. With the new knowledge and tools of the biological sciences, questions of interaction between biological and experiential factors can be readdressed. In the formulation and examination of biological–environmental questions, new and penetrating assessments of environment are especially critical. Rearing environments, we believe, can be measured well, given patience by investigators (for the data do not come quickly) and an eclecticism that is open to conceptual and methodological experimentation.

References

Ainsworth, M., Blehar, M., Waters, E., & Walls, S. *The strange situation: Observing patterns of attachment.* Hillsdale, N. J.: Erlbaum, 1978.

Anthony, E. J. The influence of a manic–depressive environment on the developing child. In E. J. Anthony & T. Benedek (Eds.), *Depression and human existence.* Boston: Little Brown, 1975.

Barrett, D. E., Yarrow, M. R., & Klein, R. E. Chronic malnutrition and child behavior: Effects of early caloric supplementation on social and emotional functioning at school age. *Developmental Psychology,* 1982, *18,* 541–557.

Baumrind, D. Parental disciplinary patterns and social competence in children. *Youth and Society,* 1978, *9,* 239–276.

Bell, R. A reinterpretation of the direction of effects in studies of socialization. *Psychological Review,* 1968, *75,* 81–95.

Block, J. H. *The child-rearing practices report.* Berkeley: Institute of Human Development, University of California, 1965.

Bowlby, J. Maternal care and mental health. *World Health Organization Monograph Series,* 1951, *2.*

Bowlby, J. *Attachment and Loss (Vol. 1).* Harmondsworth: Penguin Books, 1969.

Cairns, R. B. Social interactional methods: An introduction. In R. Cairns (Ed.), *The analysis of social interactions.* Hillsdale, N. J.: Erlbaum, 1979.

Cheyne, A. Punishment and reasoning in the development of self-control. In R. D. Parke (Ed.), *Recent trends in social learning theory.* New York: Academic Press, 1972.

Clifford, E. Discipline in the home: A controlled observational study of parental practices. *Journal of Genetic Psychology,* 1959, *96,* 45–82.

Grusec, S. E., & Redler, E. Attribution, reinforcement, and altruism: A developmental analysis. *Developmental Psychology,* 1980, *16,* 525–534.

Harlow, H., & Harlow, M. Effects of various infant-monkey relationships on rhesus monkey behaviors. In B. M. Foss (Ed.), *Determinants of infant behavior* (Vol. 4). London: Methuen, 1969.

Henry, R. M. A theoretical and empirical analysis of "reasoning" in the socialization of young children. *Human Development,* 1980, *23,* 105–125.

Hoffman, M. L. Moral development. In P. H. Mussen (Ed.), *Carmichael's manual of child psychology.* New York: Wiley, 1970.

Hoffman, M. L., & Saltzstein, H. D. Parent discipline and the child's moral development. *Journal of Personality and Social Psychology,* 1967, *5,* 45–57.

Kohlberg, L. Stage and sequences: The cognitive-developmental approach to socialization. In D. A. Goslin (Ed.), *Handbook of socialization theory and research.* Chicago: Rand McNally, 1969.

Kuczynski, L. Reasoning, prohibitions and motivations for compliance. *Developmental Psychology,* 1983, *19,* 126–134.

LaVoie, J. C. Cognitive determinants of resistance to deviation in 7, 9, and 11 year old children of low and high maturity of moral judgment. *Developmental Psychology,* 1974, *10,* 393–403.

Lytton, H. *Parent–child interaction.* New York: Plenum, 1980.

Maccoby, E. *Social development: Psychological growth and the parent–child relationship.* New York: Harcourt, 1980.

Newson, J., & Newson, E. *Infant care in an urban community.* London: Allen & Unwin, 1963.

Newson, J., & Newson, E. *Four years old in an urban community.* London: Allen & Unwin, 1968.

Newson, J., & Newson, E. *Seven years old in the home environment.* London: Allen & Unwin, 1976.

Nurnberger, J., Jr., & Gershon, E. S. Genetics of affective disorders. In R. Post & J. Ballenger (Eds.), *Neurobiology of mood disorders.* Baltimore: Williams & Wilkins, in press.

Olweus, D. Familial and temperamental determinants of aggressive behavior in adolescent boys: A causal analysis. *Developmental Psychology,* 1980, *16*(6), 644–660.

Panksepp, J., Herman, B., Conner, R., Bishop, P., & Scott, J. P. The biology of social attachments: Opiates alleviate separation distress. *Biological Psychiatry,* 1978, *13,* 607–678.

Parke, R. D. Rules, roles and resistance to deviation in children: Explorations in punishment, discipline and self control. In A. Pick (Ed.), *Minnesota symposia on child psychology* (Vol. 8). Minneapolis: University of Minnesota Press, 1974.

Patterson, G. Mothers: The unacknowledged victims. *Monographs of the Society for Research in Child Development,* 1980, *45*(5, No. 186).

Patterson, G., & Cobb, J. *Families of antisocial children: An interactional approach.* Eugene, Ore.: Castalia, 1981.

Radke-Yarrow, M., Zahn-Waxler, C., & Chapman, M. Children's prosocial dispositions and behavior. In P. H. Mussen (Ed.), *Carmichael's manual of child psychology.* New York: Wiley, in press.

Schaefer, E. A circumplex model for maternal behavior. *Journal of Abnormal and Social Psychology,* 1959, *59,* 226–235.

Sears, R. R. A theoretical framework for personality and social development. *American Psychologist,* 1951, *6,* 476–483.

Sears, R. R., Maccoby, E. E., & Levin H. *Patterns of child rearing.* Evanston, Ill.: Row, Peterson, 1957.

Spitz, R. *The first year of life.* New York: New York International Universities, 1965.

Trickett, P., & Kuczynski, L. *Children's misbehaviors and parental discipline in abusive and nonabusive families.* Paper presented at the American Psychological Association Annual Convention, Anaheim, August 1983.

Watts, J. C., & Barnett, I. C. Observing the child's environment. In B. L. White & J. C. Watts (Eds.), *Experience and environment.* Englewood Cliffs, N. J.: Prentice-Hall, 1973.

Yarrow, L. J., McQuiston, S., MacTurk, R. H., McCarthy, M. E., Klein, R. P., & Vietze, P. M. Assessment of mastery motivation during the first year of life: Contemporaneous and cross-age relationship. *Developmental Psychology,* in press.

Yarrow, M. R., Campbell, J. D., & Burton, R. B. *Child rearing: An inquiry into research and methods.* San Francisco: Jossey-Bass, 1968.

Zahn-Waxler, C., & Radke-Yarrow, M. The development of altruism: Alternative research strategies. In N. Eisenberg-Berg (Ed.), *The development of prosocial behavior.* New York: Academic Press, 1982.

Zahn-Waxler, C., Radke-Yarrow, M., & King, R. Child rearing and children's prosocial initiations toward victims in distress. *Child Development,* 1979, *50,* 319–330.

4

The "Person" Characteristics
of Children
and the Family as Environment

ELEANOR E. MACCOBY   CAROL NAGY JACKLIN

Our purpose here is to consider person–environment interaction in the context of the family as a setting for development. Part of the task will be to consider the meaning of the term *environment* in this context.

A first useful distinction is that between the physical and interpersonal environments. Family life occurs in the context of a dwelling and an area surrounding the dwelling. Family life is constrained to some degree by the size of the dwelling, the arrangement of living spaces, and the availability of safe play spaces inside and outside the dwelling. Other presumably important aspects of the physical environment include the number and kinds of books or other reading materials, the presence and location of a television set, and the number of delicate or valuable objects and furnishings. The adults with whom the child lives are the primary determiners of the child's physical enviornment. They choose the dwelling and furnish it. However, they are only partially free agents. Within any socioeconomic level, individual tastes of parents will have an influence on how they structure the child's home environment, and the kinds and number of other environmental settings into which they take the child. However, their income places fairly rigid constraints on the nature and location of the settings they provide. Thus, in some respects a child's physical environment is set by parental choices; in others the parents function more as transmitters of larger socioeconomic conditions.

With some exceptions (e.g., Bronfenbrenner, 1979), research in child development has placed relatively little emphasis on the nature and effects of the ecological niche occupied by children and their families. More central has been the *interpersonal* environment. Other family members constitute the primary

75

HUMAN DEVELOPMENT:
AN INTERACTIONAL PERSPECTIVE

interpersonal environment in which the child functions during the early years. We cannot doubt that the composition of the family—that is, the number, age, and sex of its members—has an impact in its own right. Erik Erikson (personal communication) reported, for example, that children in India, when given play materials and asked to depict a family scene, created dwellings that were densely packed with people, whereas American children of comparable age would construct dwellings in which there would be perhaps five rooms for four people. In other parts of the world, children may grow up in a compound shared by co-wives or sisters-in-law and their children. Anthropologists (e.g., Whiting & Whiting, 1975) have provided us with some insights concerning the meaning of the size and composition of co-living groups. In our own society, these matters have been of lesser interest, except for the work on father absence, on birth order (in which the effects of a child's having or not having an older sibling are studied), and the recent interest in "support system" involving the availability of members of an extended family.

However, in studies of the effects of family environment on children's development, it is not the question of who is present as a potential interaction partner that has received the most attention. Rather, most studies have dealt with the nature of adults' reactions to children's behavior and the nature of the requirements placed upon children by the adults responsible for their care. Parental childrearing characteristics have been classified according to a variety of dimensions: warm and accepting versus cold and rejecting; demanding versus indulgent; firm or lax in discipline; responsive or unresponsive; given to using suggestions rather than directives when an attempt is made to influence the child. Parental characteristics such as these have been taken to be important aspects of the child's interperson environment.

Interactions of Child and Parent Characteristics

On first thought, the question of person–environment interaction would appear to have a fairly straightforward application to the family situation. We can identify characteristics of children, such as their temperament or sex; we can identify characteristics of parents; and we can then ask whether there are main effects of each on the child's characteristics, and whether there is an interaction in the sense that a given parental characteristic has a different effect on children of one sex or temperament than on another.

An example of this kind of interaction may be found in a recent monograph by Martin (1981). Martin observed a group of infants in interaction with their mothers when the infants were 10 months old. The same mother–infant pairs were observed on two subsequent occasions: when the child had reached the age of 22 months, and again at 42 months. At 10 months, a microanalytic sequential analysis was performed, and scores for each mother's responsiveness were derived. These scores reflected her tendency to respond to changes in her infant's interactive intensity level with a corresponding change in her own intensity level. At 22 months, mother and child visited a laboratory room, in which one episode involved placing an object that made an interesting sound out of sight behind a barrier. Some of the children readily moved out of the mother's sight to explore the object, others hesitated for a time before making a move, and others remained next to their mothers without exploring. At 42 months, part of the laboratory session involved the entrance of a strange adult. The child's readiness to approach and interact with the stranger was noted. Martin found that, for girls, the children whose mothers had been most responsive at 10 months were least likely to explore behind the barrier or approach the stranger, whereas for boys the reverse was true. The interaction of sex by maternal responsiveness was significant.

The findings from Martin's monograph are consistent with some findings by Baumrind (1977, 1979). Baumrind's hypothesis is that, while the competence of children of both sexes is enhanced if the parents are both demanding and responsive, responsivity is more important in the successful socialization of boys, demandingness for girls.

In our current longitudinal work, we have assessed several aspects of children's "temperaments" (e.g., activity level, "difficultness"). We have searched for instances in which children of different temperaments have been affected differently by a given parental behavior. So far we have not found such interactions. There are a few instances where such interactions are reported in the literature. For example, in Martin's monograph, there is a significant tendency for maternal responsiveness to have a different relation to children's compliance, depending on whether the child is demanding (for boys only). And similarly, the effect of a mother's being highly involved with her infant on the child's reactions to a strange experimenter ay a later age depends on how highly involved (as distinct from autonomous) the infant was. The most positive combination was a *matching* of mother and infant involvement levels, regardless of whether the absolute levels were high or low. Another interaction between infants' temperamental characteristics and an environmental input is reported by Crockenberg (1981), who shows that social supports available to the mother have a greater effect when the infant is irritable than when it is placid. On the whole, however, there is a notable lack in the research literature of demonstrations that a given environmental input has a different effect on infants and young children of varying temperaments, and it may be that the phenomenon is not very powerful.

Recent approaches to parent–child interaction stress that each member of an interacting pair constitutes the other's interpersonal environment. If we take the child as the subject of our study, the child's sex is a person variable and the parent's sex is an environmental variable. When the parent is the focus of study, the situation is the reverse. It is possible to find a number of instances in which it is not the child's sex alone or the parent's sex alone that affects the nature of the exchanges that occur between them, but the interaction (in the

Table 1
Mean Frequency of Interactive Scores[a] from Play Session at 45 Months

	Mother–son pairs (N = 30)	Mother–daughter pairs (N = 24)	Father–son pairs (N = 30)	Father–daughter pairs (N = 24)	F tests		
					Sex of child	Sex of parent	Interaction
Thematic play	34.5	43.6	27.3	27.8	.67	8.98*	1.25
Rough and tumble play	10.8	6.4	18.5	8.0	3.78**	2.86***	1.24
Child makes influence attempt, parent complies	12.4	13.8	15.3	10.1	.66	.07	4.46*
Child makes influence attempt, parent refuses	1.0	.8	2.0	1.5	.49	4.59*	.18
Parent offers or suggests	12.1	11.2	6.9	10.0	.60	5.85*	2.34
Parent directs or demands	9.1	8.1	8.2	8.6	.01	.04	.39

[a]The scores are the number of 6-second intervals (out of a total of 150 intervals) in which the behavior occurred.

*$p = < .10$.
**$p = < .05$.
***$p = < .01$.

statistical sense) of the two. Rothbart and Maccoby (1966) reported a number of years ago that parents were likely to be more indulgent or permissive with an opposite-sex child. In our recent work, we have observed the interaction of a group of 45-month-old children with their parents. The sessions occurred at the families' homes. The experimenter provided a box of toys, and each parent in turn played with the child with these toys while the other parent was being interviewed in a separate room. Analysis of the play sessions revealed a few instances of a main effect for sex of parent; in addition, there was one instance of a main sex-of-child effect (rough-and-tumble play) and one instance of an interaction (see Table 1). For our present purposes, the finding of greatest interest is the fact that fathers were more likely to follow the suggestion or demand of a son than a daughter, whereas for mothers the sex of the child made little difference (with a slight preference for complying to daughters). Other findings from this study suggested that fathers were especially sensitive to signs of resistance from a daughter; if a girl refused to comply with a directive from her father, the total amount of interactive play (e.g., thematic play involving the enactment of integrated "pretend" roles) was considerably reduced, whereas for other parent–child pairs this effect was weak. Fathers appeared to break off interaction with resistive daughters.

The "Effective" Environment of Parent and Child

We have seen illustrations of the fact that children are in a somewhat different environment when interacting with their mothers than when with their fathers, and that the difference may depend on characteristics of the child—specifically, on the child's sex. But the approach taken so far to the issue of person–environment interaction has been rather simplistic. The biological sex of an individual is a person characteristic that can easily be defined independently of any characteristics of the environment, and the sex of a focal person's partner is an aspect of the environment that can also be defined independently of characteristics of the focal person. In many other instances, there are great complexities in achieving independent definitions of person and interpersonal environment.

Let us begin the discussion of this issue with reference to an ancient problem in psychology: the distinction between the "real" environment and the perceived or "effective" environment. In the heyday of behaviorism, there was a general assumption that stimulus situations could be defined objectively, apart from how they were interpreted by responders. There was a wholesale rejection of "black box" or "subjective" psychology, although several voices continued to insist that not all aspects of the external "stimulus situation" were in reality functioning as stimuli to the person. Koffka's (1935) famous tale of the man who confidently walked across a field of snow, believing it to be solid ground, and then dropped dead of fright when he discovered after the fact that he had walked across a thinning sheet of ice covering a lake illustrated the Gestalt position that persons' interpretations of events, not the events themselves, were the effective stimuli to which responses were made. Brunswik's (1956) distinction between distal and proximal stimuli carried the same message. With the burgeoning of cognitive psychology, it has become more and more evident that perception is highly selective and that the effect of a stimulus depends on how it is coded and stored. Thus, the neat distinction between person and environment has been replaced by a set of sequential processes in which the person acts upon stimuli to give them more or less meaning for current action. In one sense this means that more and more of the variance in behaviors is being assigned to the interactive term.

Considering these issues from the standpoint of children's development within the context of the family, a first point to note is that the effective environment depends on the capacities of the organism existing within it. A dog and a human being living in the same house cannot be said to be occupying the "same" environment. To use a Gibsonian concept, what an environment *affords* represents an interaction between organism and physical aspects of the environment. Thus, to winged creatures, certain environments have the property of "fly-throughableness." To crawling creatures it is the affordances for movement on surfaces that affect behavior. In a similar vein, the way a child utilizes the physical spaces in a house depends greatly on whether the child is crawling, toddling, or walking and running confidently. As a further example: A set of encyclopedia volumes on a shelf is only minimally a part of a 2-year-old's environment; it plays a very different role as stimulus to a child who has learned to read and has been given a school assignment that calls for looking up references. Piaget noted that children utilize a given object in quite different ways at different stages of development, and he alerted his readers to the enormous developmental changes that occur in the way objects and events are construed. The changes in how children understand and interpret the actions of other persons (e.g., their growing ability to infer others' intentions) imply progressive alteration in their interpersonal environment.

It is not only developmental changes in social cognition that affect children's effective interpersonal environment. Continued experience with a given partner affects the meaning of that partner's behavior to the subject. It is interesting to ask whether children and parents react to one another in terms of the specific action that a partner has just performed or in terms of the cumulative expectations or trait attributions that each has developed about the other. A study by Dodge (1980) illustrates the fact that among children the mutual trait attributions carry a good deal of weight. He studied storied ambiguous social events, such as a child spilling milk on another child in the school cafeteria or hitting another child with a thrown ball. Dodge found that if the agent of the action had a reputation for being aggressive, peers were likely to interpret the action as intentional mischief and to say they would react with anger, whereas if the injury was done by a person with a more benign reputation, peers would interpret it as accidental and overlook it. No doubt, parents and children develop "reputations" with one another, but there has been little research on the nature of mutual cumulative expectations and trait attributions and how they change over time, so that we can only assume that they must have a powerful effect in determining what kind of "stimulus situation" each constitutes for the other.

A related issue has to do with adaptation to a partner's behavior, so that expected behavior is not a powerful stimulus, whereas unexpected behavior is. Some years ago, Stevenson (1965) wished to determine whether there were any aspects of children's home environments—especially their parents' childrearing techniques—that determined how responsive a child would be to social reinforcement in a laboratory experiment. Many home-environment factors were examined, but the only one that proved to be related was the amount of praise used by the parents. The more praise they used, the less responsive was the child to social reinforcement (i.e., praise) in the laboratory. This would appear to be an illustration of a simple adaptation process, in which the more common praise is, the less attention it commands. Another way of looking at mutual adaptation between parent and child would be to say that each reacts to variations around the partner's baseline, and only slightly or not at all to the baseline itself. We may have an illustration of this phenomenon in a set of findings from a study of 18-month-old children interacting with their mothers. Since we will refer to this study further at several points, let me digress now to describe it briefly. We made two visits to the children's homes, 1 week apart. On each occasion, one observer interviewed the mother and gave her questionnaires to fill out, while a second observer recorded, at timer-marked intervals, any interactions that occurred between mother and child as the child moved freely about the room or made physical contact with the mother. Later in the session, the mother was asked to present several simple tasks for her child to perform, and records were made of her modes of getting the child engaged in the tasks, as well as of the child's interest in the tasks and cooperation with the mother's teaching efforts. Data from the two visits were combined to produce observational scores for both the mother and the child. At this same age, the mother filled out two 24-hr diaries in which the child's state (asleep or awake, and if awake, whether crying–fussing, quiet–calm, or happy–excited) was recorded for each 15-min interval. From the mother's questionnaire data and the diary reports, scales were constructed reflecting aspects of the children's temperaments. Data on temperament were also available for the same children at ages 9 months and 12 months, and significant correlations were found across ages 9, 12, and 18 months; thus, it was possible to construct cumulative scores reflecting stable characteristics of children over a 9-month period. The two characteristics of interest for the present report are the child's activity level and "difficultness." The latter temperamental variable is a composite based on work by Bates (1980) and combines frequency of crying, difficulty of soothing once distressed, resistance to routine caretaking procedures (e.g., diapering, dressing), intensity of negative emotional states, and not being easily distracted from undesired activities.

A sequential analysis was performed of the moment-to-moment influences of the mother's and child's behavior on one another's immediately ensuing behavior (see Martin, Maccoby, Baran, & Jacklin, 1981). It was found that the partners tended to reciprocate positive behaviors with positive behaviors, and negatives with negatives, so that each partner stimulated the other to behave in kind. Yet there are other findings from the same study that do not seem to fit this picture. Children who could be identified as "difficult" on the basis of their mothers' reports over a 9-month period did behave somewhat more negatively toward their mothers during the observational sessions at 18 months. They directed more negative actions toward their mothers, on the average, than children who were rated as easygoing on the basis of their mothers' diaries and questionnaires, and a higher *proportion* of difficult children's bids for attention were of a negative sort: whining, demanding, fussing, or obstructing the mother's activities. However, mothers did *not*, on the average, react more negatively to difficult children than to easygoing ones. Indeed, if anything, they were somewhat more positive, in the sense that they were somewhat more likely to respond to a difficult child's bids by affectionate touching and holding. We interpret this set of findings to mean that mothers were responding to moment-to-moment variations in a child's behavior around its own baseline but may have adapted to the baseline itself. Thus, although mothers may reciprocate in kind any negative behavior that is occurring at a higher rate than usual from a difficult child, the *mean* level of the child's negative behavior (which may be higher than the average for other children) is not reflected in the mother's mean level of negative responding.

The foregoing discussion has been meant to illustrate the following points: parents and children constitute one another's interpersonal environments. While each reacts to some extent to the objective behavior of the other, partner behavior is mediated by the expectations and interpretations that each has for the other's behavior, and these mediating factors change with the child's age.

Mutual Influence:
The Changing Interpersonal Environment

There is another way in which person and environment are not independent, when considered in the context of parent–child interaction. Parents and children change one another, so that the environment an individual has at a later time is a function of that individual's person characteristics at an earlier time. Such interactive effects may be seen even with respect to the physical environments that children occupy in their homes. For example, there is evidence that when parents provide developmentally advanced play materials, this accelerates children's cognitive development. But it is also true that when a child is cognitively advanced at one point in time, the probability is increased that the parent will provide advanced play materials at a later time (Bradley, Caldwell, & Elardo, 1979). Circular processes of this kind undoubtedly abound in the formation and development of interpersonal relationships within the family, so that in a sense, individuals are creating their own interpersonal environment at the same time that they are being shaped by this environment. The work of Patterson and his colleagues (see Patterson, 1980) provides a prime example of such circular processes. We can provide another from our own longitudinal work. We referred above to the study with 18-month-old children and their mothers. This same group of children was observed in a laboratory situation with their mothers at the age of 12 months. The 12-month laboratory session involved the mother's presenting a series of simple tasks to the child, and the measures were designed to identify dimensions of differences in maternal teaching styles. In addition, as noted earlier, there were mother reports, via questionnaires and diaries, concerning temperamental attributes of the child.

For our present purposes, we will focus upon one child-temperament variable, "difficultness," and one maternal variable, the amount of pressure exerted by the mother during the teaching process. At 12 months, some mothers were highly active in guiding, suggesting, making demands, demonstrating the tasks, and in calling their children back to the task if their attention wandered; others appeared to be much less involved in the teaching process and either would initiate little interaction or would play with the child in non-task-related ways in addition to whatever task-related pressure they applied. A similar measure of maternal pressure was derived from the 18-month session, utilizing both the mother's behavior during the task session and the frequency of maternal demands placed upon the child during the portion of the session when the mother was being interviewed. The availability of comparable mother-pressure measures and child-difficult measures at the two ages permits us to study whether there is bidirectional influence between an attribute of the child and an attribute of the mother.

We have performed a relatively simple form of panel analysis with these scores. We have used the two 12-month variables as joint predictors in a multiple regression to predict each of the 18-month variables in turn. Figure 1 shows that when mothers exerted considerable pressure on their sons at 12 months to perform a desired task, the boys became somewhat less difficult (or more easygoing) 6 months later, and this was true when the child's initial level of "difficultness" had been partialed out. It was also true, however, that the mothers of boys who were more difficult than average at 12 months had reduced their pressure at 18 months. The mothers of difficult boys appeared to be backing off from strong efforts to teach or to guide boys who resisted being guided. Clearly, there is the basis for an escalating cycle here in which a difficult child is creating an interpersonal environment that will not serve to modify his difficult temperament, but may instead exacerbate it.

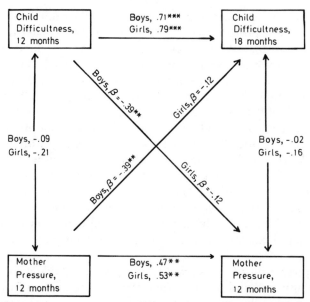

Figure 1. *Multiple regressions predicting child and mother characteristics at 18 months from matching characteristics at 12 months. Numbers on the crossbars are standardized partial regression coefficients (**p < .01; ***p < .001).*

You will note that this description applies to boys. We did not find a circular process of this kind for girls. A possible explanation might be that boys are more difficult than girls, and thus present a more intractable socialization target to their mothers. In fact, however, we do not find that children of the two sexes differ at either age in the mean frequency of reported crying, resistiveness, ease of soothing, or any of the other elements involved in our score for "difficultness." Nor did the mothers differ in the average level of pressure exerted on male as compared to female children. It is only the *relationship* between these variables that differs by the sex of the child. It should be noted that our findings for boys do not reflect the kind of relationship hypothesized by Baumrind (1977, 1979). In this instance, it is not maternal responsiveness (which we also measured), but maternal demandingness that is a positive factor for boys.

Sex differences aside, an implication of the circular process shown here is perhaps obvious, but may be worth mentioning explicitly. Studies of temperament have shown that there is probably a genetic component to the variation among children in a number of temperamental characteristics (e.g., activity, emotionality, sociability; see Buss & Plomin, 1975; Dunn, 1980). Indeed, the presence of a genetic component is taken by some writers as one of the defining characteristics of temperament. Because of the genetic component, it is easy to assume that a score on activity level or some other temperamental characteristic is an independently defined person characteristic comparable to biological sex, and one that can be studied jointly with environmental factors to obtain a relatively pure picture of the effects of person and environmental factors and their interaction. We need to remind ourselves that measures of temperament reflect both initial genetically programmed tendencies and prior influences from the environment. At any time after the day of birth, we enter the system at a point when mutually influential processes between parent and child have already occurred. Of course this does not preclude our studying the effects of parental or child characteristics at any given point in time, regardless of their history, upon the future development of the relationship.

Longer-Term Interactions

With this in mind, we turn now to some longer-range interactions between sex, temperament, and the nature of the parent–child relationship. Sixty of the children who had been studied at 12 and 18 months were observed again in interaction with their parents at the age of 45 months. We referred to the 45-month study earlier, when we examined the joint effects of sex of parent and sex of child upon their interaction. For the analysis that follows now, only the mother–child interaction scores from the 45-month session will be utilized, since our purpose is to identify any continuities from the 18-month session (when only mother–child interaction, not father–child, was observed) to the 45-month period. At 18 months, during the portion of the session when the mother was being interviewed, we distinguished "proximal" from "distal" positive mother–child interaction and scored the frequency with which each kind of interaction occurred for each mother–child pair. The proximal interaction score reflects the amount of touching and holding that occurred between the pair. Positive distal interaction refers to the exchange of smiles, the showing or giving of objects, and the exchange of social speech other than demands or protests.

A first question concerned the nature of the connections, if any, between proximal and distal interaction at 18 months and the kind of interactive play that occurred during the 45-month session. From the 45-month observational data, we derived a composite score called *mutual comply,* representing the sum of instances in which either the mother or child made an influence attempt (a suggestion, offer, directive, demand, or question) and the partner complied or answered. A still more inclusive composite combined this mutual-comply score with the frequency of interactive play (thematic play, social conversation other than influence attempts, or rough-and-tumble play); this more inclusive composite was called *total cooperative play.* As Table 2 shows, there is a modest correlation between positive distal interaction at 18 months and total cooperative play at 45 months. The amount of proximal interaction at 18 months, on the other hand, was not associated with high levels of cooperative play 2 years later. On the contrary, mother–child pairs who had done a greater-than-

Table 2
Correlations between 18-Month and 45-Month Mother–Child Interaction Scores

Interaction with mother at 45 months	Positive distal interaction at 18 months			Proximal interaction at 18 months		
	Boys (32)[a]	Girls (28)	Both sexes (60)	Boys (32)	Girls (28)	Both sexes (60)
Mutual compliance	.06	.47*	.20	−.30	−.26	−.27*
Total cooperative play	.28	.47*	.30*	−.18	−.04	−.12

[a]Values in parentheses are N.
*$p < .05$.

average amount of touching and holding at 18 months were somewhat *less* likely at 45 months to show compliance to one another's suggestions or demands (see Table 2).

Why should the early *distal* interaction show some continuity with later positive interactive behavior while early proximal interaction does not? Perhaps the lack of continuity from proximal interaction constitutes an example of a rapid developmental change in a system that has little counterpart at a later time. We had both mother reports and several observational measures of our subjects' timidity during the first year and a half of their lives. Compared to bold children, timid children and their mothers touched one another relatively often during our observation session at 18 months; we can only suspect that we were activating the familiar behavioral system whereby children seek contact with their attachment object when uneasy in the presence of a stranger. The point is that this system has a time-bound developmental course and is much less often activated at 45 months. This is an example, then, of a developmental change that diminishes continuity. Distal interaction, however, is something that can last into the period when children are no longer doing much clinging or lap-sitting.

Does temperament have anything to do with the continuities or discontinuities that occur across this 18- to 45-month time span? Here there are some surprises. Children's activity levels do seem to be implicated, at least moderately, in the interaction with their parents, but its role appears to be different for the two sexes. At 18 months, there is a tendency for a higher level of positive distal interaction to occur when the mother is interacting with either an *active* girl or a relatively *inactive* boy. The same pattern of results is found at 45 months (see Table 3).

These results are counterintuitive. We would not have been surprised if mothers had reacted more positively to relatively active boys and relatively inactive girls, on the grounds that such patterns are consistent with sex stereotypes concerning how children of the two sexes may be expected to act. Indeed, it might be argued that mothers would be motivated to interact more

Table 3
Mean Interaction Scores at 18 and 45 Months by 9- to 18-Month Activity Levels and Sex of Child

	Activity level, 9–18 months				F values for activity and sex
	Low-active boys (N = 16)	High-active boys (N = 16)	Low-active girls (N = 14)	High-active girls (N = 14)	(A × S)
Mother–child interaction at 18 months					
Positive distal interaction (mean standardized score)	.13	−.37	−.42	.85	3.57*
Proximal interaction (mean standardized score)	−.16	.68	−.43	.15	N.S.
Percentage of child bids that are positive	.47	.43	.47	.64	4.05**
Parent–child interaction at 45 months					
Mother–child: total cooperative play	146.5	113.9	128.7	148.4	5.72**
Father–child: total cooperative play[a]	141.4	112.7	86.6	137.6	7.72***

[a] The N's for father–child scores are somewhat reduced, since some single-parent families are included in the sample. The N's for this analysis are 16, 14, 11, and 13.

*p < .10.
**p < .05.
***p < .01.

positively with (i.e., reinforce) more active boys and less active girls. Finding the opposite patterns calls for some explanation. Our first hypothesis was that, even though the median split on activity level was made at the same point on the activity scale for the two sexes, it might nevertheless be the case that active boys were more active—that there were more boys at the highest end of the distribution. In this sample, this did not prove to be the case. The means and distributions on the composite measure of activity were remarkably similar for the two sexes.

As might be expected, the highly active children of both sexes made more bids for their mothers' attention at the age of 18 months than their less active counterparts, and in terms of total bids, boys and girls did not differ. However, there was some difference in the nature of the bidding that occurred: Highly active girls were different from the other three groups of children in having an especially high proportion of positive bids. That is, when they sought their mothers' attention, they tended to do so by smiling, offering objects, or vocalizing pleasantly, rather than by fussing, demanding, or obstructing (see Table 3). Thus, we see that high activity level is part of a somewhat different cluster of behaviors for the two sexes.

Is it the case that mothers have a less cooperative relationship with highly active sons, but that fathers compensate for this by showing more positive social interaction with active boys? In our data, the answer is negative. Although we did not observe fathers with their children at 18 months, we did so at 45 months, and found that fathers as well as mothers showed higher levels of total cooperative play with girls who had been relatively active during their first 2 years, and boys who had been relatively inactive (see Table 3). Especially surprising was the fact that, for both mothers and fathers, the amount of rough-and-tumble play was *less* with sons who had been above average in activity during their early years. It is as though the parents did not want to arouse active boys into a state of excitement, while they had little such compunction with girls or inactive boys.

It is worth noting that observers provided some corraboration of the positive characteristics of active girls. After the 45-month observation, the observer was asked to make an overall rating on how appealing the child was to the observer. The observers were asked to judge on the basis of the child's behavior, not appearance. The scale ranged from "very appealing" (defined as: observer would make some effort to find future opportunities to interact with this child) to "very unappealing" (i.e., never want to see this child again). The observers rated as most appealing the girls who had been in the high-activity group during the 9- to 18-month period; for the boys, current appeal was essentially unrelated to their earlier activity level (F for the interaction $= 7.57$, $p < .01$).

We do not yet have a good explanation for the way the sex and activity level of children interact to produce different kinds of relationships with their parents (and different reactions in naive observers). Our tentative hypotheses are these:

1. There may be a tendency for parents to be more interested in boys—to pay more attention to them; whether this reflects social valuings or a realistic need for more surveillance of boys, we do not know. But the tendency means that girls must take more initiative to be noticed and get parental responses. If they are passive, they will frequently be ignored. If they are active, they can engender a pattern of positive social interactions with their parents, and this is manifested, at 45 months, in characteristics that outsiders find attractive.
2. High activity levels in boys may more often be part of a cluster of behaviors associated with *hyper*activity or lack of impulse control— characteristics that are not conducive to smooth interaction with other family members.

These hypotheses are highly tentative, and alternative suggestions are invited.

Conclusions

Let us recapitulate now some of the major themes we have stressed as we have considered person–environment interaction in developing children. We noted that one can conceptualize parental behavior toward children as a major element in the children's interpersonal environments. One can study how aspects of this environment (i.e., variations in the methods of childrearing parents employ) interact with stable characteristics of the children, such as their sex or temperament, to affect the children's pattern of behavioral development. We noted that while the sex of the child, in some instances, seems to be related to the impact of a given parental input, the instances in which temperament plays this kind of interactive role are so far rare.

Our second main theme was to note the ways in which children influence their own interpersonal environment. We provided instances in which both the child's sex and temperament were implicated in this process. We noted that the child's effective environment is constantly changing for two reasons: (*a*) because maturational and other developmental changes enable the child to utilize increasingly complex inputs and (*b*) because the child's own behavior and characteristics influence the nature of the inputs received. From the time of William James, it has been observed that persons influence their own environments by choosing to participate in some activities but not others, and to enter certain settings but not others. We have attempted to expand upon this point by showing that, even when children are too young to make very effective choices about where and with whom they will spend their time, they still have an impact on their interpersonal environment by influencing the behavior of their socializers. Thus, we found that, even at the early age of 12–18 months, difficult boys can cause parents (or at least, mothers) to back off from applying socialization pressure, and active girls elicit especially positive interactive behaviors from both mothers and fathers, whereas this is not the case for active boys.

Both parent and child constitute important elements in one another's interpersonal environment. Because influence flows in both directions, neither person nor environment stands still, and this is true whether one is taking the parent or the child as the focus of analysis. For either party, both person and environment have been influenced to some degree by prior interactions between the pair. When we attempt to analyze the socialization process in terms of the familiar analysis of variance design, where variance is partitioned into the main effects for person and environment and their interaction, we need to take these complexities into account. Indeed, we have intended to raise the question of whether this conceptualization is appropriate for the analysis of processes where the presumed independent variables have a history of mutual influence.

References

Bates, J. E. The concept of difficult temperament. *Merrill Palmer Quarterly,* 1980, 26, 299–320.

Baumrind, D. *Socialization determinants of personal agency.* Paper presented at the Biennial Meeting of Society for Research in Child Development, New Orleans, March 1977.

Baumrind, D. *Sex-related socialization effects.* Paper presented at the Biennial Meeting of Society for Research in Child Development, San Francisco, March 1979.

Bradley, R. H., Caldwell, B. M., & Elardo, R. Home environment and cognitive development in the first 2 years: A cross-lagged panel analysis. *Developmental Psychology,* 1979, 15, 246–250.

Bronfenbrenner, U. *The ecology of human development.* Cambridge, Mass.: Harvard University Press, 1979.

Brunswik, E. *Perception and the representative design of psychological experiments.* Berkeley, Calif.: University of California Press, 1956.

Buss, A. H., & Plomin, R. *A temperament theory of personality development.* New York: Wiley, 1975.

Crockenberg, S. B. Infant irritability, mother responsiveness, and social support influences on the security of infant–mother attachment. *Child Development,* 1981, 52, 857–865.

Dodge, K. Social cognition and children's aggressive behavior. *Child Development,* 1980, 51, 162–171.

Dunn, J. Individual differences in temperament. In M. Rutter (Ed.), *Scientific foundations of developmental psychiatry.* London: Heinemann Medical, 1980.

Koffka, K. *Principles of Gestalt psychology.* New York: Harcourt, 1935.

Martin, J. A. A longitudinal study of the consequences of early mother–infant interaction: A microanalytic approach. *Monographs of the Society for Research in Child Development,* 1981, 46(3).

Martin, J. M., Maccoby, E. E., Baran, K. W., & Jacklin, C. N. Sequential analysis of mother–child interaction at 18 months: A comparison of microanalytic methods. *Developmental Psychology,* 1981, 17, 146–157.

Patterson, G. R. Mothers: The unacknowledged victims. *Monographs of the Society for Research in Child Development*, 1980, *45*, No. 5.

Rothbart, M., & Maccoby, E. E. Parents' differential reactions to sons and daughters. *Journal of Personality and Social Psychology*, 1966, *4*, 237–243.

Stevenson, H. W. Social reinforcement of children's behavior. In L. P. Lipsitt & C. C. Spiker (Eds.), *Advances in child development and behavior* (Vol. 2). New York: Academic Press, 1965.

Whiting, B. B., & Whiting, J. *Children of six cultures: A psychocultural analysis.* Cambridge, Mass.: Harvard University Press, 1975.

5

The Person–Environment Relationship: Lessons from Families with Preterm Infants[1]

BARBARA R. TINSLEY   ROSS D. PARKE

A variety of approaches have been utilized to characterize the person–environment relationship. The premise in this chapter is that our theoretical and empirical conceptualizations of environment need to be expanded to include a wider range of socializing agents and contexts, beyond the traditional view of the mother–child dyad to include both father–child and mother–father–child relationships. Second, recognition of the embeddedness of the family in its ecological context is needed in order to understand families' competence at differing points in development. To illustrate the interplay between person and environment, the impact of the birth of a premature infant on family functioning will be discussed. This event—the arrival of a premature infant—can be viewed as a natural experiment, which may illuminate more general processes of how families cope with stressful change.

The Impact of Children on Families: Some Recent Research Trends

A variety of modifications characterize recent research on the family's role in development, which have resulted in a sharper focus on relationships between different aspects of the individual and the environment. First, over the

[1]Preparation of this chapter was supported by NICHD Grant HEW PH5 05951, NICHD Training Grant HD 7205-01, and the National Foundation March of Dimes.

HUMAN DEVELOPMENT:
AN INTERACTIONAL PERSPECTIVE

past decade there has been a general increased concern about the limited ecological validity of our traditional methodologies, particularly our reliance on the laboratory experiment as the sine qua non of the student of social development and socialization. In fact, a "mythology of childhood," to borrow Baldwin's (1967) phrase, has evolved in which a set of effects noted in the laboratory is assumed actually to occur in naturalistic socialization contexts and is assumed to be an accurate account of how children are socialized. As a result there has been a confusion between necessary and sufficient causality; the laboratory experiments tell us only that certain variables are possible contributors to the child's social–cognitive development. However, the extent to which these hypothesized processes are, in fact, necessary and actual techniques for adequate socialization is left unanswered. To the extent that the aim is a technological one, in which the most effective techniques for modifying behavior in clinical and educational contexts are sought, the ecological validity issue is less relevant. However, if the actual developmental processes are to be elucidated, the problem cannot be dismissed. While laboratory paradigms are still widely used, the concern of contemporary researchers with the ecological validity of their questions, methodologies, and interpretations of data has led to the increased use of observational methodologies in order to assess ongoing interaction patterns in naturalistic settings (Cairns, 1979; Parke, 1979a).

A second noteworthy shift in research and theorizing in the area of parent–infant interaction is an increased recognition of the child's contribution to his or her own socialization. Traditionally, most approaches to social development have assumed a unidirectional model whereby the parent influences the child's development. Under the influence of Bell's (1968) classic article, the historical imbalance was corrected and the infant's contribution to his own socialization is now widely accepted. In part this shift occurred because of the experimental analyses of infant competencies of the 1960s that demonstrated the wide range of capacities as well as the readiness of the infant for social interaction. In fact, in our enthusiasm to correct a historical imbalance, the infant's impact on the parent became the focus, instead of the more appropriate emphasis on the reciprocal nature of the interactive process. The current zeitgeist has clearly shifted to a study of the reciprocity of interaction: The ways in which parents and infants mutually regulate each other are of central interest.

Third, the embeddedness of families in a larger network of social systems is being recognized (Brim, 1975; Bronfenbrenner, 1979). This suggests that greater attention needs to be addressed to describing the nature of these social systems and to specifying their impact on family functioning and individual development. To illustrate these trends, and the interplay between the individual and the environment, recent research on the impact of the birth of a premature infant on families will be presented.

The Impact of the Premature Infant on the
Caregiver–Infant Relationship

The birth of a premature infant is often a stressful event, as evidenced by descriptions portraying parents with infants in at-risk nurseries as shocked, angry, and otherwise emotionally distraught (Kennedy, 1973; Kopf & FcFadden, 1974; Slade, Redl, & Manguten, 1977). Furthermore, reactions to the birth of a premature infant are unlikely to be similar across families. The degree of stress associated with this event is determined, in part, by the parents' subjective perceptions of the event. In turn, it is assumed that their perceptions will influence their interactions with their infants. This cognitive–mediational approach suggests that parental knowledge, expectations, and labeling must be considered in order to understand the degree of stress as well as the parents' treatment of their infant (Leiderman, 1982; Parke, 1978b).

The survival rate of the low-birth-weight infant has increased greatly in recent years due to advances in medical care and technology (Klaus & Fanaroff, 1979). Many of these "new" survivors often have serious medical difficulties as well as a higher rate of short-term and long-term developmental problems than normal infants. Caputo and Mandell (1970) point out a number of outcomes that may make the low-birth-weight infant "at risk" for possible parental maltreatment. It should be noted that some of the outcomes may alter the parent–child relationship in the early postpartum months, while others may not affect the parent–child dyad until the child is beyond infancy.

In addition to the disequilibrium initiated by the birth of any infant, for example, additional tasks associated with caregiving, modifications of schedules and activities, and readjustment of the marital relationship (Bakan, 1971; Ryder, 1973), the birth of a premature infant has outcomes that further increase familial stress in a number of ways. First, the immature development of the infant may require special medical support procedures, which in turn may lead to separation of the mother and her infant. This shift in the usual and expected hospital procedure reminds us of the importance of considering the institutional environment in which the infant and family are embedded in studies of development (see Parke, 1978a; Richards, 1979). Although early separation may cause short-term stress on the family, follow-up studies indicate no long-term impact (i.e., 2 years) of this type of separation on the development of these infants (Leiderman, 1981, 1982).

Second, as noted earlier, the low-birth-weight, premature infant violates many parental expectations. In addition to arriving early, often before parental preparations for birth are completed, these infants differ from full terms in their appearance, cries, feeding procedures, interactional demands, and developmental progress, which, in turn, can contribute further to the stress associated with their arrival (Brooks & Hochberg, 1960; Frodi, Lamb, Leavitt,

Donovan, Neff, & Sherry, 1978). For example, in their study, Frodi *et al.* documented that, in addition to their appearance, the high-pitched cry patterns of the premature infant are rated by parents as more disturbing, irritating, and annoying. In addition, the parents reporting found prematures less pleasant and were less eager to interact with a preterm than a full-term infant.

Preterm infants place greater demands on their caregivers than term infants. For example, feeding disturbances are more common among low-birth-weight infants (Klaus & Fanaroff, 1979). Moreover, premature infants are behaviorally different than their term peers; Goldberg (Goldberg, 1979; Goldberg & Divitto, 1983) found premature infants spend less time alert, are more difficult to keep in alert states, are less responsive to sights and sounds than term infants, and provide less distinctive cues to guide parental treatment. In view of these behavioral characteristics, it is not surprising that parents have to work "harder" when interacting with a premature infant. Brown and Bakeman (1980) have documented that preterm infants are more difficult and less satisfying to feed than term infants; during feeding interactions, preterms contributed less to maintenance of the interactive flow than term infants and the burden of maintaining the interaction fell disproportionately on the mothers of these preterms. Together, these studies underscore the role that preterm infants play in shaping the behavior of their caregivers.

Not only does the preterm infant modify caregiver behavior, expectations concerning developmental timetables may be altered as well. Recently Smith, Leiderman, Selz, MacPherson, and Bingham (1981) found that mothers of preterm infants rated developmental milestones for their own child and a typical child. In rating their own children they predicted substantial lags for their own child until approximately 2 years of age. Beyond 2 years they expected more rapid development in social, psychomotor, and cognitive development than the rate of progress expected by the mothers of full-term infants. These data suggest that parents of preterm infants may have unrealistic expectations for their young children, which, in turn, may be a contributing factor in later dysfunctional parent–child relationships, such as child abuse (Egeland & Brunnquell, 1979).

In addition to the stress associated with the birth and caregiving of the premature infant, institutional arrangements for the care of the infant are problematic as well. Such procedures as the separation of the parent and infant induced by transport procedures, infant incubation in the high-risk nursery, and the extensive use of medical support equipment such as wiring and tubing affect the early parent–infant relationship (see Leiderman, 1982, and Richards, 1979, for a thorough review of the stress related to hospitalization in a high-risk nursery).

Clearly, a variety of both person and environmental characteristics conspire in altering the developmental progress of the preterm infant (see Freidman & Sigman, 1981, for a review of developmental outcomes). At the person level, the behavioral and physical characteristics and medical status of the infants merit consideration. At the environmental level, both the physical environment of the hospital and the social context (e.g., parent expectations and parent–infant interaction patterns) into which the infant is born are important. In the remainder of this chapter, it will be argued that an expanded characterization of the social world of the premature infant, beyond the mother–infant dyad, is necessary for a more complete understanding of the developmental environment of the premature infant.

Beyond the Mother–Infant Dyad: The Father–Infant Dyad and the Family Triad as Contexts for Development of the Preterm Infant

FATHER–INFANT DYAD

In recent years, the father's important role in infancy has been acknowledged (Lamb, 1981; Parke, 1979b, 1981). Fathers are active and interested participants in early infancy and competent in their execution of early caregiving tasks such as feeding (Parke & Sawin, 1976). Although the majority of studies have involved fathers with their term infants, a number of researchers have begun to recognize the special role that the father may play in the family when an infant is born prematurely.

Fathers differ in both amount of caregiving and the style of play with premature and term infants. The birth of a premature infant may elicit greater father involvement in caregiving as a result of the extra time and skill required to care for these infants. A number of recent studies confirm that fathers of preterm infants are more involved in caretaking than fathers of full-term infants (Marton, Minde, & Perrotta, 1981; Yogman, 1982).

Play patterns as well as levels of involvement in caregiving may be different for fathers of premature infants than for fathers of term infants. In a comparative observational investigation of the interaction patterns of fathers with premature and term infants in the high-risk nursery and at home shortly after the infants' discharge, styles of father–infant play with the preterm and term infants differed (Tinsley, Johnson, Szczypka, & Parke, 1982). Fathers exhibited their characteristic higher rate of physical play (bounce–stretch) than mothers—but only when the infant was born at term. When the infant was born prematurely, there was no mother–father difference in play style. The differences were particularly marked by 3 weeks; at the hospital period, there were no differences between mothers and fathers in their treatment of either term or premature infants. Possibly fathers assume that the premature infant is fragile and unable to withstand robust physical stimulation which, in turn, leads to an inhibition of fathers' usual play style.

To further illustrate the impact of prematurity on father–infant interaction, we examined one of the most consistent determinants of parental expectations, perceptions, and organizers of behavior, infant sex. There are marked and relatively consistent differences in paternal and maternal reactions to male and female infants born at term (Parke, 1979b, 1981). In general, the findings across many studies suggest that fathers stimulate their sons more than their daughters, while mothers tend to treat their sons and daughters more similarly. However, we found that when the infant is born prematurely, fathers tend to treat boys and girls in a similar fashion and no evidence of differential treatment of the sexes is evident in our research (Tinsley, Johnson, Szczypka, & Parke, 1982). Follow-up observations are currently under way to determine the stability of these patterns at later developmental points in the first year of infancy. Thus, person characteristics such as birth status combined with environmental elements such as parent behavior, perceptions, and expectations create a different socialization experience for the very young premature infant.

THE FAMILY TRIAD

Models that limit examination of the effects of interaction patterns to only the father–infant and mother–infant dyads and the direct effects of one individual on another are inadequate for understanding the impact of social interaction patterns in families and especially in families with preterm infants (Lewis & Feiring, 1981; Parke, Power, & Gottman, 1979; Parke & Tinsley, 1982).

Triadic contexts (father, mother, and infant interacting together) as well as indirect paths of mutual influence merit attention. A parent may influence a child through the mediation of another family member's impact (e.g., a mother may contribute to the father's positive affect toward his child by praising his caregiving skill). Another way in which one parent may indirectly influence the child's treatment by other agents is by modifying the infant's behavior. Child behavior patterns that develop as a result of parent–child interaction may, in turn, affect the child's treatment by other social agents. For example, irritable infant patterns induced by an insensitive and impatient mother may, in turn, make the infant more difficult for the father to handle and pacify. Thus, patterns developed in interaction with one parent may alter interaction patterns with another caregiver. In larger families, siblings can play a similar mediating role.

The importance of the relationship between family characteristics and infant status should also be emphasized. The development of at-risk infants has been demonstrated to be significantly affected by the infants' ordinal position, family background factors, parent–infant interaction patterns, and other socioeconomic factors (Caputo, Goldstein, & Taub, 1981; Drillien, 1964; Sigman, Cohen, Beckwith, & Parmalee, 1981). Parents have been shown to behave differently when alone with their infant than when interacting with the infant in the presence of the other parent. In our earlier studies (Parke, Grossman, & Tinsley, 1981; Parke & O'Leary, 1976), the presence of the other parent significantly altered the behavior of the partner; specifically, each expressed more positive affect (smiling) toward their infant and showed a higher level of exploration when the other parent was present. In our studies of premature infants and their parents, we find similar patterns (Tinsley, Johnson, Szczypka, & Parke, 1982). The family context appeared to elicit greater affective and exploratory behavior on the part of both parents. These results indicate that parent–infant interaction cannot be understood by focusing solely on parent–infant dyads, with either premature or term infants.

Other recent investigations emphasize the importance of studying the family triad in terms of the impact of the husband–wife relationship on the parent–infant interaction process and the influence of the birth of an at-risk infant on the cohesiveness of the family. In a study by Pedersen (1975), it was found that mothers of 4-week-old babies who were supported by the infant's father were rated more competent in feeding their infants. Moreover, a positive relationship between scores on the Brazelton Neonatal Assessment Scale for alertness and motor maturity and parents' marital relationship was reported. In Pedersen's view "a good baby and a good marriage go together."

Both Parke and O'Leary (1976) and Pedersen (1975) studied families with healthy, term infants. However, one would expect that a premature infant would have an even more profound impact on family interaction patterns. Of relevance to this issue is the work of Leiderman (1981) and Leiderman and Seashore (1975). These investigators examined the relationship of prematurity to marital stability. In the 2-year period following hospital discharge, marital discord, often leading to separation or divorce, was higher for the families of preterm infants who were initially separated from their mothers. As Leiderman and Seashore (1975) suggest, "separation in the newborn period does have an effect, albeit non-specific, by acting through the family as a stress that creates disequilibrium in the nuclear family structure [pp. 229–230]." While the Leiderman work provides further support for considering the family unit, the specific ways in which the birth of a preterm infant affects relationships among family members remain unclear.

Recent studies indicate the importance of the father as support figure for the mother when the infant is born prematurely. Paternal support can take a variety of forms, such as providing nurturance and emotional support for the mother as well as providing instrumental support by increased involvement in caretaking. Herzog (1979) found that fathers of premature infants provided support for the mother to facilitate her caretaking role and her positive feelings toward the infant. Further support for this position comes from a study of parental visiting patterns in an English at-risk nursery (Hawthorne, Richards, & Callon, 1978). These investigators found that mothers of premature infants were helped by fathers who became highly involved in caring for the infant. While these studies indicate that fathers assume a more active supportive role in the case of a premature infant, neither the factors that promote differential degrees of paternal involvement nor the subsequent impact of this involvement for either (a) the husband—wife relationship; (b) the mother—infant relationship or (c) the father—infant relationship have been specified.

A further clue concerning these issues comes from a recent study by Minde, Marton, Manning, and Hines (1980), who reported that the frequency with which mothers visited their hospitalized premature infants was related to the quality of the husband—wife relationship; visitation was less frequent in distressed marriages than in nondistressed families. In light of the relationship between visitation patterns and parenting disorders such as child abuse (Fanaroff, Kennell, & Klaus, 1972), and considered in combination with the findings of Minde *et al.* as discussed earlier relating maternal—infant behavior and familial relationships such as that of the mother and the infant's father, these findings assume more significance. While low frequencies of visitation by mothers may contribute to later problems possibly due, at least in part, to the lack of opportunity for the development of a strong mother—infant relationship, it is possible that the poor husband—wife relationship may be a factor in both low involvement (visitation) and subsequent parenting disorders. Alternatively, the husband in a poor marriage may not share in the caretaking activities, which may increase the likelihood of stress in mothers (Parke, 1977; Parke & Collmer, 1975). Further support for this hypothesis comes from a study of maternal adjustment to having a handicapped child (Friedrich, 1979). Marital satisfaction was found to be the best predictor of maternal coping behavior.

The importance of these findings is clear: In order to understand either the mother—infant or the father—infant relationship, the total set of relationships among the members of the family needs to be assessed. Although interviews are helpful, they are not sufficient; rather, direct observations of both mother *and* father alone with their infants as well as the mother, father, and infant together are necessary to understand the effects of prematurity on the family and the infant.

Community Support Systems and Preterm Infants

A further extension of our theoretical framework—from the dyad to the triad to the family in its ecological context—is needed to understand the environment and the development of the at-risk infant. Families do not exist as units independent of other social organizations within society. Thus, families need to be viewed within their social context; and recognition of the role of the community as a modifier of family modes of interaction is necessary for an adequate theory of early development.

To understand the specific functions that extra familial support systems play in modulating interaction patterns in families of premature infants, an appreciation of the problems associated with prematurity is necessary. Premature infants may be at risk as a result of (*a*) limited knowledge of development on the part of parents; (*b*) inappropriate infant-care skill, or (*c*) the stress associated with the care and rearing of a preterm infant. Extrafamilial support systems can function to alleviate these problems (*a*) by providing accurate timetables for the development of premature infants as well as full-term infants; (*b*) by monitoring current infant-care practices and providing corrective feedback in order to improve infant-care skills; and (*c*) by providing relief from stress associated with the birth and care of the preterm infant.

There are a variety of support systems of *special relevance* to at-risk infants and families. Two kinds of support systems operate: formal (e.g., health-care facilities, social service agencies, recreational facilities) and informal (e.g., extended families, neighbors, and co-workers). These programs serve both the educational function of providing child-care information and the mental-health function of alleviating stress associated with premature or ill infants. Support systems that serve an educational function include hospital-based courses in child care and childrearing; nurse visiting programs; well-baby clinics, follow-up programs; and parent discussion groups. Some other supportive programs that offer stress relief are family and group day-care facilities; baby-sitting services; mother's helpers,; homemaker and housekeeping services; drop-off centers; crisis nurseries; and hot lines.

Evidence in support of the role of informal and formal support systems in regulating family ability to cope with at-risk infants is limited. In the next section some illustrative studies of the role of support systems in modifying family management of infant care and development will be reviewed. Although some recent studies involve informal social support systems, many of the studies have involved primarily modification of the formal support systems available to families. Finally, in some cases, informal and formal support are provided together, which underlines the interconnectedness of these two levels of social support for families.

RELATIONSHIP BETWEEN INFORMAL
SOCIAL SUPPORT SYSTEMS
AND FAMILY INTERACTION PATTERNS

A number of studies have suggested that there is a positive relationship between informal social networks and a family's adaptation to stress. Specifically, interaction patterns among family members are influenced by the availability and utilization of informal social networks (Cochran & Brassard, 1979). In studies of abusive families, it has been found that these families are often socially isolated and lack adequate social support systems (Elmer, 1976; Garbarino & Gilliam, 1980; Parke, 1982; Parke & Collmer, 1975; Parke & Lewis, 1981). Similarly, in their study of divorce, Hetherington, Cox, and Cox (1978) found that the adequacy of the mother's social support network was positively related to her effectiveness with her children. Of more direct relevance are two recent studies of the relationship between social networks and mother–child interaction.

Powell (1979) examined the influence of social networks on mother–infant interaction in a small sample of white, low-income mothers and their young infants (under 6 months). Using the HOME Scale (Elardo, Bradley, & Caldwell, 1975) to assess interaction, Unger found that mothers who experienced high levels of stress were found to be more actively involved with their infants when they had weekly contact with friends than when they were infrequently in contact. Parents also appeared more responsive to their infants if they were receiving material resources from their network members. In a related study that also used the HOME Scale, Pascoe, Loda, Jeffries, and Earp (1981) found a positive relationship between the level of maternal social support and selected subscales from the HOME Scale in a group of families with 3-year-old children. Unfortunately, Pascoe *et al.* did not examine both intrafamilial (i.e., spouse support) and extrafamilial social support separately, which does not permit an evaluation of the relative importance of differing sources of support. However, these two studies of Pascoe *et al.* and Powell are important in view of the previously established positive relationship between the HOME Scale and mental test performance (Bradley & Caldwell, 1976). These investigations suggest that social support may affect infant and child developmental outcomes indirectly, through modifying the nature of parent–child interaction patterns.

More recently, Crockenberg (1981) found that the extent to which mothers utilized social support networks was related to the infant's pattern of attachment to her mother. Especially in the case of irritable babies (a characteristic common in many premature infants), utilization of social support was associated with secure attachment. This study provides an excellent illustration of the interplay of individual characteristics (temperament) and the role of the social environment (social support networks) on later patterns of infant–mother attachment. In view of the evidence that the quality of early attachment is associated with later peer social competence (Pastor, 1981), this finding is of particular importance.

Unfortunately, little evidence is available concerning the utilization and impact of social support systems on families of preterm infants. It is assumed that social networks will be particularly important in the families of preterm infants who are under greater initial stress than families of term infants. Although many of the children in the Pascoe *et al.* study either were born prematurely or were ill as infants, no assessments were made of the social networks of these families when their children were infants. More recent evidence (Parke, Tinsley, & Volling, 1982) indicates that parents are more likely to use social support systems when their infants are born prematurely than when their infants are born at term. However, mothers are more likely to utilize informal support networks than fathers, whereas fathers are more likely to use formal agencies for information. This suggests the importance of distinguishing informal and formal support systems and underscores the necessity of providing formal support systems for families, including fathers.

RELATIONSHIP BETWEEN FORMAL SOCIAL SUPPORT SYSTEMS
AND FAMILY INTERACTION PATTERNS

In recent years, a number of investigators have used the hospital to provide social support for parents and, in particular, the postpartum period as a convenient time-point for initiating supportive services for parents of infants. Parents are accessible at this point and often motivation for learning about infant development and caregiving skills is high during this time.

The value of hospital-based programs for mothers is illustrated in the work of Badger, Burns, and Vietze (1981). Teenage mothers who were assumed to be at risk for later parenting problems were recruited in the hospital during the postpartum period and given a series of weekly classes that included instruction in stimulating their infant's social and cognitive skills and information about infant nutrition, family planning, and health care. Results indicated that young teenage mothers (16 years or younger) and their infants profited from this intervention effort. Specifically, the infants of high-risk mothers who attended classes had normal Bayley scores at 1 year in contrast to a comparison group who had significantly lower Bayley mental scores, emphasizing that social support can indirectly as well as directly affect family members. Furthermore, the mothers who attended the classes were more physically and emotionally responsive to their infants than mothers in the comparison samples. Unfortunately, the relative contribution of the components that may account for the observed differences in infant functioning is unclear.

This early postpartum period can be effectively used to provide support for fathers as well. This is demonstrated by a recent hospital-based study (Parke, Hymel, Power, & Tinsley, 1980). During the mother's postpartum hospitalization, one group of fathers was shown a short videotape that modeled positive father–infant interaction and caretaking involvement with young infants. In comparison to a control group of fathers who saw no videotape, fathers who viewed the film in the hospital increased their knowledge about infant perceptual abilities, believed more strongly that infants need stimulation, and were more responsive to their infants during feeding and play in comparison to fathers who were not exposed to the film. Based on diary reports of caretaking activities in the home at 3 months, fathers who saw the film were more likely to diaper and feed their boy infants than fathers in the no-film control group. In summary, the film intervention significantly modified selected aspects of father behavior and attitudes both in the hospital and through the first 3 months of their infants' lives. In a related study, Parke and his colleagues (Parke, Tinsley, Power, & Hymel, 1981) directly addressed this issue through the use of a film that stressed the importance of spouses providing mutual support for one another. The level of husband–wife assistance in child care was, during the postpartum period, increased through this hospital-based intervention. Furthermore, mothers whose partners had seen a film emphasizing parental cooperation and assistance in caregiving stimulated their infants more in the hospital and the home and tended to help the fathers feed the infants more frequently in the home.

In a recent study, Dickie and Carnahan (1980) provided training to mothers and fathers of 4- to 12-month-old infants in order to increase their competence. Utilizing Goldberg's (1977; 1979) notion of competence as parental ability to assess, predict, elicit, and provide contingent response experiences for their infants, these investigators provided eight 2-hour weekly sessions. Training emphasized individual infant variation, knowledge of the infant's temperament and cues, provision of contingent experiences, and awareness of the infant's effect on the parents. Fathers who had participated in the training sessions, in contrast to fathers who had not participated, increased their interactions with their infants; specifically, they talked, touched, held, attended more, and gave more contingent responses to infant smiles and vocalizations. The infants of the trained fathers sought interaction more than infants of fathers in the control group. However, mothers in the trained group decreased their interactions; in view of this fact that training did increase the judgments of the spouses' competence, it is possible that the wives of the trained fathers encouraged "their" competent husbands to assume a greater share of the infant-care and interactional responsibilities. Interestingly, this finding underlines the reciprocal nature of the mother–father relationship and provides further support for viewing the family as a social system in which the activities of one member have an impact on the behavior of other family members. Finally, these data are consistent with nonhuman primate findings that father–infant involvement varies inversely with the degree of maternal restrictiveness (for reviews, see Parke & Suomi, 1981; Redican; 1976).

These studies and others (Zelazo, Kotelchuck, Barber, & David, 1977) show that these types of supportive interventions for increasing paternal involvement need not be restricted to the early postpartum period or to young infants. Parental behavior can be modified at a variety of time-points. The capacity of both parents and infants for continual adaptation to shifting circumstances probably overrides the paramount importance of any single time period for the formation of social relationships (Cairns, 1977), although the postpartum hospitalization period seems an important potential intervention time-point for families with a new premature infant.

Another set of studies illustrates the potential of health-care providers, such as pediatricians, to play a supportive role for parents of young children. Chamberlin (1979) reports that mothers who participated in an educational program concerning child development during pediatric well-baby visits increased their knowledge of child development and their perceptions of being supported in the caregiving role. A second study (Whitt & Casey, 1982) suggests that mothers who were provided with an office-based pediatric intervention program, emphasizing physical and preventive child care, developmental norms, and information on infant communication abilities during well-baby exams, demonstrated a more positive relationship with their infants. Again, given the problematic medical status of many premature infants, utilization of pediatric visits as support mechanisms for families of premature infants appears to be a promising form of supportive intervention. Together, these intervention studies illustrate the ways in which formal institutions such as hospitals and other health-care facilities can potentially affect infants through the modification of the skills of mother, father, or both parents.

RELATIONSHIP BETWEEN INFORMAL AND
FORMAL SUPPORT SYSTEMS

Although informal and formal support systems can make independent contributions to family functioning, a number of recent studies have shown that these two types of support systems can work in concert in supporting families. Links between formal and informal support systems can assume a variety of forms, such as (a) strengthening the informal network through formal intervention (Powell, 1979); (b) mobilizing existing social networks in times of stress (Rueveni, 1979); and (c) using informal network members to help individuals utilize formal support services (Olds, 1981).

Minde and his colleagues (Minde, Shosenberg, & Marton, 1981; Minde, Shosenberg, Marton, Thompson, Ripley, & Burns, 1980) have recently developed a program of self-help groups for mothers of premature infants, which illustrates the interplay between formal and informal systems. Each group met weekly with an experienced neonatal nurse and an experienced mother of a premature infant for 7–12 weeks following the birth of their infant. The groups provided a variety of services including opportunities to share feelings, information about the developmental and medical needs of premature infants, and assistance with daily tasks (e.g., baby-sitters' accommodations and unemployment benefits). In contrast to a control group, these mothers visited their infants significantly more in the hospital, stimulated them more, and expressed more confidence in their caretaking abilities. At 3 months after discharge, group mothers continued to show involvement with their babies during feedings and were more concerned about their general development. At 1 year, they gave their infants more general freedom and stimulation and judged their competence more appropriately to their biological abilities in contrast to mothers in the control group. In turn, the infants whose mothers participated in the intervention group showed more social and independent behaviors such as playing and self-feeding. Although the mechanisms through which these positive outcomes were achieved were not directly isolated, the role of informal social support is suggested by the finding that more mothers from the self-help group reported that their relationships with one or more significant persons in their life improved. In turn, one would expect that these mothers were able to use these significant others more effectively for support. Finally, as an illustration of the ways in which formal and informal support systems interact, Minde *et al.* reported that the "self-support" groups in this study are now being run as an independent organization, by the parents themselves.

This study illustrates the role that informal and formal social networks together can play in aiding families to adapt to stressful change. However, the details of the puzzle are only partially clear and the specific direct and indirect ways in which different types of informal and formal supportive intervention alter different aspects of family interaction and, in turn, infant development are not yet well understood. Descriptive studies of how families spontaneously use and profit from available formal and informal network resources as well as experimental interventions in which the contributions of specific parts of the network are manipulated are both useful strategies for future research.

Conclusion

In this chapter the importance of expanding our conceptualization of the social environment of the preterm infant was stressed. The ecologically sensitive expansion beyond the mother–infant to include the father–infant relationship is only a first step; an understanding of the full set of relationships among mother, father, and infant, who are recognized as part of a family system, is necessary as well. Finally, recognition of the embeddedness of the family in formal and informal social networks and of the specific direct and indirect ways in which these extrafamilial social systems can alter family functioning is necessary to improve our knowledge concerning the interplay between the individual and the environment, and to better understand the social environment of the premature infant.

Acknowledgments

We thank Sally Parsons and Jane Pritchard for their assistance in the preparation of this chapter.

References

Badger, E., Burns, D., & Vietze, P. Maternal risk factors as predictors of developmental outcome in early childhood. *Infant Mental Health Journal*, 1981, *2*, 33–43.
Bakan, D. *Slaughter of the innocents*. San Francisco: Jossey-Bass, 1971.
Baldwin, A. *Theories of child development*. New York: Wiley, 1967.
Bell, R. Q. A reinterpretation of the direction of effects in studies of socialization. *Psychological Review*, 1968, *75*, 81–95.
Bradley, R. H., & Caldwell, B. M. Early home environment and changes in mental test performance in children from 6 to 36 months. *Developmental Psychology*, 1976, *12*, 93–97.

Brim, O. G. Macro-structural influences on child development and the need for childhood social indicators. *American Journal of Orthopsychiatry,* 1975, *45,* 516–524.

Bronfenbrenner, U. *The ecology of human development.* Cambridge: Harvard University Press, 1979.

Brooks, V., & Hochberg, J. A psychological study of "cuteness." *Perceptual and Motor Skills,* 1960, *11,* 205.

Brown, J. V., & Bakeman, R. Relationships of human mothers with their infants during the first year of life: Effects of prematurity. In R. W. Bell & W. P. Smotherman (Eds.), *Maternal influences and early behavior.* Holliswood, N. Y.: Spectrum, 1980.

Cairns, R. B. Beyond social attachment: The dynamics of interactional development. In T. A. Alloway, P. Pliner, & L. Krames (Eds.), *Attachment behavior.* New York: Plenum, 1977.

Cairns, R. B. *The analysis of social interactions: Methods, issues, & illustrations.* Hillsdale, N. J.: Erlbaum, 1979.

Caputo, D. U., Goldstein, K. M., & Tabu, H. B. Neonatal compromise and later psychological development: A ten-year longitudinal study. In S. L. Friedman & M. Sigman (Eds.), *Preterm birth and psychological development.* New York: Academic Press, 1981.

Caputo, D. V., & Mandell, W. Consequences of low birth weight. *Developmental Psychology,* 1970, *3,* 363–383.

Chamberlin, R. W. *Effects of educating mothers about child development in physicians' offices on mother and child functioning over time.* Paper presented at the American Psychological Association, New York, 1979.

Cochran, M. M., & Brassard, J. A. Child development and personal social networks. *Child Development,* 1979, *50,* 601–616.

Crockenberg, S. B. Infant irritability, mother responsiveness, and social support influences on the security of infant–mother attachment. *Child Development,* 1981, *52,* 857–865.

Dickie, J., & Carnahan, S. Training in social competence: The effect on mothers, fathers and infants. *Child Development,* 1980, *51,* 1248–1251.

Drillien, C. M. *The growth and development of the prematurely born infant.* Baltimore: Williams & Wilkins, 1964.

Egeland, B., & Brunnquell, D. An at-risk approach to the study of child abuse: Some preliminary findings. *Journal of the American Academy of Psychiatry,* 1979, *18,* 219–235.

Elardo, R., Bradley, R., & Caldwell, B. The relation of infants' home environments to mental test performance from six to thirty-six months: A longitudinal analysis. *Child Development,* 1975, *46,* 71–76.

Elmer, E. *Children in jeopardy: A study of abused minors and their families.* Pittsburgh: University of Pittsburgh Press, 1976.

Fanaroff, A., Kennell, J., & Klaus, M. Follow up of low birthweight infants—The predictive value of maternal visiting patterns. *Pediatrics,* 1972, *49,* 287–290.

Freidman, S. L., & Sigman, M. (Eds.) *Preterm birth and psychological development.* New York: Academic Press, 1981.

Friedrich, W. N. Predictors of the coping behavior of mothers of handicapped children. *Journal of Consulting and Clinical Psychology,* 1979, *47,* 1140–1141.

Frodi, A. M., Lamb, M. E., Leavitt, L. A., Donovan, W. L., Neff, C., & Sherry, D. Fathers' and mothers' responses to the faces and cries of normal and premature infants. *Developmental Psychology,* 1978, *14,* 490–498.

Garbarino, J., & Gilliam, G. *Understanding abusive families.* Lexington, Mass.: Heath, 1980.

Goldberg, S. Social competence in infancy: A model of parent–infant interaction. *Merrill-Palmer Quarterly,* 1977, *23,* 163–177.

Goldberg, S. Premature birth: Consequences for the parent–infant relationship. *American Scientist,* 1979, *67,* 214–220.

Goldberg, S., & DiVitto, B. A. *Born too soon: Preterm birth and early development:* San Francisco, Calif.: W. H. Freeman, 1983.

Hawthorne, J. T., Richards, M. P. M., & Callon, M. A study of parental visiting of babies in a special care unit. In F. S. W. Brimblecombe, M. P. M. Richards, & N. R. C. Roberton (Eds.), *Early separation and special care nurseries* (Clinics in Developmental Medicine). London: SIMP/Heinemann Medical Books, 1978.

Herzog, J. M. Disturbances in parenting high-risk infants: Clinical impressions and hypotheses. In T. M. Field (Ed.), *Infants born at risk: Behavior and development.* New York: S. P. Medical and Scientific Books, 1979.

Hetherington, E. M., Cox, M., & Cox, R. The aftermath of divorce. In J. H. Stevens, Jr., & M. Matthew (Eds.), *Mother–child, father–child relations.* Washington, D. C.: National Association for the Education of Young Children, 1978.

Kennedy, J. The high risk maternal infant acquaintance process. *Nursing Clinics of North America,* 1973, *8,* 549–556.

Klaus, M. H., & Fanaroff, A. A. *Care of the high-risk neonate* (2nd ed.). Philadelphia: Saunders, 1979.

Kopf, R. C., & McFadden, E. L. Nursing intervention in the crisis of newborn illness. *Journal of Nursing Midwifery,* 1974, *16,* 629–636.

Lamb, M. E. *The role of the father in child development* (2nd ed.). New York: Wiley, 1981.

Leiderman, P. H. Human mother–infant social bonding: Is there a sensitive phase? In K. Immelman, G. W. Barlow, L. Petrinovich, & M. Main (Eds.), *Behavioral development:* The Bielefeld interdisciplinary project. New York: Cambridge University Press, 1981.

Leiderman, P. H. Social ecology and childbirth: The newborn nursery as environmental stressor. In N. Garmezy & M. Rutter (Eds.), *Stress, coping and adaptation.* New York: McGraw-Hill, 1982.

Leiderman, P. H., & Seashore, M. J. Mother–infant separation: Some delayed consequences. In *Parent–infant interaction* (CIBA Foundation Symposium 33). Amsterdam: Elsevier, 1975.

Lewis, M., & Feiring, C. Direct and indirect interactions in social relationships. In L. Lipsitt (Ed.), *Advances in infancy research* (Vol. 1). New York: Ablex Publishing Corp., 1981.

Maccoby, E. E., & Jacklin, C. N. *The psychology of sex differences.* Stanford, Calif.: Stanford University Press, 1974.

Marton, P., Minde, K., & Perrotta, M., The role of the father for the infant at risk. *American Journal of Orthopsychiatry,* 1981, *51,* 672–679.

Minde, K. K., Marton, P., Manning, D., & Hines, B. Some determinants of mother–infant interaction in the premature nursery. *American Academy of Child Psychiatry Journal,* 1980, *19,* 1–21.

Minde, K., Shosenberg, N. E., & Marton, P. L. *The effects of self-help groups in a premature nursery on maternal autonomy and caretaking style one year later.* Unpublished manuscript, University of Toronto, 1981.

Minde, K., Shosenberg, N. E., Marton, P., Thompson, J., Ripley, J., & Burns, S. Self-help groups in a premature nursery—A controlled evaluation. *Journal of Pediatrics,* 1980, *96,* 933–940.

Olds, D. L. The prenatal/early infancy project: An ecological approach to prevention. In J. Belsky (Ed.), *In the beginning: Readings in infancy.* New York: Columbia University Press, 1981.

Parke, R. D. Socialization into child abuse: A social interactional perspective. In J. L. Tapp & P. J. Levine (Eds.), *Law, justice and the individual in society: Psychological and legal issues.* New York: Holt, 1977.

Parke, R. D. Children's home environments. In I. Altman & J. Wohlwill (Eds.), *Children and the environment.* New York: Plenum, 1978. (a)

Parke, R. D. Parent–infant interaction: Progress, paradigms and problems. In G. P. Sackett (Ed.), *Observing behavior* (Vol. 1): *Theory and applications in mental retardation.* Baltimore: University Park Press, 1978. (b)

Parke, R. D. Interactional designs. In R. B. Cairns (Ed.), *The analysis of social interactions: Methods, issues and illustrations.* Hillsdale, N. J.: Erlbaum, 1979. (a)

Parke, R. D. Perspectives on father–infant interaction. In J. Osofsky (Ed.), *Handbook of infant development*. New York, Wiley, 1979. (b)

Parke, R. D. *Fathers*. Cambridge, Mass.: Harvard University Press, 1981.

Parke, R. D. On prediction of child abuse: Theoretical considerations. In R. Starr (Ed.), *Prediction of abuse*. Philadelphia: Ballinger, 1982.

Parke, R. D., & Collmer, C. W. Child abuse: An interdisciplinary analysis. In E. M. Hetherington (Ed.), *Review of child development research* (Vol. 5). Chicago: University of Chicago Press, 1975.

Parke, R. D., Grossman, K., & Tinsley, B. R. Father–mother–infant interaction in the newborn period: A German–American comparison. In T. M. Field, A. M. Sosteck, P. Vietze, & P. H. Leiderman (Eds.), *Culture and early interactions*. Hillsdale, N. J.: Erlbaum, 1981.

Parke, R. D., Hymel, S., Power, T. G., & Tinsley, B. R. Fathers and risk: A hospital based model of intervention. In D. B. Sawin, R. C. Hawkins, L. O. Walker, & J. H. Penticuff (Eds.), *Psychosocial risks in infant–environment transactions*. New York: Bruner/Mazel, 1980.

Parke, R. D., & Lewis, N. G. The family in context: A multi-level interactional analysis of child abuse. In R. W. Henderson (Ed.), *Parent–child interaction: Theory, research and prospect*. New York: Academic Press, 1981.

Parke, R. D., & O'Leary, S. E. Father–mother–infant interaction in the newborn period: Some findings, some observations and some unresolved issues. In K. Riegel & J. Meacham (Eds.), *The developing individual in a changing world* (Vol. II): *Social and environmental issues*. The Hague: Mouton, 1976.

Parke, R. D., Power, T. G., & Gottman, J. M. Conceptualizing and quantifying influence patterns in the family triad. In M. E. Lamb, S. J. Suomi, & G. R. Stephenson (Eds.), *Social interaction analysis*. Madison, Wis.: Wisconsin University Press, 1979.

Parke, R. D., & Sawin, D. B. The father's role in infancy: A re-evaluation. *The Family Co-ordinator*, 1976, *25*, 365–371.

Parke, R. D., & Suomi, S. J. Adult male–infant relationships: Human and nonhuman primate evidence. In K. Immelmann, G. W. Barlow, L. Petrinovich, & M. Main (Eds.), *Behavioral development: The Bielefeld Interdisciplinary Project*. New York: Cambridge University Press, 1981.

Parke, R. D., & Tinsley, B. R. The early environment of the at-risk infant: Expanding the social context. In D. Bricker (Ed.), *Intervention with at risk and handicapped infants: From research to application*. Baltimore: University Park Press, 1982.

Parke, R. D., Tinsley, B. R., Power, T. G., & Hymel, S. *Parent–infant interaction: Assessment and modification*. Unpublished manuscript, University of Illinois, 1981.

Parke, R. D., Tinsley, B. R., & Volling, B. *The development of the preterm infant and social support utilization*. Unpublished manuscript, University of Illinois, 1982.

Pascoe, J. M., Loda, F. A., Jeffries, V., & Earp, J. A. The association between mothers' social support and provision of stimulation to their children. *Developmental and Behavioral Pediatrics*, 1981, *2*, 15–19.

Pastor, D. L. The quality of mother–infant attachment and its relationship to toddlers' initial sociability with peers. *Developmental Psychology*, 1981, *17*, 326–335.

Pedersen, F. A. *Mother, father, and infant as an interactive system*. Paper presented to the American Psychological Association, Chicago, 1975.

Powell, D. R. Family–environment relations and early child-rearing: The role of social networks and neighborhoods. *Journal of Research and Development in Education*, 1979, *13*, 1–11.

Redican, W. K. Adult male–infant interactions in non-human primates. In M. E. Lamb (Ed.), *The role of the father in child development*. New York: Wiley, 1976.

Richards, M. P. M. Effects on development of medical interventions and the separation of newborns from their parents. In D. Schaffer & J. Dunn (Eds.), *The first year of life*. New York: Wiley, 1979.

Rueveni, U. *Networking families in crisis.* New York: Human Services Press, 1979.

Ryder, R. G. Longitudinal data relating marriage satisfaction and having a child. *Journal of Marriage and the Family,* 1973, *35,* 604–606.

Sigman, M., Cohen, S. E., Beckwith, L., & Parmalee, A. H. Social and familial influences on the development of preterm infants. *Journal of Pediatric Psychology,* 1981, 6, 1–13.

Slade, C. I., Redl, O. J., & Manguten, H. H. Working with parents of high-risk newborns. *Journal of Obstetric and Gynecologic Nursing,* 1977, 6, 21–26.

Smith, C., Leiderman, P. H., Selz, L., MacPherson, L., & Bingham, E. *Maternal expectations and developmental milestones in physically handicapped infants.* Paper read at Biennial Meetings of the Society for Research in Child Development, Boston, 1981.

Tinsley, B. R., Johnson, P., Szczypka, D., & Parke, R. D. *Reconceptualizing the social environment of the high-risk infant: Fathers and settings.* Paper presented at the International Conference on Infant Studies, Austin, Texas, March 1982.

Whitt, J. K., & Casey, P. H. The mother–infant relationship and infant development: The effect of pediatric intervention. *Child Development,* 1982, *53,* 948–956.

Yogman, M. W. Development of the father–infant relationship. In H. Fitzgerald, B. Lester, & M. W. Yogman (Eds.), *Theory and research in behavioral pediatrics* (Vol. 1). New York: Plenum, 1982.

Zelazo, P. R., Kotelchuck, M., Barber, L., & David, J. *Fathers and sons: An experimental facilitation of attachment behaviors.* Paper presented at the meetings of the Society for Research in Child Development, New Orleans, March 1977.

6

Physical and Social Environment as Factors in Development

JOACHIM F. WOHLWILL

"Trying to get Johnny to change his mind is like hitting your head against a stone wall!" Nothing could better illustrate the differentiation between the physical and social environments that we carry within us in our heads than this common figure of speech. People, that is, are different from walls—or at least are expected to be different—unless they happen to be playing football. It strikes me that this difference may be a fundamental one for developmental psychology, and for a conceptualization of environmental influences on development in particular. Just what that difference may be is quite clearly implied in the figure of speech cited in the opening sentence; before making it fully explicit, however, I should like to backtrack and examine briefly how developmental psychologists have defined the environment in the past.

From the Social to the Physical Environment—and Back

An examination of more recent writings on environmental influences in development suggests a dual set of conclusions. The first is that the term "environment" was left largely undefined throughout much of the early history of child development, including the period during the 1920s and 1930s when the heredity–environment controversy was the subject of heated and prolonged debate. The second conclusion is that, implicitly at least, child psychologists have tended to limit themselves largely to the interpersonal and social environment in their work on environmental influences—the role of parents, peers, school, culture, and the like.

HUMAN DEVELOPMENT:
AN INTERACTIONAL PERSPECTIVE

The first point emerges inescapably from a reading of the literature on the heredity–environment controversy that raged in the 1920s and 1930s, in which the term "environment" is almost invariably left undefined, much less analyzed into specific components or processes (see Barker, Kounin, & Wright, 1943, for a selection of representative studies). Where attempts were made to construct scales to measure the child's environment, the component items were typically chosen in purely pragmatic fashion, rather than based on any predefined conception of the environment. A good example is provided by Van Alstyne's (1929) scale, in which demographic characteristics of the home, such as educational status of parents, appear cheek-by-jowl with items referring to specific parental behaviors (e.g., responding to child's questions) and material possessions are juxtaposed to items that concern opportunity for contact with siblings and peers.

It is significant that Wellman (1940), in her review of alternative conceptions of the environment and approaches to measuring it, considered Van Alstyne's scale an exception in that it went beyond the material aspects of the home environment to which most of the then-current inventories had been largely restricted. This bias in these early attempts to measure the home environment most probably reflected primarily the relative ease with which features of the child's physical environment can be measured, in comparison to qualities and characteristics of the interpersonal and social environment. Yet it was this latter side of the child's environmental experience that soon after the appearance of Wellman's paper came to assume paramount significance.

Of the theoretical models that came into being, probably the three most influential ones were the socialization theory of Sears and his associates (e.g., Sears, Whiting, Nowlis, & Sears, 1953), the Lewin-derived framework of Baldwin and his co-workers (Baldwin, Kalhorn, & Breese, 1945), and, coming somewhat later, the social learning theory of Bandura and associates (Bandura & Walters, 1963). Although they differ considerably in the mechanisms or processes postulated to mediate the relationship between the child's environment and the child's behavior, they have in common an exclusive focus on the interpersonal environment—notably that of the parents in the case of the first two theorists, along with that of the child's peers in the case of Bandura. This emphasis is hardly surprising, considering the almost self-evident significance, in a phenomenal sense, of the child's interpersonal and social experience. It was virtually forced upon these theorists, furthermore, by the theoretical models espoused by them, in which parents and peers figured, respectively, as dispensers of reward and punishment (Sears), as sources of the social climate characterizing the home (Baldwin), and as the models whose behavior the child would most readily be in a position to imitate (Bandura).

While each of these theories continues, to varying degrees, to have its adherents and even to inspire research, several trends in the more recent history of the field have served to enlarge the view of children's environmental experience held by many of the major contemporary developmental psychologists concerned with experiential issues today, such as Hunt and his disciples, M. Lewis, Yarrow, and others. I should like to call attention to two such trends in particular.

First, notably through the writings of Hunt (1961, 1979) and some of his associates, the role of the environment as a source of sensory stimulation has come to be recognized and given its due in child psychology. To Hunt in particular, along with Thompson and Grusec's (1970) chapter in the *Manual of child psychology,* we owe a familiarization of child psychologists with the seminal work of Hebb and his associates at McGill on the role of early sensory experience in the individual's development, with respect to both the potentially beneficial effects of an "enriched" stimulus environment and the damaging impact of environmental conditions marked by sensory deprivation. While the Hebbian work originated exclusively in the animal laboratory, it was soon applied, somewhat indiscriminately in some cases, to accounts of the effects of institutionalization (e.g., Casler, 1961).

According to Hebb (1949), a steady input of patterned and varied stimulus input from the physical environment surrounding the organism is essential for normal development to take place, not only in the perceptual sphere, but in the realms of problem solving, maintenance of motivation, and adaptive behavior generally. His is essentially a passive-exposure conception of the role of such experience; he emphasized that it is perceptual experience per se (and predominantly visual experience) that matters, independently of any motor response by the organism, though the empirical evidence in support of that conception was conflicting at best (see Hunt, 1961, and Thompson & Grusec, 1970, for reviews).

Of greater moment with respect to the relevance of Hebb's ideas for the developmental psychologist is the implicit monotonic conception of the role of stimulation: the more, the better. While this conception *may* be applicable to the conditions of life in an institution marked by a drastic lack of sensory variation, it makes no allowance for the possibility that there may be too much, as well as too little, stimulation in a child's environment. Yet those who were dealing with children from so-called "culturally deprived" environments, such as Deutsch (1964), soon came to the realization that such children appeared to be suffering rather from a surfeit than a lack of sensory stimuli. And the work of Wachs (Wachs, 1979; Wachs, Uzgiris, & Hunt, 1971), along with related evidence (Heft, 1979), brought into the focus the issue of the possible impact of too high amounts and levels of stimulation on a child, and of background stimulation—notably in the form of noise—in particular. In the aggregate, this body of research contradicts the position that has been taken by some (e.g., Provence & Lipton, 1962) that the physical environment cannot have an effect on the child except as its role is mediated by the social environment.

Let me turn to the second of the trends that have modified our conception of the relationship between the environment and development. As noted earlier, the environment was viewed very predominantly in social terms, but even within that limitation some important shifts have taken place in our understanding of the role of social experience in the development of the child. What has changed in particular is the unidirectional conception of that role, embodied particularly in the socialization model of Sears *et al.* that was the dominant influence in the field two or three decades ago.[1] That model looked upon the role of parents, teachers, and significant others as the dispensers of the rewards and punishments or, in the modified view of Gewirtz (1969), as the sources of differential and discriminatory response learning. Little attention was paid to the reciprocal character of the parent–child bond or to the potential role of feedback from the child to the parent in modulating the latter's behavior.

Partly under the impetus of searching criticisms by Bell (1968) and others, this one-way conception has more recently given way to more positive, systematic attempts to examine the reciprocal relations between children and their caregivers (Bell & Harper, 1977; Lerner & Spanier, 1978; Lewis & Rosenblum, 1974). These, in turn, have spawned some important methodological breakthroughs in the analysis of dyadic relationships between parent and child (Bakeman & Brown, 1977; Martin, Maccoby, Baran, & Jacklin, 1981), focusing attention on sequences of contingent interactions between mother and child, and resulting in a very significant shift in our conception of child behavior. In short, the essentially reactive view of child behavior as dependent on and consequent to particular conditions of the social environment that characterized the child socialization and social reinforcement models is giving way to an explicit consideration of a child's behavior in interaction with that environment.

Physical and Social Environment Compared

It strikes me as more than a coincidence that this changeover to an interactive conception of the child's relationship to its social environment has been accompanied by a rediscovery, as it were, of the role of the physical environment in development, notably in the work of Yarrow and his colleagues (Yarrow, Rubenstein, & Pedersen, 1975) and in that of Wachs referred to previously. Yarrow, in particular, has called attention to the different patterns of relationships holding between the physical-environmental as opposed to the social-environmental variables and the behavioral measures they have studied. While neither these investigators nor others that have concerned themselves with the role of both of these sets of variables (e.g., Parke, 1978) have attempted to analyze the nature of the difference between them, one that sug-

---

[1]It is curious that Sears, who in the 1953 monograph dismissed the plausibility of a cause–effect reversal in the relationship between childrearing and child–personality measures, himself had earlier (Sears, 1951) recognized the importance of reciprocity as a principle in the analysis of social and behavioral systems.

gests itself as important is precisely the responsive character of the social environment, as contrasted to the nonresponsive one of the physical realm, to which the opening quote of the paper was meant to call attention. People emit contingent responses to children, that is, responses that themselves depend at least partially on the child's own behavior. In so doing, they place a premium on the child's recognition of and sensitivity to such feedback—a feature whose bearing on social and language development, and quite possibly on certain types of cognitive processes such as those involved in a game of checkers, is apparent. The physical environment, in contrast, generally functions in a nonresponsive manner, that is, providing an influx of stimulation, and of specific stimuli, independent of the child's response to them. This situation is particularly well illustrated by reference to the realm of noise and its impact on the individual or, in a more positive sense, the effect of a brightly colored, diversified visual background, for example, in a nursery.

We are dealing here with a basic difference, it seems, in the mode of the operation of experiential effects on development. On the one hand, the physical environment, particularly that which impinges on the individual as ambient stimulation (as opposed to the specific objects contained in it), may exert a direct influence on the perceptual, cognitive, and even motivational development of the individual by providing a substrate of stimulation required for normal behavioral development and functioning that is independent of the individual's own behavior. This is clearly of special relevance during infancy, when the individual is still to some extent a passive recipient of such stimulation, with relatively little opportunity to seek it out, to control it, or to change it.[2] Thus, it is not surprising that the most persuasive evidence for physical-environmental effects has come in infant research, notably that of Yarrow *et al.* (1975) and of Wachs *et al.* (1971) as mentioned earlier. At the same time, the work of Wachs in particular has called attention to the necessity to conceptualize these effects in terms of a presumed optimal level of stimulation, in place of the rather simplistic conception implicit in the Hebbian view, which equates the value of a given environment for the developing organism with the amount and degree of "enrichment" of stimulation that it affords to the organism. But as Wachs (1977) subsequently argued most cogently, the "optimal level" concept itself may not be adequate, unless it is treated in terms of an interaction between a given stimulus environment and the organism at a given point in its development. That is, what is "optimal" is a function, not only of the stimulation confronting the individual (in terms of amount, intensity, diversity, complexity, etc.), but also of the point of development already attained, which needs to be ascertained for each individual separately if we are to determine what is optimal.

[2]Here and elsewhere in this chapter, where the nature of the infant as a passive recipient of stimulation is stressed, it is important to interpret such statements in a relative sense. Clearly infants from a very early age on can and do engage in behavior that has the effect of changing level of ambient stimulation—through head-turning, eye-opening and closing, and the like.

There are at least two further, important qualifications to be placed on the rather simplified view of the physical environment that is being presented here. First, although it is true that the immature organism is to a degree a captive audience, so to speak, of the environmental stimulation impinging on it, this picture ceases to be adequate as soon as the organism becomes sufficiently mobile to seek out or avoid particular environments, or even to alter them through its own behavior. This point is illustrated in the widespread and diverse manifestations of exploratory activity found in most organisms, which represents a search for stimulation from particular objects and has the effect of altering the internal state of the individual as well as providing it with information about its environment. At the same time, the organism is equally able to avoid, or escape from, overly intense or unpleasant stimuli, whether by retreating into an underground burrow, in the manner of a mole, or into a room or space offering shelter from excessive levels of stimulation, as Wachs' (1979) findings suggest may be important for human infants.

The second point relates to the assumption that the physical environment is nonresponsive. While that does seem to be a general characteristic of the physical environment, it is by no means invariably so. There are certain objects, forming part of the inanimate world, that do respond to the individual's behavior, creating feedback loops of varying degrees of elaboration, and approaching the "give-and-take" character of social interaction. Such feedback-giving objects vary all the way from an infant's rattle producing sounds upon being shaken to the highly sophisticated computerized videogames that are becoming increasingly a part of a child's experience in our society. A device similar in principle was the "responsive environment" in the form of especially adapted typewriters constructed by O.K. Moore (see Moore & Anderson, 1968).

Evidence is accumulating, both from the investigations by Wachs and by Yarrow *et al.* already cited and from a number of other studies more specifically directed at this question, pointing to the important role that toys containing such a feedback property play in early cognitive development (see Parke, 1978, for a brief review of this work). It thus becomes particularly pertinent to extend our view of the physical environment to include such objects, or perhaps rather to differentiate between responsive and nonresponsive aspects of the physical environment. To that extent, the distinction between social and physical environments becomes blunted. The difference between them may be more a matter of degree than of kind; that is, feedback relations with the social environment exceed in their elaborateness and temporal extent those characterizing a child's interaction with inanimate sources of feedback.[3]

[3]The role of pets as part of children's environments, though little studied, is of interest in this regard: They clearly provide considerable feedback to the child's own responses to the pet, but in comparison to the feedback characterizing its interaction with other human beings, the feedback cycles involved are generally more rudimentary, and of shorter duration. Nevertheless, the mode of interaction of a child with a pet, at different ages, might well repay serious study, when seen from this perspective.

Conversely, it must be recognized that the social environment does not always operate in an interactive fashion; that is, feedback is often as absent from it as it is from nonreactive aspects of the physical environment. Assuredly, as long as we are concerned with a child's relations with members of its family and other individuals, such a situation is only approximated at best (or rather worst), for example, in the case of particularly uncaring or unresponsive parents. (The severity of that kind of experience is convincingly brought out by its use as an extreme form of punishment by the Amish, in their practice of "shunning." But even the Amish do not generally apply that practice to children.)

But the social environment does function in a nonresponsive manner quite frequently when considered in the aggregate, in situations in which the individual is not expected to relate to others as an individual. People at a theater, in a bus, or in a department store represent cases in point. More generally, the effects of crowding—currently a favorite topic for environmental psychologists—represent instances of this kind of impact of the aggregate social environment. It is thus particularly significant that crowding, or congestion, in the home appears to show effects similar to those of noise and of activity level in the environment, that is, acting as an aspect of ambient stimulation impinging on a child, as indicated in Wachs' (1979) findings.

The preceding analysis suggests the possibility of reformulating the distinction between the physical and social environments in somewhat different, and perhaps more useful, terms.

Developmentally Relevant Forms of the Environment–Behavior Relationship

Let us consider four different forms that the relationship between environmental forces, whether emanating from the physical or the social environment, and the child's behavioral development may take. Table 1 provides an overview of these forms, with examples of each.

A word of explanation may be helpful with reference to the term *environmental mode* as used in this table. As the title of the table indicates, the term refers not to dimensions of the environment per se, but rather to environmental characteristics that are directly implicated in the individual's behavior. This point is most obvious in the case of the first mode, since feedback is by definition a relational construct. As we will see presently, the same point applies to the concept of affordances, and to the focal-background differentiation as well, since what is focal can only be defined relative to an attending organism.

There is, admittedly, a knotty epistemological issue that arises in this regard, that is, whether, in view of the relational status of these modes, they retain any status as independently definable environmental characteristics. This has become a particular bone of contention in regard to the concept of *affordances,*

Table 1

Examples of the Environment–Behavior Relationship for Different Environmental Modes

	Examples taken from the	
Environmental mode	Physical environment	Social environment
Responsive–interactive	Infant pushing mobile Young child playing with toy typewriter Videogame play	Child interacting with parents, siblings, peers
Affordant (re objects)	Child playing with modeling clay	Infant resting on mother's arm Child sitting on father's lap
Ambient—focal	Infant fixating on mobile (out of reach) Child watching television	Teacher addressing child in directive, noninteractive mode
Ambient—background	Wall decorations providing backdrop for child's play in nursery	Sound and sight of people as backdrop for infant's waking activities in crib Crowds of children and adults around child playing on playground

so it should be helpful to discuss it in that context, however briefly, so as to allow us at the same time to become more familiar with this concept, which thus far has not had much currency in developmental psychology.

The concept of "affordances" was invented by James Gibson (1979) to deal with certain aspects of perception that concern the fit between some stimulus property or feature and the behavior associated with it. For instance, an elongated object with a sharp edge is considered to "afford" cutting; a flat rigid surface "affords" (i.e., provides support for) walking or crawling.

Gibson proposed the affordance concept, it seems, as a response to criticisms of his previous accounts of visual perception as constituting mere descriptions of the stimulus, or of the information contained in stimuli, without concern for either the mechanisms involved on the part of the organism in processing that information or the behavior consequent to the perception. This was, in effect, Gibson's attempt to come to grips with the problem of meaning in perception. Yet, characteristically, he succeeded in having his cake and eating it, refusing to abandon his stimulus-based view of perception, but arguing for the existence of certain properties belonging to the stimulus that were intrinsically tied up with specific forms of potential behaviors. Thus, he considered affordances, in contrast to such concepts as Lewin's valences or "Aufforderungscharakter," (see Marrow, 1969) to remain independent of the observer's needs or internal states (pp. 138f.).[4]

---

[4]The epistemological issues involved in Gibson's ecological theory of perception, and his use of the affordance concept in particular, are brought out in a mini-debate between Heil (1979) and Heft (1980).

For our purposes, the relevance of the concept is twofold. First, like feedback, it represents a construct that concerns relationships between particular stimulus features and behavior (see Heft, in press), which assumes a behaving organism in interaction with a stimulus, yet permits the relevant stimulus properties to be specified independently of that behavior. In contrast to feedback, however, affordances represent altogether static characteristics, eliciting, but not responding to, behavior, and for that reason represent a different level in our scheme outlined in Table 1.

The second point to note concerning affordances is that they transcend the physical–social differentiation, again resembling the responsivity characteristic in that respect. While Gibson discussed affordances primarily in regard to physical objects, he himself recognized the important role of the social environment as a provider of affordances, considering other people (along with animals) to represent the sources of the "richest and most elaborate affordances of the environment [p. 135]." Unfortunately, he did not follow through on his analysis of the social environment in any detail; in fact, he appears to have considered the principal characteristic afforded by other people as being that of reciprocity and feedback. However reasonable that view of the social environment may appear, it still seems curious that Gibson failed to recognize the important role of the human being as affording certain experienced attributes to a small infant or child purely as physical object: breasts as afforders of sucking; arms as afforders of physical support; arms, heads, and trunks as afforders of tactual comfort—as Harlow's work demonstrates so convincingly—and so forth.

A developmental extension of the application of this concept suggests itself, in fact, which would take the form of an account of perceptual development directed at the pickup of behaviorally relevant features of the child's environment (see E. J. Gibson, 1982). That is, the child presumably learns that certain kinds of stimulus variables or object characteristics afford physical support (i.e., against the forces of gravity), kinesthetic comfort, or, conversely, danger, impenetrance, and so forth. Similarly, through the child's own actions, particular features are learned as affording particular activities, such as cutting, swimming, holding, climbing, and so on. This kind of learning is apt to be important not only for the development of a child's sensitivity to the qualities and attributes of the environment, but for his or her achievement of a sense of mastery and competence. Indeed, much of exploratory activity—such as that of an infant putting objects into its mouth or throwing them out of the crib—might well be interpreted as directed toward the learning of affordances. Seen from this standpoint, it may prove possible to characterize different environments as both qualitatively and quantitatively different in regard to the opportunity provided for this kind of learning, and thus arrive at insights concerning environmental correlates of the development of competence in White's (1959) sense.

Turning now more briefly to the other two varieties of noninteractive environmental forces, that is, forms of ambient stimulation, perhaps the main point to be noted is that they are more pertinent to the physical than the social environment, although, as the examples in Table 1 show, they are not limited to the former. As was noted earlier, crowding in particular may operate in a manner similar to that of physical stimulation effects, creating changes in arousal level by dint of sheer quantity and intensity.

There is undoubtedly an ecological correlation then between the physical–social distinction and the different environmental modes presented in Table 1, in the sense that it is most characteristic of the social environment to function in an interactive mode, and conversely of the physical one to operate in an ambient mode. Yet, probably the differences among the modes should be given primary stress, since on them depends the manner in which environmental influences of either kind impact on the child. Developmentally, moreover, there appear to be important shifts with age in the relative importance of these various types of environmental forces.

Developmental Changes in the Role of Environmental Modes

Three major principles of developmental change are of particular relevance for the present analysis. They are, respectively, the increasing role of the child in exploring and self-selecting its environment; the increasing ability to attend selectively to particular stimuli, that is, to separate focal from background, or information from noise; and the increasing role of verbal communication and symbolic functioning.

INCREASING ENVIRONMENTAL EXPLORATION AND SELF-SELECTION

This principle amounts to the recognition that the developing child changes from a state of predominantly passive exposure to environmental stimulation in very early infancy to an individual who progressively exerts increasing control over his or her environment, through both self-selection and actual alteration of that environment. It hardly seems necessary to provide extensive documentation for this change, though its full extent and its implication for conceptions of child behavior, particularly beyond early childhood, have not perhaps been given the attention due them. One major reason for this relative neglect is that this particular developmental dimension requires an ecological stance conceptually, and an observational approach methodologically, if the manner in which children seek out, select, and even alter environments—both physical and social—through their spontaneous activity is to be effectively revealed. Rheingold and Eckerman's (1969) research on free environmental exploration and the less well known work on children's home range (Moore & Young, 1978; see also Schoggen & Schoggen, in press) provide good examples of research relevant to this problem.

This principle, in combination with the second one, implies that focal stimuli assume a progressively more important role with age, relative to background stimuli, since the individual increasingly determines what stimuli will be focal at any given time. Indeed, the distinction between focal and background itself is a function of the individual and his or her behavior in seeking out or selecting stimuli.

INCREASING ABILITY TO ATTEND SELECTIVELY

As just noted, this principle operates in the same direction as the preceding one to ensure an increasing impact of focal in comparison to background stimuli. In fact, the self-selection principle only serves to reinforce the selective attention one, which operates even where stimuli are not self-selected, for example, in the classroom. Again it does not require much verification qua general principle, having been amply documented in the literature (E. J. Gibson, 1969; Pick, Frankel, & Hess, 1975).

What does this principle imply, however, for the role and importance of the two environmental modes most directly concerned, that is, focal and background stimuli, during the course of development? Perhaps the most satisfactory answer to this question is to suggest a three-phase process, corresponding roughly to the periods of early infancy (i.e., up to about 8 or 9 months), later infancy and early childhood, and later childhood. During early infancy, there is a *relative* lack of differentiation between focal and background stimuli, in part because the young infant remains limited in the selectivity of its attention to environmental stimuli. It is at this time that ambient environmental stimulation conforming to the optimal-level principle as regards both intensity and diversity is presumably of greatest relevance, as Wachs *et al.* (1971) have shown. This applies both to general background stimuli and to those stimuli that, because of their placement and significance for the infant, regularly become focal for it—whether in the form of a mobile, a television set placed in close proximity, or the face of the mother. At the same time, clear perceptual segregation of focal from background stimuli should be of value to the infant in facilitating its tracking of focal stimuli and in maintaining orientation to them, and thus in providing an effective base for subsequent perceptual development.

As noted earlier, during later infancy and early childhood it becomes progressively more difficult to treat focal and background stimuli as aspects of the environment definable independently of the individual. During this second phase the child's own activity in selecting and exploring stimuli increasingly determines what is focal at any given time. But during this phase, the child remains subject to interference from background stimulation. This interference becomes greatly attenuated during the third phase, though there is no very sharp break between that phase and the preceding one. Rather, the evidence suggests that in the visual, as well as the tactual, domain (see Gollin, 1960;

Turnure, 1970) where the individual has particular responses available to ward off distracting stimuli (e.g., avoiding off-target glances), background stimuli lose their influence on task performance more rapidly than is the case for distracting auditory stimuli. But a recent study by Turnure (1981) suggests that by the age of about 12 years children's performance on discrimination and oddity learning tasks ceases to be impaired by auditory distractors (music, in the case of this study), and may even be facilitated by it.

The preceding analysis is consonant with a provocative account of early attentional development by Collins and Hagen (1979). These authors consider the infant up to the age of approximately 8 months to be operating at a preconscious level of perception characterized by a narrow, stimulus-bound mode of focusing on whatever aspects of the environment happen to be salient. They postulate a major qualitative shift taking place at about 8 months toward a more self-directed and controlled mode of attending to stimuli, which results from the integration of efferent motor processes into the perceptual system— which these authors identify with the origins of consciousness. A second transition occurs subsequently, and more gradually, involving a shift from a broadly distributed, and thus relatively unfocused, form of perception to a focal processing of information—implying of course a differentiation of functionally relevant from irrelevant stimuli. The authors cite a variety of evidence in support of their view; its correspondence to the one we have suggested above should be apparent, though theirs is concerned more with internal processes underoing development under normal environmental conditions than with the contributions of particular facets of experience to this development. Collins and Hagen's account may be directly relevant, furthermore, to the analysis of the learning of affordances, as discussed above, given that these are by definition dependent on the individual's actions with respect to particular objects and activities in particular environmental contexts. A most promising opportunity presents itself here for infusing a developmental-process view into an effective, theoretically grounded approach to the study of the role of experience in development.

INCREASING VERBALIZATION AND SYMBOLIC FUNCTIONING

The increasing role of language and symbols in the child's behavior over the course of its development hardly needs documenting. But it is of direct relevance for us insofar as it points to the increasing importance of environmental stimuli in the interactive mode—and therefore of the social environment, which, as already pointed out, represents by far the most significant source of environmental stimulation of this type. Admittedly, interpersonal communication antedates language, as various analyses of mother–infant interactions have shown (e.g., Bakeman & Brown, 1977; Jaffe, Stern, & Perry, 1973). But it is apparent that the advent of language, both passive and active, vastly increases the scope of such interactive forms of environmental stimuli, whether in the form of simple contingent chains between maternal and child behavior that may be verbally mediated (e.g., Moerk, 1975) or through ongoing conversation between a child and other individuals, both adults and peers. Thus, effects of institutionalization are plausibly attributable to a considerable extent to the reduced level and amount of such interactive stimulus experience, compared to that which we can take for granted for a normal home-raised child. Attempts by preschool intervention programs to work with the children's mothers to increase the extent of their verbal interaction with their children point in the same direction (e.g., Heber, 1978; Levenstein, 1970).

Evidence Concerning the Environment–Development Interaction

The preceding theoretical analysis of the differential operation of the various environmental modes over the course of development leads to the expectation of strong interactions between age level and the efficacy of particular environmental variables subsumable under one or another of these modes. The evidence relating to such interactions remains fairly limited, largely because few researchers have investigated the role of diverse environmental dimensions across different age levels. The work of Wachs and his colleagues, referred to repeatedly throughout this paper, represents the most notable exception to this statement; both his original cross-sectional study (Wachs *et al.*, 1971) and his subsequent longitudinal one (Wachs, 1979) provide an opportunity to look for differential relationships between specific environmental variables and behavior at different age levels. Since Wachs's work is based on field methodology (i.e., variation with respect to environmental variables is measured as it is observed across the different homes of the infants in his sample, rather than being either experimentally built in or achieved via selection of contrasting groups), the evidence consists of differential magnitudes of correlations, rather than of analysis-of-variance-based interaction terms. But it is nonetheless relevant to our question.

At the outset we may point to Wachs's "specificity" principle, enunciated in his interpretation of his findings from the longitudinal study. Wachs considers several kinds of specificity, but the one that bears most directly on our question is the tendency for the efficacy of particular items of the scale he employed (the PHSI, Purdue Home Stimulation Inventory) to be limited to particular age levels. Such an age-specific pattern actually is less clearly in evidence in the results of Wachs's longitudinal study—which appear rather to reveal an overall increase in significant correlations between the ages 15 and 24 months—than in those from his earlier cross-sectional study (Wachs *et al.* 1971). This investigation not only covers a wider age span, from 7 to 22 months, but includes a much larger set of items. While this study likewise shows a considerable rise in significant correlations with age, from 33 at 7 months to 66 at 18, dropping subsequently to 53 at 22 months, there are at the same time interesting patterns in the kinds of environmental variables that show significant correlations with some of the Piagetian scales at the various age levels. Thus, of the five items showing a significant relationship to one or another dimension of sensorimotor development at age 7 months exclusively, three referred specifically to the decor in the home: degree of patterning of the decor, amount of variation in color, and presence of at least one painting or decoration on the wall—though the correlation for the latter, curiously enough, was *negative*. A more plausible negative correlation was found for a fourth item, amount of noise in the neighborhood, while the fifth item referred to opportunity for self-feeding with a spoon.

It seems particularly interesting that the background noise item showed up significantly only at 7 months, whereas the ambient noise level in the home was (again negatively) correlated with various behavioral dimensions at ages 7, 18, and 22 months, and the inability to escape noise in the home showed up significantly at all ages except one (18 months). The first variable represents an aspect of general ambient stimulation, at an age at which differentiation between focal and background stimuli remains rudimentary. Older children may well have been able to ward off the effects of such outside noise through differential focusing of attention, as well as self-selection of their environment. These strategies would be expected to be less effective in the case of noise emanating from within the home itself, thus accounting for the maintenance of the correlations at the older age level in the case of the latter two items.[5]

Among items, on the other hand, that come into their own only at the older age levels (specifically, from 15 months on), there are two that clearly reveal the increasingly interactive nature of the child's experience, particularly in the form of mother–infant interactions: the mother's spontaneous vocalization to the child and spontaneous naming of objects for the child. Consistent with this finding is that, in the later study, the presence of feedback-giving toys correlates significantly ($p < .01$) with various behavioral variables from the age of 18 months on.

Admittedly, the items cited represent particular cases that happen to fit the thesis of an interaction between age and environmental effects. One reason for condoning such a procedure is that only a relatively small proportion of the items used by Wachs *et al.* (1971) are of clear-cut significance for our purposes, that is, in relating specifically to any of the modes of environmental-behavior reactions considered earlier. In fact, a number of those utilized in the

---

[5]Wachs (1982, personal communication) has suggested that a major reason for the potentially nefarious impact of background noise may be their affordance-less character: There is no action the individual can generally take on such noise to create a discernible effect. It is thus impossible for the child to achieve a sense of control over this kind of stimulation. (A New Year's Eve noisemaker represents, of course, a very different case, that is, an *object* that affords the creation of a particular sound.)

cross-sectional study (e.g., "home has a washing machine"; "child has had picture taken commercially at least once") presumably operate in a highly indirect manner, much as socioeconomic status does.

Conclusion

This chapter began with the premise that physical and social aspects of the environment represent very different and contrasting influences on a developing child, each acting in its own way and assuming different forms over the course of development. Subsequently, we saw that this differentiation could be profitably enlarged and subsumed under a more comprehensive categorization of different modes of operation of the environment in its relationship to the development of behavior. A classificatory scheme differentiating among ambient, affordant, and interactive modes of environmental stimulation was proposed for this purpose.

That discussion, which represents an extension and reformulation of an earlier analysis by this writer (Wohlwill, 1973), should bring out the point that experience has both a quantitative and a qualitative aspect. This point is of special relevance for attempts to construct viable measures of environmental stimulation or of situational contexts for development. The need for such scales has been recognized for some time, for instance, with reference to the interpretation of data on behavioral stability across development (Wohlwill, 1980) and more generally to study the extent to which behavior is susceptible to change as a function of environmental conditions (see Bloom, 1964). But only comparatively recently have investigators come to grips with the fact that environments do not function as unitary, monolithic entities, but comprise separable components and types of influences. The outcome of Yarrow *et al.*'s (1975) work, as well as the work conducted with the Home Observation for Measurement of the Environment (HOME) scale developed by Caldwell and her colleagues (Caldwell, Heider, & Kaplan, 1966; see Elardo & Bradley, 1981), has contributed significantly to this recognition. The factor analysis of the items of the PHSI reported by Wachs, Francis, and McQuiston (1979), which uncovered no less than 13 separable factors (of which 10 relate specifically to the physical environment), has provided information relevant to the same point.

However valuable these pioneering efforts to assess and measure the quality as well as quantity of environmental stimulation are, they are subject to at least one major limitation. There is something misleadingly simplistic, and inappropriately unidirectional in regard to causation, in the standard procedure of correlating particular items of a home-environment inventory with a set of behavioral variables. Take, for instance, two of the items used by Wachs, as part of his PHSI scale: "Home has place where child can be away from people and noise"(The "stimulus–shelter" item) and "Number of toys that make an audio-visual response when activated." These two items were among the most important in terms of showing significant correlations with various of the Piagetian sensorimotor development scales. Yet they strike one as somehow inappropriately worded, in that they fail to get at the child's activity that is necessary for each to exert an effect: the child's actual use of the room to escape from people and noise in the first case, and the child's play with the feedback-giving toys in the second. In these environmental modes, as noted above, we are dealing with environmental forces whose impact is mediated by the child's own activity, and it seems necessary to insert this activity into the environment-development equation, even at the risk of changing a "pure" S–R relationship into a more problematic form, such as $[(S \rightarrow) R]-R$, or $[(S \rightarrow) R \rightarrow S]-R$. This represents a clear challenge, as much at a conceptual level as at a measurement level. But it is one that we as developmental psychologists can hardly avoid facing up to.

Finally, in case life hasn't been made complex enough for us, it is incumbent upon us to confront the developmental dynamics of the picture in tracing the effects of experience. Specifically, we must bear in mind the cumulative and frequently mutually reinforcing action of successive environmental forces or events. Thus, suppose we were to find that exposure to and experience with feedback-producing toys in the nursery are conducive to creative thinking in preadolescence. In such a case, there is a temptation to link the early experience with the later behavioral variable in terms of a direct functional relationship. What often is too readily ignored is that a sustained experience at one age will have an impact on the child at the time of the experience, which may alter the course of its development from then on into the future, for a variety of reasons. These include (a) the impact of the original experience on the child's sense of competence with respect to the behaviors, prompting the child to seek out more such experiences in the future; (b) the likely increase in further opportunities for such experiences, as the parents, teachers, and others, recognize the child's adeptness with a particular set of materials or pursuits; (c) the possible acquisition of new skills, concepts, interests, and so on, on the part of the child that develop out of its original activity. All of these factors in combination suggest a strongly cumulative model of experience, rich in positive feedback, which operates presumably in both a positive and a negative sense, that is, to enhance development as a function of original favorable conditions as well as to retard it as a function of originally depriving conditions. The possible role of such a cumulative model in explaining some of the data on the stability of the I.Q. was pointed out in an earlier article by this writer (Wohlwill, 1980). It appears equally relevant in the present context reminding us that, when dealing with a developing organism, experience never operates at an isolated point in time, but needs to be conceived of as influencing the course of subsequent development, taken as a whole.

Acknowledgments

The author is indebted to Jay Belsky, Richard Lerner, and Theodore Wachs for valuable criticisms and suggestions based on an earlier draft of this chapter, as well as to Ross Parke for his trenchant discussion of the paper as presented at the Conference.

References

Bakeman, R., & Brown, J. Behavioral dialogues: An approach to the assessment of mother–infant interaction. *Child Development,* 1977, *48,* 195–203.

Baldwin, A. L., Kalhorn, J., & Breese, F. H. Patterns of parent behavior. *Psychological Monographs,* 1945, *58*(5, Whole No. 268).

Bandura, A., & Walters, R. H. *Social learning and personality development.* New York: Holt, 1963.

Barker, R., Kounin, J. S., & Wright, H. F. (eds.), *Child behavior and development: A course of representative studies.* New York: McGraw-Hill, 1943.

Bell, R. Q. A reinterpretation of the direction of effects in studies of socialization. *Psychological Review,* 1968, *75,* 81–95.

Bell, R. Q., & Harper, L. V. *The effect of children on parents.* Hillsdale, N. J.: Erlbaum, 1977.

Bloom, B. S. *Stability and change in human characteristics.* New York: Wiley, 1964.

Caldwell, B., Heider, J., & Kaplan, B. *Home observation for measurement of the environment.* Paper presented at meetings of American Psychological Association, New York, 1966.

Casler, L. Maternal deprivation: A critical review of the literature. *Monographs of the Society for Research in Child Development,* 1961, *26* (2, Whole No. 80).

Collins, J. W., & Hagen, J. W. A constructivist account of the development of perception, attention, and memory. In G. A. Hale & M. Lewis (Eds.), *Attention and cognitive development.* New York: Plenum, 1979. Pp. 65–96.

Deutsch, C. Auditory discrimination and learning: Social factors. *Merrill-Palmer Quarterly,* 1964, *10,* 277–296.

Elardo, R., & Bradley, R. H. The home observation for measurement of the environment (HOME) scale: A review of research. *Developmental Review,* 1981, *1,* 113–145.

Gewirtz, J. L. Mechanisms of social learning: Some roles of stimulation and behavior in early human development. In D. A. Goslin (Ed.), *Handbook of socialization theory and research.* Chicago: Rand-McNally, 1969. Pp. 57–212.

Gibson, E. J. *Principles of perceptual learning and development.* New York: Appleton, 1969.

Gibson, E. J. The concept of affordances in development: The renascence of functionalism. In W. A. Collins (Ed.), *Minnesota Symposium on Child Psychology* (Vol. 15): *The concept of development.* Hillsdale, N. J.: Erlbaum, 1982, pp. 55–81.

Gibson, J. J. *The ecological approach to visual perception.* Boston: Houghton Mifflin, 1979.

Gollin, E. S. Tactual form discrimination: A developmental comparison under conditions of spatial interference. *Journal of Experimental Psychology,* 1960, *60,* 126–129.

Hebb, D. O. *The organization of behavior,* New York: Wiley, 1949.

Heber, R. Research in prevention of socio-cultural mental retardation. In D. G. Forgays (Ed.), *Primary prevention of psychopathology* (Vol. 2): *Environment influences.* Hanover, N. H.: University Press of New England, 1978. Pp. 39–62.

Heft, H. Background and focal environmental conditions of the home and attention in young children. *Journal of Applied Social Psychology,* 1979, *9,* 47–69.

Heft, H. What Heil is missing in Gibson: A reply. *Journal for the Theory of Social Behavior,* 1980, *10,* 187–194.

Heft, H. High residential density and perceptual–cognitive development: An examination of the effects of crowding and noise in the home. In J. F. Wohlwill & W. VanVliet (Eds.), *Habitats for children: The impacts of density*. Hillsdale, N. J.: Erlbaum, in press.

Heil, J. What Gibson's missing. *Journal for the Theory of Social Behavior*, 1979, 9, 265–269.

Hunt, J. McV. *Intelligence and experience*. New York: Ronald, 1961.

Hunt, J. McV. Psychological development: Early experience. *Annual Review of Psychology*, 1979, 30, 103–144.

Jaffe, J., Stern, D. N., & Perry, J. C. "Conversational" coupling of gaze behavior in prelinguistic human development. *Journal of Psycholinguistic Research*, 1973, 2, 321–329.

Lerner, R. M., & Spanier, G. B. (Eds.) *Child influences on marital and family interaction: A life-span perspective*. New York: Academic Press, 1978.

Levenstein, P. Cognitive growth in preschoolers through verbal interaction with their mothers. *American Journal of Orthopsychiatry*, 1970, 40, 426–432.

Lewis, M., & Rosenblum, L. A. (Eds.) *The effect of the infant on its caregiver*. New York: Wiley, 1974.

Marrow, A. J. *The practical theorist: The life and work of Kurt Lewin*. New York: Basic Books, 1969.

Martin, J. A., Maccoby, E. E., Baran, K. W., & Jacklin, C. N. Sequential analysis of mother–child interaction at 18 months: A comparison of microanalytic methods. *Developmental Psychology*, 1981, 17, 146–157.

Moerk, E. L. Verbal interactions between children and their mothers during the preschool years. *Developmental Psychology*, 1975, 11, 788–794.

Moore, O. K., & Anderson, A. R. The responsive environments project. In R. D. Hess & R. M. Bear (Eds.), *Early education: Current theory, research, and action*. Chicago: Aldine, 1968. Pp. 171–190.

Moore, R., & Young, D. Childhood outdoors: Towards a social ecology of the landscape. In I. Altman & J. F. Wohlwill (Eds.), *Children and the environment (Human behavior and environment*, Vol. 3). New York: Plenum, 1978. Pp. 83–130.

Parke, R. D. Children's home environments: Social and cognitive effects. In I. Altman & J. F. Wohlwill (Eds.), *Children and the environment (Human behavior and environment*, Vol. 3). New York: Plenum, 1978. Pp. 33–82.

Pick, A. D., Frankel, D. G., & Hess, V. L. Children's attention: The development of selectivity. In E. M. Hetherington (Ed.), *Review of child development research* (Vol. 5). Chicago: University of Chicago Press, 1975. Pp. 325–384.

Provence, S., & Lipton, R. C. *Infants in institutions*. New York: International Universities Press, 1962.

Rheingold, H. L., & Eckerman, C. D. The infant's free entry into a new environment. *Journal of Experimental Child Psychology*, 1969, 8, 271–283.

Schoggen, P., & Schoggen, M. Play, exploration, and density. In J. F. Wohlwill & W. VanVliet (Eds.), *Habitats for children: The impacts of density*. Hillsdale, N. J.: Erlbaum, in press.

Sears, R. A theoretical framework for personality and social behavior. *American Psychologist*, 1951, 6, 476–483.

Sears, R. R., Whiting, I. W., Nowlis, J., & Sears, P. S. Some child rearing antecedents of aggression and dependency in young children. *Genetic Psychology Monographs*, 1953, 47, 135–246.

Thompson, W. R., & Grusec, J. Studies of early experience. In P. H. Mussen (Ed.), *Carmichael's manual of child psychology* (3rd ed.). New York: Wiley, 1970. Pp. 565–654.

Turnure, J. E. Children's reactions to distractors in a learning situation. *Developmental Psychology*, 1970, 2, 115–122.

Turnure, J. E. *Distractability and concentration of attention in children's development*. Unpublished paper, Department of Psychology, University of Minnesota (Minneapolis), 1981.

Van Alstyne, D. The environment of three-year-old children: Factors related to intelligence and vocabulary tests. *Teachers College, Columbia University, Contributions to Education*, 1929, No. 366.

Wachs, T. D. The optimal stimulation hypothesis and early development: Anybody got a match? In I. C. Uzgiris & F. Weizmann (Eds.), *The structuring of experience*. New York: Plenum, 1977. Pp. 153–178.

Wachs, T. D. Proximal experience and early cognitive-intellectual development: The physical environment. *Merrill-Palmer Quarterly*, 1979, *25*, 3–41.

Wachs, T. D., Francis, J., & McQuiston, S. Psychological dimensions of the infant's physical environment. *Infant Behavior and Development*, 1979, *2*, 155–161.

Wachs, T. D., Uzgiris, I. C., & Hunt, J. McV. Cognitive development in infants of different age levels and from different environmental backgrounds: An exploratory investigation. *Merrill-Palmer Quarterly*, 1971, *17*, 283–317.

Wellman, B. L. The meaning of environment. *Yearbook of the National Society for the Study of Education*, 1940, *39*(Pt. 1), 21–40.

White, R. W. Motivation reconsidered: The concept of competence. *Psychological Review*, 1959, *66*, 297–333.

Wohlwill, J. F. The concept of experience: S or R? *Human Development*, 1973, *16*, 90–107.

Wohlwill, J. F. [Stability of] Cognitive development in childhood. In O. G. Brim & J. Kagan (Eds.), *Constancy and change in human development*. Cambridge, Mass.: Harvard University Press, 1980. Pp. 359–444.

Yarrow, L. J., Rubenstein, J. L., & Pedersen, F. A. *Infant and environment: Early cognitive and motivational development*. New York: Wiley (Halsted Press), 1975.

III

The Person:
Cognitive Processes

In the third section of this book are four chapters concerned with the analysis of problems of the development of cognition from the perspective of interactional theory. This section includes the substantive areas of personal theories of reality (Epstein and Erskine), self-regulation (Mischel), competence and achievement (Heckhausen), and cognitive coping strategies (Sarason and Sarason).

The person–environment interaction framework recognizes several important subsystems of the person, one of the most important being the world conception held by the individual. This topic is addressed by Epstein and Erskine in the first chapter of this section. The authors posit that individuals develop for themselves a set of implicit assumptions and beliefs that constitute "theories" about reality. Such conceptions of self and the world help the individual understand a complex and changing social environment. According to the authors, a theory of reality also serves the functions of maintaining favorable self-esteem and an acceptable balance of pleasure and pain.

In Chapter 8 Mischel discusses the topic of self-control or self-regulation— an important conception in most theories of personality. This concept has been the object of investigation by Mischel and others by means of the delay of gratification paradigm. Both situational and cognitive variables have been shown to influence a child's ability to delay. Findings suggest that there is a considerable degree of temporal consistency in children's delay behaviors.

The next chapter, by Heckhausen, deals with competence and achievement at three different stages of life. Research is reported indicating that competence and achievement are determined by different aspects of the person– environ-

HUMAN DEVELOPMENT:
AN INTERACTIONAL PERSPECTIVE

ment interaction at different points in the life cycle. In the early years of life, level of development of the concept of self influences how a child responds to interference with an ongoing activity. Another important developmental period for the domain of competence occurs between the ages of 8 and 12 years. The third example of the role of person–environment interaction in achievement is taken from a study of highly motivated business executives. These examples illustrate that person–environment interactions are involved in different ways in achievement and competence throughout the life cycle.

Sarason and Sarason discuss cognitive coping strategies in Chapter 10. Characteristics of both the person and the situation contribute to the ability of an individual to cope successfully with stressful transition points that occur across the life cycle. In this chapter the Sarasons use an interactional framework to investigate the use of cognitive factors as coping strategies.

7

The Development of
Personal Theories of Reality
from an Interactional Perspective[1]

SEYMOUR EPSTEIN   NANCY ERSKINE

The essence of the scientific method is that it involves a continuous interaction between observation and conceptualization, each influencing the other and, in the process, generating an increasingly differentiated, integrated, and accurate model of the world. What is true of science, in this respect, is no less true of an effective personal theory of reality (see Epstein, 1973, 1980; Kelly, 1955; Lecky, 1945; Piaget, 1937/1954). The aim of this chapter is to explore the implications for human development of regarding an individual's conceptual system as analogous, in certain fundamental respects, to a scientific theory. Two broad principles will guide our effort. One is that a personal theory of reality develops through a continuous interaction between conceptualization and experience. The other is that personal theories of reality develop not only incrementally, in a manner corresponding to what Kuhn (1970) refers to as normal science, but also through abrupt reorganizations, in a manner corresponding to what Kuhn refers to as scientific revolutions.

The Nature of Personal Theories of Reality

It is important to note that the personal theories of reality we are discussing are implicit, not explicit, theories. They are theories that individuals unwittingly construct in the course of living. It is necessary to distinguish such personal theories, which exist at a preconscious level, from more intellectual,

[1]The writing of this article was supported by NIMH Research Grant MH01293.

conscious personal theories. Not only is the content of the two systems different, but the preconscious and conscious systems differ in their rules of logic. As noted elsewhere (Epstein, 1983), a preconscious, experiential conceptual system differs from a conscious, intellectual system in the following ways:

1. It is less abstract and more closely associated with affective experience.
2. It is more action-oriented and less contemplative.
3. It is more concerned with immediate personal welfare.
4. It is more loosely integrated and more apt to exhibit dissociation.
5. It is less well differentiated and articulated and is characterized by categorical rather than dimensional judgments.
6. It contains affective conceptual subsystems that become dominant when an emotion is experienced.
7. It is experienced passively, as if events and emotions directly impose themselves on the individual rather than being mediated by the individual's interpretative processes.

THE STRUCTURE OF PERSONAL THEORIES OF REALITY

For present purposes the following summary of the nature of a personal theory of reality will suffice. (For a more thorough discussion, see Epstein, 1973, 1976, 1979, 1980, 1981, 1983.) A personal theory of reality, like a scientific theory, does not develop for its own sake, but is a conceptual tool for solving problems. The theory develops in order to fulfill three basic needs of the individual: to assimilate the data of experience, to maintain a favorable balance of pleasure and pain over the foreseeable future, and to maintain a favorable level of self-esteem. When these functions are fulfilled, the individual experiences positive affect, and when they are not, the individual experiences negative affect. Such affective reactions are adaptive, as they provide an intrinsic source of motivation for the individual to maintain and enhance the theory when it functions well, and to modify or reorganize the theory when it fails to fulfill its functions.

A theory of reality contains two major subtheories, one concerned with the nature of the person (a self theory), and one with the nature of the world (a world theory), and propositions relating the two. An individual's self theory is not independent of his or her world theory. To a large extent, an individual's conceptualization of the world is a reflection of the individual's conceptualization of self, and the opposite is also true. If an individual views himself or herself as strong or secure, it obviously is in relationship to others and the world.

Like any theory, an individual's theory of reality consists of a hierarchy of major and minor postulates. Minor postulates are relatively narrow generalizations that pertain to specific situations. Since they are directly tied to experience, they can be relatively easily invalidated by new experience. Because they are narrow generalizations, such invalidation does not constitute a serious threat to the organization of the overall conceptual system. Major postulates, on the other hand, are broad generalizations that are usually derived from cumulative experience. As broad generalizations, they are not easily invalidated. When they are invalidated, a large network of other postulates is affected and the stability of the overall conceptual system is therefore threatened. As a result, individuals will normally go to great lengths to defend their basic preconscious beliefs.

Behavior can be understood as a compromise among the functions of maintaining a favorable balance of pleasure and pain, assimilating the data of experience, and maintaining a favorable level of self-esteem. In the case of a delusion of grandeur, for example, the accurate assimilation of the data of reality is sacrificed in order to achieve a favorable level of self-esteem. In instances where an individual maintains a low opinion of himself or herself despite disconfirming experiences, the need to maintain a stable conceptual system takes precedence over the need to maintain a favorable level of self-esteem.

Most theories of personality, including psychoanalysis and learning theory, fail to recognize the importance of the need to maintain a coherent, integrated conceptual system as a major source of human motivation that often takes precedence over the pleasure principle, or the principle of reinforcement. As a result, they have difficulty in accounting for behavior that either is manifestly self-destructive or is maintained in the absence of reinforcement. The observation of such behavior led Freud (1936) to revise drastically his theory of personality by introducing the concepts of the life and death instincts and the repetition compulsion. As examples of the repetition compulsion, Freud cited repetitive dreams in the traumatic neurosis, the repetitive play of children who reenact frightening experiences such as a visit to a doctor, the transference neurosis in psychotherapy, and the demonic fate theme, in which individuals appear to be pursued by a relentless, destructive fate. Similar observations led Allport (1961) to introduce his concept of "functional autonomy," which refers to the maintenance of behavior in the absence of reinforcement. In both cases, little more was accomplished than to attach a label to an observed phenomenon.

The repetition compulsion and functional autonomy can readily be explained by the need to maintain a coherent conceptual system as, in order to maintain their conceptual systems, people must validate their basic beliefs, or postulates. As a result, they are often driven to prove that what they most fear is true. As an example, consider a woman who was abused by her father during childhood and who, as an adult, seeks out men who continue to abuse her. If she behaved rationally, she would seek out men who are gentle and considerate. One would suspect that she, more than most, would be sensitized to people who abuse her, and would avoid them. Yet, she behaves as if the opposite were the case. When viewed in the context of a need to maintain a theory of reality, her repeated involvement with abusive men makes perfect sense. Her world theory contains postulates that suggest that men are brutal and incapable of caring, while her self theory contains corresponding postulates addressed to her own unworthiness of affection. Although her negative emotional experiences appear to be controlled by an external destiny that she is powerless to affect, she is, in fact, creating her own destiny. Her need to maintain a familiar world overrides her need to maintain a favorable balance of pleasure and pain, or self-esteem. Were she to become emotionally involved with a considerate man, her need to maintain the integrity of her theory of reality would cause her to engage in behavior that would elicit the kinds of responses from him which are congruent with her expectations. Such reactions provide an interesting example of how inner structures and external events can interact to maintain a stable system that fails to grow with experience. The critical element in this case is the basic nature of the postulate that is involved, which was learned under conditions of high emotionality.

DESCRIPTIVE AND PRESCRIPTIVE POSTULATES

Some of an individual's postulates are descriptive, while others are motivational, or prescriptive. Major descriptive postulates are broad generalizations usually derived from emotionally significant experiences about what the world is like (e.g., "the world is safe") and what the self is like (e.g., "I am worthy"). Major motivational, or prescriptive, postulates are broad generalizations usually derived from emotionally significant experiences about how to behave in the future in order to obtain what one desires and avoid what one fears. Horney's (1945) descriptions of major styles of relating to others, namely, moving toward others, moving away from others, and moving against others, are examples of broad prescriptive postulates.

Postulates formed early in the developmental process are particularly important, as they influence later experiences and the development of other postulates. In interaction with the world they often serve as self-fulfilling hypotheses. In this respect, let us consider the interaction of two children with their mothers. One of the children has the descriptive postulate, "I am lovable," the other, "I am unlovable." Both children have learned that smiling increases the liklihood they will be picked up. Now consider what happens when both children smile and are picked up. For the first child, being picked up confirms the belief of lovableness. For the second child, the resolution is more complicated. Smiling leads to getting picked up, but getting picked up does not confirm the child's belief of lovableness. Because of his or her insecurity, the second child clings to the mother for as long as she will permit. The mother eventually must put the child down, which, so long as the child is unsatisfied, validates the child's belief that he or she is unlovable. Another possibility is that the child may respond in demanding ways upon being picked up, thereby evoking a negative response in the mother, which, too, validates the descriptive postulate of being unlovable.

The above example of a self-maintaining interaction between belief and experience is not meant to suggest that once a basic postulate is formed a child is necessarily "stuck" forever in its grip. It does suggest, however, the potent influence that basic postulates have on the assimilation of experience. Ainsworth, Bell, and Stayton (1971) describe the behavior of 12-month-old babies with insecure attachment relationships who behave in a manner similar to that just described. The babies engage in contact-seeking behavior (smiling, holding arms out to mother, etc.), only to follow their initial attempts at contact with signs of resistance. For example, they push the mother away, slap away toys she offers, and squirm in attempts to get down from her lap. As a result, these infants tend to get distressed and are not easily calmed. If they had been playing before the mother appeared, they tend not to go back to playing, nor do they achieve the contact they appaently wanted upon first seeing her. As Sroufe (1979) has noted, the securely attached child behaves very differently. Such a child is more receptive of the mother's affection and is more apt to engage in exploration of the environment. Not only does the securely attached infant experience more pleasure than the insecurely attached infant, but the behavior of the securely attached infant serves to enhance the emotional bond with the mother. Moreover, its exploratory behavior provides it with the opportunity to achieve mastery of the environment, thereby fostering a positive evaluation of the self (see Chapter 2 in this volume by Ainsworth for further description of such interactions between infants and their environments).

Given the potent self-sustaining interactive effects between the infant's developing theory of reality and the responses the infant receives from primary caretakers, how, then, does one account for the changes that occur over time? It is evident that both fortuitous experiences and maturational changes can foster new conceptualizations. In order to answer this question further, it will be helpful to compare the developmental progress of a personal theory of reality and the progress of a scientific theory. A personal theory of reality, of course, differs from a scientific theory in a number of important ways. Unlike scientific theories, personal theories of reality are implicit rather than explicit, are less well articulated, and are tested more casually and in a more biased manner. Nevertheless, as previously noted, the two have enough in common to warrant the analogy. Both involve a continuous interaction between conceptualization and experience, both exist in order to solve problems, both package experience into efficient, hierarchically organized systems, both direct behavior, and both change through sudden reorganization as well as gradual growth.

The Progress of Scientific and Personal Theories

According to Kuhn (1970), scientific progress occurs in two ways: through the practice of normal science and through scientific revolutions. Scientists in an era tend to share a common paradigm that consists of a theory or model for interpreting their data and conducting research. As long as there is an agreed-upon working model, scientists can go about the business of fleshing out the details of the model by conducting normal science. Ultimately, as the model continues to stimulate additional research, it leads to its own demise, as anomalies are uncovered that cannot be assimilated. Before a theory is discarded, desperate attempts are usually made to shore it up, and it is normally retained until an alternate theory is available. Kuhn refers to the process by which a theory is invalidated and another is substituted as a scientific revolution. Scientific revolutions are fostered not only by anomalies uncovered by normal science, but also by practical demands placed on the theory with which it is unable to cope. As an example, Kuhn notes that at one point in history the need for a better calendar produced dissatisfaction with the extant theory of astronomy and provided an important impetus for developing a new theory.

Personal theories of reality, like scientific theories, undergo changes through a continuous, incremental process of learning as well as through abrupt changes in organization. Moreover, like scientific revolutions, reorganizations of a personal theory of reality occur for two reasons: the uncovering of anomalies as the conceptual system gradually interacts with the world, and practical demands on the theory as a result of socially constituted life crises.

Developmental changes in a personal theory of reality normally occur in a gradual and continuous manner. No single experience, unless of overwhelming intensity, is apt to have a significant effect. Basic postulates tend to reflect cumulative experience over extended time periods. That is, they are inductively derived from an intuitive averaging, or aggregation, of experience that occurs at a preconscious level. As noted earlier, postulates formed in early childhood are particularly important as they become higher-order postulates that influence the development of other postulates. The form in which the postulates are expressed in later life, however, differs considerably from how the same postulates are expressed in childhood, for lower-order postulates modulate their expression. As a simple example, a person's belief that he or she must wrest from the world what it will not give willingly is apt to take the form of overt aggression in a young child, but the more subtle exercise of power in an adult.

In common with Kelly (1955), we believe that individuals, to varying degrees, test their beliefs in the laboratory of everyday life. The more secure the individual, the more he or she is willing to experiment, which is a precondition for growth. By the same token, the more insecure the individual, the less the likelihood that he or she will risk invalidation of important beliefs, and the more the individual is apt to formulate untestable hypotheses.

Kuhn describes a period after the abandonment of a paradigm in which scientific effort proceeds in a random fashion, and scientists report feeling anxiety and despair. Shortly before a new quantum theory was proposed by Heisenberg, Wolfgang Pauli stated: "At the moment physics is again terribly confused. In any case, it is difficult for me and I wish I had been a movie comedian or something of the sort and had never heard of physics [Kuhn,

1970, p. 84]." The anxiety and despair experienced by scientists as the result of the disorganization or deterioration of a scientific paradigm is much less intense, of course, than the anxiety and despair experienced by individuals as a result of the disorganization or deterioration of a personal theory of reality. The scientist quoted above was despairing over the disorganized state of a portion of his life, whereas the individual who perceives his or her theory of reality as disorganizing is despairing over his or her entire range of knowing and functioning. Individuals, like scientists, have a need to maintain structure, for the only alternative to structure is chaos and overwhelming anxiety (Goldstein, 1939).

Kuhn notes that it is usually not long after a paradigm is abandoned by the scientific community that a new paradigm gains acceptance. Often what is involved is a reorganization, or "gestalt switch," where old, familiar data are no longer viewed in the same manner as previously. Kuhn (1970) states: "The scientist who embraces a new paradigm is like a man wearing inverting lenses. Confronting the same constellation of objects as before and knowing that he does so, he nevertheless finds them transformed through and through in many details [p. 122]." In the same vein, an individual who lets loose the last threads of sanity may find an unusual opportunity for new learning and the assimilation of old learning into a new ground plan of experience. Consider, for example, the following account by a schizophrenic woman.

> And once the great Madness in me found a voice, there was no stopping it. It rolled out in such a tumult I was amazed at myself; wondered where it came from. It seemed obscene and terrible that I should answer in adult language, things said to me in my childhood. Things I had forgotten, until they again began to pour about me in a flood of bitter memories. . . . As I fitted answers to all those unimportant and forgotten childish silences, they lost much of their bitterness [Jefferson, 1974, p. 213].

Of course, it is not necessary to have an acute schizophrenic reaction for major changes to occur in a theory of reality. (For further discussion of schizophrenic disorganization as a potential growth process, see Epstein, 1979.) As previously noted, postulates are constantly gradually changing. Such changes are usually subtle and imperceptible at any moment. In addition, people experience degrees of reorganization of personality that are less complete than the scientific revolutions to which Kuhn refers. With respect to personal theories of reality, and, we suspect, scientific theories as well, it is often more appropriate to talk in terms of "mini-" than of maxi-revolutions. Mini-revolutions occur when people experience demands in their lives with which their extant conceptual system is unable to cope. Some degree of reorganization is therefore required. The need for reorganization may be extrinsically determined, that is, instigated by the occurrence of new events, or intrinsically determined, that is, instigated by the cumulative process of everyday living until anomalies are uncovered. Let us examine the process further.

As a personal theory of reality continues to assimilate experience, there is the danger that it will reconstitute the world in its own image. Basic postulates serve as background variables whose influence, although usually undetectable in single situations, exerts a biasing effect, the cumulative consequences of which can be considerable. As a result, inconsistencies between an individual's conceptual system and reality that originally were undetectable and of no great consequence may become sources of major disturbance. Expressed otherwise, personal theories have within them the seeds of their own destruction. As a result, the normal process of development through the life span often consists of periods of assimilation followed by periods of reorganization. The reorganization can be either constructive or maladaptive. The dynamics of personal theories of reality can be likened to an organic growth process; there is no standing still. Such a conclusion is consistent with observations by Levinson (1978) that the adult years are often characterized by periods of stability alternating with periods of reorganization.

In the course of normal growth, as in normal science, it is important to recognize that there is a dynamic interaction between two opposing forces, one consisting of a tendency to enhance the theory through growth and change and the other of a tendency to maintain the stability of the theory and thereby avoid anxiety.

With the preceding summary as a background, let us proceed to a consideration of specific stages of development. The stages that will be considered are (a) precursors of a personal theory of reality; (b) development of a theory of reality in childhood; (c) adolescence as an important transition to adult conceptualizations; and (d) adulthood.

It was noted at the beginning of this chapter that the preconscious conceptual system is closely tied to emotional experience. In order to understand the development of the preconscious conceptual system, it will be helpful to examine the role of emotions.

Precursors to a Theory of Reality

The neonate has the capacity to attend and react to the energetic impact of direct sensory stimulation by experiencing variations in arousal and in pleasant and unpleasant feelings, and to communicate its reactions to the external world. Thus, hunger pangs are arousing, unpleasant, and elicit crying, whereas stroking reduces arousal, is pleasant, and elicits smiling. Both of these reactions set up an interaction with the external world that lays the groundwork for selective attention, the development of associations and generalizations, and ultimately the construction of a theory of reality.

The first period of the neonate's reactions to the energetic component of stimulation is followed by the second stage of development, which is characterized by the emergence of an associative component. Elsewhere, one of us

(Epstein, 1967) has noted that, in addition to simple conditioning as a source of concept development, habituation plays an important role. In the course of habituation, a constant stimulus is reexperienced over a range of arousal levels. As a result, a stimulus that was initially attended to because of its energetic component is encoded and stored, and is able to cause other related stimuli to acquire interest because of their similarity to the habituated stimulus. It is through this process as well as conditioning that rudimentary concepts are formed and that assimilation is systematically expanded to encompass an ever-widening network of stimuli. The emergence of concepts exerts an important influence on the quality of the interactions between the infant and caregiver. Smiles that were nondiscriminatory at 2 months of age are directed at the mother by 3 or 4 months of age. Such behavior has important implications for strengthening the emotional bond between the infant and the mother, as it elicits and sustains prolonged interactive exchanges between the two (Izard, 1979; Mahler, Pine, & Bergman, 1975).

The next level of functioning in the first year of life takes the infant to a much more highly differentiated mode of reaction. It is associated with the emergence of intentional behavior (Piaget, 1981) and of true emotions (Lewis & Brooks, 1978; Sroufe, 1979). It is in this third stage of development that an evaluative component comes into play so that the child is able to react with positive and negative affect not only to the behavior of others, but also to its own behavioral impulses. Thus, the precursors of self-esteem can be discerned in this stage of development.

The first year of life sets up the foundation upon which a complex, integrated theory of reality, with subdivisions of a self theory and a world theory, will later develop. The pleasure–pain ratio of experience is critical during this period, for, if the environment is too painful, the infant will have little reason to continue to maintain contact with the external world and to conceptualize itself as an independent being who is capable of being influenced by and evaluated by others and who, in turn, can influence and evaluate others as well as itself. The experience of feeling loved and cared for has important implications for the infant because it establishes the basis for a sense of optimism, or trust in the world (Erikson, 1950), and for feelings of love-worthiness, which is the most fundamental source of self-esteem. Trust and self-esteem are two of the most basic postulates in a personal theory of reality. It is intersting, in this respect, that Horney (1945) concluded that the basis of all neurosis is the belief that one is a helpless and isolated individual in a hostile world.

The emergence and communication of differentiated emotions, such as fear, anger, sadness, and affection, provide an important basis for the development of organized conceptual and behavioral subsystems. Emotions can be regarded as organized conceptual–affective–physiological systems that prepare the organism to respond to certain critical life experiences, such as attack and threat, with certain general reaction tendencies, such as fight and flight. Thus, in the normal course of living, young children can be expected to exhibit behaviors involving attack, withdrawal, avoidance, and the expression of joy and affection. Depending on the responses of others, the emotions and associated behavior will be elaborated in different ways by different children. Expressed otherwise, the interaction between the child's emotionally induced behavior and the response of the environment to that behavior will be an important source not only of the further development of the child's emotions, but also of the child's behavioral repertoire and the conceptual system associated with it. Some children may learn to approach the world predominantly in terms of withdrawal, some in terms of flight, some in terms of attack, and some in terms of nurturance and the expression of affection. It may be concluded that some of the most basic motivational postulates that individuals acquire, such as moving away from, moving toward, and moving against others (Horney, 1945), have their roots in biological predispositions, which is not to imply that such dispositions are uninfluenced by learning.

Once an integrated, rudimentary theory of self is formed, self-esteem plays an increasingly important role in an individual's balance of pleasure and pain and in the maintenance of the individual's conceptual system. There are a number of forces at work in the internalization of parental values, including their acceptance and love for the child, which, as previously noted, is regarded as the most fundamental source of the child's self-esteem. First, new experiences are assimilated according to existing concepts, and, conversely, the concepts are influenced by the experiences of the infant; that is, a dialectical interaction is established. In Piaget's (1952) terms, the child assimilates reality into its concepts and accommodates its concepts to reality. Of course, the infant is extremely limited in its ability to analyze experience. Thus, if the infant is subjected to angry and aggressive responses from its father, the infant cannot dismiss the behavior as the result of "a hard day at the office." Rather, the anger must be experienced in relation to something that is fundamental to the infant's own being. The infant can't know that there are alternate explanations, and so whatever is experienced within its own environment is taken as universal truth.

Furthermore, because the infant's very existence depends on the good will of the parents, there is a strong incentive for the child to learn to behave in a way that ensures the parents' affection (Sullivan, 1953). By internalizing the values of the parents, the child is able to correct tendencies or impulses that would otherwise cause it to behave in a manner that would incur anxiety associated with fear of disapproval or abandonment. Let us consider an example of this process. At first, when Johnny reaches for the forbidden cookie jar, his mother says "Bad Johnny" and slaps his hand. Later, when Johnny finds himself tempted to reach for the cookie jar, he says to himself, "Bad Johnny" and slaps his own hand, which helps him refrain from taking the cookie. Through this process, Johnny develops a conscience, supported by guilt and anxiety if he fails to follow its dictates. His conscience becomes as effective in controlling his behavior as fear of loss of his mother's love used to be. Instead of being controlled by fear of his mother's disapproval, from this point on he will be controlled by anxiety associated with his own disapproval.

As already noted, comparable to self-esteem in importance is a child's basic trust in the world, or optimism. Such trust is necessary for the child to have the security to engage in exploratory activity (see Chapter 2 by Ainsworth in this volume). Exploration contributes to a broadening of the child's theory of reality and, equally important, to a sense of mastery, which is an important component of self-esteem. Second, it is important that the child's interactions with the world not be entirely free of conflict, as conflict is an important source of motivation for elaborating upon and differentiating the postulates in a theory of reality. Insufficient as well as excessive stress can retard normal development. Let us examine this issue further.

To the extent that the functions of a personal theory of reality are not realized, the system is placed under stress, which is subjectively experienced as anxiety, and there is a tendency for the conceptual system to disorganize. One of the defenses against disorganization is withdrawal, which protects the child from further vulnerability, but at the cost of psychological growth. At the same time, if the child is never allowed to experience anxiety due to overprotective parents (Adler, 1927), then the child will not develop strategies for handling the diverse kinds of experiences that must eventually be confronted when the parents are not present to intervene on the child's behalf (e.g., when the child enters school). At this point, the anxiety experienced may be overwhelming for the child who is not prepared to cope with the new demands. In consequence, the child may retreat to earlier forms of behavior associated with a more conflict-free existence. Although the earlier types of behavior may be adequate as strategies for receiving positive responses from the parents, they are not apt to evoke positive responses from teachers and peers who have different expectations. An adaptive theory of reality requires additional postulates to cope with exposure to a more extended world.

The nature of the postulates that develop in childhood will be determined by the nature of the emotionally significant events to which the child is exposed. Some experiences will be unique for a particular child, but all children in a particular culture will be exposed to some potentially and highly emotionally significant experiences in common, such as toilet training and giving up a dependent relationship with the mother when entering school. Such experiences, as they impose new adjustive demands on the child's theory of reality, are important sources of descriptive and prescriptive postulates. One can begin to outline some common descriptive and prescriptive postulates by noting common critical events in a particular society as described by different personality theorists. From Freud one obtains the view that nursing, weaning, toilet training, attraction to the parent of the opposite sex, and rivalry with the parent of the same sex are important sources of basic postulates. Erikson's (1950) theory emphasizes postulates associated with trust versus mistrust, autonomy versus shame and doubt, initiative versus guilt, and industry versus inferiority. Sullivan's (1953) theory draws attention to conceptual subsystems associated with self-evaluation and evaluation of the mothering figure. Thus, Sullivan refers to the importance in the child's conceptualization of "the good me," "the bad me," "the good mother," and "the bad mother."

It is beyond the scope of this presentation to integrate the views of different personality theorists on the nature of common descriptive and prescriptive postulates at different stages of the development process. This remains an interesting challenge for a future enterprise.

Apart from the nature of the common experiences that are apt to occur at different developmental stages, it is important to consider the influence of the child's conceptual ability on the postulates that will be formed. The work of Rosenberg (1979) on self-conceptualization, Kohlberg (1963) and Loevinger (1976) on moral development, Piaget (1952, 1937/1954) on cognitive development, and Sroufe (1979) and Lewis and Brooks (1978) on emotional development all suggest that postulates in childhood tend to be relatively absolute, concrete, and undifferentiated. As the child ages, experiences more, and develops greater conceptual abilities, his or her conceptual system becomes increasingly relative, differentiated, and integrated. Basic postulates are increasingly modified by peripheral postulates that are more susceptible to change. Accordingly, over a sufficient period of time, there is often considerable change in the manifest personality of an individual. Nevertheless, the same basic postulates are apt to be present, although their degree of generality and form of expression have been considerably modified by other postulates. It should also be considered that the basic aims of the conceptual system, which are to assimilate the data of experience, to maintain a favorable balance of pleasure and pain, and to maintain a favorable level of self-esteem, do not change, although the balance among them may. In this respect, during the course of early development there is a shift away from sensory pleasure and pain as the dominant source of motivation to maintaining the integrity of the conceptual system and to maintaining a favorable level of self-esteem.

Development of a Personal Theory of Reality during Adolescence

Adolescence is a period of rapid physical growth, of important physiological changes, and of changes in role expectancies. It is a period during which an individual's identity must change from that of a child to an adult. Postulates concerned with sexual and social attractiveness, with self-reliance, and with choosing a profession become very important. As a result of the need to elaborate and change the individual's theory of reality, adolescence is often a trying period, characterized by instability and feelings of inadequacy on the one hand, and exaggerated attempts to establish stability and a favorable level of self-esteem on the other. Rosenberg (1979) has noted that a major characteristic of adolescents is their tendency to be introspective. While younger children are likely to view themselves in terms of their "social exterior," that is, their manifest behavior, physical characteristics, and accomplishments, adolescents are apt to view themselves in terms of their "psychological interior." That is, they are concerned with their emotions, attitudes, desires, and secrets. As Rosenberg (1979) has nicely summed it up, "with increasing age the child becomes less of a Skinnerian and more of a Freudian [p. 202]."

Development of a Personal Theory of Reality during Adulthood

The importance of physical and social changes in promoting psychological crises in the life of an individual is widely recognized. What is less well known is that, in the absence of physical and social changes, theories of reality tend to evoke their own crises due to the manner in which they cumulatively assimilate experience, which is biased by the individual's basic postulates. In a sense, each assimilation of an experience contains within it an inherent distortion because the emotionally salient aspects of experience receive the most attention, and these are determined in large part by the existing postulates. That is, although postulates are constantly changing in minor ways to accommodate discordant information, they are also distorting the information in the service of maintaining the stability of the conceptual system. As a result, over sufficient time, there is the danger that the individual will gradually reorganize his or her world so that it increasingly conforms to the individual's dominant basic postulates. The world then becomes a caricature of the person's most deep-seated preconscious beliefs, which can be a source of considerable stress if these beliefs are not in harmony with more conscious aspects of the conceptual system or with reality as perceived by others. On the positive side, the problems that arise from the selective compounding of experience can be a significant impetus for growth and reorganization, resulting in a more differentiated, integrated, and valid conceptual system.

Apart from intrinsically generated pressures upon theories of reality to reorganize themselves, there are also common extrinsic pressures in adulthood that provide an impetus to modify a personal theory of reality. Decisions to marry and establish a family bring new demands on the self, as does the need to perform well on a job and, eventually, to retire from it and find new sources of self-esteem and coherence. In American society, with its emphasis on youth and physical attractiveness, anxiety associated with entering middle or old age can be particularly intense. At some point, individuals must cope with the prospect of infirmities at old age and ultimately with death.

For people who have relied heavily on involvement with children as sources of stability and self-esteem, the departure from the home of children can place special stress on the individual's conceptual system, for an important aspect of the reality that has structured their life and provided a source of pleasure and self-esteem no longer exists. Moreover, interpersonal problems that were successfully avoided as long as there were children to focus upon can no longer be ignored, and this, too, may require reorganization of a personal theory of reality.

It is beyond the scope of this presentation to attempt a detailed analysis of the significant experiences people are likely to encounter as they grow older. For the moment, we simply wish to draw attention to the observation that, with each new experience, additional demands are placed upon a personal theory of reality, and that such demands can have important implications for changes in an individual's conceptual system. Depending on how such stress is coped with it can be a source of greater integration and differentiation of the conceptual system or it can produce defensive retrenchment and a corresponding increase in the rigidity of the conceptual system.

In closing, it should be noted that we do not conceive of development as proceeding according to a number of fixed stages that begin in infancy and end in early adulthood. Rather, we assume that an organic, interactive process occurs between how the individual conceives of the world and the world as it exists. From this viewpoint, adjustment is a never-ending interactive process that is organized around three basic concerns of human existence, namely, (a) the maintenance of a favorable balance of pleasure and pain; (b) the assimilation of the data of experience into a coherent conceptual system; and (c) the maintenance of a favorable level of self-esteem. So long as there is life, the process can no more be suspended than can be the need to breathe or digest food. In terms of effectiveness of adaptation, the process can either progress or regress, as people have no choice but to conceptualize their experience in one way or another.

References

Adler, A. *The practice and theory of individual psychology.* New York: Harcourt, Brace, & World, 1927.

Ainsworth, M., Bell, S., & Stayton, D. Individual differences in strange-situation behavior of one-year-olds. In H. Schaffer (Ed.), *The origins of human social relations.* London: Academic Press, 1971.

Allport, G. W. *Pattern and growth in personality.* New York: Holt, 1961.

Epstein, S. Toward a unified theory of anxiety. In B. A. Maher (Ed.), *Progress in experimental personality research* (Vol. 4). New York: Academic Press, 1967.

Epstein, S. The self-concept revisited, or a theory of a theory. *American Psychologist,* 1973, *28,* 404–416.

Epstein, S. Anxiety, arousal, and the self-concept. In I. G. Sarason & C. D. Spielberger (Eds.), *Stress and anxiety* (Vol. 3). Washington, D. C.: Hemisphere Publishing Corporation, 1976.

Epstein, S. Natural healing processes of the mind: I. Acute schizophrenic disorganization. *Schizophrenia Bulletin,* 1979, *5,* 313–321.

Epstein, S. The self-concept: A review and the proposal of an integrated theory of personality. In E.

Staub (Ed.), *Personality: Basic issues and current research*. Englewood Cliffs, N. J.: Prentice Hall, 1980.

Epstein, S. The unity principle versus the reality and pleasure principles, or the tale of the scorpion and the frog. In M. D. Lynch, A. A. Norem-Hebeisen, & K. J. Gergen (Eds.), *Self-concept, advances in theory and research*. Cambridge, Mass.: Ballinger, 1981.

Epstein, S. *The unconscious, the preconscious, and the self-concept*. In J. Suls & A. Greenwald (Eds.), *Psychological perspectives on the self* (Vol. 2). Hillsdale, N. J.: Erlbaum, 1983.

Erikson, E. *Childhood and society*. New York: Norton, 1950.

Freud, S. *The problem of anxiety*. New York: Norton, 1936.

Goldstein, K. *The organism*. New York: American Book Co., 1939.

Horney, K. *Our inner conflicts*. New York: Norton, 1945.

Izard, C. E. Emotions as motivators: An evolutionary-developmental perspective. In H. Howe & R. Dienstbier (Eds.), *Nebraska Symposium on Motivation, 1978*. Lincoln, Neb.: University of Nebraska Press, 1979.

Jefferson, L. *These are my sisters*. New York: Anchor Press/Doubleday, 1974.

Kelly, G. A. *The psychology of personal constructs* (2 vols.). New York: Norton, 1955.

Kohlberg, L. The development of children's orientations toward a moral order. I. Sequence in the development of moral thought. *Vita Humana*, 1963, 6, 11–13.

Kuhn, T. S. *The structure of scientific revolutions*. Chicago: University of Chicago Press, 1970.

Lecky, P. *Self-consistency: A theory of personality*. New York: Island Press, 1945.

Levinson, D. J. *The seasons of a man's life*. New York: Knopf, 1978.

Lewis, M., & Brooks, J. Self knowledge and emotional development. In M. Lewis & L. A. Rosenblum (Eds.), *The development of affect*. New York: Plenum, 1978.

Loevinger, J. *Ego development*. San Francisco: Jossey-Bass, 1976.

Mahler, M. S., Pine, F., & Bergman, A. *The psychological birth of the human infant*. New York: Basic Books, 1975.

Piaget, J. *The origins of intelligence in children*. New York: Rutledge & Kegan Paul, 1952.

Piaget, J. *The construction of reality in the child*. New York: Basic Books, 1954. (Originally published, 1937.)

Piaget, J. Intelligence and affectivity: Their relationship during childhood development. *Annual Reviews Monograph*, 1981.

Rosenberg, M. *Conceiving the self*. New York: Basic Books, 1979.

Sroufe, L. A. Socioemotional development. In J. Osofsky (Ed.), *Handbook of infant development*. New York: Wiley, 1979.

Sullivan, H. S. *The interpersonal theory of psychiatry*. New York: Norton, 1953.

8

Delay of Gratification as Process and as Person Variable in Development[1]

WALTER MISCHEL

Combining Experimental and Correlational Strategies

BACKGROUND AND ORIENTATION

As Cronbach noted in his 1957 American Psychological Association presidential address, psychology has chronically suffered from an unfortunate bifurcation into two virtually nonoverlapping disciplines: the experimental study of behavior in response to situational manipulations versus the search for individual differences and their correlates. The former seeks to analyze the determinants of behavior through experimental manipulation of independent variables in the situation and is the method of experimental psychology; the latter pursues the nature of individual differences through a correlational strategy and is the method of differential psychology. Modern interactionism (e.g., Magnusson & Endler, 1977) seems in many ways a contemporary attempt to bridge the gap between these two disciplines, between experimental and correlational psychology, focusing on situations as they interact with the qualities of persons. With the purpose of trying to narrow the old schism between the two kinds of psychology, my own construct validation program for delay of gratification has tried to encompass both routes. It combines an experimental strategy that manipulates independent variables ("situations") to elucidate underlying mechanisms, on the one hand, with a correlational strategy to

[1]Preparation of this chapter and the research by the author were supported in part by Grant MH-36953 from the National Institute of Mental Health and by Grant MH-09814 from the National Institute of Child Health and Human Development.

HUMAN DEVELOPMENT:
AN INTERACTIONAL PERSPECTIVE

explore relevant individual differences, on the other hand. This dual strategy has characterized the work from its beginning (e.g., Mischel, 1966). By pursuing both experimental and correlational studies in the same substantive domain, one can try to analyze in fine-grain detail the processes that seem to affect the behavior of interest in the situation, while more or less simultaneously elaborating the meaning of the behavior as a personality index.

In this research, my central commitment continues to be elucidation of the process through which the developing individual can achieve increasing freedom from environmental (situational) constraints. The enduring general question here is: How do (can) persons overcome "stimulus control" and achieve increasing mastery and volitional control over their own behavior and the conditions of their lives? Theoretically, this effort is guided by a cognitive–social learning formulation that applies and integrates constructs from the study of cognition as well as from personality and developmental psychology to analyze the phenomena of social behavior and person variables systematically (W. Mischel, 1973, 1977, 1979). Briefly, this theoretical orientation is based on a synthesis of social learning and cognitive principles strongly influenced by expectancy-value theory (e.g., Rotter, 1954; Rotter, Chance, & Phares, 1972). Applied to self-control, this formulation distinguishes between two processes (W. Mischel, 1974; W. Mischel & H. N. Mischel, 1976, 1977). On the one hand are the developmental, cognitive, and learning processes through which the competencies necessary for particular novel forms of self-control are acquired in the first place. On the other hand, one must consider the motivational and cognitive factors that regulate the individual's choices among the behavior patterns that he has already acquired and is therefore capable of performing under appropriate incentive conditions. This view, which shares the acquisition–performance or competence–action distinction proposed by several theorists (e.g., Bandura, 1977), calls attention both to the cognitive, observational, and developmental processes through which competencies are acquired and to the incentive, value, and expectancy variables—the motivational and cognitive considerations—that guide the selection or choice of potential behaviors from the array of alternatives that the person is able to generate.

The theoretical orientation that guides this research on self-control (described in W. Mischel, 1973, 1974, 1979) emphasizes the importance of social learning variables and cognitive processes for the acquisition, maintenance, and modification of self-control patterns. It further emphasizes the relative specificity and discriminativeness of self-control behaviors and hence the importance of the contextual variables that influence them—a state not unique to the personality domain (e.g., Jenkins, 1974). However, it also recognizes that under some conditions relative consistency may be found, and it seeks to identify those conditions (e.g., W. Mischel & Peake, 1982). In the analysis of complex social behavior the orientation focuses on the reciprocal interaction between personal variables and the conditions or situational variables in the psychological environment. It views situational variables as exerting their impact by providing information that influences such specific person variables as the individual's competencies, encoding strategies, expectancies, and plans (W. Mischel, 1973, 1977, 1979).

In studying self-control, we have paid special attention to the role of cognition and particularly to such mental activities as self-instructions, rules, plans, imagery, and selective attention in the process of coping with frustration, as in delay of gratification. The hope is to help shed light on such issues as the links between ideation and coping competence, the processes underlying the development of self-regulation and the organization of self-control, and the reciprocal interaction between person variables and situational conditions in the genesis, maintenance, and modification of self-control behavior at different points in the course of development.

Substantively, the aspect of self-regulation to which this research program has devoted most attention is delay of gratification. A child's preference for delayed but more valued outcomes and his or her willingness and ability actually to wait or work for those outcomes have long been recognized as potentially prototypic features of an ego strength construct in a psychodynamic framework (e.g., Freud, 1911/1959; W. Mischel, 1966). In my own perspective (W. Mischel, 1973, 1974), waiting behavior is seen as a central feature of cognitive and social competence, a basic person variable assumed to have a major role in the individual's ability to generate effective cognitions and behaviors in the coping process (W. Mischel, 1973, 1974). In earlier phases of the research, when the focus was on the child's choice preferences, we explored the social and personal correlates and antecedents of preferences for immediate smaller versus delayed but more valued outcomes and found extensive and meaningful networks of relations and antecedents (e.g., W. Mischel, 1966, 1974; W. Mischel & Staub, 1965). In the current phases of the research, interest shifted to the actual waiting process after the choice to delay has been made (e.g., W. Mischel, 1974, 1981). Consequently we have turned to the nature, causes, and correlates of waiting behavior itself and these are the focus of the present chapter.

THE WAITING PARADIGM

To study the process underlying waiting behavior and its correlates a paradigm was constructed to test the willingness of preschool children (mean age, about 4 years) to remain in an experimental room—to wait entirely alone for at least a short time without becoming upset and debilitatingly anxious. After the usual play periods for building rapport, each child was taught a "game" in which he or she would immediately summon the experimenter by a simple signal. This step was practiced repeatedly, until the children clearly understood that they could immediately terminate the waiting period in the room simply by signaling for the experimenter, who regularly returned from outside as soon as the child signaled. Next, the children were introduced to the relevant contingency. They were shown two objects (e.g., food treats), one of which was clearly preferred (as determined by pretesting). To attain the preferred object the child had to wait for it until the experimenter returned "by himself." The child was, however, entirely free throughout the waiting period to signal at any time for the experimenter to return; if he signaled he could have the less preferred object at once but had to forgo the more desirable one. In this paradigm (and its variations) our research program has systematically tested the effects of theoretically relevant cognitive and social manipulations, and of developmental changes, on children's delay behavior.

Processes Underlying Effective Delay: Situational and Cognitive Determinants

A good deal of research has shown the dramatic role of the child's attention to the rewards in self-imposed delay of gratification in this paradigm. (The results cited in this section are described and referenced more fully in W. Mischel, 1981.) Specifically, initial theorizing suggested that during delay of gratification, attention to the rewards should serve a "time-binding" function and should facilitate the child's ability to wait for them. Empirically, these expectations proved to be exactly wrong: Preschool children were able to wait 10 times longer when the rewards in the contingency were not available for attention during the delay period than when they were in view.

COGNITION DURING DELAY

To explore what caused these unexpected results, we tried to see just what the children were doing while they were waiting. Therefore, we observed them closely by means of a one-way mirror throughout the delay period as they sat waiting for their preferred outcomes in what had proved to be the most difficult situation, the one in which both the immediate and delayed outcomes faced them. These observations were helped by "Mr. Talk Box," a device that consisted of a tape recorder and a microphone that announced its name to the youngsters and cheerfully said, "Hi, I have big ears and I love it when children fill them with all the things they think and feel, no matter what." Thereafter, Mr. Talk Box adopted a Rogerian nondirective attitude and acceptingly "unhemed" and "ahad" to whatever the child said to him. In fact, many children seemed quickly to treat Mr. Talk Box as an extension of their psyche and engaged in elaborate, animated discussions with themselves.

The most effective delay strategies employed by some children were remarkably simple. These youngsters seemed able to wait for the preferred reward for long periods apparently by converting the aversive waiting situation into a more pleasant nonwaiting one. They managed this by elaborate self-distraction techniques through which they spent their time psychologically doing almost anything other than waiting. Instead of focusing their attention prolongedly on the rewards, they avoided them. Some of the children covered their eyes with their hands, rested their heads on their arms, and discovered other similar techniques for averting their gaze from the rewards. Many children also seemed to try to reduce the frustration of delay of reward by generating their own diversions: They talked quietly to themselves, sang ("This is such a pretty day, hurray"), created games with their hands and feet, and, when all other distractions seemed exhausted, even tried to go to sleep during the waiting time—as one child successfully did, falling into a deep slumber in front of the signal bell. These tactics, of course, are familiar to anyone who has ever been trapped in a boring lecture.

Our observations of the children seemed consistent with theorizing that emphasizes the aversiveness of frustration and delayed rewards. If one is experiencing conflict and frustration about wanting to end the delay but not wanting to lose the preferred, delayed outcomes, then cues that enhance attention to the elements in the conflict (i.e., the two sets of rewards) should increase the aversiveness of waiting. More specifically, when the children attend to the immediate reward their motivation for it increases and they become tempted to take it but are frustrated because they know that taking it now prevents getting the preferred reward later. When the children attend to the preferred but delayed outcome they become increasingly frustrated because they want it more now but cannot have it yet. When attention is focused on both objects, both of these sources of frustration occur and further delay becomes most aversive; hence, the child acts to end the waiting period quickly (as indeed happened). This reasoning would suggest that conditions that decrease attention to the rewards in the choice contingency and that distract the person (through internal or overt activity) from the conflict and the frustrating delay would make it less aversive to continue goal-directed waiting and thus permit longer delay of gratification. That is, just as cognitive avoidance may help one to cope with anxiety so may it help to deal with other such aversive events as the frustration of waiting for a desired but delayed outcome and the continuous conflict of whether or not to end the waiting period.

THE ROLE OF COGNITIVE DISTRACTION

This line of theorizing suggests that delay of gratification and frustration tolerance should be facilitated by conditions that help the individual to transfer the aversive waiting period into a more pleasant nonwaiting situation. Such a transformation could be achieved by directing attention and thoughts away from the frustrating components of delay of gratification. Thus, voluntary delay of reward should be enhanced by any overt or covert activities that serve as distractors from the rewards and thus ease the aversiveness of the situation. By means of such distraction the person should convert the frustrating delay-of-reward situation into a less aversive one. Activities, cognitions, and fantasy that could distract the individual from the reward objects therefore should increase the length of time that he would delay gratification for the sake of getting the preferred outcome.

But how can one influence what the child is going to think about? We made some poor starts, but soon discovered that even 3 and 4-year-old children could give us elaborate, dramatic examples of the many events that made them feel happy, like finding frogs, or singing, or swinging on a swing with mommy pushing. In turn, we instructed them to think about these fun things while they sat waiting alone for their preferred outcomes. In some of these studies the immediate and delayed rewards were physically not available for direct attention during the waiting period. We manipulated the children's attention to the absent rewards cognitively by different types of instructions given before the start of the delay period. Again the results showed that cognitions directed toward the rewards substantially reduced, rather than increased, the amount of time that the children were able to wait. Thus, attentional and cognitive mechanisms that enhance the salience of the rewards greatly decreased the length of voluntary delay time. In contrast, overt or covert distractions from the rewards (e.g., by prior instructions to think about fun things) facilitated delay of gratification (W. Mischel, Ebbesen, & Zeiss, 1972), as Figure 1 illustrates.

As the figure shows, when they were faced with the physical presence of the rewards, the children found it extremely difficult to wait unless they were distracted by thinking about "fun things." Likewise, when the rewards were

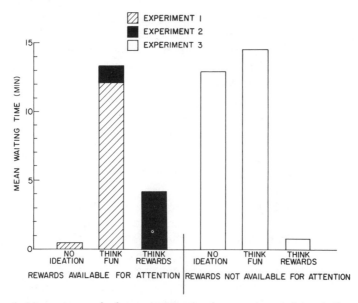

Figure 1. *Mean minutes of voluntary waiting time for treatment conditions in Experiments 1, 2, and 3, comparing different ideation instructions with controls. [From Mischel, Ebbesen, & Zeiss, 1972.]*

not physically in front of them, no special ideation needed to be supplied; the children spontaneously engaged in their own distracting ideations. However, if they were led to think about the rewards even when these rewards were physically absent, delay became as difficult as when they were physically in sight.

The overall results undermine theories that predict that mental attention to the reward objects will enhance voluntary delay by facilitating "time-binding" and tension discharge (through cathexes of the image of the object). The data also undermine any "salience" theories that would suggest that making the outcomes salient by imagery, cognitions, and self-instructions about the consequences of delay behavior should increase voluntary delay. The findings unequivocally contradict theoretical expectations that images and cognitions relevant to the gratifications sustain delay behavior. Instead, either looking at the rewards or thinking about them in their absence decreases voluntary delay of gratification. Effective delay thus seems to depend on suppressive and avoidance mechanisms to reduce frustration during the delay period; it does not appear to be mediated by consummatory fantasies about the rewards.

These findings suggest that a person can delay most effectively for a chosen deferred gratification if during the delay period he shifts his attention from the relevant gratification and occupies himself internally with cognitive distractions. Situational or self-induced conditions that serve to shift attention from the reward objects appear to facilitate voluntary waiting times appreciably. In order to bridge the delay effectively, it is as if the child must make an internal notation of what he is waiting for, perhaps remind himself of it periodically and abstractly (e.g., W. Mischel & Moore, 1980), but spend the remaining time attending to other less frustrating internal and external stimuli, thereby transforming the noxious into the easy and making "will power" manageable.

COGNITIVE TRANSFORMATIONS

Especially interesting to us was the finding in many studies that the effects of actual rewards physically present or absent in the situation could be completely overcome and even totally reversed by changing how the child represented those rewards mentally during the delay period (W. Mischel, 1974, 1981). For example, when, through pre-experimental instructions, preschoolers ideate about the rewards for which they are waiting in consummatory, or "hot," ways (focusing on their taste, for instance), they can hardly delay at all; but if they focus on the nonconsummatory, or "cool," qualities of the rewards (on their abstract or nonconsummatory qualities), they can wait for them easily and even longer than if they distract themselves from the rewards altogether. Thus, hot, reward-oriented ideation decreases delay by making it more aversively frustrative and arousing. In contrast, delay is facilitated by cool ideation focusing on the abstract (rather than consummatory) features of the rewards, as well as by distraction from the rewards altogether. In sum, attending to a blocked outcome or thinking about it in consummatory (goal-directed) ways seems to increase frustrative arousal and to make it more difficult for the child to delay (W. Mischel, 1981). Understanding that process allows one to make fairly powerful predictions about specific behavior in specific delay situations.

PERSON–SITUATION INTERACTION

How do the findings from our research program speak to the relative contribution of person and situation to the person–situation interaction? When examined closely in this context, the distinction between the power of the situation and of the person becomes somewhat fuzzy. Consider the findings that attention focused away from the rewards in the delay situation (e.g., by covering the rewards or avoiding them cognitively) potently affects and predicts delay behavior. Do these results demonstrate the power of situational variables in self-control? Yes, in the sense that they show how specific changes in the situation can make delay either very difficult or very easy. No, in the sense that our results also show how even young children can and do increase their own personal ability to control what stimuli do to them by changing how they think about these stimuli, by "reframing" them mentally or by distracting themselves from the frustrativeness of the situation while persevering in their goal-directed waiting. Once children recognize how their own ideation makes self-control either hard or easy, the option to delay or not to delay becomes truly their own. They know how to delay effectively and must merely choose whether or not they want to, by becoming increasingly immune to the physical situation and able to rearrange it psychologically, guided by their growing understanding of self-control rules (H. N. Mischel & W. Mischel, in press). Knowledge of situational variables can become a vital ingredient of each person's power over situations and can enhance the individual's ability to control stimuli purposefully rather than being controlled by the stimuli to become the victim of situations. The child's growing ability to understand and apply his or her knowledge of how the "situation" works seems an interesting province of research for the personologist as much as for the student of metacognition (e.g., H. N. Mischel & W. Mischel, in press).

Attentional focus, assessed as an activity of the person, allows impressive predictions of the individual's actual waiting behavior in the delay situation. For example, we are finding that the child's tendency to attend to the rewards, assessed by measuring what he or she is looking at, allows us to predict the majority of the variance in number of seconds of delay time (Peake & Mischel, in preparation). The more the children distract themselves from the frustrativeness of the rewards by avoiding them cognitively during the delay period, the longer they can wait for them (H. N. Mischel, 1983). Those seconds of waiting time, in turn, appear to be not at all trivial behaviors; they are, instead, remarkably robust indicators of a temporally stable human quality of considerable practical and theoretical significance. We see that from studies in related directions in which we also are pursuing the personality correlates, the cross-situational consistency, and the temporal stability of delay behavior in the same children whose delay behavior we assessed a dozen years earlier in specific, structured experimental situations when they were preschoolers (W. Mischel, Peake, & Zeiss, in preparation).

Delay Ability as a Person Variable

At the same time that we have been gathering evidence for the situational and cognitive processes underlying delay behavior and clarifying their operations, we have also been documenting the meaning of delay behavior as a quality of the person. Our aim here is to explore the cognitive and social correlates of effective goal-directed delay behavior in the course of development. As noted at the start of this chapter, the potential importance of delay of gratification as a key personality indicator has been recognized since Freud first called attention to it. In our earlier research we found a network of correlations associated with children's choice preferences for delayed, more valuable versus immediate, less valuable outcomes (e.g., W. Mischel, 1966, 1974). For example, individuals who predominantly choose larger, delayed rewards or goals for which they must either wait or work tend more to be oriented toward the future, to plan carefully for distant goals, to have high scores on "ego-control" measures, to have high achievement motivation, to be more trusting and socially responsible, to be brighter and more mature, to have a higher level of aspiration, and to show less uncontrolled impulsivity (for details see W. Mischel, 1966, 1974; W. Mischel & Metzner, 1962).

In contrast to the extensive network of correlates elaborated for delay choice preferences, little has been known until very recently about the possible correlates of actual waiting time in the delay paradigm. To help fill this void, Mischel and Peake (1982a,b) exposed preschool children (with a mean age of 53 months) at Stanford's Bing School to two versions of the delay situation. The children participated in tbe standard delay situation but with the exception that the experimenter was present during the delay period. They also participated in the standard Mischel–Ebbesen (1970) delay situation in which all procedures are identical, but the experimenter is absent during the delay period.[2] The children participated in the two situations in random order over a

---

[2]We undertook this study in part to test Bem and Funder's (1978) claim that their "template-matching" technique would be of value in efforts to demonstrate cross-situational consistency. Since they attempted to make their point in the domain of delay of gratification, we were especially interested in testing it definitively. We therefore used their version of the delay situation (experimenter present) as well as ours (experimenter absent during the delay period to avoid putting pressures for compliance on the part of the child) and followed their procedures as closely as possible. The results presented no support for their arguments (see W. Mischel & Peake, 1982a). Briefly, Bem and Funder's "distinctive Q-sort portraits" for their delay situation failed to replicate with our larger sample of subjects tested. Under virtually identical conditions we also found that the two delay situations that they predicted would be reliably differentiated by distinctive Q-sort portraits actually shared highly similar and familiar patterns of correlations. The correlation between delay behavior in the two situations was .22. The implications of the total results are discussed in W. Mischel and Peake (1982a).

period of 3 weeks. For most children, responses to the 100-item California Child Q Set, or CCQ (Block, 1961), were obtained concurrently from both parents. The composited mother–father Q-item correlates that reached or tended to approach statistical significance are shown for both measures of waiting time in Tables 1 and 2.

The correlations obtained for the "standard-delay" (experimenter-absent) procedure seemed generally similar to those for the experimenter-present version and on the whole both seem coherent with the expected high-competence, high ego strength portrait (W. Mischel, 1966, 1974). That is, as the tables show, there were some low-level but statistically significant associations between the delay measures and such ratings as "is competent, skillful"; "is planful, thinks ahead"; "has high standards of performance for self"; "can acknowledge unpleasant experiences and admit to own negative feelings"; "uses and responds to reason"; "is verbally fluent, can express ideas well in language"; "is curious and exploring, eager to learn, open to new experiences"; "is reflective, thinks and deliberates before he or she speaks or acts." In sum, these ratings illustrate the occurrence of some modest, generally theory-consistent associations between concurrent parental ratings and the preschool child's delay time on the same behaviors whose predictable responsiveness to situational and cognitive variables have been demonstrated experimentally.

Table 1

Mother and Father Composited Q-Item Correlates with Preschool Child's Delay Time, Experimenter Present Situation (N = 52), Concurrent Data

Item	r	p
Positively Correlated		
Is competent, skillful	.38	.005
Is planful, thinks ahead	.36	.01
Has high standards of performance for self	.28	.04
Is curious and exploring, eager to learn, open to new experiences	.27	.05
Uses and responds to reason	.27	.05
Is reflective, thinks and deliberates before he or she speaks or acts	.26	.06
Seeks physical contact with others	.24	.08
Develops genuine and close relationships	.23	.10
Appears to have high intellectual capacity	.23	.10
Negatively Correlated		
Tends to be indecisive, vacillating	−.30	.03
Daydreams, tends to get lost in reverie	−.27	.06
Is inhibited and constricted	−.26	.07
Is a talkative child	−.25	.08
Can recoup or recover when under stressful experiences	−.23	.10
Tends to become rigidly repetitive or immobilized when under stress	−.23	.10

Note: All p values are two-tailed unless otherwise noted throughout this chapter.

Table 2

Mother and Father Composited Q-Item Correlates with Preschool Child's Delay Time, Experimenter Absent (Standard) Situation (N = 47), Concurrent Data

Item	r	p
Positively Correlated		
Can acknowledge unpleasant experiences and admit to own negative feelings	.34	.02
Uses and responds to reason	.28	.06
Is verbally fluent, can express ideas well in language	.26	.08
Is curious and exploring, eager to learn, open to new experiences	.25	.09
Negatively Correlated		
Is calm, relaxed, easy-going	−.48	.001
Tries to be the center of attention	−.30	.04
Tends to withdraw and disengage himself or herself when under stress	−.29	.05
Is cheerful	−.28	.06
Is inhibited and constricted	−.28	.06
Is warm and responsive	−.27	.07
Gets along well with other children	−.26	.08
Is physically active	−.26	.06
Tends to be indecisive and vacillating	−.26	.08
Is physically attractive, good-looking	−.25	.08
Is eager to please	−.25	.09
Is obedient and compliant	−.25	.09
Tries to manipulate others by ingratiation	−.24	.10

Long-Term Correlates of Early Waiting Behavior

Most interesting to us is the possible association between the preschool child's delay behavior and indexes of coping and competence obtained not concurrently but years later. Such data are now becoming available. Specifically, at the same time that we pursued the experimental strategy for studying delay mechanisms we were also engaged in a longitudinal study of children who participated in these delay-of-gratification experiments when they were preschoolers in the years from 1967 to 1974 at Stanford's Bing School. During that time, over 650 preschool children (with a mean age of about 53 months) were subjects in one or more studies of waiting behavior.[3] All delay situations were versions of the standard waiting paradigm (experimenter absent during delay) (W. Mischel, 1974), on which numerous experimental variations were conducted (e.g., by manipulating the ideation instructions to the child or the presence of the rewards). Some children also were administered various measures to test individual differences. In addition, the parents of a subsample of these children provided ratings of their child's ability to delay rewards and made predictions (in minutes) of the child's probable waiting times in specific

[3]Note that this is a sample different from the children tested, years later, by W. Mischel and Peake (1982a,b) whose data are shown in Tables 1 and 2.

delay situations like those in which the child was actually tested. These ratings were obtained while the child was still in preschool. In follow-ups starting in 1979, after time intervals of about 10 years had elapsed, we also began to collect data to assess the child's cognitive and social competence and coping patterns in the adolescent years.

Our total results are beginning to provide intriguing evidence both for the discriminativeness of delay behavior (across even seemingly similar contexts) and for its temporal stability over many years. We know that the preschool child who delays effectively in some contexts may not do so in other, even slightly different, situations, showing much cross-context discriminativeness. For example, the correlation between preschool delay time with experimenter present versus experimenter absent during the delay, but otherwise identical, was .22 (W. Mischel & Peake, 1982a). But we are also finding highly significant continuities linking the preschooler's delay time while waiting for a couple of marshmallows to indexes of his or her cognitive and social competence, coping skills, and school performance years later. For example, the number of seconds preschoolers delayed the first time they had a chance to do so in our 1967–1974 preschool studies, regardless of the specific delay situation they encountered, significantly predicts their social competence as high school juniors and seniors as rated by their parents ($r = .34$, $N = 99$, $p < .001$). Sometimes even single acts *can* predict meaningful life outcomes.

This example is not an isolated finding. Although our data collection and analyses are still at early stages, a clear picture seems to be emerging of coherent adolescent correlates significantly associated with preschool delay in our experimental situation a decade earlier. To illustrate, Tables 3 and 4 show relations between preschool delay and parental composited Q-sort ratings years later.[4] (These children's mean age at first delay was 4 years, 6 months; it was 16 years, 8 months at the time of the parental Q-sorts.) Again it is noteworthy that a clearly coherent picture of perceived competence and positive coping is associated even with the single act of number of seconds the child delayed in the first delay situation assessed. A similar and somewhat enhanced picture emerges when the child's early mean delay score is the predictor. (It is not surprising that the data for first delay and mean delay are similar since most children were exposed to only one or two delay situations.) The mean number of delay occasions in this measure for the data in Table 4 was 1.65.

In both Tables 3 and 4 also note the greater strength and number of the qualities a decade later associated with early delay, compared to the concurrent correlates found for children in the preschool years. Interestingly, the characterization of children who waited in unequivocally positive terms that denote cognitive and social competence seems extensive and definitive when they are adolescents than it was when preschool children were rated. When they are adolescents, preschoolers who delayed tend to be described exten-

---

[4]These data are for transformed delay scores, as indicated in the tables. Analyses based on untransformed seconds of delay time yielded generally similar Q-correlates.

Table 3
Adolescent Q-Correlates[a] of First Preschool Delay Time (N = 77)

Item	r	p
Positive		
Uses and responds to reason	.42	.001
Is competent, skillful	.39	.001
Is attentive and able to concentrate	.37	.001
Is resourceful in initiating activities	.37	.001
Is verbally fluent, can express ideas well	.36	.001
Is curious and exploring, eager to learn, open	.36	.001
Is planful, thinks ahead	.36	.001
Is self-reliant, confident, trusts own judgment	.33	.003
Becomes strongly involved in what he or she does	.33	.003
Is creative in perception, thought, work, or play	.31	.006
Is self-assertive	.30	.008
Is persistent in his or her activities	.27	.02
Appears to have high intellectual capacity	.23	.04
Can be trusted, is dependable	.22	.06
Has high standards of performance for self	.21	.07
Negative		
Tends to go to pieces under stress, becomes rattled	−.42	.001
Reverts to more immature behavior under stress	−.41	.001
Appears to feel unworthy, thinks of himself as bad	−.30	.008
Is shy and reserved, makes social contacts slowly	−.30	.009
Tends to be indecisive and vacillating	−.29	.01
Tends to become rigidly repetitive or immobilized when under stress	−.26	.02
Attempts to transfer blame to others	−.25	.03
Tends to withdraw and disengage himself under stress	−.25	.03
Is restless and fidgety	−.25	.03
Is fearful and anxious	−.24	.04
Is inhibited and constricted	−.22	.05
Looks to adults for help and direction	−.22	.05
Tends to be sulky or whiny	−.22	.06

[a]Mother–father composite ratings.
Note: Delay scores for computing the correlations are based on *z* transformations within conditions within each delay study.

sively, in coherent positive fashion that consistently denotes cognitive and social competence and maturity. Indeed the 37 correlates in Table 4 provide a portrait that seems almost idealized, although the time spanned is from age 4 to adolescence. Moreover, these long-term links between early delay and later competence and coping strength are not confined to ratings; recall that the initial data are all the child's specific behavior, that is, the seconds of waiting time in a preschool experiment.[5]

[5]We also are exploring possible links between early delay and later objective measures of competence, such as the Scholastic Achievement Test scores. While some suggestive associations seem to be emerging, these results are still too tentative to permit conclusions. We are in the process of trying to increase the sample size of our follow-up study; all long-term correlates reported here should be viewed as preliminary, pending such expansion of the data base.

Table 4

Adolescent Q-Correlates[a] of Mean Preschool Delay Time (N = 77)

Item	r	p
Positive		
Is attentive and able to concentrate	.49	.001
Is verbally fluent, can express ideas well	.40	.001
Uses and responds to reason	.38	.001
Is competent, skillful	.38	.001
Is planful, thinks ahead	.35	.002
Is self-reliant, confident, trusts own judgment	.33	.004
Is curious and exploring, eager to learn, open	.32	.004
Is resourceful in initiating activities	.29	.01
Is self-assertive	.29	.01
Appears to have high intellectual capacity	.28	.01
Has high standards of performance for self	.27	.02
Can be trusted, is dependable	.25	.03
Becomes strongly involved in what he or she does	.25	.03
Is creative in perception, thought, work, or play	.24	.04
Is persistent in his or her activities	.23	.05
Is admired and sought out by other children	.22	.06
Tends to be pleased with, proud of his or her products	.20	.08
Negative		
Tends to go to pieces under stress, becomes rattled	−.49	.001
Reverts to more immature behavior under stress	−.39	.001
Appears to feel unworthy, thinks of himself or herself as bad	−.33	.003
Is restless and fidgety	−.32	.005
Is shy and reserved, makes social contacts slowly	−.31	.006
Tends to withdraw and disengage himself or herself under stress	−.30	.008
Shows specific mannerisms or behavioral rituals	−.27	.02
Is stubborn	−.25	.03
Turns anxious when his or her environment is unpredictable	−.25	.03
Is unable to delay gratification	−.25	.03
Attempts to transfer blame to others	−.24	.04
Teases other children	−.22	.05
Tends to be indecisive and vacillating	−.22	.05
Is easily victimized by other children	−.21	.06
Is fearful and anxious	−.21	.06
Tends to imitate and take over the characteristic manners and behavior of those he or she admires	−.21	.07
Is inappropriate in his or her emotive behavior	−.21	.07
Looks to adults for help and direction	−.20	.08
Has transient interpersonal relationships	−.19	.10
Overreacts to minor frustrations	−.19	.10

[a]Mother–father composite ratings.

Note: Delay scores for computing the correlations are based on z transformations within conditions within each delay study.

Conclusions

In conclusion, let us consider the experimental and correlational studies as a whole. Here we have a set of data in which a fine-grain analysis of the psychological situation and of the relevant basic psychological processes allows specific predictions of behavior within the delay situation itself. In these data, moreover, cross-context discriminativeness is high even across seemingly similar situations. Yet, perhaps most provocatively, these same data lend themselves to demonstrations of the temporal stabilities, that is, the threads of continuity in lives, that have become increasingly evident even over long periods of time (e.g., Block & Block, 1980). The overall findings so far, while still far from complete, suggest the following tentative conclusions.

The preschooler's waiting behavior in the delay paradigm is highly predictable from knowledge of the particular situational and cognitive variables operating in the specific context. A set of principles or rules that characterize the relevant psychological processes have emerged that allow detailed predictions of delay time in the specific situation. These rules allow one to account for a substantial portion of the variance in children's delay behavior.

Nevertheless, the same behavior is significantly predictive of the child's competence and coping as perceived by the parents when assessed a decade later in development and provides a stable network of coherent correlates. The magnitude of these relations is modest in absolute terms, generally averaging not more than about .30, and thus leaves most of the variance unexplained. But these correlations seem impressive given that they rest on a specific preschool behavior, that they span a lengthy period of development, and that they occur even for a single early act (i.e., seconds of first delay time). The demonstrations of temporal coherences and continuity in these data are based on links with the child's own preschool behavior objectively and independently assessed and therefore cannot be attributed only to stability in the rater's theories.

The attributes suggested by the adolescent correlational data are nicely congruent with the process analyses provided by the experimental research. The correlations provide a general picture of the adolescent who delayed in preschool as one who is seen as attentive and able to concentrate, able to express ideas well, responsive to reason, competent, skillful, planful, able to think ahead, and so forth. He or she is also seen as able to cope and deal with stress maturely. The process analysis provides a more detailed, specific analysis of the essential ingredient for effective delay in the waiting paradigm: the ability to divert and control attention, focusing it away from the frustrativeness of the situation and the "stimulus pull" of the rewards while maintaining the goal-directed perseverance required for their attainment. In juxtaposition, the experimental and correlational efforts provide a complementary and more complete view both of the psychological demands of the delay situation and of the qualities of the children who are likely to meet them effectively.

Taken collectively, these two sets of findings from experimental and correlational strategies within the same subjects and the same behavioral measures illustrate the conjoint operation of contextual and cognitive-personological determinants in the domain of self-regulation. The research also highlights the importance of pursuing the "two disciplines of psychology" more or less together and of undertaking process-oriented experimental studies in conjunction with person-oriented investigations of individual differences. As noted often before (e.g., W. Mischel, 1973, H. N. Mischel, 1983, in press), the investigator's purposes must guide the selection of which facet of the situation—person interaction one selects and which of the two disciplines one follows at any juncture. Neither side can be ignored in a comprehensive account.

Finally, two points must be reiterated, although space prevents their discussion here. First, the existence of long-term coherences of the sort found here implies the operation of long-lived personal qualities. The qualities suggested by the present results seem consistent with an attribute like "cognitive and social competence" that was proposed earlier as the first of five person variables in a cognitive social learning approach to personality (W. Mischel, 1973). The specific structure and composition of this competence variable seem well worth analyzing closely. For example, we will want to try to see what links may exist between the parents' perceptions of the child's qualities and the child's current competencies.

Second, the existence of stabilities over time and coherences among indexes of cognitive and social competencies should not be mistaken as an answer to a different problem: the nature of cross-situational consistencies in the behavioral referents for trait categories. Indeed, as discussed in W. Mischel and Peake (1982a) and Mischel (1983, in press), the analysis of temporal coherences and enduring qualities on the one hand, and of cross-situational consistencies in behavior on the other, involves a host of issues about the structure and construction of behavior that unfortunately have too often been lumped together and now must be untangled.

References

Bandura, A. *Social learning theory*. Englewood Cliffs, N. J.: Prentice-Hall, 1977.

Bem, D. J., & Funder, D. C. Predicting more of the people more of the time: Assessing the personality of situations. *Psychological Review*, 1978, *85*, 485–501.

Block, J. *The Q-sort method in personality assessment and psychiatric research*. Springfield, Ill.: Charles C Thomas, 1961.

Block, J., & Block, J. The role of ego-control and ego resiliency in the organization of behavior. In W. A. Collins (Ed.), *The Minnesota Symposia on Child Psychology* (Vol. 13). Hillsdale, N. J.: Erlbaum, 1980.

Cronbach, L. J. The two disciplines of scientific psychology. *American Psychologist*, 1957, *12*, 671–684.

Freud, S. Formulations regarding the two principles in mental functioning. In *Collected papers* (Vol. 4). New York: Basic Books, 1959. (Originally published, 1911.)

Jenkins, J. J. Remember that old theory of memory? Well, forget it! *American Psychologist,* 1974, *29,* 785–795.

Magnusson, D., & Endler, N. S. Interactional psychology: Present status and future prospects. In D. Magnusson & N. S. Endler (Eds.), *Personality at the crossroads: Current issues in interactional psychology.* Hillsdale, N. J.: Erlbaum, 1977.

Mischel, H. N. From intention to action: The role of rule knowledge in the development of self-regulation. Presented at the Biennial Meeting of the Society for Research in Child Development, Detroit, Michigan, 1983.

Mischel, H. N., & Mischel, W. The development of children's knowledge of self-control strategies. *Child Development,* in press.

Mischel, W. Theory and research on the antecedents of self-imposed delay of reward. In B. A. Maher (Ed.), *Progress in experimental personality research.* (Vol. 3). New York: Academic Press, 1966.

Mischel, W. Toward a cognitive social learning reconceptualization of personality. *Psychological Review,* 1973, *80,* 252–283.

Mischel, W. Processes in delay of gratification. In L. Berkowitz (Ed.), *Advances in experimental social psychology* (Vol. 7). New York: Academic Press, 1974.

Mischel, W. On the future of personality measurement. *American Psychologist,* 1977, *32,* 246–254.

Mischel, W. On the interface of cognition and personality: Beyond the person–situation debate. *American Psychologist,* 1979, *34,* 740–754.

Mischel, W. Metacognition and the rules of delay. In J. Flavell & L. Ross (Eds.), *Cognitive social development: Frontiers and possible futures.* New York: Cambridge University Press, 1981.

Mischel, W. Alternatives in the pursuit of the predictability and consistency of persons: Stable data that yield unstable interpretations. *Journal of Personality,* 1983, in press.

Mischel, W., & Ebbesen, E. Attention in delay of gratification. *Journal of Personality and Social Psychology,* 1970, *16,* 329–337.

Mischel, W., Ebbesen, E., & Zeiss, A. R. Cognitive and attentional mechanisms in delay of gratification. *Journal of Personality and Social Psychology,* 1972, *21,* 204–218.

Mischel, W., & Metzner, R. Preference for delayed reward as a function of age, intelligence, and length of delay interval. *Journal of Abnormal and Social Psychology,* 1962, *64,* 425–431.

Mischel, W., & Mischel, H. N. A cognitive social learning approach to morality and self-regulation. In T. Lickona (Ed.), *Moral development and behavior: Theory, research, and social issues.* New York: Holt, 1976.

Mischel, W., & Mischel, H. N. Self-control and the self. In T. Mischel (Ed.), *The self: Psychological and philosophical issues.* Oxford, England: Basil Blackwell, 1977.

Mischel, W., & Moore, B. The role of ideation in voluntary delay for symbolically-presented rewards. *Cognitive Therapy and Research,* 1980, *4,* 211–221.

Mischel, W., & Peake, P. K. Beyond deja vu in the search for cross-situational consistency. *Psychological Review,* 1982, *89,* 730–755. (a)

Mischel, W., & Peake, P. K. In search of consistency: Measure for measure. In M. P. Zanna, E. T. Higgins, & C. P. Herman (Eds.), *Consistency in social behavior: The Ontario symposium of personality and social psychology* (Vol. 2). Hillsdale, N. J.: Erlbaum, 1982. (b)

Mischel, W., Peake, P. K., & Zeiss, A. R. *Long-term correlates of early waiting behavior.* Manuscript in preparation, Stanford University.

Mischel, W., & Staub, E. Effects of expectancy on working and waiting for larger rewards. *Journal of Personality and Social Psychology,* 1965, *2,* 625–633.

Peake, P. K., & Mischel, W. *Work as distraction: The effects of attention to rewards in working and waiting situations.* Manuscript in preparation, Stanford University.

Rotter, J. B. *Social learning and clinical psychology.* Englewood Cliffs, N. J.: Prentice-Hall, 1954.

Rotter, J. B., Chance, J. E., & Phares, E. J. (Eds.) *Applications of a social learning theory of personality.* New York: Holt, 1972.

9

Concern with One's Competence: Developmental Shifts in Person–Environment Interaction

HEINZ HECKHAUSEN

Much has been said about the "interaction" between person and situation in order to explain the seeming contradiction between intraperson consistency of behavior across situations and simultaneous situational specificity (e.g., Magnusson & Endler, 1977). The contradiction vanishes for the most part if we let the individuals themselves define the equivalence, and nonequivalence, of the situations they encounter as well as which of their behaviors are equifinal. That is, one can avoid what Bem and Allen (1974) have called the "nomothetic fallacy."

This line of reasoning is rather reassuring for trait psychologists in the tradition of Allport (1937), in that it lets behavior remain highly person specific and, at the same time, highly responsive to specific situations, as the individual perceives them. Research on achievement motivation, for instance, has been a convincing example of an interactional approach ever since its beginnings in the 1950s, although the approach has hardly been noted by motivation researchers until recently (Nygård, 1981).

However, when we turn from personality in general to personality development, the theme of this book, the problem becomes more thorny because the subjective meaning of one's own behavior and those of the situations one encounters are not preestablished but, instead, are acquired in a long string of transactions. Many meanings may still be altered by unanticipated or contradictory experiences, such that the course of development is steered in part by objective reality. Independent of what individuals expect or believe, their behavior may or may not have physical and social effects on the environment. They must grapple with the unanticipated repercussions of their doings, and by

167

HUMAN DEVELOPMENT:
AN INTERACTIONAL PERSPECTIVE

so doing they acquire new knowledge, refine old skills, and establish norms and values that incite and guide their future actions.

To conceive of ontogenetic development from a person–environment perspective is therefore more complicated than to explain why mature personalities deal with situations the way they do. Ontogenetic development capitalizes on inconsistent behaviors that, when confronted with the same situation, attain a better transactional match. The processes of assimilation and accommodation, as postulated by Piaget (1936), construct reality anew and ever more adequately in each individual's development. These processes are aided partly, and are sometimes spurred on, by an orderly sequence of maturational changes in the organism—particularly in the early span of life. In later phases of life we face normative, that is, age-related, shifts in the opportunities offered by the environment that elicit new learning and engagement as well as relearning and disengagement.

To demonstrate developmental change in person–environment interactions, I have chosen examples from three periods of the life span. My first example refers to the emergence of the self-concept of competence in the first years of life. I want to show how the attained level of self-concept development causes children to react differentially to identical kinds of interference.

My second example focuses on a late accomplishment in the development of the ability concept at the threshold of the second decade of life. With the comprehension of a compensatory causal schema, the effects of being praised or blamed for one's achievement outcomes can turn around.

The last example shows how a change in person–situation interaction may be initiated by a normative shift in responsiveness of the environment. I refer to observations about a midlife trap for successful top-level executives who are highly achievement-motivated.

The Developing Self as an Agent of Change in Coping with Interactions

It is well known from two observational studies, those by Goodenough (1931) and Kemmler (1957), that there is an early age span between $1\frac{1}{2}$ and $2\frac{1}{2}$ years during which a temper tantrum is easily aroused when the child's ongoing activity is interrupted or thwarted by a familiar adult. Kemmler has observed temper tantrums of 71 children as they occurred in the daily settings of families or institutions. Nearly all cases of temper tantrum were triggered by a request or an intervention of the adult that interfered directly with what the child was just about to do. Obviously, the blocking of the impending execution of an anticipated activity step or of the attainment of an intended goal causes a severe emergency reaction of the disruptive type.

Kemmler suggests that, in this early stage, the disruptive temper tantrum is a result of a developmental dilemma, in that two different abilities progress with uneven pace. The result is a temporary non-fit among two aspects of the child: an advanced ability to plan one's action, and a relative inability to communicate one's plans verbally or to delay them in the face of social requests. Such an explanation is corroborated by the fact that temper tantrums become increasingly rare after the age of $2\frac{1}{2}$, if one disregards temper tantrum behavior that is displayed and intentionally maintained owing to its reinforcement value.

In an early study, one of my students attempted to set up situations that would be frustrating. However, instead of blocking, the experimenter took over the child's activity with the words "I will do it now!" in order to provoke milder reactions which we called "wanting-to-do-it-oneself" (Klamma, 1957). If the task was not too difficult for the child, children who had reached the age of 2 rejected such an interference and insisted upon completing the task themselves.

One might explain the developmental shift in the child's reaction to interference with its activity as a progressive development of coping behavior. Kemmler has suggested a similar explanation for the fact that temper tantrums disappear before children reach 3 years of age. In other words, what develops are executive skills, while person and situation as well as their interaction remain basically unaltered. Progression of executive skills is the most common or at least the most popular view of how early development works. I intend to show that, at least in the present context, such a view is fallacious or, to say the least, irrelevant; in a longitudinal perspective, however, it is hard to exclude the contribution of advancing executive skills.

As Geppert and Küster (1981) have demonstrated in our laboratory, it is a development in the conception of one's own self that appears to be responsible for the age-correlated but dramatic shifts in children's reactions to interference with their ongoing activities. To put it in terms of interactional psychology: An irreversible developmental change within the person has changed the person–situation interaction with regard to objectively unaltered situations; this, in turn, leads to a shift ("inconsistency") in behavior.

As to the concept of self, ingenious tests have been designed to trace its development in children who are not yet verbal. In such tests the ability for some form of self-awareness can become manifest either by self-recognition of one's reflection in a mirror (Amsterdam, 1972; Dixon, 1957), or of other representations of the self, or by taking account of one's own body when changing its present position is required for the solution of a task.

As to self-recognition, it is worth noting that, among primates, only humans and the great apes, such as chimpanzees and orangutans, are capable of recognizing their own mirror images (Gallup, 1970). Other monkeys can learn to deal efficiently with mirror images when reaching out for reflected objects but they are unable to learn to use their own reflections in the mirror for responding to themselves (Tinklebaugh, 1928). Bertenthal and Fisher (1978) have designed mirror tasks for the developmental sequence or self-recognition of infants between 6 and 24 months of age. Lewis and Brooks-Gunn (1979) have employed, in addition, still pictures and video representations (live versus non-live) in order to infer early forms of a "categorial self." As soon as there are behavioral indexes of self-recognition, the child must already have at its disposal an image of its outer appearance, that is, of a rudimentary form of self as object, of a "categorial self."

Geppert and Küster (1981) have administered two tests for identifying the self-concept development stage. The blanket test is modeled after an observation Piaget reported about his daughter Jacqueline (Piaget, 1936, Observation No. 168). The child is placed on a blanket and asked to present the blanket to the mother. It is judged to be a positive index of a (categorial) self-concept if the child understands that it must first step off the blanket in order to be able to present it. Such a behavior corresponds to tertiary circular reactions. For this fifth stage in sensorimotor development, Piaget claims that the target object of activity can be singled out from the executive scheme of the activity so that the object can also be reached or manipulated in an altered way. To the extent that a child can single out the blanket as a target object, then, correspondingly, it should also be able to single out its own body in perceiving its momentary position as an impediment for the attainment of the task goal.

The other test was the "rouge task," which, according to Bertenthal and Fisher, is an index of the next, the sixth, stage of sensorimotor development. Unnoticed by the child, the tip of its nose was marked with rouge. It is then observed whether the children, when placed in front of a mirror, touch their noses.

In the Geppert and Küster study 41 children between 9 and 78 months of age were tested. The age between 16 and 18 months turned out to be a transitional age. Children below that age did not master both tests. For the sake of brevity I will call this stage in the development of self "the unaware self," because if there is already some sort of self, the child has not yet become aware of it. Children within the transitional age solved only the blanket test. Since these children are not yet able to recognize their images, but can already take account of their bodies in an instrumental way, this transitional stage may be called "the instrumental self." From 19 months onward all children passed both tests. I will distinguish and name two further stages in a moment.

The children were engaged in various attractive play activities such as un-packing and packing up of building blocks, doing puzzles, building a tower, and so forth. The experimenter first introduced the child to the respective activity by showing the child how to do it. Once the child was engaged in the activity, the experimenter interfered in two ways: offering unrequested help, and taking over the child's activity. Help was offered at moments when the child encountered some slight difficulty. Each of the two kinds of intervention was performed alternately in two modes, either announced in advance in question form (e.g., "May I help you?" "Will you let me do it, now?") or by an intruding action accompanied by verbal comment (e.g., "I will help you" "Now it's my turn").

All episodes were videotaped. The analysis comprised the children's reactions to the experimenter (*a*) showing the child how to do it; (*b*) offering and extending help; and (*c*) announcing and then taking over. The results showed a surprising correspondence between stage of development of self and the children's reactions to the different kinds of intervention to their ongoing activities.

The youngest children in the stage of the *unaware self* (i.e., who were still unable to take account of their impeding bodies in the blanket test and who did not recognize themselves in the mirror) accepted all kinds of intervention without protest or disturbance. They tolerated the offered and extended acts of helping and the taking over of their activities. The children in the transitional stage of the *instrumental self* (who mastered the blanket test, but not yet the rouge task) accepted both modes of help, that is, offered as well as executed. They protested, however, against announced or performed taking over. They attempted to prevent taking over by quarreling over the same object. For instance, they moved the respective toy away or grabbed back what they already had in their hands. The protest sometimes reached the level of a temper tantrum.

All other children between 1½ and 6½ years of age who had mastered both tests showed three behaviors in common. First, they were very eager to take over the task and refused to be shown at length how to do the tasks. Second, they demanded to do the last step of a task. Third, they reacted in more flexible ways to the experimenter's interventions. With increasing age they more often tolerated help and taking over in that they took account of the intervention by continuing with the next step of the action sequence. They insisted, however, on performing the last step to attain the goal. From 2½ years on, some children stated rules for cooperative taking of turns.

Besides these commonalities, there are further developmental shifts. These shifts are, on the one hand, marked by verbal indicators for two successive stages of development of self. When children protested against the experimenter's attempts to take over, those in the age group of 19 to 26 months were the youngest ones to use the personal pronoun *I* or their first names in order to make clear that they insisted upon doing the task alone. This can be interpreted as the verbal expression of a feeling of efficacy—of feeling like an *origin* (de Charms, 1968). We may therefore term this stage in the development of self the *originating self*. Older children between 2½ and 4 expanded their utterances to "I can do it" or "I am able to do it alone." These utterances reveal, in addition to the idea of originating, a self-concept of competence or, in other words, a categorial self with one of its first psychological properties, the concept of one's competence. We may therefore call this stage the *competent self*.[1]

---

[1]One may argue that it is hazardous to infer stages of self-development from the first appearance of spontaneous verbal utterances. What children say may be a belated message of what they have known or have felt for a long time. However, we have independent evidence from expressive behavior after success and failure that children hardly have at their disposal a self-concept of competence before the age of 2½ (Heckhausen, 1981, 1982).

On the other hand, the reactions to help and taking over changed correspondingly with changes in the developing self. To begin with, I should first point to the growing power of time-binding in the children's organization of their actions. While to children in the stage of the instrumental self it did not matter which action step was interfered with, children in the stage of the originating self insisted most vehemently on doing the very last step of the task themselves. In the next stage of the competent self, children went even further and wished to do the whole task until finished.

These time-binding accomplishments appear to be a progression of accomplishment, like an executive skill, and, in our present context, it is even more interesting to consider the effects of the two different kinds of interventions on children. Help and taking over had contrasting effects in the two stages of originating and competent self. Let us first consider help. Whether offered or extended without a prior offer, help was accepted nearly invariably by the children in the stage of the originating self, whereas taking over (i.e., being put temporarily out of business) made them angry at the experimenter. In the subsequent stage of the competent self, however, the impact of both interventions had reversed. With the emergence of a self-concept of competence from $2\frac{1}{2}$ years on, offered help had become the threatening event, whereas taking over was in most cases placidly accepted while the child continued the task (as the child also did when help was simply given without asking). This contrast is further highlighted by behavior differences in the face of task difficulties. The younger children in the first three stages of self-development (the unaware, instrumental, and partly originating selves) asked the experimenter for help. Children in the stage of the competent self did not ask for help but increased, instead, their persistence. Instead of tolerating the receipt of help, they preferred to choose the active role in helping, and actually helped the experimenter.

The interpretation of the development-based alterations in the behavior-arousing properties of the same situation appears to be straightforward. For the competent self, the acceptance of help devalues the intensely felt sense of one's competence, whereas letting another person "take a turn" does not throw into question one's competence. In the earlier stage of the originating self, giving up the task activity to another person to become inactive is a threat, whereas receiving help while one is still active does not spoil the pleasure in pursuing the goal.

It is evident from the reported findings that early development cannot always and only be conceived of as an inevitable progression of executive skills. Some developments consist of dramatic shifts of the meaning of the situations, that is, transformations of motivating incentives. In our example, the meaning of offered help or taking over of one's own activity by another person changed substantially, as could be inferred from behavioral reactions. The orderly sequence went, first, from the general indifference of the unaware self to the agitated defense of the instrumental and originating selves against an intruder's attempts to take over the child's ongoing activity, and, finally, to the rejection of help from the competent self. The agent of change of all of these transmutations is the young individual's developing awareness of self.

A Developmental Step Reversing the Implications of Being Praised or Blamed

With the emergence of the self-describing category of competence at age $2\frac{1}{2}$, a long development of the concept of ability begins. Adults—and among them psychologists, too—conceive of ability as constant within individuals but variable between individuals. Unlike the concept of effort, which is variable within individuals, the concept of ability can hardly be experienced by the individual as actor. Rather, it is a construct explaining why people differ with respect to handling difficulties of tasks that they still do master, and also why it is that these observed rank orders in competence remain stable across time and across repeated social comparisons.

It takes 7 to 10 years for children to conceive of ability as a dispositional construct in the sense of an internal and stable cause of their own achievement outcomes. A firm indication for such an accomplishment is the mastering of the causal schema of compensation (Kelley, 1972); this means that, to a certain extent, a lack of ability can be compensated for by effort and persistence (effort compensation), and a lack of effort or persistence by ability (ability compensation).

The mastery of the compensatory causal schema has been tested using different procedures. Nicholls (1978) showed children between the ages of 5 and 13 several films, that, with social comparison, displayed violations of a simple covariation between amount of effort and outcomes. In the first film, two children achieved the same outcomes, although the first, older, child worked continuously and the second only part of the time. In the second film, the child who worked only part of the time achieved a better outcome than the older child. Afterward, the subjects were asked (*a*) if both children in the film had exerted the same or different amounts of effort; (*b*) if they were equally smart, or if one was smarter than the other; (*c*) if the results would have been the same if the first child had worked hard but the other had not; and (*d*) who would do better if they both really exerted themselves.

Using a content analysis, answers were assigned to one of four stages. These stages appear to correspond to Piaget's sequence ranging from preoperational thought to formal operation and are roughly summarized as follows: *Stage I*—a global concept of competence, with an undifferentiated mixture of effort, ability, and outcome, centering on visible differences in effort or outcome (most 5- and 6-year-olds); *Stage II*—covariation of effort and outcome, effort alone causes the outcome (most 7- through 9-year-olds); *Stage III*—ability begins to be seen as autonomous, but still tends to be coupled with effort, and there are clear signs of ability compensation (most 10-year-olds); *Stage IV*— systematic use of ability compensation, and the idea that ability can compensate for lack of effort in explaining as well as predicting outcomes (12 years and older).

Another procedure to test for both schemata of compensation gives the child information about the outcome and either of the two causal factors and asks for the magnitude of the other causal factor. Effort compensation has been observed in children between 5 and 10 years of age, but ability compensation always emerges at a later age, roughly between 6 and 12 years (Karabenick & Heller, 1976; Kun, 1977; Surber, 1980; Tweer, 1976). Generally, the compensatory causal schema will appear earlier if the information given to the child is as simple as possible and is aided visually (i.e., appears in the format of a story) and if the dependent variable is assessed by paired comparison, not by scaling. Still more important, there is an orderly sequence in which false responses are also revealing (see Heckhausen, 1982). Younger children tend to infer effort from outcome by letting effort covary with outcome (and neglect the given information about ability). Older children let effort correctly compensate for fixed levels of ability; however, they are not yet able to compensate for fixed levels of effort with the necessary amount of ability. Instead, they let ability covary with the given levels of effort and neglected the outcome given.

Figure 1 represents cross-sectional data obtained by Tweer (1976) on the development of the compensatory causal schema and of the two wrong responses: ability inferred as a covariate from effort, and effort inferred as a covariate from outcome. Tweer had her subjects perform first a real task of "ring the bell." After the subjects had practiced for some time they were asked to compare two hypothetical cases with (in Fig. 1) equal outcomes and either one of the two causal factors. As can be seen, 6-year-olds inferred ability as a

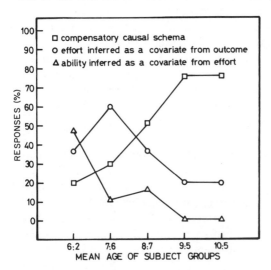

Figure 1. *Percentage of correct responses (compensatory causal schema) and of false responses (effort inferred as a covariate from outcome; ability inferred as a covariate from effort) in five age groups between the ages of 6 and 10. [After Tweer, 1976, p. 58.]*

covariate of the given levels of effort, whereas most 7-year-olds let effort covary with the given levels of outcome. Both false responses clear the way for the emergence of the compensatory causal schema that was used by the majority of the 9-year-olds.

From the various studies cited earlier, we may draw the following conclusions:

1. Young children tend to perceive effort, rather than ability, as correlated with outcomes.
2. They derive ability from effort rather than the reverse, effort from ability.
3. They do not yet distinguish sufficiently between ability and effort; effort appears to play the major role in a diffuse competence concept.
4. The compensation of ability through effort precedes the compensation of effort through ability.
5. The transitional age span during which children attain full mastery of the compensatory causal schema extends from 9 to 13 years.
6. Within the same age span, realistic self-ratings of attainment levels in school closely correlate with the attained stage of development of ability compensation (Nicholls, 1978).

Thus far I have sketched the cognitive development that initially protects the young child against depressing inferences of a lack of one's competence. This stage of development eventually results in the turning around, or reversal, of the child's affective reactions to praise and blame. The protective function rests on the young child's systematic error to infer ability from exerted effort. The more effort is expended at an easy task, even to attain a modest result, the more able will the young child perceive himself or herself.

With such a happy reasoning error, it is hard to discourage young children when tasks require high effort and long persistence. Rholes, Blackwell, Jordan, and Walters (1980) have investigated the extent to which a long series of failures can make children between 5 and 11 years of age "helpless," as manifested by deterioration of performance and decrease of persistence. The helplessness-inducing program of Rholes *et al.* succeeded only in the oldest age group of 10- and 11-year olds. These fifth-graders, as the only age group, already had at their disposal a compensatory causal schema. In all other age groups, most children inferred their ability from the expended effort. This was particularly the case among the 5- and 6-year-olds, who even after repeated failure showed no greater drop in estimated ability than did a comparison group under a success condition.

Similarly, young children draw benign but erroneous conclusions about their competence when they are praised by an adult for a successful achievement outcome. Many studies have shown that children are not just praised for any success and blamed for any failure. Adults also take into account the perceived causes of the outcome, as has been shown, for instance, by Weiner and Kukla (1970) and by Rest, Nierenberg, Weiner, and Heckhausen (1973). A success is praised all the more explicitly the more it can be attributed to effort to the exclusion of ability, because compensating for what is beyond one's ability through an outburst of effort is seen as clearly laudable. Conversely, a failure is blamed the more explicit the less it can be attributed to the child's lack of ability than to lack of effort or persistence.

As far as children become aware (and there is no reason to assume that they do not) that an adult bases praise and blame mainly on cues for effort attribution or lack thereof, respectively, they infer from praise given to hard-attained success that the adult perceives them to be incompetent and, conversely, from blame at a negligent failure that the adult regards them to be competent. While attribution to effort is decisive for the evaluation of an achievement outcome by another person, it has repeatedly been found that, in self-evaluation, attribution to ability generates more affect than does attribution to effort (Heckhausen, 1978; see compiled evidence in Heckhausen, 1980).

However, as soon as children are able to grasp the compensatory causal schema, a praised success conveys to them that, in the opinion of the praising adult, the mastered task has nearly overtaxed their ability and a blamed failure indicates a task difficulty for whose mastery they possess sufficient ability. By this token, praise indicates that one's competence has approached its limits, and blame contains the reassuring message that the respective failure should not be mistaken as a sign of a lack of ability. If there are, in addition, independent cues for the difficulty level of task, the child can directly infer what the praising or blaming adult thinks of the child's ability. The most distressing inference about one's ability results from being praised for solving a very easy task, and the most ego-boosting inference results from being blamed for failing a very difficult task.

In several studies, Meyer (1978, 1982; Meyer, Bachmann, Biermann, Hempelmann, Plöger, & Spiller, 1979) has confirmed the negative effects of praise for success at easy tasks as well as the positive effects of blame for failure at difficult tasks, using perception of one's ability as a dependent variable. In one simple study, for instance, the subjects were informed that two students were successful at a very easy task that everybody in the class should be capable of mastering (Meyer, 1978). However, the teacher reacted differently to the two students: one of them was praised, but the other was informed merely that his result was correct. The subjects had then to indicate which of the two students the teacher regarded as more able.

As Table 1 shows, most subjects beyond 10 to 12 years of age based their judgments on the compensatory causal schema: They believed that in the teacher's view the nonpraised student was more able than the praised student. In other studies on the effects of blame, of unrequested help, and of the assignment of easier tasks, Meyer (1982) has collected corresponding findings. The dependent variables range from ratings of ability to ratings of probability of success and of affect.

Table 1
Percentages of Subjects in Successive Age Groups Who Regard the Praised or the Non-praised Student to Be More Able in the Eyes of the Teacher

Grade	Age (years)	N	Student regarded to be more able (%)	
			Non-praised	Praised
3	8–9	27	19	81
4	9–10	25	56	44
5	10–11	55	56	44
6	12–13	17	47	53
7	13–14	18	56	44
8	14–15	15	80	20
9	15–16	19	84	16
12 13	17–19	43	81	19

Note: From Meyer (1978, p. 77).

Although we do not yet have longitudinal data or case studies, we may assume that some children stumble into a self-esteem crisis when the compensatory relation between ability and effort suddenly dawns upon them for the first time and the teacher's generous praise implies bad news. At any rate, we should be struck and satisfied by the wisdom of development that protects so long the less able children against the negative implications of being praised for success and not being blamed for failure at an easy task. However, other indirect communications from adults to children that unintentionally may carry messages of low ability—such as excessive but unrequested help or the expression of pity for failure (Weiner, Meyer, & Taylor, in press)—are perhaps already understood at an earlier age. The asynchronic effects of such different situations must be traced longitudinally in order to discover when these situations become equivalent in the child's perception and how they interfere with each other in the child's earlier experience.

A Midlife Trap for Achievement-Motivated Executives at the Top Level

Before presenting some observations, I will dwell first on a theoretical point, namely, a clarification of the term "outcome." I wish to underscore a basic distinction between how far the attainment of a goal depends on one's own competencies and how far it depends on the responsiveness of the environment. For more than two decades, research on achievement motivation has neglected such a distinction between outcome and consequence, whereby outcome is dependent on an individual's competence while consequence is contingent on a certain outcome but dependent on the responsiveness of the environment. It is notable that applied research in industrial psychology has stimulated the recognition of this distinction, namely, in Vroom's (1964) instrumentality theory.

Meanwhile, I also make a strict distinction between action outcome and outcome consequences, and I further assume that all of the motivating incentives reside in the outcome consequences and not in the action outcome per se (Heckhausen, 1977). Outcome consequences, intended and anticipated, are therefore the ultimate criteria for equifinality in the interaction of people with their environments. The consequences help us to sort situations as well as behaviors into classes of equivalence for the individual.

How can a distinction between outcome and its consequences be justified? Besides a notable increase in predictive power (Heckhausen & Rheinberg, 1980), there are three evidently compelling reasons for the distinction. First, each single action outcome elicits, as a rule, several incentive-laden consequences. Second, the same outcome has, as a rule, different consequences for different individuals. Third, outcomes can be influenced directly by the individual (e.g., by ability, effort, etc.), but many outcome consequences cannot be influenced so directly because they depend on the responsiveness of the environment, that is, on built-in contingency regularities of the social world. (Therefore, we must distinguish between at least two kinds of expectancies: action-outcome expectancy, for which the individual can be held responsible, and outcome-consequence expectancy, or instrumentality, for which environmental forces, not the individual, can be held responsible.)

However, one must distinguish between different classes of consequences, each with their respective instrumentalities. One important class consists of self-evaluative emotions, such as pride or shame after a successful or unsuccessful action outcome, respectively. Such consequences are achieved by the individuals themselves and are independent of the responsiveness of the environment, and they depend on the discrepancy between the outcome and the personal standard as well as on the causal attribution of the outcome. Other classes of motivating consequences, however, are mediated by the environment, such as evaluation and reward by others, approaching supraordinate goals, or emerging extrinsic side effects. All of these have their specific incentive values and their respective outcome-consequences instrumentalities (which may vary between +1 and −1, where −1 indicates that a certain outcome totally precludes a desired consequence).

I will not go into how all of these value and expectancy terms are combined into a motivation model predicting action (see Heckhausen, 1977). For what follows I want to stress only the distinction between the action outcome and its incentive-laden consequences, both of which are confounded in such popular constructs as Rotter's (1966) "personal control." We can disaggregate this construct into its core notion of action-outcome control and take the other component, instrumentality of outcome for desired consequences, as a separate issue. However, since personal control in the sense of action-outcome control becomes useless when the established instrumentality for desired consequences breaks down or becomes unpredictable, there is an indirect loss of action control, which might be called "hopelessness" (not helplessness) or resignation; both of these result in disengagement or even in disengagement cycles as Klinger (1975) has described them. In contrast, helplessness ensues when one realizes one's own inability to achieve the intended outcome.

I also wish to point to a few regular disengagement phenomena in the highly specific setting of large corporations in capitalist countries. These phenomena derive from an interaction between personality factors (different motives) and a segment of the life course that is keyed to age for certain occupational roles. The evidence that I report is anecdotal but suggestive and was accumulated over quite a few courses, each lasting several days and given for top-level business executives of large corporations.

The courses were intended to determine each participant's stage of life cycle. The total sample consisted of about 150 male volunteers between 45 and 55 years of age. The courses were offered by a prestigious agency in a European capital. All observations were made by Siegbert Krug, a co-worker of mine who served as trainer in these courses.

At the beginning of each course, Thematic Apperception Test (TAT) motive measures were taken, among them the needs for power and achievement. Roughly three motive patterns turned out to be typical for this group of course participants: About 50% of them were dominated more by concerns for power than for achievement—let us call them power-motivated. For 30% of the participants the reverse was true: They had a strong achievement motive and a weak power motive—let us call them achievement-motivated. The remaining 20% scored high on both motives.

A few words are in order concerning the two motive measures and their real-life correlates. The dominance of each of the two motives refers to a separate domain of current concerns, of predominant incentives, and of specific competencies (see Heckhausen, 1980).

A dominant achievement motive is directed toward challenging tasks, is fundamentally not a social motive, and has to do with competing with standards of excellence—doing better than other people or than the individual has done before.

A dominant power motive is directed toward persons, groups, or institutions and incites these individuals to acts that will ultimately serve certain goals transcending individualistic concerns or self-interest, for example, the productivity of a work group, the benefit of the company, a group climate of comfortableness or of enthusiasm, and the stabilization of social structures and their effectiveness. All of this resembles McClelland's (1975) notion of "social power"; that is, the power is not coercive or egoistic. The individual evinces strong interest in having other people act in the service of a certain common goal. Specific abilities of power-motivated executives are high social competence; a quick awareness of other people's motive bases, that is, of those incentives that make them behave in a way they would not do otherwise; keen empathy; veridical motivation attribution; and skills for smooth and agreeable social interactions.

The results show that course participants can be distinguished according to two levels of success thus far achieved. A first group is successful, but not as much as would have been possible. The supraordinate goal of being promoted successively to the highest probable level is, at their stage of life, no longer attainable. Accidental factors aside (such as timely openings), the corporations' promotion policies are based on two rules. The first is the wisdom of a rather naive developmental psychology: people become less dynamic as they get older. The second is of an economical nature: Further investments in preparing an individual for higher level positions have diminishing returns the older the person is.

The achievement-motivated executives in this group bitterly experienced a contradiction between the two kinds of personal control: They were still highly effective and attained excellent action outcomes so that personal control as to action-outcome expectancy was still intact and self-confident. On the other hand, excellent action outcomes were no longer followed by the consequences striven for, namely, a steady rise in position, responsibility, and competence-related prestige. The outcome-consequence expectancy decreased to zero. It no longer mattered as much how competent or efficient they were in achievement-related terms. Most of the motivating, incentive-laden feedback loops, such as promotions, raises, new and more challenging tasks, and so forth, had broken down, with the single exception of self-evaluative consequences, but these are ordinarily highly contingent on evaluative consequences mediated by superiors and agencies of the corporation. These executives finally saw their abstract, supraordinate goals slipping from their grasp. With all of their professional and specialized competencies and merits, they felt blocked and hopeless, and they felt resignation. Ironically, their bitterness reinforced the corporations' decisions to decline further promotion.

The power-motivated executives in this group presented another picture. They had not been as successful as their achievement-motivated colleagues. For them, achievement-related accomplishments had only instrumental or extrinsic incentive values, in order to rise within the power structure of the corporation to such levels where work roles lose their specificity in favor of a general leadership, of assigning others to tasks so as to maximize efficiency, etc. When they became aware that they would not make it to the top, their fate was usually less gloomy because they made use of compensatory activities in power structures outside their corporations. They became leading figures in many sorts of political and quasi-political associations and societies (some corporations explicitly support such compensatory activity outlets).

In a study on 68 medium-level executives of a large chemical corporation, Börgens (1980), a student of mine, collected data on compensatory changes during midlife. She studied three age groups: up to 39, 40–49, and older than 50. Börgens found an age-related linear drop in power-related incentives, such as influence, prestige, promotion, and leadership responsibility, as well as in achievement-related incentives, such as work satisfaction and self-evaluation. Correspondingly, there was an increase in other incentive values, such as extra-occupational interests, leisure time, cooperation with colleagues, and salary.

The question in this study is whether an age-dependent drop in power-related opportunities leads to a reorientation in favor of extraoccupational self-actualization values. Such a process would appear to be compensatory—implying disengagement from goals that appear to be no longer attainable. The causality could, of course, operate the other way around: Extraoccupational self-actualization incentives could gain in strength with age in their own right. The latter possibility would represent a benign kind of self-management.

The answer is that not only did the incentive values drop, but the respective instrumentalities did also—particularly in the middle-aged group of 40 to 49. The correlation between the two variables was .52. Therefore, a realistic and adaptive disengagement appears to be the best guess for these cross-sectional data.

Returning to the training course observations, I will now discuss the larger group of course participants, those who had reached the highest level of promotion realistically to be attained. The achievement-motivated people among them had reached their supraordinate goal. However, their ceiling position confronted them with a drastic change in occupational demands. There were no longer achievement-related and innovative challenges. If there were such tasks they would already be delegated to other persons—to subordinates. These participants were keeping themselves free from all specific tasks, free from their mastery-oriented incentives in order to ensure a generalist's all-around view. In short, achievement-motivated incentives dropped out and power-motivated goals were called for, along with the respective competencies. They now had to motivate other people, to bolster their positions within the power structure, to develop a feeling for delicate balances between sub-institutions within the corporation, to improve the relations among the many forces within and without, etc.

As a result, they were faced with a threefold loss of personal control. First, they had lost the motivating incentives of their achievement-related supraordinate goals as well as of their self-evaluative satisfactions. Second, with regard to the power-related objectives that were instead required, the respective action-outcome expectancies were alarmingly low: these individuals lacked self-efficacy and even felt repulsed by the activities necessary for the power game. Moreover, they had difficulties in abstaining from achievement-related actions and delegating them to specialized subordinates. Thus, they became hooked on niceties, as seen from their present position. Third, if they attempted the power game, they turned out to be rather inexperienced and clumsy. Therefore, whatever they did—whether they played the achievement or the power game—the respective outcome-consequences expectancies tended to be rather low and insecure, although for different reasons in both cases. With respect to achievement success, the environment became unresponsive, and with respect to power-related actions success was improbable.

For these executives the changed occupational demands constituted a depressing state of relative hopelessness, which often was increased by bitter reflection on the past. They became aware that they had sacrificed their families, friendships, leisure time, and hobbies in the service of high achievements and rapid advancements. Moreover, some of them began to face problems within their neglected families, with bitter wives and children leaving home. Some began to think of quitting the corporation to set up their own small firms, but ran into the problem of lack of financial support.

Quite the contrary held for the power-motivated executives. After they had worked hard but without inner devotion for many years, they had finally "made it." They began to bloom and devote their full capacities and time to their new occupational roles. They experienced a remarkable increase in personal control, that is, in action-outcome expectancies as well as in outcome-consequence expectancies. The top position finally opened for them all of the power resources they had sought during their lifetimes.

Finally, in regard to the small group of executives who were strong in both motives, their life situation was still somewhat unclear. However, I can safely say that they had particular leadership difficulties because they set extremely high standards for their co-workers. Therefore, they were rather unpopular with their workers and were unable to create a climate of high morale and dedication, a climate that their power-motivated colleagues with weaker achievement motives were so able to create.

The picture I have drawn is, of course, somewhat simplified and exaggerated but, as I said, suggestive, though of course cross-sectional. We do not yet know how successful individuals ultimately cope with such radical and age-bound shifts, if not reversals, in the occupational opportunity structures as presented in the environment of large business corporations. One may wonder how much achievement-motivated executives may struggle to extricate themselves from the trap that appears in their careers after a long sequence of successes. What we now need are longitudinal observations.

Conclusions

The three examples given are apt to underscore the fact that concern with one's competence is a lifelong theme in people's interactions with their environments, a theme that is often called achievement motivation. In addition, I have tried to make a special point with each of the three examples.

The first example demonstrated a developing sequence of interactions that is not constricted to the development of executive skills. Instead, personality development takes the lead in transmuting established interactions. In this sense, the developing self-concept dramatically changes the effects of interfering interventions on the reactions of toddlers.

The second example showed how progress in information integration skills entirely reverses the behavioral implications of environmental feedback. Outcome-contingent praise and blame are eventually, and then irreversibly, appraised in a more veridical way. We are mistaken if we regard praise and blame to be nothing but sheer and invariable reinforcers.

The third example of a midlife trap stresses the distinction between action outcome and outcome consequences in order to understand more fully person–environment interactions. The environment may offer or withhold its responsiveness to certain personal endeavors and accomplishments according to normative rules for age-bound positions and domains.

I note finally that the first two examples refer to universal developments of the early life cycle, whereas the third example reveals interindividual differences in the developmental fate of later phases of the life cycle. Developmental fates, such as the described midlife crisis (which results in altered interactions with the environment), are normative and depend on age, but they are not universal or inevitable. In principle, they can be changed and overcome either by redesigning the opportunity structures of the environment or by rearranging the person's primary concerns.

Acknowledgment

I am grateful to Robert A. Wicklund for helpful comments while preparing the manuscript.

References

Allport, G. W. *Personality: A psychological interpretation.* New York: Holt, 1937.
Amsterdam, B. Mirror self-image reactions before age two. *Developmental Psychobiology,* 1972, *5,* 297–305.
Bem, D. J., & Allen, A. On predicting some of the people some of the time: The search for cross-situational consistencies in behavior. *Psychological Review,* 1974, *81,* 506–520.
Bertenthal, B. I., & Fisher, K. W. Development of self-recognition in the infant. *Developmental Psychology,* 1978, *14,* 44–50.
Börgens, B. Wechselwirkungen zwischen individueller Motivstruktur und betrieblichen Anreizbedingungen. Diplomarbeit, Psychologisches Institut der Ruhr-Universität. Bochum, 1980.
de Charms, R. *Personal causation.* New York: Academic Press, 1968.
Dixon, J. Development of self recognition. *Journal of Genetic Psychology,* 1957, *91,* 251–256.
Gallup, G. G., Jr. Chimpanzees: Self-recognition. *Science,* 1970, *167,* 86–87.
Geppert, U., & Küster, U. *The emergence of "wanting to do it oneself": A precursor of achievement motivation. International Journal of Behavioral Development* (in press).
Goodenough, F. L. Anger in young children. *University of Minnesota Institute of Child Welfare Monographs,* 1931, No. 9.

Heckhausen, H. Achievement motivation and its constructs: A cognitive model. *Motivation and Emotion*, 1977, *1*, 283–329.

Heckhausen, H. Selbstbewertung nach erwartungswidrigem Leistungsverlauf: Einfluß von Motiv, Kausalattribution und Zielsetzung. *Zeitschrift für Entwicklungspsychologie und Pädagogische Psychologie*, 1978, *10*, 191–216.

Heckhausen, H. *Motivation und Handeln*. Berlin: Springer, 1980.

Heckhausen, H. Developmental precursors of success and failure experience. In G. d'Ydewalle & W. Lens (Eds.), *Cognition in human motivation and learning*. Leuven: Leuven University Press; Hillsdale, N. J.: Erlbaum, 1981. Pp. 15–32.

Heckhausen, H. The development of achievement motivation. In W. W. Hartup (Ed.), *Review of child development research* (Vol. 6). Chicago: University of Chicago Press, 1982.

Heckhausen, H., & Rheinberg, F. Lernmotivation, erneut betrachtet. *Unterrichtswissenschaft*, 1980, *8*, 7–47.

Karabenick, J. D., & Heller, K. A. A developmental study of effort and ability attributions. *Developmental Psychology*, 1976, *12*, 559–560.

Kelley, H. H. *Causal schemata and the attribution process*. New York: General Learning Press, 1972.

Kemmler, L. Untersuchung über den frühkindlichen Trotz. *Psychologische Forschung*, 1957, *25*, 279–338.

Klamma, M. Über das Selbermachenwollen und Ablehnen von Hilfen bei Kleinkindern. Vordiplomarbeit, Psychologisches Institut der Universität, Münster, 1957.

Klinger, E. Consequences of commitment to and disengagement from incentives. *Psychological Review*, 1975, *82*, 1–25.

Kun, A. Development of the magnitude-covariation and compensation schemata in ability and effort attributions of performance. *Child Development*, 1977, *48*, 862–873.

Lewis, M., & Brooks-Gun, J. *Social cognition and the acquisition of self*. New York: Plenum, 1979.

McClelland, D. C. *Power: The inner experience*. New York: Irvington, 1975.

Magnusson, D., & Endler, N. S. (Eds.), *Personality at the crossroads: Current issues in interactional psychology*. Hillsdale, N. J.: Erlbaum, 1977.

Meyer, W. -U. Der Einfluß von Sanktionen auf Begabungsperzeptionen. In D. Görlitz, W. -U. Meyer, & B. Weiner (Eds.), *Bielefelder Symposium über Attribution*. Stuttgart: Klett-Cotta, 1978. Pp. 71–87.

Meyer, W. -U. Indirect communications about perceived ability estimates. *Journal of Educational Psychology*, 1982, *74*, 888–897.

Meyer, W. -U., Bachmann, M., Biermann, U., Hempelmann, M., Plöger, F. -O., & Spiller, H. The informational value of evaluative behavior: Influences of praise and blame on perceptions of ability. *Journal of Educational Psychology*, 1979, *71*, 259–268.

Nicholls, J. G. The development of the concepts of effort and ability, perception of academic attainment, and the understanding that difficult tasks require more ability. *Child Development*, 1978, *49*, 800–814.

Nygård, R. Toward an interactional psychology: Models from achievement motivation research. *Journal of Personality*, 1981, *49*, 363–387.

Piaget, J. *La naissance de l'intelligence chez l'enfant*. Neuchâtel: Delachaux et Niestlé, 1936.

Rest, S., Nierenberg, R., Weiner, B., & Heckhausen, H. Further evidence concerning the effects of perception of effort and ability on achievement evaluation. *Journal of Personality and Social Psychology*, 1973, *28*, 187–191.

Rholes, W. S., Blackwell, J., Jordan, C., & Walters, C. A. A developmental study of learned helplessness. *Developmental Psychology*, 1980, *16*, 616–624.

Rotter, J. B. Generalized expectancies for internal versus external control of reinforcement. *Psychological Monographs*, 1966, *80* (1, Whole No. 609).

Surber, C. F. The development of reversible operations in judgments of ability, effort, and performance. *Child Development*, 1980, *51*, 1018–1029.

Tinklebaugh, O. L. An experimental study of representative factors in monkeys. *Journal of Comparative Psychology*, 1928, *8*, 197–236.

Tweer, R. Das Ökonomieprinzip in der Anstrengungskalkulation: Eine entwicklungspsychologische Untersuchung. Diplomarbeit, Psychologisches Institut, Ruhr-Universität, Bochum, 1976.

Vroom, V. H. *Work and motivation*. New York: Wiley, 1964.

Weiner, B., & Kukla, A. An attributional analysis of achievement motivation. *Journal of Personality and Social Psychology*, 1970, *15*, 1–20.

Weiner, B., Meyer, W. -U., & Taylor, E. S. Social cognition in the classroom. *Harvard Educational Review*, (in press).

10

Person–Situation Interactions in Human Development: Cognitive Factors and Coping Strategies[1]

IRWIN G. SARASON   BARBARA R. SARASON

The viewpoint that behavior is the product of the interaction of the person and the situation, and that in many contexts neither element is as important as their interactions, has been a productive one for psychological research. However, merely looking at behavior as the joint product of person variables and situational factors may be unnecessarily limiting. In this chapter, we (*a*) discuss the idea of person–situation–behavior relationships within interactional systems; (*b*) examine and exemplify person–situation interaction from a developmental perspective; and (*c*) provide research examples of interventions within person–situation–behavior systems.

Person–Situation Interactions

Behavior sometimes seems to be a product of stable person variables, while at other times it seems to be powerfully influenced by situational factors (Magnusson & Endler, 1977). This fact has been discussed and explained by reference to cognitive processes (e.g., how the situation is perceived, expectations, competencies).

Rather than being viewed as producing an end state or outcome, the person–situation interaction can be viewed as a part of a system in which each interaction may alter both the person's typical response and his or her subse-

[1]Preparation of this chapter was supported by the United States Office of Naval Research Contract N00014-80-C-0522, NR170-908.

quent perception of the situation. To put it another way, the person interacts with the situation, and the resultant behavior alters the person's perception of his or her own characteristics and of the next situation in a kind of self-perpetuation of change.

Looked at in terms of this paradigm, elements of both continuity and change in personality can be understood. In some ways, this idea is similar to a basic idea of learning theory, that reinforcement or the lack of it changes the expectancy for response. But this Person × Situation (P×S) view differs in the prominence it gives to the cognitive element. The response is different not just because of the expectancy of reinforcement, but because the reinforcement or experience may change what a person thinks both about his or her competencies and about a particular type of situation. This kind of analysis leads to the conclusion, reached by researchers in a variety of fields, that the way people think about situations and their competencies with respect to situations change both their view of the situations and their responses (Beck, 1974; Ellis, 1962; Meichenbaum, 1977; Sarason & Sarason, 1981a).

These changes can occur for a number of reasons. It may be that a person's attributions are altered. For example, a noisy environment has negative performance effects or stress-producing qualities for those people who feel the situation is not under their control (Glass & Singer, 1972; Schmidt & Keating, 1979). Those people who believe they can control the noise level do not report stress, and their behavior is not adversely affected. The same is true of reaction to crowded environments (Gochman, 1977). With a change in view about controllability of the situation may come a change from interfering, non-task-related thoughts to those that are task related (Sarason, 1973). Preoccupation with worries, other thoughts unrelated to the task, or even generalized thoughts of self-reassurance ("it doesn't matter anyhow") can have deleterious effects on performance (Sarason & Stoops, 1978; Siegel & Loftus, 1978). Why is performance affected? It may be because valuable time is used that should be devoted to problem solving. It may also be that necessary cues in the situation are distorted or not perceived accurately because of the preoccupations of the individual.

Interactions and Continuity versus Change

How do these ideas fit in with personality change? A survey of the data available on change and continuity in personality and adaptation of the individual leads us to the conclusion that both continuity and change are characteristics that are predominantly determined by (a) the point or points in the life span on which one is focusing (that is, whether the focus is on a stage or a transition period); (b) what general environmental factors are present at the time; (c) what characteristics are studied; and (d) the particular persons selected for study.

Knowledge of these parameters is important for anyone interested in investigating the issue of continuity and change. It also behooves researchers interested in interventions pointed toward behavior change to take these factors into account in deciding on populations and variables for study. What does this mean in practical terms? First, it means that researchers should look at periods of developmental transition as likely spots for intervention. Schaeffer and Bayley (1960), in their investigation of young children, pointed to the great changes from one developmental period to another. Levinson (1978), in his investigation of a quite different sample, adult males, also presented data that suggest that there are periods of considerable flux between developmental stages, and that these include changes by the person in ways of dealing with the environment. In his studies of young children, Kagan has concluded that the only personality characteristic that endures from childhood to adulthood is passivity, or, as he more recently tentatively termed it, "inhibition in the face of uncertainty [1982, p. 18]."

When we apply the interactionist paradigm discussed earlier to development, the relationship of person and situation might be stated as follows: While certain things have to be possible for development to take place, *development makes certain things possible.* To say this another way, many stage theorists (e.g., Piaget) believe that certain maturational changes must have occurred before a gain in development, as defined by transition to another developmental stage, is possible. It also seems clear that, in addition to a particular degree of maturation, certain kinds of skills of a learned variety must be present to enable an individual to cope successfully with environmental challenges. Whether the coping process is successful or not is also a factor in whether development will take place, since one aspect of development is change in self-appraisal of personal competence.

We can define coping as the ability to respond effectively to the environment. Several factors contribute to this effective response: the ability to assess the environment accurately, the possession of the requisite skills needed to deal with the situation, and, finally, the inclination or confidence to use those skills in the situation. We might express these last two ideas as both knowing what to do and how to do it and having the appropriate cognitive set, that is, for task-oriented action rather than for internal monitoring or preoccupation.

Intervention and Person–Situation Interaction Systems

The remainder of this chapter will deal with two research projects that illustrate how interventions using the interactionist viewpoint, with special emphasis on cognitive coping mechanisms, can be linked to the concepts of development of the individual throughout his or her life span (especially the idea of stages and transition periods) and the impact of life events.

A basic component of the studies to be discussed is the emphasis on accurate perception of the environment. Inaccuracy is defined here as deviation from the consensus view of the relevant reference group. Why do people perceive the environment inaccurately? Individuals may lack information that enables them to know what to look for. For example, some people can accurately gauge their peers' view of a situation, but have no awareness of the point of view or the internal agenda of non-peers. A second reason for inaccurate perception is preoccupation with an internal agenda that dominates the person's attention. These preoccupations may be peculiar to specific situations in which an individual believes his or her skills are lacking, or they may be generalized, as in the case in which they are associated with a particular cognitive style, such as self-attributions of generalized helplessness (Abramson, Seligman, & Teasdale, 1978; Hammen & Krantz, 1976). Both those who lack knowledge and those whose appraisals are inaccurate can profit by being taught alternative coping responses. For those in the first group, this should result in supplying a skill they do not possess. In the second group, such training should help to change the focus from ineffective cognitions to those that enable already existing skills to be utilized.

The developmental-stage paradigm has pointed toward certain age-related transition points where different behaviors tend to appear. Consensus has not been achieved as to whether environmental factors also typically impinge more heavily at those points. In addition to these maturational landmarks, points of change may originate from situationally based stressors. Some of these events may be related to age. They may take the form of institutionally related events, such as entering a new school level. Some may be independent of age, for example, a serious accident. Other events may be only somewhat related to age, for example, those in which considerable choice exists but which have higher probabilities during certain age periods. These include such things as joining a new organization, marriage, and parenthood. All these types of events present a series of challenges to the individual that are likely to demand responses not already in the behavioral repertoire. Perhaps more important, they are likely to demand new cognitions from the individual relating to personal competencies and to the understanding of new situational demands. This approach stretches the idea of transitional periods to include both person (age) and situational (life-change) factors.

Another important developmental idea is that behavior and competencies are mutable throughout the entire life span, not just during the early years (Schaie & Strother, 1968). A third important consideration in promoting change is that of *salience*. The success of intervention depends not only on timing but on whether the person is interested in behavior change. For this to be the case, the individual must perceive the situation as one in which change is required and, furthermore, as one in which change can be useful. The change must also be perceived as possible. Thus, the cognitive appraisal of the situation is critical.

The interactionist model described earlier predicts that new cognitive appraisals can result in replacement of one behavior by another in a particular situation. This change can also generalize to other situations, because the person then perceives his or her own competencies differently. A different interaction pattern in a new situation may result both because of new approach methods and because of new perceptions of the situation.

THE HIGH SCHOOL STUDY

This intervention study involved students from an inner-city high school (Sarason & Sarason, 1981a). Most of these students were in the ninth grade, a period of transition between the different cognitive and social demands of middle school and high school. The students were also making the transition between early and late adolescence.

The high school project grew out of earlier work with a slightly older but otherwise demographically similar group of males who were incarcerated in an institution for delinquents. The delinquency project demonstrated that modeling techniques were useful in providing information about effective ways of handling common problem situations (Sarason, 1968, 1978; Sarason & Ganzer, 1973). In addition to increasing information, the modeling procedure produced behavioral changes reflected in better institutional adjustment and, more important, in lower recidivism rates computed as long as 6 years after the intervention.

The high school study followed the same approach, using modeling as the intervention technique. However, in order to increase the power of the treatment and the generalizability of the skills learned, the modeling focused on how cognitions affect behavior and the kinds of cognitions that are most effective. The subjects saw demonstrations of both effective overt responses (e.g., how to ask the teacher a question) and the cognitive antecedents of effective behavior (e.g., deciding between alternative courses of action). Emphasis was placed on the consequences of an action, the alternatives available in a situation, the effect of the individual's behavior on others and increased understanding of others' points of view, and communication skills (particularly communications with non-peers).

The situations used for the modeling scenes and the areas of emphasis listed earlier were determined by an extensive program of interviews with students, teachers, and employers who frequently hired students from this school for part-time jobs. All three groups agreed about problem areas and which skills were important but often lacking.

The intervention consisted of using 13 sessions of a ninth grade health class for a course in "Decision Making." Some students saw peer models act out the scenes "live." Others saw videotape performances of the scenes by the same students. The sessions were highly structured; the group leaders emphasized the four areas of consequences, alternatives, effect on others, and communication at each session and related them to the script. The students role-played the scenes after viewing them. The group leaders then led a discussion covering a series of points: (a) highlighting the importance of weighing alternatives; (b) pointing out how decisions, on the basis of the alternatives and their consequences, should be made; (c) noting the need to think about what is actually happening and not deciding on a course of action simply on the basis of his or her feelings and emotions.

The live and televised modeling groups and the control group were compared in a number of ways. Cognitive differences related to the experimental conditions were assessed by using a version of the Means–Ends Problem Solving (MEPS) measure devised by Spivak, Platt, and Shure (1976). This MEPS-type test was made up of three situations. For each, the problem situation and the outcome were described. The task for the subject was to supply the behavioral steps that led to the outcome.

Another measure was a specially devised Alternatives Test that required the subject to list the various ways in which a particular problem might be handled. This measure consisted of two problem situations. For each, subjects were asked to list all the alternative solutions they could.

Both the MEPS and Alternatives tests were scored by independent raters for the adaptiveness of subjects' responses. Table 1 gives the mean ratings for these measures. For both measures, modeling was associated with higher adaptiveness ratings. Subjects who participated in the course on social and cognitive skills were better able to (a) solve the MEPS-type problems and (b) think of more (and often better) alternatives to problematic situations than were control subjects. They also handled themselves better in an actual job interview situation than did controls. The interviews occurred a few months after the conclusion of the course on social and cognitive skills and, from the interviewee's perspective, seemed unrelated to it.

It seemed desirable to gather longer term follow-up information on subjects in the three different groups. The three measures evaluated were school absences, tardiness, and behavior referrals to psychologists and counselors during the year subsequent to conduct of the experiment. Subjects in the modeling groups had significantly fewer instances of absences, tardiness, and behavioral referrals than did the control subjects. The results were somewhat stronger for the live than for the televised modeling group.

Table 1
Mean Adaptiveness Ratings for MEPS and Alternatives Tests

Group	N	MEPS	Alternatives
Live modeling	32	5.47	10.28
Televised modeling	43	5.05	9.86
Control	33	3.82	7.65

Note: Adapted from Sarason and Sarason (1981a). Copyright 1981 by the American Psychological Association. Adapted by permission.

This study's findings suggest that social and cognitive skills of low-achieving high school students are amenable to change through the behavioral methods of modeling and role playing. The small number of hours necessary to produce behavioral change suggests that many individuals, even those who do not initially seek out behavior change for themselves, may profit from cognitive modeling programs that deal with topics they see as relevant. The follow-up data suggest that there may be generalized results of the program in preventing maladaptive behavior.

THE MARINE RECRUIT STUDY

Marine recruits are entering a new situation that demands new behaviors, just as are the high school students. They are also in a transition developmental phase, between late adolescence and early adulthood. The principal difference between the student and recruit situation is one of level of stress. The recruit training period is one of total immersion, without respite; the demands made are not only more intense, but failure to meet them has much severer implications.

From the moment the recruit steps off a commercial plane and is met by Marine personnel, he encounters an environment composed of strange and unfamiliar sights, sounds, faces, and rules. It is likely that the first 24 hours constitute the maximum stress period for most recruits. Bourne (1967) noted that, during this time, most men exhibit a picture of dazed apathy, and he cited research showing that during this period there is a dramatic elevation in recruits' 17-hydroxycorticosteroid levels. These elevated readings are comparable to those of schizophrenic patients during incipient psychosis.

As was true in the high school study, preparation of the experimental intervention in this Marine study required careful analysis of cognitive factors that played a role in success of training. Information concerning these factors was gained from direct observation and interviews with a variety of Marine personnel, particularly the recruits. Attention was also given to the salience of the various training demands.

Almost as soon as he arrives at the training facility, the recruit finds much of his previously learned verbal and nonverbal behavior to be inadequate and inappropriate. Any display of emotion brings an immediate negative reaction. Any attempt to exert personal control over a situation, other than in response to a command, results in personal criticism. Coupled with exposure to multiple unexpected demands is a low sense of self-efficacy. Especially during the early days of basic training, the recruit finds he cannot do anything right.

Attrition or loss of recruits varies considerably among platoons. This differential rate does not seem to be associated with differences among the recruits in each platoon or in the level of performance achieved by the platoon members. Rather, it seems to be associated with the particular drill instructor in charge (Cook, Novaco, & Sarason, 1980; Sarason, Novaco, Robinson, & Cook, 1981).

The interaction of drill instructor and recruit characteristics is important, and it is illustrated by the results of a study in which four groups of recruits were compared with regard to attrition (Sarason *et al.,* 1981). Recruits who did not graduate from high school had a higher attrition rate than did graduates; however, this difference was statistically significant only for platoons led by drill instructors with histories of having high recruit attrition (8% versus 23%). Thus, high school graduation is a significant factor, but only in conjunction with the drill instructor variable.

A traditional reaction to recruit attrition is that a relatively high rate may be desirable because it serves to eliminate recruits who are doomed to ultimate failure. The research described here does not support this generalization. On the contrary, platoons led by drill instructors with histories of low recruit attrition performed better as recruits and later as Marines than did those led by high-attrition drill instructors. Thus, the interaction of the drill instructor, or situational variable, with individual characteristics persists beyond the original training situation.

It is useful to think of platoons as social environments. The drill instructors' levels of self-confidence and sense of personal responsibility in shaping recruits into Marines are communicated to recruits and, in turn, influence recruits' level of self-confidence, commitment, and motivation. These changes are probably most important to the least well-prepared recruits. The drill instructor may appear to them to be a mentor who both provides a role model and functions as a supportive figure during the stresses of the transition–growth period inherent to basic training.

As training progresses, marked cognitive changes occur in the recruits of all platoons. In units with low or medium attrition, the recruits become more internal in their locus of control; that is, they see situational outcomes as functions of their own actions. In high-attrition platoons, recruits tend to become more external or to see events proceeding independently of their own efforts. Over time, successful recruits tend to reappraise and reinterpret the environment. For example, as training proceeds, they begin to recognize that tasks and drills that may have seemed to be irrelevant nuisances at first do have a purpose.

Simply observing the cognitive changes that occur in the recruits as training progresses gives evidence that cognitive coping skills are used and prove effective for them. It can also be seen that successful drill instructors help in bringing about these cognitive changes.

In an effort to assist recruits in cognitive change and in developing useful coping skills, an intervention film was prepared. It might be thought that a film simply emphasizing what experiences were to come in training would be useful to recruits. However, in earlier research, a film consisting of film clips from an army training film, "This Is How It Is," resulted in an increase in expected distress immediately after viewing and no decrease in distress, compared to a control group, during training (Datel & Lifrak, 1969). Datel and Lifrak's discussion of their negative results is of interest: "Perhaps, in other words, all

[the] film did was make the S's momentarily anxious . . . . Perhaps to give them a cognitive structure on which to focus their anxieties. Maybe the work of worrying has no preparatory value if one is not taught specifically what to worry about [p. 2879]."

The film used in the present research effort was constructed by randomly selecting 10 recruits as focal individuals. They were tracked by a photographer and two assistants with tape recorders through all aspects of their first 5 days of training. After a major portion of the training was completed, their first days as recruits were recreated for these men by slides and a coordinated sound track, and interviewers sought to learn how they had coped with recruit training. Segments of their videotaped interviews were incorporated in the intervention film, and some of the sound track was used as voice-overs for other video material to convey stress-related cognitions and coping strategies juxtaposed to video scenes of training circumstances. This produced a film with two key themes: the self-controlled regulation of emotion and effectiveness of task performance. The coping skills related to these themes are highlighted by phrases or key words superimposed on the screen and also by modeling of adaptive cognitive coping statements. The film, in summary, attempts to augment the recruits' skills for coping with stress by acknowledging the presence of distress, providing useful information about the environment, promoting an adaptive cognitive orientation, offering suggestions about coping techniques, and modeling successful coping behaviors.

This 28-minute film, shown early in the training period, constituted the complete intervention in one study. When the effect of this film was compared to several other conditions, the results bore out the effectiveness of the cognitive coping skill approach as a way to reduce the negative effects of stress. Groups seeing the film, called "Making It," see the challenges of training as being greater than do groups that do not see the film. However, they also have higher expectations of how they will perform in training and report less trouble adjusting to the demands of drill instructors. Seeing the film also increased the internal locus of control of recruits who were originally external. On the other hand, those in a control group who were originally external and who did not see the film became more external during training. This is important because earlier research showed that externals generally have a higher rate of attrition and are more negative in their self-appraisals (Novaco, Cook, & Sarason, 1981). The experience of seeing the film may also have longer-term effects. Githens (1981) reported a study showing that recruits who saw "Making It" had less attrition during the training period than did control and comparison groups.

Summary and Conclusions

We have described two examples of psychological intervention employed at transitional points in development. In the high school study, the transition was that not only from a simpler to a more complex school environment, but also from early to late adolescence. For example, our subjects were becoming highly interested in getting jobs in order to have money that would facilitate their widening social involvements. The Marine recruits, while older than the high school subjects, also were confronted by a new, complex environment and were also engaged in a developmental transition, that from late adolescence to early adulthood. Thus, in both studies, situational challenges and developmental transitions could be easily identified.

Also common to both studies were interventions that were directed toward specific needs and problems identified by the subjects. We believe that this fact is of great importance. Broadly speaking, change can be brought about in two ways. Environmental influences can be brought to bear on people in such a way as to impel behavioral change. Token economies and other reinforcement regimens illustrate this way of bringing about change. The person who is being influenced is confronted with a problem that is imposed.

A more appealing, less authoritarian way of bringing about change is through a problem-solving approach whose hallmarks are the individual's identification of a problem or goal and his or her motivation to solve the problem or to achieve the goal. These two factors were present in the two projects we have described. What the subjects needed were problem-solving strategies applicable to the problems they had identified. Because they knew what they wanted (part-time jobs, how to deal with peer pressure, the ability to ask for help effectively, not to be yelled at by the drill instructor), they were highly attentive to demonstrations of effective problem-solving strategies and eager to apply what they were learning. In addition, the outcome of the work with Marine recruits has emphasized the importance of the acquisition of skills as well as the effect of role models or mentors on the recruits' success. The presence of these positive, supportive, yet demanding figures had an interactive effect with the recruits' own characteristics.

The materials and topics we used in the two projects were highly salient for the subjects. In most situations, we know very little about either the determinants of salience or its cognitive ingredients. Developmental transitions represent challenges and opportunities that highlight the salience of adaptive responses. In our research, we were able to capitalize on the heightened salience that certain situations already had for our subjects.

Characteristic cognitive styles (such as attributional processes) and defensive maneuvers (such as the need to avoid unpleasantness) may direct the person's attention to problems and problem-solving strategies that are irrelevant to the real problems of personal growth. This research was directed at showing these subjects how altering their cognitive style or defensive maneuvers could be of immediate use to them. The practical consequences were apparent, as was their heightened motivation to relieve the increased situational stress.

Both of these intervention studies illustrate how cognitive coping skills can be taught to adolescents and young adults and how, having learned them, the individuals behave more effectively in stressful situations including, but not limited to, those which have been specifically presented. This approach seems to facilitate not only situation-specific, but generalized adaptive behavior. We have suggested that the adaptive behavior occurs not only because the individual has learned certain specific skills, but, more important, because both the individual and the situation have been altered owing to the changed cognitions directed toward each.

References

Abramson, L., Seligman, M. E. P., & Teasdale, J. D. Learned helplessness in humans: Critique and reformulation. *Journal of Abnormal Psychology*, 1978, *87*, 49–74.

Beck, A. T. The development of depression: A cognitive model. In R. J. Friedman & M. M. Katz (Eds.), *The psychology of depression: Contemporary theory and research*. Washington, D. C.: V. H. Winston, 1974.

Bourne, P. G. Some observations on the psychosocial phenomena seen in basic training. *Psychiatry*, 1967, *30*, 187–196.

Cook, T. M., Novaco, R. W., & Sarason, I. G. *Generalized expectancies, life experiences, and adaptation to Marine Corps recruit training* (Technical Report AR-002). Seattle: University of Washington, April 1980.

Datel, W. E., & Lifrak, S. T. Expectations, affect change, and military performance in the army recruit. *Psychological Reports*, 1969, *24*, 2855–2879.

Ellis, A. *Reason and emotion in psychotherapy*. New York: Lyle Stuart, 1962.

Githens, W. *Evaluation of "Making It."* Personal communication, Navy Personnel Research & Development Center, San Diego, 1981.

Glass, D., & Singer, J. *Urban stress: Experiments on noise and social stressors*. New York: Academic Press, 1972.

Gochman, I. R. Causes of perceived crowding unrelated to density. *Dissertation Abstracts International*, 1977, *37*, 3675B (University microfilms N077-576).

Hammen, C. L., & Krantz, S. Effect of success and failure on depressive cognitions. *Journal of Abnormal Psychology*, 1976, *85*, 577–586.

Kagan, J. This week's citation classic. *Current Contents*, 1982, *4*, January 25, 1982.

Levinson, D. J. *The seasons of a man's life*. New York: Knopf, 1978.

Magnusson, D., & Endler, N. S. Interactional psychology: Present status and future prospects. In D. Magnusson & R. S. Endler (Eds.), *Personality at the crossroads: Current issues in interactional psychology*. Hillsdale, N. J.: Erlbaum, 1977.

Meichenbaum, D. *Cognitive-behavior modification*. New York: Plenum, 1977.

Novaco, R. W., Cook, T. N., & Sarason, I. G. *Military recruit training: An arena for stress coping skills* (Technical Report AR-003). Seattle: University of Washington, March 1981.

Sarason, I. G. Verbal learning, modeling and juvenile delinquency. *American Psychologist*, 1968, *23*, 245–266.

Sarason, I. G. Test anxiety and cognitive modeling. *Journal of Personality and Social Psychology*, 1973, *28*, 58–61.

Sarason, I. G. A cognitive social learning approach to juvenile delinquency. In R. Hare & D. Schalling (Eds.), *Psychopathic behavior: Approaches to research*. London: Wiley, 1978.

Sarason, I. G., & Ganzer, V. J. Modeling and group discussion in the rehabilitation of juvenile delinquents. *Journal of Counseling Psychology*, 1973, *20*, 442–449.

Sarason, I. G., Novaco, R. W., Robinson, G. L., & Cook, T. M. *Recruit attrition and the training unit environment* (Technical Report AR-004). Seattle: University of Washington, April 1981.

Sarason, I. G., & Sarason, B. R. Teaching cognitive and social skills to high school students. *Journal of Consulting and Clinical Psychology,* 1981, *49,* 908–918. (a)

Sarason, I. G., & Sarason, B. R. The importance of cognition and moderator variables in stress. In D. Magnusson (Ed.), *Toward a psychology of situations: An interactional perspective.* Hillsdale, N. J.: Erlbaum, 1981. (b)

Sarason, I. G., & Stoops, R. Test anxiety and the passage of time. *Journal of Consulting and Clinical Psychology,* 1978, *46,* 102–109.

Schaeffer, E. S., & Bayley, N. Consistency of maternal behavior from infancy to preadolescence. *Journal of Abnormal and Social Psychology,* 1960, *61,* 1–6.

Schaie, K. W., & Strother, C. R. A cross sequential study of age changes in cognitive behavior. *Psychological Bulletin,* 1968, *70,* 671–680.

Schmidt, D. E., & Keating, J. P. Human crowding and personal control: An integration of research. *Psychological Bulletin,* 1979, *86,* 680–700.

Siegel, J. M., & Loftus, E. F. Impact of anxiety and life stress upon eyewitness testimony. *Bulletin of the Psychonomic Society,* 1978, *12,* 479–480.

Spivack, G., Platt, J. J., & Shure, M. *The problem solving approach to adjustment.* San Francisco: Jossey-Bass, 1976.

IV

The Person: Biological Processes

Section IV comprises five chapters primarily concerned with the biological bases of behavior. The first two chapters present a general overview of genetics and endocrinology and their relation to behavior. First, Rasmuson makes a strong argument for the position that behavior genetics complements psychology and the social sciences; genetic factors interact with various aspects of the environment in a very complex way in affecting resultant behavior. In Chapter 12 Eneroth presents some of the basic concepts of endocrinology that are relevant for behavioral processes. The endocrine system influences psychological processes both directly and indirectly and, at the same time, is affected by environmental events as well.

The third chapter, by Mednick and associates, is also concerned with interaction between genetic and environmental factors as determinants of schizophrenia, alcoholism, and crime. Results of several studies are summarized, including a large-scale investigation of criminal behavior conducted by Mednick with adoptees in Denmark. Suggestions are offered in the chapter concerning the specific biological mechanisms that may mediate the relation found between genetic factors and deviant behavior.

In Chapter 14, Meyer-Probst, Rösler, and Teichmann report a longitudinal study designed to investigate the joint effect of biological and psychosocial factors in the mental development of children judged to be "at risk" at birth. An important finding was the interactive nature of the risk factors: the detrimental consequences of biological risk factors depended on the unfavorableness of the psychosocial conditions.

HUMAN DEVELOPMENT:
AN INTERACTIONAL PERSPECTIVE

The last chapter in this section (Lewis and Michalson) examines the interaction between unlearned aspects of facial expressions and the socialization of emotional behavior. There does seem to be an innate biological basis for emotional responses, but how the social environment shapes the expression of emotion at different ages and in different cultures remains an important problem.

11

The Role of Genes as Determinants of Behavior

MARIANNE RASMUSON

Genes and Development

The ontogeny of an organism is the joint result of genes and environment and can be seen as the stepwise unfolding of the genetic message in the zygote, the product of union of an egg cell and sperm nucleus. This genetic message is responsible for an individual's entire life cycle, from its beginning as a single cell to its death as an aged, extremely complicated organism. Genes control the differentiation in multicellular organisms, the subsequent division of labor among different organs and tissues, and the timing mechanisms that regulate the different stages of development.

Thanks to the work of molecular geneticists over the past 20 years, we are now better informed about the first steps in the long chain of events that occur between the intermingling of genes to the appearance of a fully functioning organism. We know how the DNA is transcribed to m-RNA, which is then processed and deposited in the cytoplasm where its uncoded message is used to produce protein molecules, enzymes, hormones, and structural proteins, which build up the cells and keep the metabolism going.

The later stages of the development of a multicellular organism include growth, morphogenesis, and differentiation, which are all controlled by cellular processes. Development means production of the right substances at the right time in the right place.

The production of substances can be controlled at a number of stages from the transcription of DNA to the final folding of the polypeptide molecule. Various feedback models are assumed whereby products in the metabolic

HUMAN DEVELOPMENT:
AN INTERACTIONAL PERSPECTIVE

chain act as activators or inhibitors for previous steps. Such loops can be limited to reactions in the cytoplasm, but, in general, the nuclear processes are also involved. One of the most important control points is that of transcription. However, control may also be exerted outside of the genes, but still within the organism, by regulating hormones, and may even be exerted from outside the body, as, for instance, by the pheromones in social insects. Abiotic factors such as temperature and oxygen concentration may influence the sequence of chemical reactions in the cells, thus allowing an adaptation to external factors. An unwanted effect of external influences sometimes brought on in pregnant woman is sensitivity to a drug, which may lead to teratogenic effects.

The timing process is crucial in development. Among the many conceivable bottlenecks in the rate of synthesis in a metabolic chain, the availability of m-RNA is certainly one of the most important. When large quantities of a protein are needed immediately, the release of these proteins can be accurately timed if m-RNA is available in an inactivated form, ready to be turned on at the right moment, which is the case in the early stages of embryonic development. In mice, as probably in humans, proteins are translated by use of the maternal m-RNA up to the eight-cell stage, when the embryonic genome gradually takes over control of development. m-RNA is usually rapidly denatured but may occasionally be longer lived. In bone marrow, erythroid stem cells are stimulated by a special hormone to become erythroid cells, where m-RNA for hemoglobin is synthesized. After three or four cell divisions, immature red blood cells are produced and, at this point, but not before, hemoglobin is synthesized, from m-RNA that is by then about 2 days old. Other devices for a rapid production of proteins are repeated gene sequences and gene amplification, whereby special parts of the genome undergo extra replications, resulting in numerous gene copies ready to start transcription.

Genes may be activated at very different phases of the life cycle. Single genes are known for which action is delayed a whole life cycle, so that their effects are revealed only in the offspring of the organisms carrying the gene (e.g., shell coiling in the snail *Limnea* and the mutant "grandchildless" in the fruitfly *Drosophila melanogaster*). There are other genes with delayed actions that regulate the length of the postreproductive period of the life cycle. Evolution cannot proceed without the death of organisms and their replacement by means of new births, thus natural selection will favor genes that increase the chances of death after a particular age. Death and senescense occur through a breakdown of the soma, which occurs in a variety of ways, such as increased susceptibility to a particular disease, tissue changes (cancer), and organ malformations.

The secondary consequences of a gene that is active early in the development are expected to be more severe than those of genes with late effects, and the selection against early defects is accordingly stronger. This in turn leads to greater variability during later stages. Young individuals of two species resemble one another more than adults of those species, and young people show less variation than old people.

Sex Determination

The best-known and most intensively studied example of far-reaching consequences of a genetic switch is sex determination, which occurs from a series of sequential interactions between the genetic machinery and the regulatory factors. The only genetic entity exclusive for one sex in humans is the Y chromosome. Since this chromosome can be disposed of without lethality, it cannot contain many essential genes. This is also surmised from an evolutionary perspective, because it is important that both sexes be able to benefit from selective advantages that may appear in only one. The sex-determining mechanism—even when producing a marked sexual dimorphism—must therefore maintain a minimum of genetic differences between the sexes.

The mechanism by which sex of the organism is determined has been found to function in the same way in all mammals and seems to be carried over very strongly during evolution (Ohno, 1976). In the 1950s, a special male antigen, H-Y (histocompatibility-Y) antigen, was found in inbred male mice that caused rejection by isogenic females of skin grafts from males. When a serological assay method became available, it was confirmed that the same antigen was present in males of all investigated mammalian species, including man. The H-Y antigen is produced by a gene on the Y chromosome, is bound to the plasma membrane of the gonadal cells, and acts as a short-range hormone, turning the indifferent gonad of the embryo into a testis at about 6–8 weeks of embryonic age. The chromosomal sex has thereby determined the gonadal sex, and the role of the Y chromosome is essentially over. For secondary sex determination, the male steroid hormone, testosterone, plays the principal role. The synthesis of testosterone begins when the testes are formed and, at this stage, it is irrelevant what the chromosomal sex of the cells is, since they are all normally endowed with androgen receptors, a protein probably controlled by an X-linked gene. Absence of this gene product causes the "testicular feminization" syndrome, whereby the external phenotype is female but there are testosterone-producing testes and the chromosomal sex is male.

No corresponding mutations have been found that result in deficient estrogen receptors, probably because estrogen is essential for the successful implantation of the embryo and for its survival. Both male and female embryos produce estrogen temporarily at early stages.

Besides testosterone, fetal testes also produce an anti-Mullerian hormone, which destroys the Mullerian ducts that otherwise would develop into ovaries. This sequence of events has been established by experiments on animals and on human cell cultures, and by studies of mutations that interfere with the normal sex differentiation. The hormones exert their cellular actions after passive diffusion into the target cells, where they bind to the receptor proteins. This complex then enters the nucleus and interacts with specific structural genes, causing repression or transcription followed by the appropriate protein synthesis.

At the end of embryogenesis, in the postnatal stage, gonadotrophins from the pituitary gland regulate the rates of production of male and female sex hormones in the ovaries and testes. This hypothalamus–pituitary regulation of hormone production is also sex-dependent. There is a rather constant flow of gonadotrophins in males, whereas the output in females is cyclic. This indicates, that at least the part of the brain that regulates the sex hormones is different in males and females, and the sex differences may well include other parts of the brain, thus extending the sex dimorphism also to perception and behavior.

I mention the possibly biologically caused sexual differences in behavior because they illustrate the long and complicated chain of events that lies between the gene action and the final consequences for behavior, and this complicated chain is probably common to all gene–behavior pathways. In the case of gender, the presence or absence of the Y chromosome is the prime determiner, and, for males, it, along with the X-linked gene for androgen receptors, directs the developmental course that follows conception.

Single Genes Can Affect Behavior

Mutants are valuable tools that aid the process of elucidation of developmental pathways. For instance, lack of receptors, and perhaps lack of an active transmembrane transport, may be two physiological bases for certain genetic defects. Once these possibilities are verified, the detection of many other such variants may be made possible.

Single gene mutations can also create genetic blocks that interfere with normal mental development. The blocks may cause an accumulation of toxic substances leading to progressive brain damage, as in Tay-Sachs, Niemann-Pick, and Gauchers diseases.

Special dietary measures, when administered sufficiently early, may protect patients from mental disturbances resulting from genetic blocks, as has been possible for phenylketonuria and galactosemia. The sensitive period is limited to the first years of life; treatments that are begun at a later stage seem to be without effect. In order to accomplish a successful reversal of the effects of such monogenic inborn errors, certain prerequisites must be met: (a) the sensitive period must occur after the child is born; (b) the defect must be diagnosed before the damage is done; and (c) the primary genetic defect causing the disease must be understood. It can be supposed that progress will be made in this line of clinical genetics during the years to come, but many attempts will be unsuccessful because one or other of these prerequisites is not met.

For a large category of familial mental disorders the genetic mechanism is not understood and it has not even been possible to decide whether or not the inherited disease is monogenic (due to a single mutant gene). The difficulties are partly due to limitations of the methodologies available at present to study

human behavior, but they are also due to the long pathway that exists between the gene and its possible behavior phenotype, and it is this length that makes possible the varieties of interaction both with other genes and with environmental factors. This variety of interaction almost inevitably leads to pleiotropism, which means that the presence of a single mutant gene may have many phenotypic consequences. One example is the light hair color and small head size that accompany phenylketonuria; another is the many behavioral abnormalities associated with the porphyrias.

Pleiotropism may sometimes aid the clinical diagnosis, whereas genetic heterogeneity and variable phenotypic expression are obstacles for genetic analysis. When two or more different genotypes result in almost identical phenotypes or syndromes, much confusion as to the origin can be caused. For a general diagnosis, for instance congenital deafness, the causes can be nongenetic as well as genetic, with recessive or dominant genes at various loci. However, syndromes with more precisely identifiable causes may be genetically heterogeneous, for instance, partial (red–green) color blindness. Color blindness has been divided into two types, protan and deutan, which are probably due to recessive mutants in one or the other of two loci on the X chromosome. The genetic heterogeneity in this case was confirmed by comparisons of incidences in males and females. Two loci should give fewer female homozygotes than one locus. If q_1 and q_2 are the male frequencies of the two types, the female frequency should be $(q_1)^2 + (q_2)^2$ in the case of two loci and $(q_1 + q_2)^2$ in case of one locus. Observations showed that the first model gave the best fit.

The phenomenon that certain individuals with the genetic qualifications for a certain trait nevertheless do not show the expected phenotype is called incomplete penetrance. The causes for this are in most cases unknown. Furthermore, among different individuals who have inherited the same trait, there can be a vast variety of in phenotypic expression, and both quantitative and qualitative differences are common. One aspect of differences in expressivity is that the onset for the symptoms of a genetic disease may occur at very different ages. Huntington's chorea can appear from 15 to 65 years of age for those who have inherited the gene, and cases of hereditary macular degeneration, which are definitely caused by the same mutant gene, become apparent between ages 1 and 2 years and 50 years and older (Nordström, 1974).

Multifactorial Background and Threshold Traits

Differences in penetrance and expressivity may lead to lack of confirmation of Mendelian inheritance for some monogenic traits, but most failures in this respect can be supposed to be due to a *polygenic* background, where genes at several loci interact, or to a *multifactorial* background, where environmental as well as genetic factors are of importance. While the genetic diseases known to be monogenically inherited still number fewer than 2000, there are almost no human defects or diseases where hereditary factors are wholly unimportant.

The model behind the multifactorial predisposition for a certain trait is an underlying continuous scale of *liability,* and a threshold beyond which the trait is expressed. The liability may be thought of as the concentration of some substance or the rate of some developmental process. It is in principle measurable, although unknown. Since related persons are expected to share both genes and environment to a higher degree than random pairs from the population, relatives to probands showing a certain trait are theorized to have a higher average liability than the population as a whole and therefore also a higher incidence of the trait. From observations of incidence in different types of relatives (sibs, parents, half sibs, and cousins), a statistical estimate of the heritable contribution can be made, in spite of the lack of quantitative information concerning the liability.

This type of analysis has been found to be reliable for congenital deformities such as clubfoot, pyloric stenosis, and cleft palate, which have mainly a hereditary basis. One factor of importance is sex, since the risk factor is different for male and female relatives. When this type of analysis is applied to the common mental disorders, it is still not possible to determine if the genetic component is due to one major gene or many additive gene effects, nor is it possible to answer to such questions for antisocial behaviors such as criminality and drug abuse. Genetic heterogeneity most probably is involved, and a statistical approach may have to await better diagnoses and better discrimination among various types. Further progress may be forthcoming from biochemical research and identification of major genes by means of linkage to known polymorphic genetic markers.

Quantitative Traits

For much of the observable variation in behavior it is difficult to obtain a quantitative measure. Often it is possible only to define different types of deviations from normal behavior, and then a threshold analysis must be used, sometimes with an expansion to several thresholds if the deviations can be graded in, for instance, mild, medium, and severe. In a few cases, however, it has been possible to obtain a reliable quantitative value of mental properties. By "reliable" here I mean a measure that gives relatively constant values on repeated testing and is stable over longer periods of a person's life. The best-known example is, of course, the IQ value, but personality traits such as neuroticism and extraversion have also been given quantitative values. The aim when analyzing such data is to estimate the different components of phenotypic variation and to test hypotheses about the importance of biological and cultural factors.

The population under study must consist of related persons of some kind, nuclear families, twins, and adoptees with biological and foster parents. The properties that can be estimated for the trait are means, variances, and covariances. Some methods rely on variances within and between groups, others on correlations between pairs of related persons.

In a linear additive model, the phenotype (P) is dependent on two factors, genes (G) and environment (E), which may be correlated. Thus, phenotypic variation (V_P) is equal to $V_G + V_E + 2\text{covGE}$. However, a realistic model of human behavioral traits must include a division of the environment at least into home environment and residual environment. The genetic component can be divided into parts due to additive, dominant, and epistatic gene effects. In addition, the possibilities of assortative mating and parental correlation, gene–environment correlation, and nonadditive gene–environment interaction may be considered.

Usually some of these components must be sacrificed in the analysis in order to simplify the model, and among those that have been considered of minor importance are dominance and epistasis, gene–environment correlation, and nonadditive interaction of genes and environment. Of course, this elimination may be more or less justifiable, and must depend on previous knowledge of the trait. A wrongly applied model can sometimes be detected by special tests for goodness of fit.

The most consistent and logical model available at present seems to be that of Rao and Morton (1978). It is summarized in the pathway diagram shown in Figure 1, which includes a nuclear family with father (F), mother (M), and child (C). The observed entities are the phenotype (P) and an index for family environment (I), and these are influenced by three variables, genotype (G), home environment (C), and residual environment (not shown in the diagram). The complete model has 14 independent parameters, but if maternal effects are assumed to be negligible 10 parameters remain. Such null hypotheses can be tested. Since there are 16 correlations that can be estimated, the data show extra degrees of freedom for testing the goodness of fit of the model. Furthermore, independent estimations of correlation can be obtained if other types of relatives are included, such as twins and adoptees.

When the model was applied to independently collected data on family resemblance for IQ, Rao and Morton confirmed what had been observed by Wright (1978) many years earlier, that the genetic part of the variation in IQ is much larger for children (69%) than for adults (30%), for which home environment is the main cause of variation (55% for adults against 16% for children). Accordingly, heritability estimates from adult sibs should be smaller than those from sibs tested in childhood, but the sib–sib correlation might increase with age.

This model has recently been modified by Rao, Morton, Lalouel, and Lew (1982) to include some further parameters. When analyzing the same data on IQ, they now find conflicting results as to both the relative importance of genetic and cultural influences and the estimates of parameters for children and adults. Further data and models will obviously be needed before consensus can be reached in these matters.

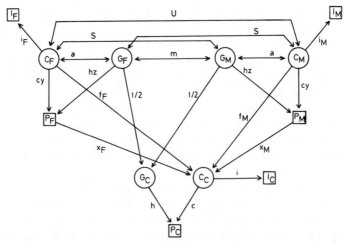

Figure 1. *Pathway diagram for a nuclear family. The subscripts F, M, and C denote father, mother, and child, respectively. G is genotype, C is home environment with index I, and P is phenotype. Paths from residual environment to phenotypes are not shown, since they do not contribute to family resemblance. (a = correlation between individual's genotype and childhood family environment; m, s, u = correlations between parents; i = effect of family environment on child's index; h = effect of genotype on child's phenotype [square root of heritability]; hz = effect of genotype on adult's phenotype; c = effect of family environment on child's phenotype; cy = effect of childhood family environment on adult's phenotype; f = effect of parent's childhood family environment on environment of children; x = effect of parent's adult phenotype on environment of children; ½ = correlation between genotype of parent and genotype of child.) [After Rao & Morton, 1978.]*

There are some rather unique data on IQ that illustrate the question of the importance of school systems, as formed by social policy in countries with and without social class structures. A sample of twins from prewar Russia (Halperin, Rao, & Morton, 1975) did not reveal any decrease in the influence of home environment in that egalitarian setting. Another investigation in Warsaw performed in 1974 (Firkowska, Ostrowska, Sokolowska, Stein, Susser, & Wald, 1978) aimed at an estimation of the importance of the social factors that remained after social policy had removed differences in extrinsic factors such as housing, school quality, and residence. It was clearly shown that the remaining differences—education and occupation of the parents—had a marked influence on the results of intelligence tests, which maintained a strong and regular increase from low to high index of parental occupation and education.

Taken together, these results emphasize the strong genetic basis for IQ variations in school-age children. It is well known that IQ test results for children below 2 years of age are unstable and have low predictive value. It seems that the adult age values may also be unpredictable and strongly influenced by cultural factors, but as yet there is a severe lack of data for adult relatives.

Many studies from different countries indicate that mental capacity is nega-

tively influenced by inbreeding. This holds for IQ as well as school performance and incidence of mental retardation. If consanguinity is not confounded
with variation in social environment, this association is a valid proof of genetic
effects. For IQ, the decline amounts to about 3 units when the parents are first
cousins, and for mental retardation the statistical risk for normal parents to
have a retarded child increases from about 1% to 6% if they are first cousins
(Morton, 1978). The probable cause is the occurrence of rare, recessive, deleterious genes, which are maintained by recurrent mutations. Morton estimated the number of contributing loci in a population to above 300, all with a
very low gene frequency.

Gene–Environment Interaction

The occurrence of a nonadditive gene–environment interaction complicates
the kinship correlation models and is often disregarded. Nonadditive interactions have, however, been observed in plants and animals, where specially
designed experiments can be performed. For behavioral traits, such interaction
is plausible, but its existence and importance for mental traits in humans
remains to be demonstrated. Jinks and Fulker (1970) have devised a method to
estimate the importance of such gene–environment interactions from data on
monozygotic twins. If a correlation between intrapair sums and intrapair differences can be shown to exist, then a gene–environment nonadditive interaction is indicated. The sums estimate the combined effects of genes and environment, whereas the differences estimate the magnitude of the variation due to
home environment and residual environment if the twins have been reared in
separate homes, or to variance in residual environmental only if the twins have
lived together. A correlation between sums and differences indicates that these
environmental components of variance are not independent of the phenotype
or, it can be assumed, of the underlying genotype. High phenotypic values may
be associated with large or small differences according to the type of interaction.

A test of this model on a rather small sample gave negative but nonsignificant correlations for verbal performance test results for pairs reared both
together and apart. A survey of the four major studies on monozygotic twins
reared apart (122 pairs) yielded a correlation of $-.15$ for IQ, which also is
nonsignificant (Jensen, 1970). It is thus indicated that low performers are more
vulnerable to environmental risks than are high performers, but that the interaction for these traits is of minor importance.

Another way to study this question is to follow twins during a longer period
of time and compare the intrapair similarity of monozygotic and dizygotic
twin pairs. No difference in similarity level would indicate that the genetic
background is without importance for the variation, but this seems to be a very
improbable situation, for the similarity is almost always higher within mono-

zygotic pairs. Constant and high within-pair correlations for monozygotic twins and constant but lower values for dizygotic twins suggest that genetic factors are the primary cause of variation, and that development follows a genetic plan that is well buffered from environmental influences. If the similarity remains constant for monozygotic pairs but deteriorates for dizygotic pairs, this may indicate a nonadditive gene–environment interaction. Assuming similar environments within pairs, the monozygotic twins, with their equal genotype, react alike to this environment, whereas the different genotypes of the dizygotic twins cause varying reactions to the same environment, that is, a nonadditive interaction.

Longitudinal studies done on the mental development of twins of from 3 months to 6 years age (Wilson, 1978) have shown that monozygotic twins become increasingly concordant with age, whereas this is not the case for dizygotic twins. These results can be compared with a Swedish study of twins, who were followed from 10 to 18 years of age (Fischbein, 1979). Physical measurements of height and weight as well as tests for performance at different ages were undertaken. The similarity trends for monozygotic and dizygotic twins ran parallel during the whole period for height, and the two tests of inductive reasoning given to boys at 12 and 18 years age showed equal monozygotic–dizygotic differences. For weight, verbal tests, and standard achievement tests in mathematics, however, the within-pair correlation decreased in the dizygotic pairs.

Another finding in these studies was that the monozygotic twins showed a high degree of synchrony in spurts and lags during development for both mental and physical measurements. For instance, the difference in age at maximum growth was less than half a year for monozygotic twins but more than 8 months for dizygotic twins. This gives evidence for a genetically controlled rate of maturation, and variations in such timed gene actions can be seen as an alternative to the assumption of a nonadditive gene–environment interaction. If during development different genes take part in the regulation of a trait, these gradually unfolding genetic effects should not differentiate monozygotic twins, but they are likely to have a multiplicative effect and therefore increase the phenotypic differences between dizygotic twins, even if genetic and environmental influences are additive.

An Evolutionary Perspective

The recent debate concerning sociobiology has vitalized questions about the genetic adaptation behind behavior. In this connection it should be emphasized that genetic control is an indispensible prerequisite in all hypotheses of natural selection as the cause of evolution. Only if the apparent variation has a genetic component can selection working in one generation have lasting effects on later generations. Man's most distinguishing characteristic is his mental capacity. Given that we share a common biological origin with all living organisms, we therefore must assume a genetic control of human behavior and mental development. This evolutionary perspective on human adaptation does not rule out the cultural influence on behavior. The strength of the human mind is flexibility, with long maturation times and therefore possibilities for adaptation to varying environmental situations. The genetic program unfolds in a specific setting and answers to the stimuli of that environment, with lasting consequences for personality and behavior.

One result of the modern way of living is a change in the distribution of genetic variation. Small populations with rigid conditions for survival become genetically homogeneous and differentiated from each other. Race differentiation can be seen as a long-lasting consequence of former isolation and genetic adaptation to varying climatic and other factors. The tendency today is toward large, heterogeneous populations instead of the small, isolated, genetically homogeneous groups of the past. This has probably neither increased nor decreased genetic variation, but it certainly has redistributed it.

Our environment is very different from that of our ancestors. It is characteristic for most contemporary Western countries that the childhood environment is rather homogeneous from nutritional, educational, and social viewpoints. Consequently, the relative importance of genetic variation will be greater than in a more heterogeneous environment, and the possibility of tracing gene–behavior pathways may thus be increased.

In a long-term perspective, what will follow from the situation at present is probably an accumulation of more genetic variants. Mutation rates will probably increase, the tolerance limits for deviations will expand, and the survival chances for the less physically and mentally fit will become greater. This, however, is a very slow process, and it is uncertain if the present state of civilization will continue long enough for such effects to be realized.

Conclusions

Taking the previously discussed aspects of our evolutionary situation into consideration, it is impossible to neglect the impact of genetic variation on all human matters. Behavior genetics is therefore a necessary complement to psychology and the social sciences. From a rather obscure position, this field of genetics has gained attention and prestige over the last 20 years. It is true that many of the methods that have made behavior genetic studies of animals so successful are not available to study humans. Systematic inbreeding along with comparison of behavior between lines of genetically identical individuals is one powerful design, breeding experiments to ascertain genetic homology and the hereditary nature of variants is another, and selective breeding is a third. In research on humans, these must be compensated for by less efficient designs of twin and pedigree analyses and kinship correlation studies. However, for other techniques, the situation is more equal. It has been possible to perform chromosomal studies on small samples of blood cells since the 1950s, and these have led to the discovery of the chromosomal trisomy behind Down's syndrome and of sex chromosome aberrations. Even if we do not understand how the extra chromosome exerts its influence during development, the cytological approach has widened our knowledge about genetic control of human behavior.

The accumulated knowledge of human physiology, neurology, histology, and anatomy is greater than for any other species, and genetic variants are described in a number surpassed only by those described for *Drosophila*, the favorite animal of geneticists. Where cell functions and biochemistry of cells are concerned, the use of cell cultures and the new hybridoma technique makes human cells fully available for research.

Thus, the prognosis for research into human behavior genetics is in many ways good. The possibilities for furthering our knowledge of brain function and mental development are a question of relating the genetic knowledge and methodology to the knowledge of psychology.

References

Firkowska, A., Ostrowska, A., Sokolowska, M., Stein, Z., Susser, M., & Wald, I. Cognitive development and social policy. *Science,* 1978, *200,* 1357–1362.

Fischbein, S. Heredity–environment influences on growth and development during adolescence: A longitudinal study of twins. *Studies in Education and Psychology* (Vol. 4). GOTAB Lund Sweden: CWK/Gleerup, 1979.

Halperin, S. L., Rao, D. C., & Morton, N. E. A twin study of intelligence in Russia. *Behavior Genetics,* 1975, *5,* 83–86.

Jensen, A. R. IQs of identical twins reared apart. *Behavior Genetics,* 1970, *1,* 133–148.

Jinks, J. L., & Fulker, D. W. Comparison of the biometrical, genetical, MAVA, and classical approaches to the analysis of human behavior. *Psychological Bulletin,* 1970, *73,* 311–349.

Morton, N. E. Effect of inbreeding on IQ and mental retardation. *Proceedings of the National Academy of Sciences,* 1978, *75,* 3906–3908.

Nordström, S. Hereditary macular degeneration—A population survey in the county of Västerbotten, Sweden. *Hereditas,* 1974, *78,* 41–62.

Ohno, S. Major regulatory genes for mammalian sexual development. *Cell,* 1976, *7,* 315–321.

Rao, D. C., & Morton, N. E. IQ as a paradigm in genetic epidemiology. In N. E. Morton & C. S. Chung (Eds.), *Genetic Epidemiology.* New York: Academic Press, 1978.

Rao, D. C., Morton, N. E., Lalouel, J. M. & Lew, R. Path analysis under generalized assortative mating. II American IQ. *Genetical Research,* 1982, *39,* 187–198.

Wilson, R. S. Synchronies in mental development: An epigenetic perspective. *Science,* 1978, *202,* 939–948.

Wright, S. *Evolution and the genetics of populations* (Vol. 4). Chicago: University of Chicago Press, 1978.

12

Endocrinology and Behavior

PETER ENEROTH

During early fetal life influences from the outside world are already interacting with the developing organism. At certain stages of development the gradually maturating cells under the combined influence of the genes and messenger substances start responding to stimulation. There is, however, one prerequisite. The cells must have developed specific receptors for the messenger substances in order to be able to respond to the message. In order to respond to an activated receptor, a definite number of enzyme systems within the cells must have been synthesized, again at the command of the genes. The activity of these enzymes in turn may be modulated by key metabolites in the energy-producing steps involved in the breakdown of food. This latter process appears to be the most important single factor in the development of the fetus. Development at this stage means growth. Growth signifies multiplication of the cells, and the building blocks for cells must be manufactured, which calls for a great deal of energy. The only source of energy available to the fetus is the nourishment derived from the maternal blood, and this transfer process is governed by the placenta (Baconfield & Baconfield, 1979; Laga, Driscoll, & Munro, 1974). This fabulous organ, which is a combination of many separate adult organs (primarily liver and kidney), is also an endocrine organ cooperating with the immature organism to form what is referred to as the fetal–placental unit (Diczfalusy, 1964).

HUMAN DEVELOPMENT:
AN INTERACTIONAL PERSPECTIVE

Receptors

Having established that the sources of energy are fundamental factors in development, let us go back to the cellular receptors, because they determine when and to what extent a cell will interact with its environment. Cellular receptors interact with individual molecules or molecular complexes in the fluid medium of the cells, and current data also indicate that cells which are to form a future specialized tissue link together in a "lock and key" type of process whereby complementary receptor structures anchor cells to one another (Johnson, Smith, & Klyne, 1978). This recognition system is organ-specific, but it is also a system with individual-specific features, such that all the individual cells recognize "self" from "non-self." Once cells of the same type (i.e., destiny) have established edge-to-edge contact, they may also create intercellular connections via microchannels and can thus exchange information (Petozinsky, Chabrodsky, & Hilson, 1977). Cells from different organs may also contain rejecting or repelling receptors that prohibit, for instance, kidney cells from developing inside the pancreas, and so on. We may conclude that cell recognition is another important aspect of development.

Growth of an organ does not progress forever. Organs generally grow until the organism within which they function has reached adulthood, at which time most organs have also reached their maximal sizes. From then on, aging sets in, which leads to nonsynchronous functioning of the organ systems, which in turn leads to death of the whole system and thus of the body.

We can see that cells and organs develop up to a limit. We like to think that the setting of an end point is genetically controlled, but that outside factors can narrow the range with inhibiting factors such as understimulation (e.g., limitations in fuel supply). But data available today indicate that the organism releases specific growth-stimulating factors for each organ system (Mizuno, Share, & Tanaka, 1981) in a way that one organ might control the growth of other perhaps anatomically or functionally related organs. If the final levels of synthesis of these growth factors are predetermined by genetic mechanisms, that fact would readily explain why there is a limit to growth and development of the organs. Furthermore, as one organ grows under the influence of another organ, which may be at a distance from this first one, a communication system would naturally have to be established to monitor the progress of growth of the organ being influenced. If a receipt substance is produced by the stimulated organ that inhibits the distant production of the growth stimulant, a balance can be reached. This is a classic feedback control system, and it serves to integrate the functions of separate organs. However, this type of coordination of function is not enough, although it may be sufficient for many autonomous processes.

During fetal development, relatively constant conditions prevail under the supervision of the placenta but, after birth, the number of possible changes in the milieu becomes so high that it is hard to see how control of all these factors could be genetically foreseen and programmed unless the individual were to seek an environment that is rigidly controlled. Thus, to interact with the total environment available to an individual, an overriding control over organ function must be developed. This is obviously based on sensitive detection of essential characteristics of the environment, but, more important, these data must be evaluated before new and subtle corrections of autonomous functioning of the organ is effected. It is probably not a coincidence that vital sensory systems such as sight, hearing, and smell are located close to or as part of the central nervous system.

Some individual functions are of such foreseeable importance in the life of an individual that they have been genetically determined. The most striking one is the determination of sex of the organism at conception; other developments seem to be left for later stages. In this context, I draw attention to the imprinting concept (Gustafsson & Stenberg, 1974), that is, the situation whereby a stimulus rapidly induces a long-lasting programmed behavior in an individual. An example that is easy to comprehend is the induction of parent identification in a newborn bird. Another is the imprinting of sexual behavior in the rat (Södersten & Hansen, 1977). It seems in this particular case as if the expression of the genetically determined sex can be anything from subtle correction of the behavior (both in the true sense of the word and in metabolic terms) to complete suppression or even inversion of male or female functioning. Imprinting of sex characteristics seems to occur both during fetal life and during the neonatal period, with further modifications taking place during childhood and puberty; these continual modifications may be thought of as check-stations. For instance, if the Leydig cells in the fetal testes do not function properly, and secrete insufficient amounts of testosterone, the development of secondary sexual organs will not occur properly and future male performance will be impaired (Lester, Bruder, & Kögelsdorf, 1975). It is conceivable that the developing individual may, at the time of imprinting, have available to him alternative modes of action to correct, at least in part, the imbalance. From present knowledge, it is believed that imprinting is mediated by cellular receptors, perhaps by setting the genetic machinery at such a point that cells in the male organism will be equipped with androgen receptors at all times, whereas in the female none or very few androgen receptors will be found on cells (Pousette, 1978). The number of receptors on cell surfaces can be altered, however, especially by drastic changes in the environment. For instance, species-foreign compounds may mimic the action of endogenous molecules or attach to receptors in an irreversible way, thereby preventing the natural compounds from transmitting their message to the cell. When receptors are overstimulated, a so-called "down-regulation" of receptors occurs; that is, the receptors are destroyed or their synthesis is stopped. An example of this is down-regulation of the adrenergic β-receptor by terbulatin, which thus induces its own biological inactivity (Jönsson & Batra, 1982). There are also examples of induction of receptors for another class of messengers: High enough levels of progesterone increase not only the availability of its own receptors, but may also cause increased formation of estrogen receptors (Banlien, 1980). It is not known whether this represents an unintended cross-reaction in the initiation of receptor biosynthesis or is actually a way to integrate the function of two separate classes of steroid hormones. For instance, sexual puberty is preceded by maturation of the adrenal gland (Ritzén, Karlsson, & Fredriksson, 1979). Gradually elevated corticosteroid levels might eventually induce receptors for luteinizing hormone (LH) in the Leydig cells, thereby leading to onset of testosterone formation.

Having come this far, I will summarize the following concepts. Provided there are sufficient energy-producing substrates, cells develop and multiply. Cells do not respond to outside messenger substances unless there are receptors for these messengers. Synthesis of enzymes for energy production and building units as well as receptors is genetically controlled. Both enzyme and receptor biosynthesis might be modified by environmental factors, and the fitness of enzymes and receptors may also be influenced by environmental compounds. The time span in terms of capacity for receptor biosynthesis is genetically predetermined, and limitations in the use of this span are induced by events in the process of adaptation to the environment. Some induced receptor functions may be long-lasting (some throughout life) after triggering by some key stimuli. This may be the basis for the imprinting process, which can be said to represent an enhanced or favored learning by fundamentally important environmental factors. The outcome will be a preprogrammed behavior that, after the initial imprinting, can be modified only slightly.

Cyclicity

As mentioned earlier, man's total environment may vary enormously and with short notice. To maintain a capacity to respond to environmental demands, our endocrine system continuously challenges the responsiveness of target organs by test signals secreted in a pulsatory fashion (Wetterman & Seagram, 1979). This seems to be true, in particular, for hormones or messengers released in or from the central nervous system. Thus, sudden, sharp, minute-long pulses in the release of pituitary growth hormone may be easily observed. The pulses themselves may show a regular pattern over hours or days, and there is a night and day rhythmicity as well. In terms of blood corticosteroid levels, we wake up in a state of pronounced stress and fall asleep with corticosteroid levels that resemble severe adrenal cortical hypofunction. During sleep, some organs are permitted to rest. For instance, the tonus of the uterus decreases and the regular contractions of this organ stop, only to start again as soon as the woman awakens (Lundström, Granström, & Eneroth, in press). Before waking, during the REM phase of sleep, vigorous release of prolactin from the pituitary occurs.

Cyclicity lasting for several days or a week is most easily noticed in fertile women who are exposed to increasing estrogen levels from Day 7 to Day 13 of the menstrual cycle, after which estrogen levels fall and progesterone secretion increases to reach a maximum at Day 21, after which the progesterone levels drop to a low at Day 28. In between the estrogen peak and the onset of progesterone production from the ovary, LH from the anterior pituitary is released to induce ovulation. According to recent data, this is not only caused by the gradual day-to-day increase in plasma estrogens: Pulsatile ovarian secretion during the day, which is superimposed on the continuous and steady day-to-day estrogen increases, seems to carry additional information, possibly serving as specific identification signals that ovulation—and no other process—is approaching.

The endocrinological events described for menstruation in all likelihood represent a genetically determined, neonatally imprinted, receptor-governed, autonomous process. What are the behavioral aspects? It has been established that in periovulatory periods coital frequency reaches a peak. During the premenstrual day, with falling progesterone levels, some women experience a syndrome of premenstrual tension characterized by increased irritability, a strong feeling of discontent, and a noticeable aggressivity recognized by the French judicial system, which regards crimes committed by women during this phase of their menstrual cycle as less severe than those taking place during other parts of the menstrual cycle. Obviously, autonomous endocrine processes influence mood and behavior. In many endocrine disturbances a loss of rhythmicity and cyclicity can be noticed, but selected stimulation can restore these functions to the system. One may conclude that cyclicity induced by environmental challenges is necessary to bring about normal development and functioning in an individual.

When the genetically predetermined number of oocytes is depleted, menopause occurs, and the loss of estrogen and progesterone causes discomfort in many women.

Do environmental processes affect imprinted endocrine events? Again, we use menstruation as an example. It is well established that environmental factors, that is, changes causing marked alternations in an individual's normal behavior, such as traveling, may induce menstrual disturbances.

Although abnormal intake of food is almost certainly due to previous disturbances to personality, caloric intake affects the menstrual cycle. Thus, when the body weight reaches an abnormally high level, menstruation ceases and the female remains infertile as body weight increases. When eating is curtailed and body weight declines, menstruation begins again at about the same body weight that it was halted. A low caloric intake (or none) with loss of normal body weight soon leads to amenorrhea also, which is well known from studies on anorexia. Furthermore, there are data to indicate that vigorous physical training in young women may lead to cessation of ovulation, perhaps owing to an androgen level that is too high to meet anabolic demands.

With respect to male sexual performance and behavior, cyclicity has been difficult to demonstrate. There seems to be a seasonal difference in circulating testosterone levels and slight indications that a male period may exist with a duration of some 60 days. Somewhere between the ages of 55 and 60 there are changes in the secretion pattern of steroids, which indicate the possibility of a male menopause (Sköldfors, 1978). However, these changes are probably attributable to adrenal function rather than to testosterone secretion. Loss of androgen leads to a number of side effects. Such patients report primarily a loss of initiative and fighting spirit and tend not to respond to provocation with aggression; libido is gradually lost. Replacement therapy restores male performance characteristics. Administration of estrogens to men induces some female sex characteristics, and androgens given to women cause varying degrees of virilization.

Although glands such as the thyroid, adrenal, and parathyroid are similar in appearance in men and women, they probably function in a sex-specific way. Recent data also indicate that "non-endocrine" organs such as the liver and kidney also function in a sex-specific way (Fleetwood, Landgren, & Eneroth, unpublished observations, 1982; Gustafsson, Modé, Eneroth, Hökfelt, & Norstedt, 1981). In fact, all organs seem to excrete messenger substances, making a division into endocrine and non-endocrine organs less meaningful. However, in one sense there is a difference. Classic endocrine organs have specific stimulators, trophins, which govern their function. Extracts from the pituitary display a very complex composition, as do the trophins from the pituitary; the trophins that have been isolated and identified from the pituitary are primarily those that cause acute effects (e.g., ACTH) or that have an effect on most organ functions (e.g., human growth hormone [hGH]). Typically, prolactin, which does not cause acute effects and does not play such a fundamental role as GH, was the most recently discovered pituitary hormone. Since the hypothalamus exerts a major control over the anterior pituitary function, the releasing and inhibiting factors found there are, of course, those connected to the known pituitary hormones. Abnormalities associated with this region clearly change the behavior of the patient in a way that seems specific for the endocrine axis damaged. Thus, clinicians can readily differentiate an acromegalic patient with excessive release of GH from a patient with hyperprolactinoma. The former is often extroverted and cooperative, whereas the latter is sullen and complaining. Often patients do not notice their own gradually developing disease, but when treatment is effective they usually claim that they recall how they felt before the illness and that they now can distinguish between the healthy and diseased states (S. Werner, personal communication, 1982).

Conclusions

As indicated in this chapter, the number of hormones or messengers discovered over the last decade has been growing exponentially. We now know of endogenous substances that induce sleep, anorexia or hyperphagia, and anesthesia, just to mention a few (Noda, 1982). Most messengers do affect behavior, and the induced behavior in turn brings about changes in secretion of the messengers. We are dealing with an integrated system that, at present, is impossible to comprehend as a whole because it is common practice to study one or a few "endocrine axes" at a time. One may doubt that there is a definable beginning of endocrine events that can be pinpointed in a meaningful way. It is like asking where the ocean begins. In the continuity of the life of an individual selected information in extreme cases of malfunction can be discerned, but we can only guess, and rarely, what might have been the trigger event. It is absolutely meaningless to divide an individual's life into somatic and nonsomatic influences; this would be like trying to determine both the location and the speed of an electron: We do know that the electron has both a location and a certain speed, but we have to settle for a measurement of only one of these criteria during each experiment, which creates uncertainty as to the whereabouts of electrons, as depicted by Heisenberg. The same goes for the human mind, where development and degeneration are continuous processes that are hard to distinguish from one another. To me, degeneration means loss of cyclicity, loss of capacity, reliance on imprinted behavior, and an incapacity to adjust to environments. Studies that have been done on a monkey colony on an isolated island might help to illustrate this: One day people who used to transverse the lagoon to feed the apes happened to drop the food into the water. Some of the monkeys waded into the water and caught the food. Further studies revealed that those who could adjust to this new way of feeding were below a certain age in their life spans. Older monkeys remained on the beach walking uneasily around, displaying much distress. It is my sincere hope that we who participated in the meeting from which this book was culled are not the ones remaining on the beach.

References

Baconfield, S., & Baconfield, J. (Eds). *Placenta: An experimental animal.* New York: McGraw-Hill, 1979.

Banlien, E. E. Induction of estrogen receptors by high progesterone doses (*Nobel Symposia No. 14*). Stockholm: Almqvist and Wiksell, 1980. Pp. 118–139.

Diczfalusy, E. Endocrine functions of the human fetoplacental unit. *Federation Proceedings*, 1964, *23*, 791–798.

Gustafsson, J.-Å., Modé, A., Eneroth, P., Hökfelt, T., & Norstedt, G. Sex-dependent hepatic function in the rat. In G. Persson (Ed.), *Neurobiology of the brain.* New York: Raven, 1981. Pp. 80–103.

Gustafsson, J.-Å., & Stenberg, Å. Imprinting of hepatic metabolism of steroid hormones in the rat. *Journal of Steroid Biochemistry*, 1974, *21*, 95–103.

Johnson, T., Smith, E., & Klyne, V. Connections between cells. *Trends in Biochemistry*, 1978, *2*, 21–23.

Jönsson, S., & Batra, T. Down-regulation of β-adrenergic receptors during treatment with an agonist. In *Abstracts of the XII International Meeting of Gynaecology and Obstetrics.* San Francisco, 1982.

Laga, E. A., Driscoll, S. G., & Munro, H. N. Human placental structure: Relationships to fetal nutrition. In J. B. Josimovich, M. Reynolds, & E. Cobo (Eds.), *Lactogenic hormones, fetal nutrition and lactation.* New York: Wiley, 1974. Pp. 143–182.

Lester, C., Bruder, A., & Kögelsdorf, S. F. Arrest of sex-organ development by antiandrogens. In X. Castrino (Ed.), *Serono symposia: Sexual differentiation of the male genital tractus.* New York: Wiley, 1975. Pp. 181–199.

Lundström, V., Granström, E., & Eneroth, P. Diurnal variations in uterine contractibility. *Acta Endocrinologica,* in press.

Mizuno, H., Share, L., & Tanaka, K. Tissue growth stimulators. *Cell,* 1981, *14,* 308–319.

Noda, H. *Peptide research.* New York: McGraw-Hill, 1982.

Petrozinsky, V., Chabrodsky, W., & Hilson, J. W. Evidence for cell-to-cell contact via microchannels. *Cell Physiology,* 1977, *29,* 906–912.

Pousette, Å. *Androgen receptors in various organs from male to female rats.* Unpublished doctoral thesis, Karolinska Institute, Stockholm, 1978.

Ritzén, M., Karlsson, K., & Fredriksson, S. Adrenal engagement in the advancement of puberty. In S. Shamrock (Ed.), *Puberty.* New York: Plenum, 1979. Pp. 261–283.

Sköldfors, H. *Hormone levels in older men.* Unpublished doctoral thesis, Karolinska Institute, Stockholm, 1978.

Södersten, P., & Hansen, S. Imprinting of sexual behavior in the rat. *Journal of Endocrinology,* 1977, *81,* 516–522.

Wetterman, A., & Seagram, J. Cyclicity in hormone release. In B. Z. Chockburn (Ed.), *Rhythm investigation in endocrinology.* New York: Raven, 1979.

13

The Inheritance of Human Deviance

SARNOFF A. MEDNICK   TERRIE E. MOFFITT   VICKI POLLOCK
SHARON TALOVIC   WILLIAM F. GABRIELLI, JR.
KATHERINE T. VAN DUSEN

All human behavioral characteristics are products of an interaction between life experiences and a conglomerate of genetic factors. It is not unusual to consider the effects of genes as limiting normal behavior, as in rare states such as Down's syndrome, phenylketonuria (PKU), or Huntington's disease, where single genes directly determine whether the disease will appear. But, even in these cases, the environment helps shape the behavioral symptoms and the course of the illness.

Genes and environment also interact to produce behaviors that are not symptoms of disease states. One example is the genetic coding for eye structure and central nervous system processing, interacting with nutrition and visual environmental stimulation, which enable normal visual perceptual behaviors to take place. In actuality, without genetic coding, no behavior at all would exist.

If other behaviors are partially genetically determined, it does not seem unreasonable to test the hypothesis that gene–environment interactions also might influence deviant behaviors. In this chapter we review the evidence for a genetic component in the etiologies of three of the deviant states that are most troublesome to society: schizophrenia, alcoholism, and criminal offending. We shall emphasize the topic of criminal behavior in particular because we have new, unpublished findings to report here.

In each of three sections, schizophrenia, alcoholism, and criminal offending, we review results of studies from three approaches to genetic investigation. The first, family studies, provide valuable information about increased risk for deviance found among family members of affected individuals. However, fam-

HUMAN DEVELOPMENT:
AN INTERACTIONAL PERSPECTIVE

ily studies provide few conclusions about genetic etiology because members of families share environments as well as genes. A second approach, the study of twins, offers a somewhat better separation of genetic and environmental effects. The twin studies compare identical, monozygotic (MZ) twins, who are genetically identical, to fraternal, same-sex, dizygotic (DZ) twins, who have no more genes in common than other siblings (50%). The research design assumes that the effect of hereditary factors is demonstrated if the MZ twins have more similar outcomes (concordance for deviance) than DZ twins. In almost all studies, the twins were reared together, and the method assumes that the environmental influences upon MZ twins are no different from those upon DZ twins. The possibility exists, however, that MZ pairs were reared more similarly than DZ pairs because of their identical appearances (Dalgaard & Kringlen, 1976).

A third approach, the adoption study, overcomes the possibility of confounding genetic and environmental factors, which limit inferences from the results of twin studies. In this method, the deviance outcomes of adopted children (separated from birth from their biological parents) are compared to the outcomes of their adoptive parents and their biological parents. Similarity in outcome between adoptees and biological parents indicates a genetic effect. In addition, with the application of cross-fostering analysis, relative contributions to deviance from genetic family and from family of rearing may be compared and interactions between genetic and environmental factors may be examined.

Genetics in the Etiology of Schizophrenia

Numerous researchers have emphasized the importance of genetics in the etiology of schizophrenia. From Meehl (1954), who noted that the genetic contribution was the "uniformly most potent" contributor to the etiology of schizophrenia, to Kety, who quips, "If schizophrenia is a myth, it is a myth with a heavy genetic component" (1974), we see the importance given to genetics.

FAMILY STUDIES

The incidence of schizophrenia in the general population is about 1%. The risk for schizophrenia is decidedly higher in relatives of a schizophrenic, ranging from 2 to 46 times higher, depending on the number of genes shared with the schizophrenic (Rosenthal, 1970; Slater & Cowie, 1971). Thus, among first-degree relatives, the risk for schizophrenia is about 8–10%; the risk for third-degree relatives is about 2%; and the risk for second-degree relatives is slightly more than this.

Moreover, the risk for schizophrenia increases as the genetic loading increases. Children with two schizophrenic parents have a 46% risk, whereas children with only one schizophrenic parent have about a 10–16% risk, depending on severity of the parent's illness (Kallman, 1938).

TWIN STUDIES

Twins have a much higher rate of concordance for schizophrenia if they have the same genetic makeup (MZ twins) than if they are no more alike genetically than ordinary siblings (DZ twins). The risk is about 40–50% for MZ twins and 10–15% for DZ twins (Fischer, Harvald & Hauge, 1969; Gottesman & Shields, 1982; Kringlen, 1968; Pollin, Allen, Hoffer, Stabenau, & Hrubec, 1969; Tienari, 1971).

ADOPTION STUDIES

Because the less-than-perfect concordance in MZ twins reveals that environmental factors also play a role in the etiology of schizophrenia, studies have attempted to separate the relative influences of heredity and rearing environment. Heston (1966) found that, of 47 foster-reared children of schizophrenic women, 5 had become schizophrenic, as compared to 0 of 50 foster-reared children of psychiatrically normal women. In addition, Rosenthal (1974) found that 30% of 76 children of a schizophrenic parent who were adopted at an early age developed a schizophrenia spectrum disorder (e.g., borderline schizophrenia, schizoid personality, schizophrenia) in contrast to 17.8% of 67 control adoptees. Thus, even though all children were raised in adoptive homes (with index and control cases being matched for age, sex, age at transfer to adopting family, and SES of adopting parents), a higher rate of pathology was found in children with a schizophrenic biological parent than in children with normal parents.

Both Heston and Rosenthal conclude that offspring of a schizophrenic have the same risk for schizophrenia whether or not they are raised by their schizophrenic parent. The logical questions that arise in response to these two studies are, "What were the adoptive parents like?" and "Could the adoptive rearing environments help account for the development of schizophrenia?"

Kety, Rosenthal, Wender, and Schulsinger (1974) are conducting a major adoption study in Scandinavia, where national record-keeping policies and procedures make possible the study of very large cohorts, which allows for greater generalization of results. Their study is based on a register of all non-familial adoptions that took place in Denmark in the years 1924–1947. The register includes information on 14,427 adoptees and their adoptive and biological parents, a total of more than 70,000 persons. Kety *et al.* (1974, 1975) found that schizophrenia spectrum disorders were no more common in the adoptive relatives of children who developed schizophrenia than of those of normal children. Yet, consistent with prior findings, the occurrence of schizophrenia spectrum disorder in biological relatives did differentiate schizophrenic from normal offspring. The 33 schizophrenic offspring had 13 biological relatives (parents, sibs, half-sibs) who had a schizophrenia spectrum disorder. The 33 normal offspring had 3 biological relatives with the disorder. Kety's initial findings were based upon review of psychiatric hospital records that listed all relatives (adoptive and biological) who were admitted.

Rather than rely only on hospital records, Kety chose to further investigate genetic contribution to the schizophrenia spectrum via psychiatric interviews of all the relatives, performed by a Danish psychiatrist who did not know to which group a relative belonged. Kety found even more marked contrasts. Of 118 biological relatives of index cases, 37 had a schizophrenia spectrum disorder, in contrast to 19 out of 140 for controls, a difference of 21.4% to 10.9%. Again, index and control subjects had adoptive relatives who had very little pathology, 5.4% and 7.7%, respectively. To be even more certain that control subjects themselves did not possess a schizophrenic disorder that was undetected because the individual had not been hospitalized for it, Kety interviewed the subjects. He excluded 10 control subjects and found that the rate of schizophrenia spectrum in the biological relatives of this "screened" control group, 6.4%, was lower than before and stands in stark contrast to the 21.4% for index cases. Thus, it wasn't the adoptive environment that differentiated schizophrenics from controls, but rather biological background. Given a relatively normal rearing environment, individuals who develop schizophrenia have a genetic disposition to do so. But what of those individuals who have no such biological predisposition but are reared by an adoptive schizophrenic parent?

Wender, Rosenthal, Kety, Schulsinger, and Welner (1974) investigated this very question. Three groups were contrasted: (a) 69 adoptees with a biological parent who was schizophrenic (index group); (b) 69 matched adoptees with biological parents who had no psychiatric history (control group); and (c) 28 adoptees who had nonschizophrenic biological parents but who had an adoptive parent with a schizophrenia spectrum diagnosis (cross-fostered group). Upon interviewing all adoptees, Wender et al. found no differences between the control and cross-fostered groups in their degree of psychopathology. Yet both groups were lower in psychopathology than the index group. This clearly suggests that a rearing environment with schizophrenic parents does not exert nearly as strong an influence as a biological predisposition.

Rosenthal, Wender, Kety, Schulsinger, Welner, and Reider (1975) pursued this question further by rating the degree of child psychopathology and the quality of parent–child interaction for four groups representing differing combinations of genetic predisposition and "schizophrenic" rearing environment. The four groups were control adoptees (1), index adoptees (2), cross-fostered adoptees (3), and index children reared by their schizophrenic parent (4).

The most severe psychopathology was exhibited by all individuals with a biological predisposition (Groups 1 and 2) regardless of where they were reared. The worst parent–child relations were found in both groups reared in a schizophrenic environment (Groups 1 and 3), regardless of biological predisposition. The relation between child diagnosis and quality of parent–child interaction was strongest in Groups 3 and 4, which did not have the biological predisposition. Thus, the rearing environment predicted child diagnosis better in individuals without a genetic loading for schizophrenia than it did for individuals with such loading.

Acute Schizophrenia.   There has been the suggestion in the literature that sudden onset, or acute, schizophrenia may not have the same genetic loading that the chronic schizophrenia does. Rosenthal and Kety (1968), for example, report that adoptees with a diagnosis of acute schizophrenic reaction had relatively few schizophrenia-like disorders among their biological relatives as compared to the biological relatives of chronic and borderline schizophrenics. Rosenthal (1974) concludes that the classical subtypes of schizophrenia, as well as the less disturbed schizoid and borderline personalities, are genetically related; but the true reactive schizophrenics, those with good premorbid histories and good outcomes, probably do not share the same genetic background. A recent statement by Gottesman and Shields (1982) questions whether the "splitting" of the schizophrenia diagnosis will prove to have genetic justification.

Taken together, the adoption studies certainly reveal the importance of genetics in the development of schizophrenia and help to clarify the relative contribution of environmental variables. Given a genetic predisposition, parent–child interaction in the rearing environment contributes relatively little to a prediction of schizophrenia in offspring. For those individuals without a genetic predisposition (which characterizes the majority of eventual schizophrenics) rearing environment does play an important role in prediction of schizophrenic outcome.

It may be that better techniques of assessing genetic predisposition (e.g., biological markers) or methods of assessing other environmental influences (e.g., affective stability of home environment) will add significantly to our understanding of the relative contribution *and* the interaction of hereditary and environmental influences.

Genetics in the Etiology of Alcoholism

FAMILY STUDIES

There are two important findings that emerge from family studies of alcoholism. One concerns the rates of alcoholism among biological relatives of alcoholics, and the other concerns the specificity of alcoholism as a psychiatric disorder among the alcoholics' relatives. Both findings, however, depend on the sex of the alcoholic.

More men are alcoholic than women. The prevalence of alcoholism among males is approximately 3–5%, but only .1–1.0% for females. It is likely that these estimates reflect genuine differences in the population and are not due to methodological or cultural biases against diagnosing females alcoholic (Goodwin, 1981).

The first important finding to emerge from family studies of alcoholism is that rates of alcoholism among biological relatives of alcoholics are higher than those observed in the general population. Cotton (1979) reviewed 39 studies on familial alcoholism, providing information on 6251 alcoholic and 4083 nonalcoholic families. In two-thirds of those studies, 25% of the alcoholics had alcoholic fathers. The combined findings of these reports are impressive because, in spite of numerous methodological inconsistencies, they permit the conclusion that biological relatives of alcoholics constitute a high-risk group for alcoholism.

Interestingly, Cotton's review also indicated a trend in the difference of alcoholism rates among relatives of male and female alcoholics. The biological relatives of female alcoholics tended to have higher rates of alcoholism than those of male alcoholics. This trend underscores the importance of distinguishing the sexes for studying etiological factors in alcoholism.

The second important finding to emerge from familial studies of alcoholism concerns alcoholism as a specific syndrome. Are the biological relatives of alcoholics more prone to develop alcoholism specifically, rather than other types of psychiatric disorders? If the relatives of alcoholics show higher rates of alcoholism than any other type of mental illness, this would provide tentative evidence that alcoholism constitutes a specific disorder that may have a genetic origin. The evidence must be considered tentative in as much as the families share their environment as well as genetics.

The empirical evidence bearing on this issue is complex, but the answer to the question is straightforward. The evidence strongly suggests that families of alcoholics have higher rates of alcoholism rather than any other type of mental illness. But here the complexities creep in. The biological relatives of alcoholics also exhibit more psychopathological symptoms, especially those indicative of affective disorders, than do relatives of nonalcoholics. The issue becomes especially murky if one examines family research literature on female alcoholics. The course of alcoholism in women is such that the diagnosis of alcoholism is often secondary to depression (Goodwin, 1981). Furthermore, the daughters of male alcoholics often exhibit depressive symptomatology. Attempts to resolve these findings are hampered by the small numbers of female alcoholics that have been studied. Nonetheless, the most important point is that alcoholism is the most frequent disorder manifested by the relatives of alcoholics; other types of psychiatric disorders appear less frequently.

In summary, family studies of alcoholism provide evidence consistent with the hypothesis that alcoholism is genetically influenced.

TWIN STUDIES

The first major twin study of alcoholism was conducted by Kaij (1960) in Sweden. Kaij classified each member of 48 MZ and 126 DZ twins according to their severity of alcohol abuse. Each individual was classified into one of four categories of alcohol use, ranging from average to severe. Kaij found that 54.2% of MZs received the same classification, as compared to 31.2% of DZs. These results indicate that MZs exhibit more similar patterns of alcohol use than DZs.

It is possible that Kaij's results reflect conservative estimates for similarity of alcohol use among twins, because the sample did not include twins who abstained from alcohol, or who consumed very little. This is important, because in another twin study, the highest heritabilities were obtained for two features predisposing against alcohol use. Loehlin (1972) reported the highest heritabilities for hangovers and not abusing alcohol, while the heritability for excessive use of alcohol was lower.

Other twin study findings also emphasize the importance of studying alcohol abuse as well as abstinence. Partanen, Brunn, and Markkanen (1966) studied 902 male twins' drinking practices. Factor analyses yielded three variables that described their drinking behaviors: (*a*) frequency of ethanol consumption; (*b*) amount of ethanol consumed per drinking session; and (*c*) loss of control over drinking. Heritabilities for the first two factors were .39 and .36, respectively. This result indicates that quantity and frequency of ethanol consumption are under substantial genetic control, a conclusion also warranted by Jonsson and Nilsson's (1968) study of 750 male twin pairs. The strongest evidence for genetic influence was observed when drinkers and abstainers were compared.

The observation that MZ twins show more similarity in amount and frequency of ethanol consumption as compared to DZs may be related to ethanol metabolism rate. It is widely acknowledged that ethanol metabolism rates are genetically determined (Kissin, 1979); it is therefore not too surprising to find that MZ twins show more similarities in terms of amount and frequency of ethanol consumption than DZ twins.

The twin study findings suggest two important considerations to be addressed in research on alcoholism. First, it is important to consider factors that mediate abstinence from alcohol as well as those that contribute to alcoholism. Second, the studies suggest that alcoholism (or abstinence from alcohol) may be mediated by genetically determined biological features. Studying biological characteristics may prove a useful avenue for identifying etiological factors involved in the development of alcohol abuse.

ADOPTION STUDIES

Persuasive evidence for genetic factors in the etiology of alcoholism is derived from results of adoption studies on alcoholism. With one exception, adoption studies of alcoholism among females provide such small samples that the results do not permit firm inferences. The majority of literature reviewed here is limited almost exclusively to males.

Goodwin, Schulsinger, Moller, Hermansen, Winodur, and Guze (1974) conducted an adoption study of alcoholism in Denmark. They used material derived from interviews with adoptees, as well as information available on alcohol abuse among adoptees and both sets of their parents through information maintained by the Danish government. Goodwin found that the adopted-away sons of alcoholics were four times more likely to develop alcoholism than control adoptees. Since Goodwin's report, all subsequent adoption studies of alcoholism furnish results consistent with his. Cadoret and Gath (1978) found higher rates of alcoholism among adoptees ($N = 84$) with a biological history of alcoholism as compared to controls. Bohman (1978) used information on 2000 adoptees available through Swedish governmental sources and obtained a significant positive association between biological parents' alcohol abuse and their adopted-away sons' extent of alcohol use.

The distinction between alcoholism and heavy drinking is an important one. Roe (1944) conducted an adoption study of alcoholism in the United States. Adopted children whose biological parents were heavy drinkers ($N = 27$) were compared to foster control children ($N = 22$) on the basis of their adult drinking problems. No significant differences in adult drinking problems were found to distinguish the two groups of adoptees.

Although Roe's findings appear inconsistent with the bulk of adoption study results on alcoholism, Goodwin attempted to resolve the discrepancy. Goodwin (1977) used the data he acquired in Denmark to compare rates of heavy drinking by adopted-away sons of alcoholics to control adoptees, and found no differences between the two groups. It was only when a strict definition of alcoholism was used that the adopted-away sons of alcoholics showed higher rates of alcoholism than controls; heavy drinking did not distinguish them.

An elegant adoption study of alcoholism was recently reported by Cloninger, Bohman, and Sigvardsson (1981) that supports and refines previous findings of adoption studies of alcoholism. Results led Cloninger et al. to postulate a provocative hypothesis. They speculate that there are two types of alcoholism with different extents of genetic and environmental influence.

According to the authors, one type of alcoholism is strongly influenced by genetic factors, but is less influenced by environmental ones. They termed this type of alcoholism "male-limited." These adoptees had been classified as moderate alcohol abusers, and while their biological fathers were severe alcohol abusers, their biological mothers were essentially normal.

The other type of alcohol abuse is, according to Cloninger et al., influenced by both genetics and environment. They termed this type of alcoholism "milieu-limited." These milieu-limited adoptees were mild or severe alcohol abusers. Both their biological mothers and fathers evidenced signs of mild alcohol abuse.

There are two considerations that suggest it may be premature to conclude that the etiological factors influencing mild and severe alcohol abuse are similar. The considerations concern the ages of the adoptees at the time of the study and interpretation of the cross-fostering analysis.

At the time of the study, the subjects ranged in age from 23 to 43 years old. Cloninger *et al.* (1981) included statistical adjustments for adoptees' age, and state that age had "no detectable effect on observed risks" and "made no contribution to any results [p. 862]." These statements pertain to results of statistical tests, but there is no way for statistical tests to account for the fact that 23-year-old men have not had the same amount of time to become registered for alcohol abuse as 43-year-old men. It is possible, and maybe even probable, that 23-year-old men presently classified as mild or moderate alcohol abusers could receive additional registrations or treatment for alcoholism during the next 20 years that would result in reclassifying them as severe alcohol abusers. Previous observations do suggest that symptoms of severe alcohol abuse increase during the 30- to 40-year age bracket (Goodwin, 1981). Cloninger *et al.* do not present mean ages of adoptees classified as mild, moderate, or severe alcohol abusers, which would shed some light on this issue.

Careful inspection of the cross-fostering analysis also suggests something a little bit peculiar about emphasizing the similarities of mild and severe alcohol abusers. Only 10.3% of adoptees with positive genetic and environmental influences predisposing to alcoholism manifest severe alcohol abuse, whereas 7.1% of the adoptees with only positive genetic predispositions (not environmental ones) manifest severe alcohol abuse. The corresponding percentages for adoptees classified as mild alcohol abusers are different: 26.7% of those with positive genetic and environmental influences predisposing to alcohol abuse manifest mild symptoms, but for those with only positive genetic predispositions (not environmental ones) 10.4% manifest symptoms indicative of mild alcohol abuse. In conjunction with consideration of the age influence, the cross-fostering analysis results suggest it may be useful to retain a distinction between mild and severe alcohol abuse at present.

Finally, the Swedish group has recently conducted the first adoption study of alcoholism among females with a large enough sample size to permit some tentative conclusions, and these data should be available shortly.

Genetics in the Etiology of Criminal Behavior

FAMILY STUDIES

It has long been observed that antisocial parents raise an excessive number of children who also become antisocial. In the classic study by Robins (1966), one of the best predictors of antisocial behavior in a child was father's criminal behavior. In terms of genetics, very little can be concluded from such family data since it is difficult to disentangle hereditary and environmental influences.

TWIN STUDIES

In the first twin-criminality study, the German psychiatrist Lange (1929) found 77% concordance for criminality for his MZ twins and 12% concordance for his DZ twins. Lange concluded that "heredity plays a quite preponderant part among the causes of crime [p. 41]." Subsequently, studies of twins (until 1961 there were eight in all) have tended to confirm the direction of Lange's results. About 60% pairwise concordance has been reported for MZ and about 30% concordance for DZ twins (see Table 1). For a detailed discussion of these twin studies, the reader may turn to Christiansen (1977a).

These eight twin studies suffer from the fact that their sampling was rather haphazard. As mentioned earlier, many were carried out in Germany or Japan during a politically unfortunate period. They report too high a proportion of MZ twins. Concordant MZ pairs are more likely to be brought to the attention of the investigator. Twinship is usually easier to detect in the case of identical twins, especially if they end up in the same prison. All of these factors tend to inflate MZ concordance rates in nonsystematic studies.

More recently, Christiansen (1977b) has reported on the criminality of a total population of 3586 twin pairs from a well-defined area of Denmark. He found 35% pairwise concordance for criminal behavior for male–male identical twin pairs and 12% concordance for male–male fraternal twin pairs. This result suggests that identical twins inherit some biological characteristic (or characteristics) that increases their common risk of being registered for criminal behavior.

ADOPTION STUDIES

Limitations of the twin method in decisively separating genetic and environmental effects have led to hesitation in the full acceptance of the genetic implications of twin research. The study of adoptions better separates environment and genetics; if male criminal adoptees have disproportionately high numbers of criminal biological fathers (given appropriate controls), this would suggest a genetic factor in criminality. This is especially true since in almost all instances the adoptee has never seen the biological father and does not know who he is; the adoptee may not even realize he has been adopted.

Two United States adoption studies have reported highly suggestive results. Crowe (1975) found an increased rate of criminality in 18 Iowan adoptees with criminal biological mothers. Cadoret (1978) reported on 246 Iowans adopted at birth. Reports of antisocial behavior in these 246 adoptees are significantly related to antisocial behavior in the biological parents.

In a study of Swedish adoptees, Bohman (1978) originally found no significant relationship between criminality in the biological parents and in the adoptees; further analysis distinguishing between biological parents' levels of severity of criminality has yielded evidence of a genetic relationship (Cloninger, Sigvardsson, Bohman, & Von Knorring, 1982).

NEW RESULTS FROM OUR ADOPTION STUDY

The present study is being conducted in the context of the cohort of 14,427 Danish adoptees described earlier in our discussion of adoption studies in

Table 1
Twin Studies of Psychopathy and Criminality in MZ and Same-Sexed DZ Twins Only

Study	Location	Monozygotic			Dizygotic		
		Total pairs	Pairs concordant	Percentage concordant	Total pairs	Pairs concordant	Percentage concordant
Lange, 1929	Bavaria	13	10	77	17	2	12
Legras, 1932	Holland	4	4	100	5	1	20
Rosanoff, 1934	U.S.A.	37	25	68	28	5	18
Stumpfl, 1936	Germany	18	11	61	19	7	37
Kranz, 1936	Prussia	32	21	66	43	23	54
Borgstrom, 1939	Finland	4	3	75	5	2	40
Slater, 1953 (psychopathy)	England	2	1	50	10	3	30
Yoshimasu, 1961	Japan	28	17	61	18	2	11
Total		138	92	67.2	145	45	31.0

schizophrenia (Kety *et al.* 1974). We hypothesized that registered criminality in the biological parents would be associated with an increased risk of registered criminal behavior in the adoptees.

Results. Court convictions were utilized as an index of criminal involvement. In order to access these records it is necessary to know the place of birth, as well as the date of birth, and, of course, the individual's name. When subjects were lost to the investigation it was usually because of lack of information or ambiguity regarding their place of birth. Table 2 presents the numbers of adoptees, biological parents, and adoptive parents for which we have complete information. The levels of court convictions for each of the members of the "adoption family" are also given in Table 2. It seems that, in this time period in Denmark, individuals who gave their children up for adoption, and the children themselves, evidenced higher rates of court convictions than did the adoptive parents, whose convictions rates are very near the conviction rates for men and women in the general population of Denmark (Wolf, Kaarsen, & Hogh, 1958).

Cross-Fostering Analysis. Because of the size of the population, it is possible to segregate subgroups of adoptees who have combinations of criminal and noncriminal biological and adoptive parents. Table 3 presents the four groups in a design that is analogous to the cross-fostering paradigm used in behavior genetics. As can be seen in the lower right-hand cell, if neither the biological nor adoptive parents are criminal, 13.5% of their sons are criminal, but if the biological parents are not criminal while the adoptive parents evidence criminality, this figure rises to 14.7%. In the lower left-hand cell of Table 3 note that 20.0% of the sons are criminal if the adoptive parents are *not* criminal and one of the biological parents is criminal. If at least one biological parent and at least one adoptive parent are criminal, we observe the highest level of criminality in the sons, 24.5%. The comparison analogous to the cross-fostering paradigm favors a partial genetic etiology hypothesis. We must caution, however, that simply knowing that the adoptive father has been convicted of a crime does not tell us how criminogenic the adoptee's environment had been. On the other hand, at conception, the genetic influence of the biological father is already complete. Thus, this analysis does not yield a fair comparison between environmental and genetic influences included in the table. But this initial analysis does indicate that sons who have never seen their criminal biological fathers have an elevated probability of becoming criminal. This suggests that some biological characteristic is transmitted from the criminal biological father to the son that increases the son's risk of obtaining a court conviction for a criminal law offense.

A series of log-linear analyses of the frequencies observed in Table 3 have shown that the adoptive parent criminality is not associated with a significant increment in the son's criminality. In view of the low frequency of court

Table 2
Conviction Rates of Completely Identified Members of the Adoptee Families

Family member	Number identified	Number not identified	Percentage of criminal law court convictions			
			0	1	2	3 or more
Male Adoptee	6,129	571	.841	.088	.029	.040
Female Adoptee	7,065	662	.972	.020	.005	.003
Adoptive Fathers	13,918	509	.938	.046	.008	.008
Adoptive Mothers	14,267	160	.981	.015	.002	.002
Biological Fathers	10,604	3,823	.714	.129	.056	.102
Biological Mothers	12,300	2,127	.911	.064	.012	.013

Table 3

"Cross-Fostering" Analysis: Percentage of Adoptive Sons Who Have Been Convicted of Criminal Law Offenses

	Are biological parents criminal?	
	Yes	No
Are adoptive parents criminal?		
Yes	24.5	14.7
	(of 143)	(of 204)
No	20.0	13.5
	(of 1226)	(of 2492)

Note: The numbers in parentheses are the total Ns for each cell.

convictions in the adoptive parents, in the analysis to be reported below we will report only on associations between biological parents' crime and adoptees' crime in cases where the adoptive parents are free of court conviction. This is done to facilitate interpretation. Analyses of biological parental influence upon adoptee crime rates including the convicted adoptive parents yield identical results.

Figures 1 and 2 present the relationship between degree of recidivism in the biological parent and criminality in the sons. The relationship is positive. Note also in Figure 2 that the relationship mainly affects property crimes in the adoptee. Log-linear analyses reveal that the relationship is highly significant for property crimes and not statistically significant for violent crimes. This may reflect a lack of heritability for violence or may be due to the relatively low level of violent crime in Denmark.

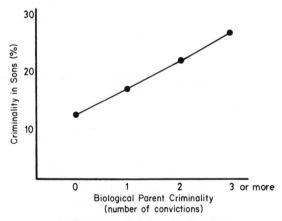

Figure 1. *Percentage of male adoptee criminality by biological parent criminality (cases in which adoptive parents are non-criminal) based on criminal law convictions.*

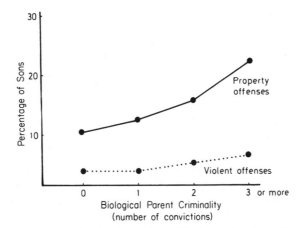

Figure 2. *Percentage of male adoptee property offenders and violent offenders by biological parent criminality (cases in which adoptive parents are non-criminal) based on criminal law convictions.*

The Chronic Offender.   The chronic offender has been shown to commit a markedly disproportionate number of criminal offenses. The extremely high rate of offending in the chronic offender suggests that perhaps the environment may play a smaller role in the etiology of his offending. We examined the relationship between the criminal behavior of the chronic adoptee offender and his biological parents.

In an important United States birth cohort study (Wolfgang, Figlio, & Sellin, 1972), the chronic offender was defined as one who had been arrested five or more times; these chronic offenders comprised 6% of the males and had committed 56% of the offenses. In our adoption cohort we have recorded court conviction, rather than arrest data. If we select as chronic offenders those with three or more court convictions, this includes 4.09% of the male adoptees. This small group of recidivists accounts for 69.4% of all of the court convictions for all of the male adoptees. This is a high concentration of crime in a very small fraction of the cohort.

Table 4 shows how the chronic offender, the other offenders (one or two convictions), and the nonoffenders are distributed as a function of level of crime in the biological parents. As can be seen, the stated hypothesis is supported: The proportion of chronic adoptee offenders increases as a function of level of recidivism in the biological parents.

Another way of expressing this concentration of crime is to point out that the chronic adoptee offenders with chronic biological parent offenders number only 37. They comprise 1% of the 3691 adoptees; they are responsible, however, for *30%* of the male adoptee convictions. We should also note that the mean number of convictions for the chronic adoptee offenders increases sharply as a function of biological parent recidivism. The biological parents with 0,

Table 4

Proportion of Chronic Offenders, Other Offenders, and Non-offenders in Male Adoptees as a Function of Level of Crime in the Biological Parents

	Number of biological parent convictions			
	0	1	2	3 or More
Number of male adoptee convictions				
Non-offenders (no convictions)	.87	.84	.80	.75
Other offenders (1 or 2 convictions)	.10	.12	.15	.17
Chronic offenders (3 or more convictions)	.03	.04	.05	.09
Number of adoptees	2492	547	233	419

Note: Table excludes cases in which adoptive parents have been convicted of criminal law violation.

1, 2, or 3 or more convictions have male adoptees with means of .30, .41, .48, and .70 convictions, respectively.

Controlling Genetic Influence Better to Examine Environmental Effects.

In many psychological investigations genetic variance is not considered. In some analyses, this may contribute error; in some cases it may produce erroneous conclusions. Thus, separation from a father is associated with increased levels of delinquency in a son (Robins, 1966). This has been interpreted as a result of failure of identification or lack of consistent discipline. As we can see from Table 2, fathers who permit themselves to be separated from their child (e.g., biological fathers of adoptees) tend to have high levels of criminal conviction. The higher levels of delinquency found in "separation" studies might be partially due to genetic transmission of criminogenic predispositional characteristics. If this genetic variance were partially accounted for, the environmental hypothesis could be more precisely tested. We have utilized such partial genetic control better to study an important criminologic variable, social class. In a recent study by Van Dusen, Mednick, and Gabrielli (in press) we separated the variance ascribable to "genetic" social class and rearing social class. We examined adoptee crime as a joint function of biological parents' social class and adoptive parents' social class. The result for male adoptee crime may be seen in Table 5. It is clear from inspection of Table 5 that male adoptee crime varies as a function of both genetic and environmental social class, and log-linear analyses reveal that both effects are statistically significant. While the genetic effect is of interest, we wish to emphasize that, to our knowledge, this is the first controlled demonstration that *environmental* aspects of social class influence the social class–crime relationship. This finding suggests that, regardless of genetic background, improved social conditions are likely to lead to reductions in criminal behavior.

Table 5

Percentage of Male Adoptees with Criminal Convictions as a Function of Adoptive and Biological Parents' SES[a]

	Biological parents' SES			
	High	Middle	Low	Total
Adoptive parents' SES				
High	9.30	11.52	12.98	11.58
	(441)	(903)	(775)	(2099)
Middle	13.44	15.29	16.86	15.62
	(320)	(870)	(795)	(1985)
Low	13.81	17.25	18.04	17.19
	(210)	(568)	(787)	(1565)
Total	11.64	14.31	16.00	14.55
	(971)	(2341)	(2337)	(5649)

Note: Tabled values are percentage of adoptees with criminal convictions. Numbers in parentheses are total cell Ns.
[a]Data gathered from Van Dusen, Mednick, and Gabrielli (in press).

What Is Inherited in Deviance?

The preceding reviews have demonstrated that genetic factors can and do influence three types of deviance: schizophrenia, alcoholism, and criminal offending. What are the implications of this knowledge? To the list of environmental factors that are commonly acknowledged to contribute to deviance, we must now add biological factors, for it is through heritable biological structures and processes that the genes exert their influence. Identification of specific biological factors that must be involved in the etiology of deviance is the next goal, and this goal suggests the kinds of research that might now be profitably undertaken. The remainder of this chapter describes current efforts to identify the biological factors that act specifically in schizophrenia, alcoholism, and criminal offending.

SCHIZOPHRENIA

One train of research that we have followed in Copenhagen, Denmark, is the possibility that schizophrenics may be genetically predisposed to greater vulnerability to brain damage from prenatal and birth complications. This damage may be due to genetically determined arterial insufficiency in specific brain areas. Computerized axial tomography (CAT) scans performed on a small group of individuals with a genetic risk for schizophrenia revealed definite evidence of this type of brain damage in the brains of chronic schizophrenics. Presence of enlarged ventricles is associated with pregnancy and birth complications recorded at the children's births (Parnas, Schulsinger, Teasdale,

Schulsinger, Feldman, & Mednick, 1982). While all other data reported here from the Danish research projects have been prospective in nature, the CAT scans were performed recently. However, the association of the specific type of brain damage with pregnancy and birth complications over a 20-year time period seems to suggest that enlarged ventricles may be a precursor of adult schizophrenia, and not a result of the illness or its treatment. These results are tentatively reported as a suggestion of how we can search for possible genetic predispositions. We plan to perform CAT scans on our entire high-risk sample of 311.

ALCOHOLISM

We have preliminary findings from two prospective studies on alcoholism that included biological measures. The findings are preliminary because the individuals examined in the studies are still too young to manifest symptoms severe enough to warrant receiving a diagnosis of alcoholism.

In each study, we compared a group at high risk for alcoholism with control subjects. Individuals at high risk (HR) for alcoholism were defined as offspring of alcoholics, and control subjects were matched to HR subjects for sex, age, and social class. The HR and control subjects' brain wave activities, measured by electroencephalographic (EEG) techniques, were used to compare the two groups.

In the first study, Gabrielli, Mednick, Volavka, Pollock, Schulsinger, and Itil (1982) found that biological sons of alcoholics had more relative fast EEG activity than controls when they were 11 to 13 years of age. Since components of the EEG in man are genetically influenced (Zuckerman, Buchsbaum, & Murphy, 1980), this finding is consistent with the hypothesis that genetic factors are involved in the etiology of alcoholism. Furthermore, they suggest a possible hypothesis as to the nature of the genetic predisposition: abnormally fast brain activity. In view of the fact that alcohol intake slows brain activity and the fact that slower brain activity (such as slow alpha) is associated with pleasant subjective states, it seems reasonable to hypothesize that genetically controlled fast brain activity may predispose to alcoholism.

We also considered the possiblity that the alcoholic may be an individual with an especially sensitive brain response to alcohol. In a second study, we administered low doses of alcohol to HR and control subjects and studied their EEGs prior to and subsequent to drinking. We evaluated three different measures of alpha activity and found that all three distinguished HR and control subjects' responses to alcohol. All three alpha measures indicate that HR subjects were more physiologically sensitive than controls to the EEG-slowing effects of alcohol. One interpretation of these results is that a genetically determined central nervous system sensitivity to alcohol may characterize persons with a biological predisposition to develop alcoholism.

CRIMINAL OFFENDING

Our work in Denmark suggests that one biological mechanism involved in a genetic predisposition toward criminal offending may be responsiveness of the autonomic nervous system (ANS). Mednick (1977) has proposed a theory that includes relatively sluggish ANS responsiveness and slow ANS response recovery as critical components. There exists a literature supporting the notion that adult criminal offenders do exhibit lower arousal and slower recovery than non-offenders (Mednick & Volavka, 1980). Twin studies are available that have demonstrated that the critical ANS components are heritable (Bell *et al.*, described in Mednick, 1977). We have found the children of criminal offenders to show patterns of ANS responding that we would predict their parents to have had (Mednick, 1977). Thus, we know that slow ANS responding is characteristic of adult criminal offenders and their children, and that ANS responsiveness can be partially genetically determined. Can ANS responsiveness, measured prospectively, predict later antisocial behavior in the same individuals? Two of our studies provide evidence that ANS can predict in this way. Low responsiveness has predicted delinquency and recidivism over a 10-year period in a Danish study (Loeb & Mednick, 1977). Also, in a study we are conducting on the island of Mauritius, half recovery rate assessed in 3-year-olds is predictive over a 6-year period of behavioral precursors for delinquency such as fighting and bullying (Clark, 1982). These studies continue to reveal information useful in answering the question of what specific factors account for the results of family, twin, and adoption studies in criminal offending.

Conclusion

The argument is made from time to time that there is little use for genetic research into deviance, because only the environmental influences are susceptible to alteration. The misconception is that a "genetic" problem is predetermined and unyielding to treatments applied after the genetic code is set; therefore, it is said, the information that schizophrenia, alcoholism, or criminal offending have heritable components is certainly interesting, but not very useful. If genetic research ceased at the point of demonstrating heritability of deviance, this argument would be quite true. The real task is to identify the biological mechanisms through which heritable predispositions toward deviance are expressed. These mechanisms may suggest appropriate interventions and, most encouraging of all, *preventive* interventions.

Let us consider an example. Phenylketonuria (PKU), a disease that causes mental retardation, was not identified as a heritable disease separate from other forms of retardation until 1934, when Folling conducted a study of sisters in Norway. Infants with PKU could then be identified, but identification was useless; the mechanism by which the genes produced PKU retardation was unknown. Not until 1958 was the mechanism, a deficient enzyme, discovered. Discovery of the specific biological mechanism opened the way for development of a diet intervention. Since that time, 1 of every 100 children genetically destined to suffer mental retardation has been spared this fate (Harsanyi & Hutton, 1981). The example of PKU is an optimistic one. The etiologies of human deviances such as schizophrenia, alcoholism, and crime will most probably not be ascribable to some single enzyme. Let us proceed therefore with tempered optimism. Current research into the genetics of deviance is beginning to point to possible mechanisms of inheritance. Interventions, such as more attentive perinatal care for infants at risk for schizophrenia, are tentatively suggesting themselves. The progress of this research, and similar research on alcoholism and antisocial behavior, will be exciting to watch.

References

Bohman, M. Some genetic aspects of alcoholism and criminality. *Archives of General Psychiatry,* 1978, *35,* 269–276.

Borgstrom, C. A. Eine Serie von Kriminellen Zwillingen, *Archiv fur Rassenbiologie,* 1939.

Cadoret, R. J. Psychopathy in adopted away offspring of biological parents with antisocial behavior. *Archives of General Psychiatry,* 1978, *35,* 176–184.

Cadoret, R. J., & Gath, A. Inheritance of alcoholism in adoptees. *British Journal of Psychiatry,* 1978, *132,* 252–258.

Christiansen, K. O. A review of studies of criminality among twins. In S. A. Mednick & K. O. Christiansen (Eds.), *Biosocial bases of criminal behavior.* New York: Gardner Press, 1977, 45–88. (a)

Christiansen, K. O. A preliminary study of criminality among twins. In S. A. Mednick & K. O. Christiansen (Eds.), *Biosocial bases of criminal behavior.* New York: Gardner Press, 1977, 89–108. (b)

Clark, F. *Relationship of electrodermal activity at age 3 to aggression at age 9: A study of a physiologic substrate of temperament.* Unpublished manuscript, University of Southern California Library, 1982.

Cloninger, C. R., Bohman, M., & Sigvardsson, S. Inheritance of alcohol abuse. *Archives of General Psychiatry,* 1981, *38,* 861–868.

Cloninger, C. R., Sigvardsson, S., Bohman, M., & vonKnorring, A. Predisposition to petty criminality in Swedish adoptees. *Archives of General Psychiatry,* 1982, *39,* 1242–1247.

Cotton, N. S. The familial incidence of alcoholism. *Journal of Studies on Alcohol,* 1979, *40,* 89–117.

Crowe, R. An adoptive study of psychopathy: Preliminary results from arrest records and psychiatric hospital records. In R. Fieve, D. Rosenthal, & H. Brill (Eds.), *Genetic research in psychiatry.* Baltimore: Johns Hopkins University Press, 1975.

Dalgaard, O. S., and Kringlen, E. A. Norwegian twin study of criminality. *British Journal of Criminology,* 1976, *16,* 213–232.

Fischer, M., Harvald, B. A., & Hauge, M. D. Danish twin study of schizophrenia. *British Journal of Psychiatry,* 1969, *115,* 981–990.

Gabrielli, W. F., Mednick, S. A., Volavka, J., Pollack, V. E., Schulsinger, F., & Itil, T. M. Electroencephalograms in children of alcoholic fathers. *Psychophysiology,* 1982, *19,* 404–407.

Goodwin, D. W., Schulsinger, F., Moller, N., Hermansen, L., Winodur, G., & Guze, S. B. Drinking problems in adopted and non-adopted sons of alcoholics. *Archives of General Psychiatry,* 1974, *31,* 164–169.

Goodwin, D. W. Family and adoption studies of alcoholism. In S. A. Mednick & K. O. Christiansen (Eds.), *Biosocial bases of criminal behavior.* New York: Gardner Press, 1977. Pp. 143–159.

Goodwin, D. W. *Alcoholism: The facts.* New York: Oxford University Press, 1981.

Gottesman, I. I., and Shields, J. *Schizophrenia: The epigenetic puzzle.* New York: Cambridge University Press, 1982.

Harsanyi, Z., & Hutton, R. *Genetic prophecy: Beyond the double helix.* New York: Rawson, Wade, 1981.

Heston, L. L. Psychiatric disorders in foster home reared children of schizophrenic mothers. *British Journal of Psychiatry,* 1966, *112,* 819–825.

Jonsson, A. E., & Nilsson, T. Alkoholkonsumption hos monozygota och dizygota tvillingar. *Norduk Hygienisk Tidskrift,* 1968, *49,* 21–25.

Kaij, L. *Alcoholism in twins.* Stockholm: Almqvist & Wiksell, 1960.

Kallman, F. J. *The genetics of schizophrenia.* New York: J. J. Augustin, 1938.

Kety, S. S. From rationalization to reason. *American Journal of Psychiatry,* 1974, *131,* 957–963.

Kety, S. S., Rosenthal, D., Wender, P. H., & Schulsinger, F. The types and prevalence of mental illness in the biological and adoptive families of adopted schizophrenics. In S. A. Mednick, F. Schulsinger, J. Higgins, & B. Bell (Eds.), *Genetics, environment and psychopathology.* Amsterdam: North Holland/Elsevier, 1974, 159–166.

Kety, S. S., Rosenthal, D., Wender, P. H., Schulsinger, F., & Jacobsen, B. Mental illness in the biological and adoptive families of adopted individuals who have become schizophrenic: A preliminary report based on psychiatric interviews. In R. R. Fieve, D. Rosenthal, & H. Brill (Eds.), *Genetic research in psychiatry.* Baltimore: Johns Hopkins University Press, 1975, 147–166.

Kissin, B. Biological investigations in alcohol research. *Journal of Studies on Alcohol,* 1979, *Suppl. No. 8,* 146–181.

Kranz, H. *Lebensschicksale kriminellen zwillinge.* Berlin: Julius Springer, 1936.

Lange, J. *Verbrechen als schicksa.* Leipzig: George Thieme, 1929.

Legras, A. M. *Psychese en criminaliteit bij twellingen.* Utrecht: Kemink en Zoon N. V. 1932.

Loeb, L. & Mednick, S. A. Asocial behavior and electrodermal response patterns. In S. A. Mednick & K. O. Christiansen (Eds.), *Biosocial bases of antisocial behavior.* New York: Gardner Press, 1977.

Loehlin, J. C. An analysis of alcohol related questionnaire items from the National Merit Twin study. *Annals of the New York Academy of Sciences,* 1972, *197,* 117–120.

Mednick, S. A. A bio-social theory of the learning of law-abiding behavior. In S. A. Mednick & K. O. Christiansen (Eds.), *Biosocial bases of criminal behavior.* New York: Gardner Press, 1977. 1–8.

Mednick, A. S., & Volavka, J. Biology and crime. In N. Morris & M. Tonry (Eds.), *Crime and justice: An annual review of research* (Vol. II). Chicago: University of Chicago Press, 1980.

Meehl, P. E. *Clinical versus statistical prediction: A theoretical analysis and a review of the evidence.* Minneapolis: University of Minnesota Press, 1954.

Parnas, J., Schulsinger, F., Teasdale, T. W., Schulsinger, H., Feldman, P. M., & Mednick, S. A. Perinatal complications and clinical outcome within the schizophrenia spectrum. *British Journal of Psychiatry,* 1982, *140,* 416–420.

Partanen, J., Brunn, K., & Markkanen, T. *Inheritance of drinking behavior.* New Brunswick: Rutgers University Center of Alcohol Studies, 1966.

Pollin, W., Allen, M. G., Hoffer, A., Stabenau, J. R., & Hrubec, Z. Psychopathology in 15,909 pairs of veteran twins. *American Journal of Psychiatry,* 1969, *126,* 597–609.

Robins, L. N. *Deviant children grown up.* Baltimore: William & Wilkins, 1966.

Roe, A. The adult adjustment of children of alcoholic parents raised in foster homes. *Quarterly Journal of Studies on Alcohol*, 1944, *5*, 378–393.

Rosanoff, A. J., Handy, L. M., & Rosanoff, F. A. Criminality and delinquency in twins. *Journal of Criminal Law and Criminology*, 1934, *24*, 923–934.

Rosenthal, D., *Genetic theory and abnormal behavior*. New York: McGraw-Hill, 1970.

Rosenthal, D. The genetics of schizophrenia. In S. Arieti and E. Brody (Eds.), *American handbook of psychiatry* (2nd ed., Vol. 3). New York: Basic Books, 1974.

Rosenthal, D., and Kety S. (Eds.) *The transmission of schizophrenia*. Oxford, England: Pergamon, 1968.

Rosenthal, D., Wender, P. H., Kety, S. S., Schulsinger, F., Welner, J., & Reider, R. O. Parent–child relationships and psychopathological disorder in the child. *Archives of General Psychiatry*, 1975, *32*, 466–476.

Slater, E. The incidence of mental disorder. *Annals of Eugenics*, 1953, *6*, 172.

Slater, E., & Cowie, V. *The genetics of mental disorders*. London: Oxford University Press, 1971.

Stumpfl, F. *Die ursprunge des verberchens: dargestellt am lebenslauf von zwillingen*. Leipzig: George Thieme, 1936.

Tienari, P. Schizophrenia and monozygotic twins. *Psychiatrica Finnica*, 1971, 97–104.

Van Dusen, K. T., Mednick, S. A., Gabrielli, W. F., & Hutchings, B. Social class and crime in an adoption cohort. *Journal of Criminal Law and Criminology*, in press.

Wender, P. H., Rosenthal, D., Kety, S. S., Schulsinger, F., & Welner, J. Cross-fostering: A research strategy for clarifying the role of genetic and experiential factors in the etiology of schizophrenia. *Archives of General Psychiatry*, 1974, *30*, 121–128.

Wolf, P., Kaarsen, J., & Hogh, E. Kriminalitetskyppigheden i Danmark. *Nordisk Tidsskrift for Kriminalvidenskab*. 1958, *46*, 113–119.

Wolfgang, M. E., Figlio, R. M., & Sellin, T. *Delinquency in a birth cohort*. Chicago: University of Chicago Press, 1972.

Yoshimasu, S. The criminological significance of the family in the light of the studies of criminal twins. *Acta Criminologiae et Medicinae Legalis Japanica*, 1961, 27.

Zuckerman, M., Buchsbaum, M. S., & Murphy, D. L. Sensation-seeking and its biological correlates. *Psychological Bulletin*, 1980, *88*, 187–215.

14

Biological and Psychosocial Risk Factors and Development during Childhood

BERNHARD MEYER-PROBST   HANS-DIETER RÖSLER
HELFRIED TEICHMANN

All sciences concerned with man converge on a common point—the problem of sociobiology. Dialectical and historical materialism, which established the social character of man and the science of history, has basically clarified the sociobiological problem at the philosophical level. Acceptance of the primarily socially determined nature of the human personality includes acceptance of the biologically preformed conditions of existence. The unique, precise interlacing of these two spheres in the case of man is so complex that it has so far virtually defied illumination by individual sciences. The question of the factors causing differences and changes in personality presses for concrete answers. The conscious planning of social life demands knowledge both biological fundamentals and socialization processes, and thus requires that the barriers between the natural and the social sciences be overcome.

Medicine developed as part of the natural sciences and has been concerned mainly with the art of healing, with a primarily biologically oriented causality concept. The social sciences were defined on the basis of theories of society and ignored the biological characteristics of individual development. The rapid social progress associated with the revolution in science and technology showed vividly that socially induced changes modify the biological nature of man and that biological processes are to a great degree socially mediated (for instance, changes in mortality and morbidity structures, acceleration of physical and mental development). Almost all branches of medicine have, in the meantime, realized that social aspects are important factors of influence and have arrived at a broader and more differentiated notion of illness. The biological nature and the social essence of man are inseparable. Research into the

HUMAN DEVELOPMENT:
AN INTERACTIONAL PERSPECTIVE

relationship between healthy and ill or between normal and abnormal is an elementary concern of the human sciences.

The purpose of the longitudinal study performed at Rostock was to reveal the causes of, and factors influencing, differences among individuals and their value for long-term prognosis using the development of at-risk children as an example. It was intended to throw light upon the interaction between cerebral laod factors sustained during early childhood and environmental climate.

In the course of the 1960s the terms risk factor, risk pregnancy, risk birth, and risk child rapidly became widespread, although the theoretical basis of the risk concept was unable to keep pace with its practical propagation (Joppich & Schulte, 1968; Perzianinow, Kyervschenkow, Frolovà, Nikolaeva, & Chushkowa, 1976). But the growing feeling of responsibility for the healthful development of infants pressed for answers to questions such as (a) Which risk factor must be considered particularly grave? (b) What chances of development do risk children have? (c) How can risks and their consequences be reduced or avoided?

The number of publications dealing with specific risk factors has continued to grow, but the results of follow-up studies have shown a singular lack of uniformity. In this connection, there can be little doubt that differences in methodology have made the comparison of results difficult. Furthermore, the manifestation of risk effects depends on the child–environment interaction. This relation, however, will be hindered not only by biological but also by psychosocial risks. Both are usually investigated separately; nevertheless, there are relationships. In this study, therefore, they were observed for the same children and compared together.

The Rostock Longitudinal Study on Two-Year-Olds

OBJECTIVE AND METHODS

When the children were examined by us at the ages of 2 and 6, objective findings from the perinatal period were available. A new way of organizing scientific work had been introduced that permitted the data recorded during a national research project to be taken over for use in our study. The result was that a wealth of material was available for each child. These data, even for the perinatal period, stemmed from special examinations undertaken on the basis of a uniform scheme, specifically with the aim of performing follow-up studies. We were forced to examine the children as if for a dummy experiment—an approach that could only be of benefit as far as the objectivity of the follow-up examinations was concerned.

From the start we restricted our attention to the 1000 registered children who attended a day nursery when the first follow-up examination was undertaken at age 2.0–2.3 years. All 294 children born in the course of a year who were attending such a nursery were examined at the nursery they attended. This ensured that the examinations took place in surroundings familiar to the children.

The follow-up examination was not only physical in nature. The children also performed a psychometric test developed by Schmidt-Kolmer and Zwiener (Schmidt-Kolmer, 1977) specifically for use in nurseries in the German Democratic Republic. The medical examinations were performed by Brigitte Heider. The children had been assigned to the categories "risk child" and "non-risk child" by the midwives involved in delivery and by neonatalogists after birth. The total sample consisted of every risk child and every fourth non-risk child classified in this way.

RESULTS

Biological Risks.   The great expectations that had been placed in this experimental design failed to materialize at first. As a group, the risk children differed only slightly from the non-risk children in terms of mental development. The non-risk children serving as a control group had a mean developmental quotient (DQ) of 97.4, and the mean DQ of the risk group was 94.7, that is, only 2.7 DQ points lower. Does this mean that it is impossible to give a prognosis for mental development immediately after birth? Or do perinatal risks too rarely have persistent deleterious effects on development to permit their detection with certainty by comparing DQ means?

The biological risk spectrum included 55 risk factors. However, not every child who was exposed to one of these factors was automatically classed perinatally as a risk child. Hence, the subjects in the control group had also, at least in some cases, been exposed to risks. This consideration prompted us to combine our risk and non-risk groups to form a single group.

The number of recorded biological risks to which a child had been exposed in the course of its life was termed the biological risk index and varied from 0 to 14. Only 6.5% of the children had developed completely without exposure to biological risks. On the average, each child had been exposed to 3.7 risks. Retrospective consideration of only those risks that our study had proved to have inhibited development resulted in a revised distribution with a mean risk exposure of 2 risks per child.

The next step was to check each risk separately for its effect as a monocausal factor inhibiting mental development. The mean DQ of the combined group (96.1) and the mean DQ of the children who had never been exposed to any risk (98.9) were used as control values. The lowest scores were those of underweight children (less than 2500 g at birth) with a mean DQ of 80.2, which again shows the importance of premature birth. But the other risks also led to scores that were significantly lower than those of the controls; birth longer than 24 hr after loss of amniotic fluid (86.2); gynecological operation on uterus and adnexus (86.4); respiratory distress (87.3); hemorrhage during the second half of pregnancy (87.9); placental infarct covering over one-third of the total surface (89.8); less subcutaneous fat than normal (92.8); cyanosis (not generalized) (93.3); hematomous petechial hemorrhages (93.4); normalization of Apgar[1] values after the fifth minute of life (93.7).

It was found that 27 biological risks retard development. The list of these factors in the order of the gravity of their effects proved to be extremely unstable, probably because it is rare for any single factor to act on its own. Simply the elimination of one risk from a group of risks leads to an increase in the mean DQ of the risk group concerned, but this improvement is not the same for all risk groups and, consequently, the rank of eliminated risk in the list is subject to variation. This is illustrated by the following example.

Children who have suffered from cyanosis have a mean DQ of 93.3. However, this score immediately rises to 97.2 (i.e., higher than the lower of the control scores) if all children of below-average weight at birth are taken out of the cyanosis group. This seems to imply that cyanosis is not a risk factor at all. But, as the next comparison shows, this is not so: The mean DQ of children who weighed 2500 g or less at birth is 80.2, but the mean DQ of the children who were underweight at birth and subsequently suffered from cyanosis is only 75.7. In other words, the effect of cyanosis after the second hour of life (which did not occur in generalized form in any of the children belonging to our sample) is not intensive enough to produce any significant difference in means when acting alone. It is rather a factor that assumes the nature of a definite risk only when it occurs concurrently with other risks.

Every biological risk factor, however, was found to interact in a statistically significant way with, on the average, seven others, and it is impossible to clarify the effects of such compound risk factors by discussing the effect of each risk factor separately. A single biological risk factor is like the tip of an iceberg: It may be the external sign of an underlying assemblage of risk factors. Moreover, biological risk factors also interact with psychosocial risk factors, although these interactions are weaker and less frequent.

Psychosocial Risks. Empirical sociological research during the past decades has revealed many load factors that lead to retardation of behavioral disturbances in only some of the subjects concerned. We have called these factors psychosocial risk factors and define them as all kinds of nonbiological risk factors that can inhibit physical or mental development. Although our sample can be considered completely nonselective as far as psychosocial risk factors are concerned, exposure to such factors again proved to be higher than expected.

The psychosocial risk index (which is defined analogously to the biological risk index) varied between 0 and 13. Only 12.9% of the children in our sample

---

[1]Apgar Index: heart frequency, respiration, reflex excitability, muscular tonus and color of the skin (see Apgar, 1953).

had developed completely without exposure to psychosocial risks. On the average, each child had been exposed to 3.1. Retrospective consideration of only those risks that our study proved to inhibit development again gave a revised distribution which showed that, on the average, each child was exposed to 2 risk factors. The psychosocial risk factors were also first checked for their effects when considered singly. The mean DQ of the combined group (96.1) and the mean DQ of the children who had developed without exposure to psychosocial risks (99.4) were used as control values in this case.

Intellectual retardation in 2-year-olds was found to be greatest, despite attendance at a nursery, when one of the parents concerned is antisocial in character, that is, where it is known (to the nursery staff) that the domestic environment of the child is disturbed by alcoholism, criminality, or neglect. The mean DQ of children with an antisocial mother was 80.1, antisocial father 81.7. It was found that 25 psychosocial risks lead to developmental retardation, significant in the following: mother did not successfully complete 8th grade (83.9); large family (4 children or more) (86.1); father did not successfully complete 8th grade (86.3); single-parent family (89.8); poor standards of sanitation facilities at home (no bath, no indoor toilet) (90.1); disharmonious marriage (91.1); child not desired (92.6); mother undergoing treatment for mental trouble (93.0). The listing of psychosocial risks in the order of the gravity of their effects once again proved to be extremely unstable for the same reasons as noted in connection with biological risk factors. Each of the 36 psychosocial risk factors studied were found to have a statistically significant interaction with, on the average, 9 others. When any risk factor was eliminated from a group of such factors the mean DQ immediately increased. We will again furnish one illustration of this.

The children from large families (four or more children) in our sample had a mean DQ of 86.1. However, we find that in this group the children whose mother was employed in a skilled occupation and stated that she had wanted the child had a normal DQ (96.2). In contrast, children from large families whose mother was employed in an unskilled trade and had not wanted the child had a mean DQ of only 80.1. In other words, the size of the family on its own has no bearing on mental development.

Children from single-parent families also have a DQ lower than our control score of 96.1: Their mean DQ is only 89.8. But if we consider only single-parent children whose mothers, apart from being without a partner, are able to give little intellectual stimulation (mother with an unskilled occupation) or exhibit behavioral patterns that lie outside the social norm we find that their mean DQ is even lower (79.0). On the other hand, children from the single-parent group whose mother does not exhibit the conditions outlined above have a mean DQ of 96.0, that is, within the normal range for the group as a whole. This result provides an ideal argument for use in reducing prejudice against single-parent children, which in the past has apparently been pseudo-scientifically confirmed by monocausal interpretation of results.

However, in view of our results, how can we explain the fact that many children who are mentally retarded or show signs of aberrant behavior come from large, single-parent families? Our comparison also supplies one answer to this question. Where the two factors "large family" and "single-parent family" act concurrently, the mean DQ of the children is only 72.2. In other words, a woman who has to cope alone with four or more children is chronically overstressed. This implies that "large family" and "single-parent family" can be considered separately as risk factors only if some other psychosocial risk factor acts at the same time. Such families have little compensation ability when confronted with additional loads. At this point we can draw the conclusion that a reduction in the number of psychosocial load factors allows better adaptation in the same way as a reduction in the number of biological risks to which a child is exposed.

Interaction.   In connection with encouragement at an early age it is essential to know the extent to which biological risks with an inhibitory or negative effect on development can be influenced by psychosocial factors. The interactions playing a role in this connection can be demonstrated in numerous cases. In view of the interest currently being paid to the problem of premature birth, we shall use this biological factor as a model.

It again shows the mean DQ for the whole group of children who were below average weight at birth (DQ = 80.2). In this group, the children who were additionally exposed to four or more psychosocial risks had a mean DQ of only 74.7, while those who developed under more favorable psychosocial conditions reached a mean DQ of 86.8. Does this mean that the considerable retardation we have observed is merely an effect of simultaneous action? After all, it is known that social deprivation hinders development. To check this we calculated the mean DQ of all children in the combined group whose psychosocial risk index was 4 or higher. It turned out to be 93.1, that is, 3 DQ points below the control value. The score of 74.7 cannot simply be calculated from the sum of the biological and psychosocial loads (96.1 − 80.2; 96.1 − 93.1). The sum of these differences gives a figure of around 77. The actual score of 74.7 is even lower. In other words, the retardation resulting from unfavorable psychosocial conditions is superadditive and illustrates clearly the particular susceptability of risk children to the influences of their milieu. At the same time, the difference between premature children from good and average psychosocial conditions (86.6−80.2) can be interpreted as the compensatory effect of a favorable psychosocial environment.

The mutual aggravation of biological and psychosocial load factors can also be shown in a way that permits important practical conclusions to be drawn. The mean DQ of children with antisocial parents is 85.2. The question that interests us is, does the degree of their biological load have no effect on the mental development of these children?

Children with antisocial parents and four or more biological load factors have a mean DQ of only 80.1. Children who had been exposed to fewer biological risk factors, on the other hand, reached a mean DQ of 88.6 despite the considerable influence of the milieu to which they were exposed. Here again we see that the effects of the risks are superadditive. After all, in the combined group, children with four or more biological risk factors reached a mean DQ of 94.0. Summation of the two retardations (96.1–85.2; 96.1–95.0) results in a DQ of 83. The actual DQ reached by these children is even lower (80.1).

Here we must leave our illustrations of biosocial relationships based on specific risk groups and turn to the underlying patterns that we describe in more generalized form (Figure 1), and which will be discussed in more detail in the following section relating our data from 6-year-olds. It can be seen from Figure 1 that the DQ decreases continuously as the numbers of both biological and psychosocial risks increase. We can thus describe mental development as a function of both biological and psychosocial risk load, this being shown cogently by our two straight lines of regression.

In other words, the results of our follow-up studies on 2-year-olds prove that mental development is functionally dependent upon the cumulative number of risks to which the child is or has been exposed. In a specific case, and thus for a particular risk as a clinical problem, it is less important to identify the risk factor that is obviously acting or has acted than to identify which other risk factors are acting concurrently. In the case of 2-year-olds, this applies not only to psychological parameters but also to physical parameters, such as body weight, body length, and frequency of infection, but these aspects cannot be dealt with in the framework of this chapter due to the restriction of its topic. We must, however, draw attention in this respect to the results obtained by Tonkowa-Jampolskaja (1979), which are fully consistent with ours.

DISCUSSION

From the significance of risk cumulation for the manifestation of retardation and its symptoms, we can draw the following conclusions that are of some

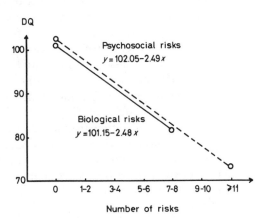

Figure 1. *Mental development as a function of number of biological and psychosocial risk factors to which 2-year-olds have been exposed.*

relevance in connection with the avoidance of risk factors and compensation for their consequences.

1. The retarding effect of biological risk factors on development becomes weaker unless additional biological risk factors come into play.
2. The retarding effect of psychosocial risk factors on development becomes weaker unless additional psychosocial risk factors come into play.
3. The retarding effect of biological risk factors on development becomes weaker if the child is exposed to a favorable psychosocial environment.
4. The retarding effect of psychosocial risk factors becomes weaker if the load resulting from previous exposure to biological risk factors is small.
5. Some risk factors do not retard development unless accompanied by other risk factors.
6. As a rule, the degree of retardation is greater than the sum of retardations that would accrue from the different risk factors acting on their own, thus explaining the increased susceptibility of children to their social environment after exposure to risks.
7. Adaptation following exposure to psychosocial risks is similar to that following exposure to biological risk factors because both impair brain functioning. This is why they have a mutually aggravating effect.

It is apparent that in the past the effects of biological risks on development have been considered to be permanent and immutable, when in fact they are not. This is of great importance for a long-term prognosis: Brain damage sustained at birth is not necessarily permanent damage. If the effects of biological risk factors depend on factors that do not belong to the scope of perinatal examinations and in many instances cannot even be sought within the organism, the prognosis must be very uncertain unless such conditions can be taken into account.

The psychosocial conditions we have considered represent an overall framework in which the actual influencing factors accumulate. From the etiopathogenetic standpoint they can be split into three groups:

1. Overstressing risk factors that act directly (for instance, those that can arise from inappropriately high expectations regarding behavioral patterns or the sudden separation of parents) effect strong emotions and disturb neural regulation systems.
2. Understressing, lack of stimuli, and lack of information lead to inadequate differentiation in the development of the personality that may even be reflected in the morphological development of the brain (Akert, 1979; Frotscher, Mensfeld, & Wenzel, 1975).
3. Forms of socialization that promote conflict situations do not directly induce disturbances in brain function, but sooner or later they give rise to actions by the child that lead to conflict situations and are based on the previously learned behavioral patterns that are not appropriate to the particular situation.

At present, neurobiological and neuropsychological research is fascinating, especially the results now accumulating from both man and animals that demonstrate the astonishing capability of organisms to compensate for disturbed functioning of the central nervous system (Prechtl, 1976). The degree of this ability to compensate depends on developmental age and the stimuli supplied by the milieu. Medicine has traditionally been concerned with creating conditions that permit the dormant counterregulatory forces of the organism itself to come into action, that is, with treatment aimed at promoting organismic compensation and the activation of the compensatory capability of the organism.

However, socially mediated compensation can also exploit yet another counterregulatory principle inherent in the organism: It can, by repeatedly and gradually increasing the load, increase the scope for compensation. It is common knowledge that an increase in capacity is usually accompanied by an increase in the ability to bear stress. As early as Meumann (1922) and his coworkers, during their studies on learning, came to the conclusion that mental capacity can also be trained actively and by stimulation in the same way as can physical capacity. This leads to the conclusion that is of importance in connection not only with prevention, but also with teaching, treatment, and rehabilitation: Compensation can be trained, for instance, by carefully increasing the load on physical and mental functions; this has the added advantage that a transfer effect exists between the increased ability to bear stress and the capacity for compensation obtained in this way.

Directly acting psychosocial compensation is characterized by compensatory substitution, which involves the elimination of deficiencies that the organism cannot rectify on its own. It is a unique mode of development that is specific to man and is called acquisition (Leontjew, 1967). Acquisition is used to compensate by substituting correct programs for adopting modes of behavior where such programs are absent, and by correcting or eliminating inappropriate programs. A healthy self-consciousness and self-confidence gained by successful progress in active adaptation are of immense value for strengthening the will to compensate. The child therefore requires the educational tolerance appropriate to its individuality to permit such success.

Thus, investigation of single risks has finally led to knowledge of the general framework governing biosocial adaptation. This approach has permitted order to be brought into the mosaic of negative conditions and compensatory factors and has allowed a scientifically based prognosis to be formulated. Only the laws governing biosocial adaptation can explain the pathology of disturbances in life arising from disparity between stress and the ability to cope with stress and leading possibly to disturbances both in regulatory mechanisms within the organism and in social behavior. Can the mechanisms that we found in our follow-up studies on 2-year-olds still be detected at the age of 6 years? What remains constant, and what changes? Will new relationships be found? These questions will be answered in the following section.

The Rostock Longitudinal Study on Six-Year-Olds

OBJECTIVE AND METHODS

As a result of the study on 2-year-olds presented in the preceding section, a more differentiated and fundamental approach was adopted for dealing with the central problem. The original question, which was of much interest to pediatric psychologists, concerned the development of the child after exposure to specific biological risks; in this study on 6-year-olds the terms of reference were subsequently broadened to accommodate a large-scale check on variables and discussion of sociobiological problems. The following four questions were studied within this framework.

1. Can the interrelationships found between biological and psychosocial factors in past clinical psychological studies still be detected in 6-year-olds?
2. How do biological conditions affect psychological development?
3. How do psychosocial conditions affect psychological development?
4. How does the interaction between biological and social factors manifest itself?

Of the original 294 children, we were able to examine 279 (140 male and 139 female) at 6 years of age (95% of the original sample). The acquisition and analysis of data were, as before, organized in such a way that the study had the nature of a blind experiment; that is, the staff performing the examinations had no knowledge of the previous results and there was no exchange of results. The psychological methods used were designed to give various indexes characterizing performance, to include comprehensive assessment scales and scores for behavior, and to permit uniform scaling. In view of this, the Wechsler Test for preschoolers, the Raven Test, a learning test, pictures for figure–ground differentiation, a test for linguistic articulation, and three standardized questionnaires concerning the behavior of the child and the style used by the mother to bring up the child were used. The questionnaires were filled in by the nursery staff and the mothers.

The medical data were obtained from the extensive documentation drawn up by the perinatalogists at the time of birth, the information obtained by interviewing the mothers at both follow-up examinations, and the functional and diagnostic indications considered to be criteria for assessing brain damage sustained during early childhood, that is, neurological findings, state of motor development, electroencephalogram, echoencephalogram, and radiograms of the skull and wrist bones. The medical examinations were performed by Gudrun Cammann.

The wealth of data (some 2000 data per child) made it necessary to establish integrated indexes for the severity of the biological and psychosocial loads (factors of influence) and the degree of developmental retardation and behavioral adaptation (target quantities). These indexes were

1. Biological risk index (BRI): the number of risks to which the child was exposed during pregnancy and delivery; the spectrum encompassed 55 single risks ($\bar{x} = 3.7$; SD = 3.2)
2. Brain damage index (BDI): the number of pathological signs indicating brain damage; the spectrum consisted of 8 signs ($\bar{x} = 2.6$; SD = 1.5)
3. Psychosocial risk index (SRI): the number of psychosocial risks from a spectrum of 36 single risks to which the child had been exposed ($\bar{x} = 2.6$; SD = 2.7)
4. Developmental quotient (DQ at 6 years): an integrated index reflecting the psychological and mental states of development on the basis of 14 test and questionnaire variables ($\bar{x} = 100.0$; SD = 14.9); comparable to DQ at 2 years
5. Axis syndrome index (ASI): the number of negative characters from a spectrum of 26 scaled behavioral characters considered to be typical symptoms of the axis syndrome after Göllnitz (1975) ($\bar{x} = 7.4$; SD = 4.5)

RESULTS

Relationships between Biological and Psychological Factors. We shall now consider groups with completely different clinical psychological results in order to determine the questions to be answered. In this section we compare the covariations of the previously defined indexes with regard to three levels of intelligence, concentration, social behavior, age at which the children started speaking, and enuresis. The children were split into three groups based on intelligence level by means of the Wechsler Test: above average ($C \geq 8$), average ($C = 5$), and below average ($C \leq 2$). The differences are naturally reflected clearly in the developmental quotient (DQ at 6 years). As a rule, those who showed poor intelligence at age 6 years had already shown retardation in development at age 2. As the axis syndrome index (ASI) shows, high intelligence is associated with better behavioral control. The biological risk index (BRI) increases slightly as intelligence decreases, with the brain damage index (BDI) increasing considerably at the same time. The psychosocial risk index (SRI) also increases with decreasing intelligence, with the difference between the SRIs for normally and below normally intelligent children being particularly large.

For the next step of the analysis, the children were grouped on the basis of a concentration test that requires cards to be stored as quickly as possible according to certain rules. Poor concentration is associated with a low level of development (DQ at 6 years = 89). As far as the intellectual aspects of the test are concerned, it is obviously of little importance whether the subject has very good or only average concentration ability. The differences between the groups with average and poor concentration are of differential diagnostic value. Ability to concentrate seems to play a major role in behavioral control (ASI). This comparison also shows that the BRI, BDI, and SRI increase with decreasing concentration.

For the third step, the children are grouped according to "social adaptation" on the basis of a "sociality" scale in a questionnaire filled in by the nursery staff. The level of social behavior correlates well with the overall state of development as expressed by the DQ. High intelligence is associated with good adaptation capacity and conscious control of behavior. The larger the number of biological risks to which the children were exposed (BRI) and the larger the number of brain damage indicants (BDI), the lower was the assessment of social adaptation. The number of psychosocial risk factors acting on the child (SRI) increased at the same time.

The ages at which the mothers stated that their child spoke his or her first word were divided into three categories: up to 15 months, up to 18 months, and up to 24 months. Delay in learning to speak is a serious sign of retardation, as indicated by the later level of development (DQ at 6 years). Delays in learning to speak are also reflected in behavioral control (ASI). The groups do not differ in terms of the number of biological risks to which the children had been exposed (BRI), but increasing delays in learning to speak were accompanied by increases in brain damage load (BDI) and psychosocial risk load (SRI). On the average, children who still wet their beds at age 6 years have higher biological risk and brain damage indexes than normal, are exposed to a worse psychosocial climate than normal (SRI), are more retarded than normal in their mental development (DQ), and show more signs of behavioral disturbances than normal (ASI).

The selected examples shown here, which can be augmented by many others and reveal a further range of psychological properties and characters, form the empirical basis for the following rule: Differences among individuals in terms of intelligence and manifestly abnormal behavior at preschool age are decisively influenced by objective indicants showing the presence of biological and psychosocial loads. Having set out the different groupings based on clinical psychological findings, we shall now discuss the question from a different angle.

The Influence of Biological Conditions on Psychological Parameters.   The number of brain damage criteria (BDI) detected during medical examination at age 6 is a more reliable indicator of the biological load than the sum of the biological risk (BRI). We shall therefore use these two indexes for the purpose of illustration. The groups compared combine children exhibiting none (0), 1 or 2, 3 or 4, 5 or 6, and 7 or 8 positive signs of brain damage, respectively. The state of development at age 6 (DQ at 6 years ranges from 110 to 69) follows the brain-organic load remarkably well. The graduation in psychic function is also remarkably independent of age because even at age 2 the developmental quotient decreases with a similar uniformity (from 102 to 79). The effect of the brain-organic load is also reflected in the decreasing motoricity quotient and the increasing number of signs of the axis syndrome (ASI).

The mean number of biological risks increases systematically from 2.6 to 7.5, thus stressing the causal relationship between early damage and subsequently detected somatic manifestation. The slow but steady increase in psychosocial risk (from 2.4 to 4.8) is also remarkable. We shall return to this problem later. This example shows clearly that the level of psychological and mental development decreases as the number of objective brain-damage criteria increases. On the condition that diagnosis involves the assessment of many factors (and only on this condition), it is possible to prove convincingly that organic factors inhibit development. We shall now turn our attention to the psychosocial sphere.

The Influence of Psychosocial Conditions on Psychological Parameters. We can restrict our attention to a single example that is representative of the effects of numerous factors on socialization during childhood. We have chosen the success of the mother at school as one factor that is known to have a major influence on the intellectual atmosphere in the family. The level of development of the children decreases from 106 to 82 as the scholastic success of the mother drops from university entrance to successful completion of tenth grade to failure to complete tenth grade to failure to complete eighth grade. Extremely poor standards of success at school (failure to complete the eighth grade successfully) had extremely grave consequences for the children at both 2 and 6 years.

The scholastic success of the mother is also reflected in the psychosocial risk index of the children, while the number of biological risks (BRI, 3.1–5.7) and signs of brain damage (BDI, 2.3–3.6) also increase regularly with diminishing scholastic success of the mother. This again draws attention to the important sociomedical, as well as methodological, problems involved in the coupling of biological and psychosocial factors. The example can be corroborated by numerous other forms of analysis based on socioeconomic parameters, particular features of family structure, and mode of upbringing. In all cases these analyses underscore the known fact that sociocultural influences have a major impact on the expression of differences in performance and in behavior.

Interaction. Since biological and psychosocial risk loads do not, as a rule, appear independently, as suggested by the tables, their interdependence remains vague. In this section we shall examine the interrelationships. One approach is to select four extreme groups from among the combined sample on the principle of the four-field table: (*a*) low biological risk (lB); (*b*) high biological risk (mB); (*c*) children reared under favorable family conditions (lS); and (*d*) children reared under unfavorable family circumstances (mS).

Comparison of the indexes for these four groups shows that our classification into groups exposed to many or to a few risks is least correct. The biological risk index is clearly related to the number of positive brain damage criteria because the two severely loaded groups (2 and 4) contain considerably more findings that deviate from the norm. For children 6 years of age, the rank orders showing the strength of the influences on DQ are

1. No or slight risk load   (lB + lS)   = 106
2. Exclusively biological risk load (mB + lS)   = 102
3. Exclusively psychosocial risk load (lB + mS) = 97
4. Double load   (mB + mS) = 88

These rank orders should be considered as a general law because they reproduced for all factors considered in our studies, whether they were the results of tests, questionnaire scales, examinations made by the school medical officer, or the marks received during the first grade.

Groups 1 and 2 compare children with a slight and major biological risk load (lB and mB) who grow up under social conditions that are conducive to development (lS). The DQ scores differ only slightly ($106 - 102 = 4$ points) and thus demonstrate clearly the compensatory influence of a favorable family milieu. In contrast, groups 3 and 4 compare children with a slight and a major biological load (lB and mB) who grow up under unfavorable social conditions (mS). The clear difference between the DQ scores ($97 - 88 = 9$) and the low level of the DQ show that development of the child is particularly endangered when biological and social risks act together (mB + mS). These differences, resulting from the flexibility of the central nervous system, characterize a basic rule regarding compensation and decompensation in psychic development: Favorable psychosocial conditions reduce, and unfavorable conditions increase, the consequences of biological risk loads.

Compensation is governed by three main components: (*a*) the mutual effects of biological and psychosocial influences; (*b*) the magnitude of the risk load; and (*c*) age. Children who have been exposed to five or more psychosocial risk factors (N = 30) are, on the average, retarded with respect to overall development (DQ = 91.1). If the children in this group are split into subgroups based on the number of biological risks to which they have been exposed, we find that the mean DQ of the group with a major biological risk load (index > 4) is 84.4, whereas the members of the group with only a slight biological risk (index ≤ 4) have almost compensated for their psychosocial deprivation (mean DQ of 96.2). However, since a large number of biological risks alone has no great effect on development (DQ = 93.5), the degree of decompensation can be considered a consequence neither of primarily biological risks nor of an additive effect of biological and psychosocial risks (this expectation value would be a DQ of 89.7); it is, rather, "superadditive" as a result of mutual negative effects.

The effect of an accumulation of risk on the state of development is illustrated in Figure 2. The harmful influence of risks on development can be plotted as a function of the number of risks. The unbroken regression line shows this for biological risks, and the broken line for psychosocial risks. As a general rule, it can be stated that, at both ages, the larger the number of risks,

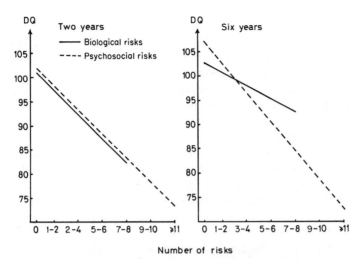

Figure 2. *Connection between the developmental quotient (DQ) and number of biological and psychosocial risk factors to which 2- and 6-year-olds have been exposed.*

the more retarded will be the development, as shown by the figure that the lines decreased. This illustrates the principle of risk cumulation.

At age 2 (Fig. 2, left side), an increase in both biological and psychosocial risks leads to a considerable and almost constant reduction in development quotient, as indicated by the closely spaced and almost parallel straight regression lines. However, a similar comparison at age 6 (Fig. 2, right side) reveals an important fact: The straight regression lines intersect. In other words, the biological risks (solid line) are subject to relative compensation over the course of development, whereas the psychosocial risks remain steady or even increase their inhibitory effect on development.

DISCUSSION

The investigations described here are, in the final analysis, a definite contribution by a single science to the dialectics of biological and social factors. However, we shall dispense with a detailed discussion of the findings in favor of more general remarks. The advantage of field studies of this kind, as compared to experimental studies, is that changes in development are recorded, genuine interactions are reflected, and multifactorial relationships are brought to light. The questions of if, to what extent, and under what conditions cerebral lesions are associated with mental consequences require unreserved acceptance of the fact that the intellect is in a state of constant interaction with the reality of life. The resultant multifactorial fabric formed by the different components turns cause and effect into relative terms.

As we have shown, biological risk load, deficiencies in family milieu, difficulties in learning, and abnormalities in behavior are mutually interwoven in terms of effect, joint effect, and mutual interference. Any attempt to consider them in isolation without consideration of these interactions leads to false conclusions. Mechanistic thinking in the sense that some "exterior" causality can be introduced to explain things is, although still widespread, wide of the mark. Biosocial dualism is an inadequate approach a priori. The biological nature and the social essence of man are inseparable aspects of the same phenomenon. Social determination takes place only within the framework of what is biologically possible.

The environmental flexibility of mental properties is, in the final analysis, an essential biological character of man. Damage to the biological substrate can impair the effective acquisition of social experience just as an intact biological substrate responds sensitively to changes in the environment. Our own results show particularly clearly that these take effect precisely during the period when development is especially dynamic (preschool age).

Biological and psychosocial factors can have a mutually aggravating effect because both can either stimulate or inhibit brain function. Even Wygotsky (1964), the father of the study of brain defects, considered damage to be essentially sociobiological in nature and regarded compensation not only as an intraorganismic but also as a socially mediated process. The decisive long-term role of social interactions in connection with compensatory learning and regulation of behavior shows the importance of an optimal sociocultural and psychosocial environment for development. It is no accident that "emotional education" of children (and their educators) is considered so important (Jankova, 1980; Zaregorodzew & Jerochin, 1979) and that the question of social adaptation is being placed in the spotlight (Schmidt-Kolmer, Tonkowa-Jampolskaja, & Atanassowa, 1979).

However, individual behavior is not, as is regrettably often assumed, a reflection of social conditions alone; it depends also on the "biological constitution" (Dölling, 1979). The borders between the human sciences are becoming increasingly blurred as our knowledge of sociobiological problems increases. Social and natural scientists, basic researchers, and clinicians are all confronted with the fact that the main subject of their research, man, is affected by both biological and social influences, and that these therefore require mutual consideration.

References

Akert, K. Probleme der Hirnreifung. In R. Lempp (Ed.), *Teilleistungsstörungen im Kindesalter.* Stuttgart: Verlag Hans Huber, 1979.

Apgar, V. A proposal for a new method of evaluation of the newborn infant. *Current Researches, Anesthe. Analg.* 1953, *32,* 260.

Dölling, I. *Naturwesen-Individum-Persönlichkeit.* Berlin: VEB Deutscher Verlag der Wissenschaften, 1979.

Frotscher, M., Mensfeld, B., & Wenzel, J. Umweltabhängige Differenzierung der Dendritenspines an Pyramidenneuronen des Hippocampus (CA 1) der Ratte. *Journal für Hirnforscheng*, 1975, *16*, 443–450.

Göllnitz, G. *Neuropsychiatrie des Kindes und Jugendalters*. Jena: VEB G. Fischer Verlag, 1975.

Jankova, S. A. Faktoren der Stabilität der Familie. *Sowjetwissenschaft/Gesellschaftswissenschaftliche Beiträge*, 1980, *1*, 60–70.

Joppich, G., & Schulte, F. J. *Neurologie des Neugeborenen*. New York: Springer-Verlag, 1968.

Leontjew, A. N. *Probleme der Entwicklung des Psychischen*. Berlin: Volk und Wissen Volkseigener Verlag, 1967.

Meumann, E. *Vorlesungen zur Einführung in die experimentelle Pädagogik und ihre psychologischen Grundlagen*. Leipzig: Engelmann Verlag, 1922.

Perzianinow, L. S., Keryvschenkow, A. P., Frolova, O. G., Nikolaeva, E. I., & Chushkowa, I. S. Faktoren und Gruppen hohen Risikos schwangerer Frauen. *Akuscherstwo i ginekologija*, 1976, *10*, 7.

Prechtl, H. F. R. Leichte frühkindliche Hirnschädigung und das Kompensationsvermögen des Nervensystems. *Bulletin der Schweizerischen Akademie der Medizinischen Wissenschaften*, 1976, *32*, 99–113.

Schmidt-Kolmer, E. *Zum Einfluss von Familie und Krippe auf die Entwicklung von Kindern in der Frühen Kindheit*. Berlin: VEB Verlag Volk und Gesundheit, 1977.

Schmidt-Kolmer, E., Tonkowa-Jampolskaja, R., & Atanassowa, A. *Die soziale Adaptation der Kinder bei der Aufnahme in Einrichtungen der Vorschulerziehung*. Berlin: VEB Verlag Volk und Gesundheit, 1979.

Tonkowa-Jampolskaja, R. W. Untersuchungen zur Adaptation der Kinder anden Aufenhalt in der Krippe. Untersuchungen in der UdSSR. In E. Schmidt-Kolmer, R. W. Tonkowa-Jampolskaja, & A. Atanassowa (Eds.), *Die soziale Adaptation der Kinder bei der. Aufnahme in Einrichtungen der Vorschuleerziehung*. Berlin: VEB Verlag Volk und Gesundtheit, 1979.

Wygotsky, L. S. *Denken und Sprechen*. Berlin: Akademie-Verlag, 1964.

Zaregorodzew, L. J., & Jerochin, W. G. Die sozial-biologische Determination in der Medizin. *Sowjetwissenschaft/Gesellschaftswissenschaftliche Beiträge*, 1979, *32*, 637–649.

15

From Emotional State to Emotional Expression: Emotional Development from the Perspective of Person–Environment Interaction

MICHAEL LEWIS   LINDA MICHALSON

Emotional development involves a complex interaction between dispositional factors of the species and the social environment of the young child. The effects of these forces are apparent in the emotional expressions of the members of any particular group. The examples that follow illustrate this perspective.

Example 1. Lucy is 20 months old. While her mother is working on a law brief at home, Lucy is playing in the backyard. Through the window the mother witnesses the following scene: Lucy runs to get a toy at the far end of the yard. She falls on her knees and starts to cry. Immediately she looks up, but seeing that no one is paying any attention, she stops crying and walks to the back door. As she approaches the door, she begins to cry again.

In this example, facial and vocal expressions are not totally determined by the precipitating event. While Lucy's first cry is probably related to her pain, her subsequent cry has more to do with an attempt to communicate a specific message to her mother. This conclusion is supported by the fact that Lucy looked around first to see if anybody was watching. Lucy's ability to produce her facial expression and vocal behavior at will suggests that these behaviors are under her control and not necessarily related to an underlying state of pain.

Example 2. Matthew, a 14-month-old, is playing in the living room. He toddles over to a reading table and reaches for a lamp. As the lamp tips precariously, his mother pulls it away from him, saying, "No, don't touch that!" Matthew screams and his body shakes with rage. He waves his arms and tries to push his mother away. Her response to this outburst is to pick him up roughly and put him in his crib. She then leaves him alone in his room.

261

HUMAN DEVELOPMENT:
AN INTERACTIONAL PERSPECTIVE

This example illustrates the negative reinforcement of emotional expressions that are deemed socially inappropriate in a specific context. The reinforcement of specific emotional behaviors begins early in children's lives and can be seen to modify particular emotional expressions. In this case, Matthew's screaming, fist-shaking, and other violent displays of anger were not tolerated by his mother, who will extinguish them through negative reinforcement. The extinction of behaviors can occur through direct reinforcement by parents, siblings, teachers, and peers or, more indirectly, through modeling the behaviors of other people. For example, in families in which laughing is unusual, young children may learn to eliminate the vocal components of joy by modeling their parents' behavior. In this example, Matthew is learning to express his anger through behaviors other than fist-shaking, screaming, and pushing.

> *Example 3.* Casey has gone to his grandfather's house for the weekend. At 2 years, Casey is a verbally precocious child who enjoys being with other people. His grandfather, an actor, encourages Casey's dramatic flair. One game they play together is "make a face." In this game, the grandfather asks Casey to make different faces. For example, he may ask Casey to make a sad face. Casey makes something resembling a sad face, narrowing his eyes and frowning. Next, the grandfather may ask Casey to make a happy face. For an instant, Casey's face resumes its neutral position and the frown of the sad face disappears. His eyes then open wide and a grin appears. Casey's grandfather continues to request other faces including, possibly, a sleepy face and an angry face. Before he becomes bored with this game, in each instance Casey produces a face that approximates the adult expression.

This example reflects the fact that, by 2 years, some children can produce different facial expressions on request. Furthermore, these children have verbal labels for at least some emotions. Had we continued to observe the game between Casey and his grandfather, we might have heard the grandfather ask Casey what kind of face a little boy would make if he got a big, chocolate ice cream cone. We would have seen Casey produce a happy face, either as a consequence of a learned association between ice cream cones and good feelings when receiving them or as a consequence of knowledge about what people generally feel in certain situations. Thus, either as a function of past associations, as a function of the knowledge of situations associated with particular emotions, or as a function of empathy Casey can produce facial expressions appropriate to imagined situations. Specific events and facial expressions are mediated through cognitive processes that may be as simple as associations or as complex as empathy.

These three examples raise an issue that we wish to address, which is the developmental relationship between emotional expressions and emotional states. The examples underscore the fact that there is not necessarily an isomorphic relationship between emotional elicitors, states, and expressions. In fact, we would argue that emotional expressions reflect the interplay between an innate, complex, biologically programmed neuromusculature (the person factor) and the socialization rules that govern the expression of behavior in any particular society (the environmental factor). Viewing emotional development from the perspective of a person–environment interaction, we suggest that the unlearned, biologically determined neuromuscular patterns constitute universal attributes, whereas the socialization rules represent an environmental contribution to development. Emotional development is posited to be an interaction between these two factors. To understand emotional development both the person factor and the environmental factor must be considered.

Emotional development has been characterized in a variety of ways. In the following discussion we will contrast the view of emotional development as the consequence of a biological program of evolutionary significance with a view that considers emotional development as the consequence of both biological forces and environmental influences. Biological models are noninteractive inasmuch as they portray emotional development to be an invariant unfolding of emotional expressions according to a timetable that is little affected by environmental factors. In contrast, socialization models focus on the person–environment interaction.

To understand the differences between the noninteractive, biological approach to emotional development and the interactive, socialization approach it is necessary to define the various components that together comprise "emotion." Elsewhere, we have labeled these components elicitors, receptors, states, expressions, and experiences (Lewis & Michalson, 1983; Lewis & Rosenblum, 1978). *Emotional elicitors* refer to situations or events that trigger an organism's emotional receptors. These stimuli may be internal or external, and the capacity of these elicitors to evoke responses may be innate or learned. *Emotional receptors* are relatively specific loci or pathways in the central nervous system (CNS) that mediate changes in the physiological or cognitive state of the organism. The process through which these receptors attain their emotional function and the types of events that trigger their activity may be genetically encoded or acquired through experience. *Emotional states* are the changes in somatic or neuronal activity that accompany the activation of emotional receptors. Emotional states are largely specific, transient, patterned alterations in ongoing levels of physiological activity. *Emotional expressions* are the potentially observable surface changes of the face, body, voice, or activity level that accompany emotional states. The constituent elements and their patterning may be either learned or innate. Finally, *emotional experiences* are the individual's conscious or unconscious perception, interpretation, and evaluation of his or her own emotional state and expression. This cognitive process is influenced by a range of prior social experiences in which the nature of the eliciting stimuli and the appropriateness of particular expressions have been articulated and defined, in part, for the individual by others.

The Noninteractive, Biological Approach to Emotional Development

The noninteractive approach to emotional development is derived from Darwin's (1872) theory that emotional behavior has adaptive significance; emotional expressions, states, and receptors are structures with an evolutionary history and biological program. In the case of facial expressions, the evolutionary trend appears to involve an increasingly differentiated neuromusculature, the primary function of which seems to be the production of different emotional expressions. From this perspective, emotional development occurs as a consequence of strong biological forces and maturational changes rather than cultural factors. Noninteractive interpretations of emotion posit (a) specific elicitor–receptor connections, such as innate releasing mechanisms; (b) specificity of CNS receptors; and (c) unlearned connections between receptors and states, between states and expressions, and among states, expressions, and experiences.

The biological interpretation of emotional development is currently represented in the writings of Izard (1971, 1977; Izard & Dougherty, 1982). His view of a direct connection between states, expressions, and experiences allows little room for environmental or socialization factors to influence emotional development. To the extent that socialization factors enter the process at all, they are seen as forces that can later alter innate facial configurations or emotional expressions once they have emerged (Ekman, Friesen, & Ellsworth, 1972; Izard, 1978).

The assumptions of noninteractive models concerning the development of elicitor–receptor connections, the specificity of receptors, and the connections between receptors and states and between states and expressions are all based on the same data. States are defined by expressions; thus, a one-to-one correspondence between them is assumed. This assumption in turn suggests the specificity of emotional states based on a demonstration of differences in emotional expressions. Specific states require the assumption of receptor specificity insofar as specific elicitors produce specific expressions. Evidence of the universality of emotional expressions is used to argue that these expressions are not culturally controlled but are determined by biological mechanisms. The data for such claims are limited to the demonstration that discrete emotions have specific expressions (Ekman *et al.*, 1972; Izard, 1977).

The maturation of the neuromusculature of the face and facial expressions of emotion can be viewed as co-occurring with, although independent of, the growth of other processes and structures, which are primarily cognitive. In some sense, then, noninteractive models of emotion, at least as they involve facial expressions, may require two separate processes: the development of the neuromusculature of the face and the simultaneous development of some other process(es). At this point, it is difficult to separate biological forces from cognitive influences.

Implied in the discussion of the limitations of the noninteractive approach is the assumption that states and expressions, states and experiences, and expressions and experiences are not necessarily isomorphic, at least in adult members of a particular society. This notion is the basic premise of interactive models of emotion. Indeed, the literature on the socialization of feeling rules (i.e., social rules that govern the expression of personal feelings) suggests that children as young as 3 years are capable of disassociating their expressions from their internal emotional states (Lewis & Michalson, 1983; Saarni, 1980, 1982). Indeed, we are familiar with examples of how our own emotional expressions do not necessarily correspond to the way we feel. Clinical psychologists often find that the conscious awareness of people and their emotional states are discordant. Indeed, part of the therapeutic process may involve teaching patients to identify correctly and to monitor their internal states.

The socialization rules that affect the development of emotional expressions, states, and experiences are quite complex (Lewis & Michalson, 1982, 1983). After considering emotional development as an interactive process that occurs between biological and environmental factors, we will consider two important feeling rules: how to express emotions and when to express emotions. Data that illustrate the acquisition of these feeling rules will be presented.

An Interactive, Socialization Model of Emotional Development

In the preceding analysis we suggested that emotional development involves an interaction between the person and the environment. This analysis raises two questions: When are emotional expressions the consequence of biological variables and isomorphic with emotional states? What is the role of the environment in emotional development, which affects the expression of emotional behaviors and influences the connection between emotional expressions and states?

In the model we have developed, the interaction between the person and the environment is reflected in a curvilinear relationship between emotional expressions and states. Emotional development proceeds through three phases, or periods, in which expressions and states are at first asynchronous, then undergo a time of synchrony, which is followed by another asynchronous period (see Fig. 1).

In the first period, internal emotional states are generally undifferentiated and independent of differentiated facial configurations. Examples of the early asynchrony between states and expressions are found in research on early infant smiling (e.g., Emde & Koenig, 1969; Wolff, 1963). An infant's earliest smiles are considered "endogenous" because they do not occur in response to external elicitors and do not seem to be related to positive states. Endogenous

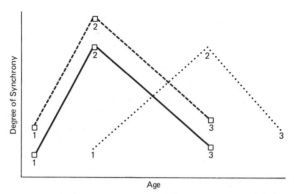

Figure 1. *The developmental relationship between emotional state and emotional expression. (The solid line refers to Emotion A; the dashed line refers to Emotion A'; and the dotted line refers to Emotion B.)*

smiles often are observed when infants are asleep and appear to be correlated with spontaneous CNS activity and REM sleep. One is reluctant to think of these facial expressions as related to anything more than a general excitation of the nervous system.

A similar explanation may apply to observations of the discrete expressions observed in very young infants. (Izard, Huebner, Risser, McGinnes, & Dougherty, 1980; Oster & Ekman, 1978). In this period the changes in an infant's neuromusculature and the patterning of facial expressions that we observe are probably related to a "start-up" or "rehearsal" mechanism in which facial expressions share little synchrony with underlying emotional states.

Alternatively, asynchrony may exist if the neuromusculature of very young infants is insufficiently developed and does not correspond with the set of discrete emotional states that some theorists assume exists early in infancy. Whether the early emotional states of the infant emerge from an undifferentiated state (Bridges, 1932; Emde, Gaensbauer, & Harmon, 1976; Sroufe, 1979) or emerge as differentiated from the start (Izard, 1978) is an unsettled issue. In either case, asynchrony could exist if the facial musculature of the infant is either more differentiated than the internal states (in the first case) or less differentiated than the internal states (in the second case).

The second period of development is marked by a greater synchrony between facial expressions and emotional states. In this phase, different patterns of facial expressions correspond (to a large degree) with differentiated emotional states. This relationship may exist because (*a*) biological factors have joined states with expressions and socialization factors have not yet divorced the two and (*b*) children's cognitive structures have not matured sufficiently to enable them to control their emotional expressions apart from underlying states. That is, even if social reinforcement and socialization rules were operative, the cognitive structures necessary for emotional deceit may not yet exist and the situational knowledge about the appropriate social behavior may not yet be acquired. During this second period, then, one is likely to find the greatest synchrony between facial expressions and internal emotional states. Implied in this view is the assumption that there is a biological force that automatically creates a synchronous relationship between emotional expressions and states. Equally likely is the possibility that the socialization experiences of the child may create the synchronous relationship between states and expressions (Brooks-Gunn & Lewis, 1982).

In the third period of emotional development, facial expressions and internal emotional states are again independent. Unlike Period 1, however, when the lack of correspondence was due to either undifferentiated internal states or an inability to express discrete states through a finely articulated facial musculature, the asynchrony of Period 3 is probably due to the acquisition and maturation of cognitive structures and to the cumulating effects of socialization pressures. Although children may have a particular emotional state and the corresponding facial expression, they may have learned to mask the state by disengaging the "appropriate" facial expression from it (Saarni, 1980, 1982). The end result is that the relationship between expressions and states is a function of the interaction between the person and the environment.

The three periods are schematized in Figure 1 in terms of the child's age and the amount of synchrony between facial expressions and internal emotional states. The courses of two different emotions (A and B) are depicted in Figure 1, from which several points can be made. First, asynchrony may exist at different times for different reasons: (a) the biological immaturity of the organism (in Period 1) or (b) the impact of environmental and cognitive forces (in Period 3).

Although all emotions follow the three-stage process, different emotions may develop according to different time schedules. Because each emotion has its own timetable (determined in part by both biological and environmental factors), it is not possible to state the specific ages for the emergence and developmental sequence of emotions. Synchrony may exist for one emotion at the same time another emotion is in a period of asynchrony. Emotions that emerge early from an undifferentiated state will probably reach the period of synchrony earlier than emotions that appear later. Thus, a fear face that reflects a fear state probably appears earlier than a guilt face that reflects guilt. In fact, for any particular child, the fear face that corresponds to an internal state of fear (Period 2) might occur at the same time as the guilt face that does not correspond to an internal state (Period 1). If this is the case, *the assumption cannot be made that, by demonstrating a correspondence between a facial expression and an internal state for one emotion, we have learned anything about the correspondence for any other emotion.* Each emotion has a unique temporal sequence in terms of when the facial expression first appears and its correspondence with an internal state. There is no reason to believe that all emotions should follow the same timetable even though they follow the same developmental course.

Implicit in our discussion to this point has been the notion that the time frame between any two developmental periods is equal and independent of the specific emotion. This may not be the case, however. The third point illustrated in Figure 1 is that emotions may differ not only in their time of emergence but also in the rate at which they pass through the three periods. Thus, for Emotion A the amount of time between Periods 1 and 2 is shown to be shorter than for Emotion B, whereas the time between Periods 2 and 3 is longer for Emotion A than for Emotion B.

Furthermore, the asynchrony of the third period may vary, with some emotions (e.g., Emotion B in Figure 1) retaining more synchrony than others (e.g., Emotion A). The degree of asynchrony in the third period may be a function of (a) the nature of the particular emotion; (b) the degree to which the emotional expression has been the target of socialization; (c) the particular situation that elicits the emotion; and (d) the degree to which the expression is under the child's cognitive control.

Finally, two levels of Emotion A (A and A') are portrayed in Figure 1. The course of Emotion A' suggests that greater synchrony is possible as a function of the intensity of the eliciting stimulus (and thus the intensity of the underlying state). It may be difficult to disassociate facial expressions from very intense emotional states. Thus, intense stimuli are more apt to produce a greater synchrony between facial expressions and internal emotional states than are less intense stimuli (Lewis, Brooks, & Haviland, 1978). In fact, one way to judge the power of an emotional elicitor may be to establish the degree of synchrony between the subsequent emotional expression and state.

In studying facial configurations and their relationship to internal emotional states, it is crucial to keep this developmental sequence in mind. With this analysis, researchers can study emotional development while at the same time recognizing that faces and states may not be related to one another for very different reasons.

Socialization Rules

Given our belief that the relationship between emotional states and expressions is influenced by environmental factors as well as by a biologically programmed neuromusculature, the explication of these environmental factors is of some interest. Some aspects of the socialization of emotional expressions will be examined in order to clarify the developmental relationship between emotional states and expressions as it is mediated by the environment.

Elsewhere, we have described in detail five particular feeling rules that are subject to socialization forces (Lewis & Michalson, 1982, 1983). The two rules that we shall consider here involve *how* to express emotions and *when* to express emotions. It is clear that adults sometimes express humor by laughing at an employer's joke, even when they do not find the joke funny. Just as often they suppress expressions of internal states that they judge to be inappropriate in a particular situation. For example, boys learn early in life to suppress expressions of fear in order to demonstrate their bravery.

Ekman and Friesen (1969) list four categories of modification of facial expressions, which Saarni (1979) has adapted to describe the rules used by young children to disguise their internal states. Personal or idiosyncratic display rules are familial and individual rules that result from a child's personal history. Deception is a second category that, as its label implies, involves intentionally falsifying an internal state through deceptive behavior. Cultural display rules pertain to the ways that cultures differ in the rules governing emotional expressions. For example, the neutral resting face of the Occidental contrasts with the neutral smiling face of the Oriental. Finally, dramatic rules for pretense are theatrical rules that involve "putting on" a particular expression.

Recently, we conducted two studies on the ways in which emotional expressions may be socialized. One focuses on how children learn to express emotions and the other on what children know about when to express emotions.

HOW TO EXPRESS EMOTIONS: A STUDY OF MOTHER–INFANT INTERACTION

In the first study, we looked at three sets of behaviors in mother–child interactions in the first 2 years of life: mother or infant vocalizing, mother or infant smiling, and infant crying (Brooks-Gunn & Lewis, 1982). Interesting developmental patterns were found in the mothers' socialization rules. During the first 6 months of the infant's life, mothers were significantly more responsive to infant crying than they were in the second 6 months or the second year of the infant's life. This decrease in responsivity to infant crying occurred despite the fact that maternal responsivity to other behaviors increased over this same period. For example, maternal responses to infant smiling increased between the time the infant was 6 and 12 months of age and then showed little developmental change: Mothers were as responsive to their infant's smile when the child was 1 year old as when the child was 2 years old. These data suggest that different socialization rules may govern the children's expressions of positive and negative emotions. To wit, mothers increase their responsiveness to positive emotions but become unresponsive to negative emotions as children get older. The data on a small sample of handicapped children were similar to those of the nonhandicapped sample, showing a reduction in responsivity to infant crying over the first 2 years of the infant's life.

These data are important to the study of emotional development for several reasons. First, they indicate that maternal responsivity to distress decreases as children grow older. The rule seems to be "it is inappropriate to express distress through crying; other 'more appropriate' means should be used."

Feiring and Lewis (1979) showed that expressions of infant distress, elicited by placing a barrier between the infant and the mother, change from crying to asking for help over the second year of the infant's life. This developmental change may correspond to the decrease in maternal responsivity to infant crying and the increase in maternal responsivity to infant vocalization that we observed during this same age period.

Second, mothers were less responsive to the crying of male infants than to the crying of female infants with the developmental function being steeper for males. This finding indicates a socialization rule dictating (at least in our culture) that "boys should not cry."

Third, the data showed differences in maternal socialization rules as a function of the status of the child. In this particular study, the status of the child was defined in terms of nonhandicapping versus handicapping characteristics. In both conditions crying was less reinforced as the appropriate expression of distress but there was a tendency for it to be less reinforced for handicapped children. Other differences in maternal responsivity suggest that the socialization rules may be modified according to the developmental level of the child. In short, maternal reinforcement patterns in response to children's early emotional expressions appear to underlie some of the known feeling rules that govern children's later emotional behavior.

WHEN TO EXPRESS EMOTIONS: A STUDY OF SOCIAL KNOWLEDGE

A second way in which emotional states and expressions might be disengaged is through a person's *knowledge* of the social and cultural rules that govern emotional expressions. This knowledge underlies a second feeling rule, which is when to express emotions. Children's knowledge about how other people feel in certain situations is a topic of considerable interest because it overlaps with two other important research areas: the development of social knowledge and empathy. Whether knowledge of other people's feelings is derived through empathy or other learning processes is a complex problem beyond the scope of this chapter. Of specific interest to a discussion of the socialization of emotions are studies showing that very young children know something about how others feel in certain circumstances.

The source of children's knowledge may be their understanding of facial expressions or other expressive behaviors rather than an explicit understanding of the emotions associated with a situation per se. For example, children may know about emotions in situations by observing another person's *behavior* in that situation. The observation of emotional expressions in turn provides information about the situation.

Alternatively, children may understand the situational requirements *apart* from the participant's emotional expressions. For our purposes, the studies most relevant to children's knowledge about when to express emotions are those that do not include emotional behaviors as cues to the emotion associated with the situation, if we are primarily interested in what children know about when to express emotions and not if children are able to recognize the facial expressions of others.

In most research on this topic children are told a brief story and shown a picture of the situation (e.g., Borke, 1973; Feshbach & Roe, 1968). For example, the story might be about a birthday party or a toy breaking. The subject is asked, "How does the child in the story feel?" or "How would you feel?" The extent to which the pictures do not contain clues about emotional behavior is the extent to which the subject's answers reflect knowledge of situations apart from knowledge of emotional expressions. The results of such studies suggest that by 4 years of age, and sometimes by 3, children know what would be considered by adults to be the correct response to the situation (Borke, 1971, 1973; Mood, Johnson, & Shantz, 1974). In a review of this literature Shantz (1975) suggests that by 4 years children reliably understand simple situations that elicit happy responses. Between 4 and 7 years children show an increasing ability to recognize situations that elicit fear, sadness, and anger.

The process of identifying emotions appropriate to particular situations appears to be enhanced by a similarity between the subject and the child in the story. When the person in the situation is more like the subject (e.g., similar in age or gender), the subject's ability to report the "correct" emotion is facilitated (Shantz, 1975). Such findings suggest that empathy may be an important aspect of the process.

It is interesting to note that when both situational and facial cues are provided in the story, younger children rely more on the information provided by the situational cue. Studies containing ambiguous situational and facial cues have shown that children use situational and facial cues differentially in judging the emotion of the person in the story. In one study, preschool children were found to base their judgments on situational cues, whereas elementary school children (5 to 7 years old) used expressions more often (Burns & Cavey, 1957). Too few data exist on this topic to confirm a developmental trend, especially since there is evidence that adults, like younger children, frequently use situational cues (Taguiri, 1969) and that situational cues have a more powerful effect on adults' emotional responses than do their own facial expressions (Laird, 1974). Nevertheless, regardless of the source, it appears that by 4 years of age children already have some situational knowledge about when emotions should occur.

Recently, we conducted a pilot study with eight children, 2, 3, and 4 years of age. We first asked the children to make different faces, after which they could ask the experimenter to make a face. The faces the children were asked to make included happy, angry, sad, surprise, sleepy, scared, afraid, silly, and "like when you eat something that doesn't taste good" (i.e., disgust). We did this to determine whether children this young could associate verbal labels with particular facial configurations. With the children's permission, photographs were taken of each face they made. The children were then told several stories in which the chief character (a girl named Felicia) is involved in activities that are likely to produce specific emotions. For example, in one story Felicia drops an ice cream cone. The subjects were asked to describe the way Felicia might feel ("what kind of face would Felicia make?"), to make a face like Felicia might make, and to select from a set of four pictures of Felicia making different faces the face that she would show in the situation.

Our preliminary findings suggest that by 2 years some children are capable, when asked, of making appropriate faces that approximate adult faces, although the facial expressions of the 2-year-olds were less differentiated than those of the 4-year-olds. The 2-year-olds produced happy, sad, angry, and surprise faces. By 4 years the children had little trouble making happy, sad, angry, funny, surprise, and scared faces. This result may be due to several factors: First, the facial musculature of 2-year-olds may be less differentiated than that of 4-year-olds and they may have less control over it. Second, 2-year-olds may know fewer verbal labels for faces; thus, they may have produced fewer faces not because they were less capable but because they could not associate the verbal label with the face. Finally, the 2-year-olds may have become bored with the game faster than the older children and therefore they made fewer faces. The preliminary findings also showed that 2-year-old children could point to faces that are likely to occur in particular situations. The 2-year-olds identified happy, sad, angry, and disgust faces appropriate to the story. These data lend some support to the proposition that children acquire knowledge about the contexts of socially appropriate emotional expressions quite early.

The feeling rules about how and when to express emotions, illustrated in the studies described in this chapter, are two topics in the study of the socialization of emotional expressions. The demonstration of socialization influences on expressive behavior returns us to our original proposition, namely, that emotional expressions must be viewed as the combined result of innate biological factors and environmental effects.

Implications for Personality Development and Psychopathology

Both the socialization history of the individual as well as a biologically programmed neuromusculature influence emotional development and the relationship between emotional expressions and states. As has been pointed out by others, emotional expression is a communicative process, the function of which is to inform others (as well as oneself) about personal feelings (Buck, 1981, 1982; Ekman & Friesen, 1975; Izard, 1977; Tomkins, 1962, 1963). The social environment interprets the internal states of its members by observing their behaviors in particular contexts. Thus, it can be said that the social environment has an impact on children (*a*) by prescribing the nature of their emotional expressions and (*b*) by interpreting their emotional states through an observation of their expressions in context.

Personality development and psychopathology involve a complex set of factors, including individual differences in temperament and cognitive abilities. Deviations in the normative socialization practices of a culture may also have an impact on personality development and psychopathology. Idiosyncratic childrearing practices may occur during the socialization of particular emotional expressions. Some children may not learn how or be able to express fear or distress if such behaviors are negatively reinforced.

What might be the result of eliminating or altering some components? Several consequences in particular may contribute to psychopathology. First, the absence of certain types of emotional expressions may directly affect emotional experience. An individual's emotional experience is determined by perceiving and interpreting (*a*) his or her own expressions and states; (*b*) situations; and (*c*) the behaviors of others. The degree to which an expressive component is missing is the degree to which the ability to experience an appropriate state may be impaired. Second, the idiosyncratic socialization of emotional expressions may affect how others react to the individual. Insofar as emotional expressions communicate the individual's feelings to other people, the inappropriate socialization of these expressions (inappropriate vis-à-vis the cultural norms) might cause the individual to be misinterpreted by others.

Another way in which the socialization of emotional expressions may be related to subsequent personality deviations pertains to the interpretation given those expressions by significant others. For example, it may be the case that a child's emotional expressions are appropriate in the context of cultural norms. However, the caregiver's interpretation of these expressions may not be appropriate. In a recent study we looked at how mothers label their 1-year-old children's distress behaviors (Lewis & Michalson, 1982). By monitoring children's emotional expressions in a context of distress, mothers generally adopted what we consider to be a normative interpretation. There were several occasions, however, in which a mother's labeling behavior contradicted our judgments of a child's emotional expression. For example, one mother labeled a frightened child "angry," while another mother labeled a frightened child "sad." The mislabeling of children's emotional states has important implications for any model of developmental psychopathology. Since psychopathology may be the consequence of both the child's characteristics and the interpretation of people around the child, evidence of a discrepancy or "mismatch" between these two factors might be used to identify children at risk for later psychopathology. Misinterpretation of children's emotional expressions and states (both in mothers' labeling and in their behavioral response toward children) has the potential for affecting children's development in two ways. First, it violates the normative values of the society and therefore puts children "at risk" with respect to deviant behavior toward others. Second, it teaches children inappropriate labels for their internal states. While our analysis is only speculative, it suggests an interactive model of psychopathology based on deviations in the normal socialization of emotions. The interactive model is applicable if we subscribe to the fact that emotional states and expressions are not always isomorphic and that the socialization of emotional expressions may produce deviant behavior as well as socially appropriate emotions.

The discussion of emotional development in terms of the relationship between emotional expressions and states forces us to consider the interaction between the biological characteristics of the person, in this case the species-specific neuromusculature of the face, and the social demands of the environment. The evolutionary-adaptive significance of facial expressions attests to an interaction between organisms and their environment in emotional development. Likewise, the socialization of facial expressions is predicated on an interaction between biological characteristics of the organism and the socialization of feeling rules prescribed by the environment. The study of emotional development in terms of the relationship between emotional expressions and internal states provides the opportunity to study one aspect of person—environmental interactions.

References

Borke, H. Interpersonal perception of young children: Egocentrism or empathy? *Developmental Psychology,* 1971, *5,* 263–269.

Borke, H. The development of empathy in Chinese and American children between three and six years of age: A cross-cultural study. *Developmental Psychology,* 1973, *9,* 102–108.

Bridges, K. M. B. Emotional development in early infancy. *Child Development,* 1932, *3,* 324–334.

Brooks-Gunn, J., & Lewis, M. Affective exchanges between normal and handicapped infants and their mothers. In T. Field & A. Fogel (Eds.), *Emotion and early interaction.* Hillsdale, N. J.: Erlbaum, 1982.

Buck, R. The evolution and development of emotion expression and communication. In S. S. Brehm, S. M. Kassin, & F. X. Gibbons (Eds.), *Developmental social psychology.* New York: Oxford University Press, 1981.

Buck, R. *Nonverbal communication and emotion communication.* New York: Guilford Press, 1982.

Burns, N., & Cavey, L. Age differences in empathic ability among children. *Canadian Journal of Psychology,* 1957, *11,* 227–230.

Darwin, C. R. *The expression of the emotions in man and animals.* London: Murray, 1872.

Ekman, P., & Friesen, W. The repertoire of nonverbal behavior: Categories, origins, usage, and coding. *Semiotica,* 1969, *1,* 49–98.

Ekman, P., & Friesen, W. V. *Unmasking the face.* Englewood Cliffs, N. J.: Prentice-Hall, 1975.

Ekman, P., Friesen, W., & Ellsworth, P. *Emotion in the human face.* New York: Pergamon, 1972.

Emde, R., Gaensbauer, T., & Harmon, R. Emotional expression in infancy: A biobehavioral study. *Psychological Issues,* 1976, *10* (1, Whole No. 37).

Emde, R. N., & Koenig, K. L. Neonatal smiling and rapid eye-movement states. *Journal of the American Academy of Child Psychiatry,* 1969, *8,* 57–67.

Feiring, C., & Lewis, M. Sex and age differences in young children's reactions to frustration: A further look at the Goldberg and Lewis subjects. *Child Development,* 1979, *50,* 848–853.

Feshbach, N. D., & Roe, K. Empathy in six- and seven-year-olds. *Child Development,* 1968, *39,* 133–145.

Izard, C. E. *The face of emotion.* New York: Appleton, 1971.

Izard, C. E. *Human emotions.* New York: Plenum, 1977.

Izard, C. E. On the development of emotions and emotion-cognitive relationships in infancy. In M. Lewis & L. A. Rosenblum (Eds.), *The development of affect.* New York: Plenum, 1978.

Izard, C. E., & Dougherty, L. M. Two complementary systems for measuring facial expressions in infants and children. In C. E. Izard (Ed.), *Measuring emotions in infants and children.* New York: Cambridge University Press, 1982.

Izard, C. E., Huebner, R. R., Risser, D., McGinnes, G. C., & Dougherty, L. M. The young infant's ability to produce discrete emotion expressions. *Developmental Psychology,* 1980, *16,* 132–140.

Laird, J. I. Self-attribution of emotion: The effects of expressive behavior on the quality of emotional experience. *Journal of Personality and Social Psychology,* 1974, *29,* 475–486.

Lewis, M., Brooks, J., & Haviland, J. Hearts and faces: A study in the measurement of emotion. In M. Lewis & L. A. Rosenblum (Eds.), *The development of affect.* New York: Plenum, 1978.

Lewis, M., & Michalson, L. The socialization of emotions. In T. Field & A. Fogel (Eds.), *Emotion and early interaction.* Hillsdale, N. J.: Erlbaum, 1982.

Lewis, M., & Michalson, L. *Children's emotions and moods: Developmental theory and measurement.* New York: Plenum, 1983.

Lewis, M., & Rosenblum, L. A. Introduction: Issues in affect development. In M. Lewis & L. A. Rosenblum (Eds.), *The development of affect.* New York: Plenum, 1978.

Mood, D., Johnson, J., & Schantz, C. U. *Affective and cognitive components of empathy in young children.* Paper presented at the southeast regional meeting of the Society for Research in Child Development, Chapel Hill, N. C., 1974.

Oster, H., & Ekman, P. Facial behavior in child development. In A. Collins (Ed.), *Minnesota symposia on child psychology* (Vol. 11). Hillsdale, N. J.: Erlbaum, 1978.

Saarni, C. Children's understanding of display rules for expressive behavior. *Developmental Psychology,* 1979, *15,* 424–429.

Saarni, C. *Observing children's use of display rules: Age and sex differences.* Paper presented at the Annual Meeting of the American Psychological Association, Montreal, September 1980.

Saarni, C. Social and affective functions of nonverbal behavior: Developmental concerns. In R. S. Feldman (Ed.), *Development of nonverbal behavior in children.* New York: Springer-Verlag, 1982.

Shantz, C. U. The development of social cognition. In E. M. Hetherington (Ed.), *Review of child development research.* Chicago: University of Chicago Press, 1975.

Sroufe, L. A. Socioemotional development. In J. D. Osofsky (Ed.), *Handbook of infant development.* New York: Wiley, 1979.

Taguiri, R. Person perception. In G. Lindzey & E. Aronson (Eds.), *The handbook of social psychology* (Vol. 3). Reading, Mass.: Addison-Wesley, 1969.

Tomkins, S. S. *Affect, imagery, consciousness* (Vol. 1): *The positive affects.* New York: Springer-Verlag, 1962.

Tomkins, S. S. *Affect, imagery, consciousness* (Vol. 2): *The negative affects.* New York: Springer-Verlag, 1963.

Wolff, P. H. Observations on the early development of smiling. In B. M. Foss (Ed.), *Determinants of infant behavior* (Vol. 2). New York: Wiley, 1963.

V

Social Adaptation:
The Person in the Environment

This section consists of five chapters that are organized around the theme of the individual's social adaptation and maladaptation. The interactional perspective provides a useful model for analyzing and interpreting behavioral problems or lack of optimal adjustment of individuals.

In the first chapter, Lerner describes a model based on the degree of congruence between characteristics of the individual and the demands of the situation or context. According to this model, the greater the "goodness of fit" between the individual and the environment, the "better" or more adaptive the behavioral outcomes will be. Lerner focuses on temperament as being a particularly important person factor in research on children's behavior.

In the second chapter, Rutter considers the psychological mechanisms involved in the person–environment interaction that may mediate between negative experiences in childhood and maladaptive behavior in adulthood. Results are presented from several studies to illustrate the different types of person–environment mediating processes that can occur. The author emphasizes that interactions are heterogeneous and should not be thought of as being a single process.

Chapter 18 by Jessor discusses the results of a longitudinal study of the social adjustment of individuals followed over 12 years (from adolescence to young adulthood). The central issue of this chapter is how to explain both continuity and change in development. Jessor offers a theoretical analysis that stresses the developmental continuities that occur in the process of changing from adolescence to adulthood.

Chapter 19, by Vaillant, deals with the role of coping styles or defenses as a

277

HUMAN DEVELOPMENT:
AN INTERACTIONAL PERSPECTIVE

factor in social adaptation and maladaptation in connection with a discussion of two large prospective longitudinal studies of two different adolescent samples. A hierarchy of defenses is posited that vary in their relative immaturity. Evidence showed that maturity of intrapsychic defenses in middle life is correlated positively with mental and physical health in adulthood.

In the last chapter in this section, Olweus reports a study that has methodological implications for research dealing with person—environment interaction. It has often been assumed that low educational achievement is causally related to aggression among boys in school. By using sophisticated statistical techniques with longitudinal data, alternative interpretations of any relation between the variables were rigorously assessed. This analysis should serve as a warning in drawing too fast conclusions about the direction of effects between factors involved in the developmental process.

16

A "Goodness of Fit" Model of Person–Context Interaction[1]

RICHARD M. LERNER

Human developmentalists who favor an interactionist approach to the study of behavioral and change phenomena have won a battle of words but have not, to date, won one of theory. Today, almost all major contributors to theory and research in human development use the term *interaction;* yet, there are several different theoretical uses of the term (see Lerner, in press, and Overton, 1973, for a discussion of these).

The concept of interaction, which guides the conceptual and empirical work I will discuss, has been labeled a *strong* concept of organism–environment interaction (R. M. Lerner, 1978; R. M. Lerner & Spanier, 1978, 1980; Overton, 1973). The concept is associated with a contextual world view (Pepper, 1942) and, as such, stresses that organism and context are always embedded each in the other (R. M. Lerner, Hultsch, & Dixon, in press). The context is composed of multiple levels, ranging from the biological to the sociocultural and physical–ecological, all changing interdependently across time (i.e., historically). Because changes in the context promote changes in the organism and, simultaneously, because the developing organism fosters changes in its context, the potential for change is present across life. Moreover, because organisms influence the context that influences them, they are producers of their own development. Consequently, as compared to what I have elsewhere argued to be the case in organismic-maturational developmental theories, the strong concept of interaction associated with contextually derived views of

[1]Work on this chapter was supported in part by a grant from the John D. and Catherine T. MacArthur Foundation.

279

HUMAN DEVELOPMENT:
AN INTERACTIONAL PERSPECTIVE

human development sees the organism as efficacious in playing an active role in its own development (R. M. Lerner & Busch-Rossnagel, 1981).

Moreover, the strong concept of interaction suggests not only that developmental change may be a life-span phenomenon, but also that, because organism and context are always involved in reciprocally influenced exchanges, the focus of developmental analysis should be the *relation* between organism and context, and not merely on either as separate, independent entities or "elements" (Looft, 1973; Riegel, 1976). Because of the embeddedness of organism and context, the same organismic attribute will have different implications for developmental outcomes in the context of different contextual conditions (because the organism attribute is actually transformed, it is only given its functional meaning, by virtue of its relation to a specific context). In turn, the same contextual condition will lead to alternative developments in that different organisms interact with it. To state this position in other, somewhat stronger terms, a given organismic attribute only has meaning for psychological development by virtue of its relation to a particular set of contextual conditions and, in turn, the import of any set of contextual conditions for psychosocial behavior and development can only be understood by specifying the context's relations to the specific features of the organisms within it.

A call for the study of the relation between organism and context, as opposed to these two elements per se (as is forwarded as the focus, for instance, in moderate interaction views; R. M. Lerner & Spanier, 1980), has been made repeatedly over the last decade (e.g., Lewis & Lee-Painter, 1974; Looft, 1973; Riegel, 1976; Overton, 1978). Nevertheless, such appeals have not led to many programmatic attempts at such study. However, my colleagues and I have recently initiated a series of studies aimed in part at using this relational interactive concept in studying the role of temperamental individuality for adaptive psychosocial development. We have used what we term a "goodness of fit" model to conceptualize the relation between an organism's temperamental attributes and features of the organism's context. We believe that this instance of a strong interaction concept leads to significant advances in theory and research pertinent to temperament. In addition, we believe that our perspective has important implications for optimizing human development.

The "Goodness of Fit" Model

The conception that the relationships between an organism and its context must involve congruence, match, or simply fit in order for adaptive transactions to exist is an idea traceable at least to Darwin (1859). As explained by White (1968), this idea has permeated American and to some extent European social science, albeit in formulations as seemingly diverse as those of G. S. Hall (1904), Clark Hull (1952), and George Herbert Mead (1934). For example, one current instance of this conception is the self-role congruence model used in social psychology (Sarbin & Allen, 1968; Smelser, 1961), and another is the model of Group × Place transaction used in environmental psychology (Stokols, 1981). The version of this idea that I have employed rests on an appreciation of the contextual significance of a person's characteristics of individuality for development.

ORGANISMIC INDIVIDUALITY AND CONTEXTUAL DEMANDS

Just as a person brings his or her characteristics of individuality to a particular social setting there are demands placed on the person by virtue of the social and physical components of the setting. These demands may take the form of (*a*) attitudes, values, or stereotypes held by others in the context regarding the person's attributes (either his or her physical or behavioral characteristics); (*b*) the attributes (usually behavioral) of others in the context with whom the person must coordinate, or fit, his or her attributes (also, in this case, usually behavioral) for adaptive interactions to exist; or (c) the physical characteristics of a setting (e.g., the presence or absence of access ramps for the motorically handicapped) that require the person to possess certain attributes (again, usually behavioral abilities) for the most efficient interaction within the setting to occur.

The person's individuality, in differentially meeting these demands, provides a basis for the feedback he or she gets from the socializing environment. For example, considering the demand "domain" of attitudes, values, or stereotypes, teachers and parents may have relatively individual and distinct expectations about behaviors desired of their students and children, respectively. Teachers may want students who show little distractibility, since they would not want attention diverted from the lesson by the activity of other children in the classroom. Parents, however, might desire their children to be moderately distractible, for example, when they require their children to switch from watching television to eating dinner or going to bed. Children whose behavioral individuality was either generally distractible or generally not distractible would thus differentially meet the demands of these two contexts. Problems of adaptation to school or to home might thus develop as a consequence of a child's lack of match (or "goodness of fit") in either or both settings.

Similarly, considering the second type of contextual demands, problems of fit might occur when a child who is highly irregular in his biological functions (e.g., eating, sleep–wake cycles, toileting behaviors) interacts in a family setting composed of highly regular and behaviorally scheduled parents and siblings. In turn, considering the third type of contextual demands, a child who has a low threshold for response and who also is highly distractible might find it problematic to perform efficiently in a setting with high noise levels (e.g., a crowded home, a school room situated near the street in a busy urban area) when tasks necessitating concentration or attention (e.g., studying, taking an examination) are required.

Thomas and Chess (1977, 1980, 1981) and J. V. Lerner (in press) believe that adaptive psychological and social functioning do not derive directly from either the nature of the person's characteristics of individuality per se or the nature of the demands of the contexts within which the person functions. Rather, if a person's characteristics of individuality match (or "fit") the demands of a particular setting, adaptive outcomes will occur. Those people whose characteristics match most of the settings within which they exist should receive supportive or positive feedback from the contexts and should show evidence of the most adaptive behavioral development. In turn, of course, mismatched people, whose characteristics are incongruent with one or most settings, should show alternative developmental outcomes.

Thus, temperament should not be measured alone. Instead, researchers must move to a second level of abstraction, measuring both the person's temperament and the contextual demands. If the demands of the context change or if the person is in contexts that have different demands, then an adaptive person would, if possible, alter his or her behavioral style. One conclusion here then is that attempts to measure the phenomenal stability of temperament attributes alone are of limited usefulness from a contextual view of temperament (see J. V. Lerner & R. M. Lerner, in press). A second conclusion is that unless one has knowledge of the demands of a particular setting one cannot adequately predict or explain the absence or presence of a relation between temperament and psychosocial functioning.[2]

Empirical Support for the Goodness of Fit Model

Much of the research literature supporting the use of the goodness of fit model either is derived directly from the Thomas and Chess NYLS or is associated with independent research that has adopted their conceptualization of temperament. We consider first the contribution of the NYLS data set.

THE NEW YORK LONGITUDINAL STUDY

In their New York Longitudinal Study (NYLS) of the psychosocial significance of temperamental individuality, Thomas and Chess (Thomas & Chess, 1977; Thomas, Chess, Sillan, & Mendez, 1974) have prospectively studied, for over 25 years, a core sample of 133 white, middle-class, largely Jewish children of professional parents. In addition, a sample of 98 New York City Puerto

---

[2]In trying to measure this relation one interesting but as yet unresolved issue is how close a fit must be to be regarded a "fit" or a "match." Some statistical answers exist (e.g., a temperament score "fits" a demand if the discrepancy between temperament and demand is less than the standard error of measurement) but they are presently atheoretical. But, provocative conceptual issues—such as whether, for optimum interest or motivation in a context, a slight discrepancy rather than complete congruence is advantageous—remain unaddressed.

Rican children of working-class parents have been followed for about 14 years. Each sample was studied from at least the first month of life onward. Although the distribution of temperamental attributes in the two samples was not different, the import of the attributes for psychosocial adjustment was quite disparate.

To illustrate, let us consider the impact of low regularity or rhythmicity of behavior, particularly in regard to sleep–wake cycles. The Puerto Rican parents studied by Thomas and Chess (Thomas & Chess, 1977; Thomas *et al.*, 1974; Korn, 1978) were quite permissive. No demands in regard to rhythmicity of sleep were placed on the infant or child. Indeed, the parents allowed the child to go to sleep at any time the child desired, and permitted the child to awaken at any time as well. The parents molded their schedule around the children. Thus, because parents were so accommodating, there were no problems of fit associated with an arrhythmic infant or child. Indeed, neither within the infancy period nor throughout the first 5 years of life did arrhythmicity predict adjustment problems. In this sample arrhythmicity remained continuous and independent of adaptive implications for the child (Thomas *et al.*, 1974).

In the white, middle-class families, however, strong demands for rhythmic sleep patterns were maintained. Thus, an arrhythmic child was not fit with parental demands and, consistent with the goodness of fit model, arrhythmicity was a major predictor of problem behaviors both within the infancy years and across time through the first 5 years of life (Thomas *et al.*, 1974). However, the parents in the white, middle-class sample took steps to change their arrhythmic children's sleep patterns; since most of these arrhythmic children were also adaptable, low rhythmicity tended to be discontinuous for most children.

Thus, in the white, middle-class sample, early infant arrhythmicity tended to be a problem during this time of life but proved to be neither continuous nor predictive of later problems of adjustment. In turn, in the Puerto Rican sample, infant arrhythmicity was not a problem during this time of life, but it was continuous and—because in the Puerto Rican context it was not involved in poor fit—it was not associated with adjustment problems in the first 5 years of life. However, to underscore the importance of considering the context of development, I should note that arrhythmicity did begin to predict adjustment problems for the Puerto Rican children when they entered the school system. Their lack of a regular sleep pattern interfered with their getting sufficient sleep to perform well in school and, in addition, often caused them to be late for arrival to school (Korn, 1978).

Another example may be given of how the differential demands existing between the two family contexts provided different incentives for adaptation. This example pertains to differences in the demands of the physical contexts of the families. As noted by Thomas *et al.* (1974), as well as Korn (1978), overall there was a very low incidence of behavior problems in the Puerto Rican sample children in their first 5 years of life, especially when compared to the corresponding incidence among the core sample children. However, if a problem was presented at this time among the Puerto Rican sample it was most likely to be a problem of motor activity. However, in the core sample's clinical group only one child (a child with brain damage) was characterized in this way.

What appears to differentiate those children whose (high) activity level scores are associated with the occurrence of clinically diagnosed motor activity problems is not their scores per se, but whether the children are from the Puerto Rican or core sample families. And what appears to differentiate these families, in regard to the relation of this behavioral style characteristic to problem behavior, are the physical features of their homes.

In the Puerto Rican sample the families usually had several children and lived in small apartments. Even average motor activity therefore tended to impinge on others in the setting. Moreover, even in the case of the children with high activity levels, the Puerto Rican parents were reluctant to let their children out of the apartment because of the actual dangers of playing on the streets of East Harlem. In the core sample, however, the parents had the financial resources to provide large apartments or houses for their families. There were typically suitable play areas for the children both inside and outside the home. As a consequence, the presence of high activity levels in the homes of the core sample did not cause the problems for interaction that they did in the Puerto Rican group. Thus, as Thomas *et al.* (1963, 1974) emphasize, the mismatch between temperamental attribute and physical environmental demand accounted for the group difference in the import of high activity level for the development of behavioral problems.

In sum, the data described above are not fully consonant with the methodological requirements prescribed for a direct and complete test of the goodness of fit model (J. V. Lerner & R. M. Lerner, in press). For example, although the NYLS is a longitudinal study and involves multiple cohorts, controls for retesting effects were not included. However, in spite of these limitations, the above analyses of the NYLS data set provide results conceptually compatible with the goodness of fit model. Data independent of the NYLS also provide some support.

DATA SETS INDEPENDENT OF THE NYLS

Support both for the generalizability of the temperamental attributes studied by Thomas and Chess (1977, 1980, 1981) and for the goodness of fit model is provided in a cross-cultural study by Super and Harkness (1981). Super and Harkness studied infants in a rural farming community in Kenya, named Kokwet, and infants in suburban families living in the metropolitan Boston area.

Super and Harkness (1981, p. 79) report that the dimensions studied in the

NYLS "are not, by and large," artifacts of the American setting. In both the Kokwet and the Boston samples, the dimensions of mood, adaptability, intensity of reaction, and rhythmicity were identified in both interview and naturalistic observational data. However, because of the cultural differences between these two settings, the import of these temperamental attributes were quite different.

Among the people of Kokwet (the Kipsigis), the baby in the first few months of life is in the exclusive care of the mother and, in fact, is rarely separated from physical contact with her. Such constant and close physical contact is not at all characteristic of the mother–infant relation in the Boston sample. Moreover, in Kokwet the mother is rarely alone with the infant. During the day an average of five additional people are in the house with her and the infant.

Some of the impact of these cultural differences may be seen by considering the dimensions of rhythmicity and adaptability. An infant who does not show rhythmicity of biological functions, like sleeping and eating, would not have a problem of fitting the cultural demands imposed by the Kokwet setting. However, an infant in the Boston setting, who had the same low level of rhythmicity, would not fit well with the demands imposed on him or her. That is, in the Boston sample, the infant's activities were typically highly scheduled. Moreover, if this American infant were low in adaptability the problems for fit, for example, to the schedule the mother tried to impose would be enhanced, and the potential problems for adequate development would be increased. In turn, an infant in Kokwet who had a low adaptability score would not have a poor fit because there is no schedule imposed on him or her to which adaptation is required.

Super and Harkness (1981) point out that there are several developmental consequences of these cultural differences in the meaning of temperament. For example, although it starts out similarly, by 4 months of age the sleep–wake cycle of Boston and Kokwet infants is quite different, with the average Boston infant sleeping for 8 hours at night, and the average Kokwet infant continuing to wake briefly and nurse. In addition, maternal impressions of the infant are different in each setting. The Kokwet mothers are not concerned with characteristics like negative mood, low rhythmicity, and low adaptability, and do not view them as indicative of long-term problems. However, the American mothers in the Super and Harkness (1981) sample have precisely the opposite evaluation of these temperamental attributes. Thus, as in the NYLS data set, we see that the same temperamental characteristic has a different impact on others as a consequence of its embeddedness in a different cultural context.

In several studies my colleagues, students, and I have assessed the use of the goodness of fit model among samples from the late childhood to late adolescent age range. In all studies we have followed a general procedure. First, we assess temperament by use of the Dimensions of Temperament Survey (DOTS), an instrument developed by R. M. Lerner, Palermo, Spiro, & Nesselroade (1982) to measure multiple dimensions of temperament: activity level, rhythmicity, adaptability/approach—withdrawal, attention span—persistence/distractability, and reactivity—an attribute composed of items relating to threshold, activity level, and intensity. The DOTS has been designed to obtain either self-ratings of temperament or ratings about a person provided by another, when it is the case that raters may have sufficient knowledge of a target person's behavioral style—as may be the case for a mother of her infant or young child. In some of our research (e.g., Palermo, 1982) we have obtained both self-ratings and ratings by mothers in order to assess the role of sources of ratings on the contribution of temperament or goodness of fit for the prediction of adaptation. In addition to the temperament ratings, we also typically measure the demands of the context, most often the attitudinal/expectational demands held by significant others in the child's context. In all of our studies we have taken steps to ensure that our measures of temperament, of demands, and of outcome were not derived solely from a single source (e.g., from a mother's ratings).

In the first study completed in our laboratory, J. V. Lerner (in press) used a version of the DOTS to measure eighth-graders' temperaments. She also assessed the demands for behavioral style in the classroom maintained by each subject's classroom teacher and peer group. Those subjects whose temperaments best matched each set of demands had more favorable teacher ratings of adjustment and ability, had better grades, more positive peer relations, fewer negative peer relations, and more positive self-esteems than did subjects whose temperaments were less well matched with either teacher or peer demands. Moreover, fit in one context predicted fit in the other context and, as such, temperamental fit with teacher (or peer) demands predicted teacher-related outcome measures, and too the outcome measures derived from the other independent context, the peer (or teacher) one.[3]

As implied earlier, it is quite important to note that the source of the temperament ratings (in this study, the students' self-appraisals) differed from the source of the contextual demands (the classroom teacher and classroom peer group) and, as explained, from the source of the outcome measures. This methodological feature is included to appraise whether the temperament—adaptation relations are merely perceptions of the rater of temperament, as suggested by Bates (1980), for instance. Since in the J. V. Lerner (in press) study the sources of temperament ratings, of contextual demands, and of adjustment/adaptation outcomes are derived from independent sources, there is seemingly little basis for insisting that temperament—adaptation relations or goodness of fit—adaptation relations are within-person perceptions.

---

[3]The "school" is a cultural or normatively based context. In such contexts it is likely that most people—especially by the time they have reached late childhood or early adolescence—will show attributes more congruent than incongruent with the context. As a consequence, those children who manifest incongruent fit between temperament and contextual demands are at the same time deviant from the norms of the social situation. Thus, their poorer performance can be due to (a) deviation from the norm; (b) lack of good fit; or (c) some combination of the two.

Further support for the use of the goodness of fit model is derived from a study by J. V. Lerner, R. M. Lerner, and Zabski (in press). This study also provides evidence that temperament–context fit covaries with actual academic abilities. That is, the J. V. Lerner (in press) study demonstrated a relation between peer and teacher ratings, and teacher-assigned grades and goodness of fit. However, no relation between actual academic abilities and fit was assessed. Such a relation was found by J. V. Lerner *et al.* (in press), however. That is, for several dimensions measured by the DOTS, and most notably for reactivity, fourth-grade students whose self-rated temperament best fit teacher demands not only had better teacher ratings of ability and adjustment but also scored better on two standardized achievement tests (the Stanford Achievement Test for Reading and the Comprehensive Test of Basic Skills) than did less well fit children.

Moreover, this study underscores another methodological feature of our approach to testing the goodness of fit idea, that is, our multivariate conception of fit. Although it may prove useful in some instances to collapse across temperament attributes and demands in order to get a global fit score, we believe such an approach may mask important information. Specifically, information would be lost about which temperament–demands relations best predict particular outcome measures in a specific context. As such, our procedure is to assess how a discrepancy between each of the temperament attributes we measure on the DOTS and each corresponding demand for temperament predicts our array of outcome measures. The use of this multivariate approach is to provide a more detailed indication of precisely which features of behavioral style may be salient, and which irrelevant, for adaptation in a particular context.

For instance, in the nine fourth-grade classrooms studied by J. V. Lerner *et al.* (in press), fit scores relevant to adaptability/approach–withdrawal were not related to any outcome measure; fit scores related to attention span–persistence/distractability were related only to teacher ratings (with students meeting or exceeding teachers' demands having better ratings); and fit scores regarding reactivity were, as noted, related to both teacher-rated and actual abilities (with students who met teachers' demands for reactivity or who showed even less reactivity having better ratings and test scores).

In another study completed in our laboratory, Palermo (1982) assessed fifth-graders' ratings of their own temperaments, the fifth-graders' mothers' ratings of their children's temperaments, and the demands for behavioral style held by the teachers and mothers of the fifth-graders. Outcome measures included teacher ratings of classroom ability and adjustment, classroom peers' sociometric appraisals of each subject's positive and negative peer relations, and mother's reports of problem behaviors shown at home. Although the children's self-ratings were obtained in their classrooms and their mother's ratings were obtained independently in mailed questionnaires completed in the home, there was little evidence of difference in the two appraisals of temperament. The mean scores for four of the five DOTS attributes provided by the children and by their mothers were not significantly different and, more important, the two sets of temperament ratings, and fit scores derived from them, were found to be virtually interchangeable in the prediction of teacher evaluations, peer relations, and maternal identification of problem behaviors in the home. Again, better fit children had more favorable scores on teacher-, peer-, and mother-derived outcome measures than did less well fit children. Most interestingly, the best predictors of *all* outcome measures—that is, of outcome measures derived from teacher-, peer-, and mother-ratings—were fit scores computed between mother-rated temperament and teacher demands. In other words, we have in Palermo's (1982) data the best indication that temperament is not a within-the-person phenomenon and, especially, is not a maternal perception: discrepancy scores derived from temperament rated by one source (mother) and demands derived from another independent source (teacher) were the best predictors not only of adaptation within the mother- and teacher-rated contexts but also within a third, and independent (peer) context.

The Palermo (1982) study extended our research, beyond the school context, to the home setting. Kacerguis (1983) continued with this emphasis, and focused on the pre- versus postpubescent daughter–mother dyad. Steinberg and Hill (1978) found that parental responses to their children differed in relation to the child's pubertal status, e.g., more problematic parent–child relations existed in parent–child dyads having a postpubescent child. Such findings led Kacerguis (1983) to speculate that the source of parent–child conflict differed among pre- versus postpubescent daughter–mother dyads; that is, that parents of prepubescents expect different behaviors of their children than do parents of postpubescents; as a consequence, Kacerguis predicted that to the extent that temperamental differences were involved in these different behavioral expectations, temperament should be differentially linked to parent–child conflict in the two puberty groups.

Studying a group of 53 prepubescent daughter–mother dyads and a group of 42 postpubescent daughter–mother dyads, Kacerguis (1983) obtained ratings by the mothers of the level of conflict in the parent–child relationship. In turn, through use of the DOTS, all adolescents rated their own temperaments. Kacerguis's predictions were strikingly confirmed. Among the prepubescent daughter–mother dyads higher levels of activity, rhythmicity, and reactivity were significantly related to higher levels of conflict (disattenuated r values $= .54, .79,$ and $.81,$ respectively; $p < .001$ in all cases) and higher levels of attention and adaptability were significantly related to lower levels of conflict (disattenuated r values $= .66$ and $.70,$ respectively; $p < .001$ in both cases). However, the relations between temperament and parent–child conflict were markedly different among the postpubescent daughter–mother dyads. First, two significant reversals in direction of correlation occurred: Higher activity level and rhythmicity scores were associated in this group with lower conflict scores (disattenuated r values $= .35$ and $.43$; $p < .05$ and $p < .01$, respectively). Second, no significant correlations between either attention, adaptability, or reactivity and parent–child conflict were found, and all three of these correlations differed significantly from the corresponding ones among the prepubescent daughter–mother dyads ($p < .001$ in all cases).

Finally, in regard to the most recent study completed in my laboratory, Windle and Lerner (1982) followed for two months 83 dyads involved in exclusive dating relationships. Each dyad member's temperament and expectation for partner's temperament were measured by the use of DOTs forms. It was predicted that (a) congruence in behavioral style between dating partners would be associated with greater relationship maintenance; and similarly that (b) dyadic congruence for expectations about temperament would be associated with relationships of greater duration. Consistent with these predictions, dyads that remained intact over the two-month period had partners who were more similar in their temperaments and expectations than were the dyads that dissolved over this period. That is, the dyads that dissolved over the course of two months had DOTS scores when first measured which were significantly correlated on only one attribute (i.e., adaptability, $r = .38$, $p < .05$), whereas the dyads that remained in contact over the two-month period had when first measured three DOTS scores which were significantly correlated (i.e., adaptability, $r = .42$, $p < .001$; rhythmicity, $r = .46$, $p < .001$; and reactivity, $r = .45$, $p < .001$.) Similarly, the dyads that dissolved over the two-month period had when first measured no correlations between dyad members' expectations for partner's temperament that were significant, whereas the dyads that remained in contact had when first measured four of the five correlations between dyad members' expectations for partner's temperament that were significant (i.e., activity level, $r = .75$, $p < .001$; adaptability, $r = .39$, $p < .01$; rhythmicity, $r = .46$, $p < .001$; and reactivity, $r = .77$, $p < .001$.)

In sum, the data derived from the studies done to date in our laboratory have several methodological shortcomings; most notably, they are not longitudinal. In addition, although we have extended the study of the import of temperament–context fit into the adolescent period we have not looked beyond this period. Nevertheless, we believe that our data, joined with the longitudinal analyses from the NYLS, provide initial support for the use of the goodness of fit model and encourage its further use. Indeed, we believe an appropriate inference from our research is that at a given point in development neither children's attributes per se nor the demands of their setting per se are the key predictors of their adaptive functioning. Instead, the *relation* between child and context seems most important in their peer, home, and school settings. If differential goodness of fit does provide a basis for contrasting psychosocial functioning, then interventions aimed at enhancing fit are appropriate to initiate. As such, the concluding section of this chapter focuses on the relevance of the goodness of fit model for theory and practice in intervention.

Enhancing Goodness of Fit

Interventions aimed at enhancing goodness of fit, and thereby also enhancing the psychosocial functions that result from good fit, may be targeted at the level of the individual or at the level of the context. First, in regard to the context, one may attempt to modify one or more of the three demand domains (attitudes, values, stereotypes of others; behavioral characteristics of others; physical characteristics of the setting) we have discussed. For example, among infants and very young children, caregivers may have to be informed about the contextual nature of temperament and the role of fit with contextual demands in the infant's psychosocial development. Here the cognitive developmental level of the caregiver is itself an issue (Sameroff, 1975), since such educational interventions with the caregiver may be expected to vary in their success as a consequence of the caregiver's cognitive abilities to deal with such concepts as "bidirectional influences," "goodness of fit," and "behavioral individuality." As such, a complete intervention repertoire, aimed at altering the context of the individual children through affecting his or her caregivers, might need to include behavior modification and parent education techniques as well as cognitive or cognitive/behavioral ones.

In turn, if one targets the individual for intervention, then one may focus one's efforts on altering the person's actions *in or on* the context, and thereby changing the goodness of fit. This latter alternative is the one we favor. There are two reasons for this. First, people have different levels of goodness of fit because of the impact of their characteristics of individuality on the context. Since it is the individuality of the person that is the initiator of "circular functions," and a key basis of the level of fit that results, work focused on the individual is therefore directed to a major basis of the developmental process with which we are concerned.

Thus, second, with the individual so central in his or her own developmental processes, it is important to enhance the person's ability to regulate his or her own further development. If we changed a particular context for the person, but did not give him or her those behavioral or cognitive abilities to continue to alter *either self or context,* then it is unlikely the person would be able to have appropriate self-regulation when new contexts or demands were encountered. Simply, one cannot anticipate all the contexts and all the demands someone may encounter in his or her life; thus, it may be most efficient to focus one's intervention efforts on providing bases for the individual to change self *or* context. Moreover, a person's perceptual "filtering" of contextual demands is an important component of the ways in which demands create incentives for fit; and this role of the individual, as a key part of his or her own context, underscores the appropriateness of targeting interventions at the individual level of analysis. Thus, by enhancing those self-regulatory functions involved in allowing the person to become an active producer of his or her own development, I believe I would be most appropriately and efficiently providing the means to enhance goodness of fit. Note, however, that I am *not* saying that I wish to eliminate individual differences in order to allow people to meet contextual demands. Rather, my goal is to provide the means by which people could alter themselves *or* the contextual demands imposed on them.

Here, I should make the point that, by itself, the goodness of fit concept describes only the status of the relation between the person and his or her context at a particular point in time. However, a life-span developmental perspective emphasizes process and, as a consequence, a key concern in the application of the goodness of fit notion is the identification of the antecedent changes that resulted in a particular fit at a specific time and, in turn, specification of the consequences of this fit for later development. Only with such information can appropriate interventions be instituted. However, as emphasized by Kendall (1981), intervention should only proceed after necessary assessments are made; there are several cognitive and behavioral variables that would have to be assessed before one could intervene to enhance goodness of fit.

One would have to assess whether the person could appropriately evaluate (*a*) the demands of a particular context; (*b*) his or her stylistic attributes; and (*c*) the degree of match that exists between the two. In addition to these cognitive assessments, other cognitive and behavioral and skill assessments are necessary. One has to determine whether the person has the ability to select and gain access to those contexts with which there is a high probability of match and to avoid those contexts where poor fit is likely. In addition, in those contexts that cannot easily be selected, for example, family of origin or assigned elementary school class, one has to assess whether the person has the knowledge and skills necessary to either change himself or herself to fit the demands of the setting or, in turn, alter the context to better fit his or her attributes (Mischel, 1977; Snyder, 1981). Moreover, in most contexts there will be multiple types of demands impinging on the person, and not all of them will provide identical incentives. As such, assessment needs to be made of whether the person can detect and evaluate such complexity. Furthermore, the absence or presence of skills in selecting those demands to which one will adapt (when all cannot be met) needs to be ascertained. Finally, it should be noted that in order for all these individual assessments to be useful, continuous assessments must be made of the contextual demands within a setting.

Appropriate interventions after such individual and contextual assessments might involve skill training, behavior modification, or various cognitive– behavioral changes (e.g., see Bandura, 1980a,b; Kendall, 1981). The common goal of all procedures would be to enhance the person's ability for self-regulation and thereby increase the ability to enhance actively his or her own fit.

In sum, an array of strategies exists for giving a person those cognitive and behavioral skills necessary to change self, context, or both (see J. V. Lerner & R. M. Lerner, in press, for an overview). Thus, rather than being "passive recipients" of the fit immediately afforded them as a consequence of their characteristics of temperamental individuality, assessments and interventions associated with a process view of the goodness of fit idea can provide people with those abilities necessary to *create* a good fit for themselves, and thus enhance their own further development. A contextual view of temperament thus not only allows us to understand adequately how this facet of human individuality contributes to development, but in so doing it provides an excellent illustration of the way in which individuals themselves contribute to their own development. As such, it also offers an important example of the potential flexibility of human development and, as a consequence, of the potential for successfully intervening to enhance human life.

Acknowledgments

I thank Jacqueline V. Lerner for her assistance in all phases of writing this chapter. I also thank David F. Hultsch, Susan McHale, and Joachim F. Wohlwill for their helpful reviews of an earlier draft of this chapter.

References

Bandura, A. Self-referent thought: A developmental analysis of self-efficacy. In J. H. Flavell & L. D. Ross (Eds.), *Cognitive social development: Frontiers and possible futures*. New York: Cambridge University Press, 1980. (a).

Bandura, A. The self and mechanisms of agency. In J. Suls (Ed.), *Social psychological perspectives on the self*. Hillsdale, N.J.: Erlbaum, 1980. (b)

Bates, J. E. The concept of difficult temperament. *Merrill-Palmer Quarterly*, 1980, 26, 299–319.

Hall, G. S. *Adolescence*. New York: Appleton, 1904.

Hull, C. L. *A behavior system*. New Haven: Yale University Press, 1952.

Kacerguis, M. A. *Child–mother relations in early adolescence: The roles of pubertal status, timing of menarche, and temperament*. Unpublished dissertation, The Pennsylvania State University, 1983.

Kendall, P. Cognitive-behavioral interventions with children. In B. Lahey and A. E. Kazdin (Eds.), *Advances in child clinical psychology* (Vol. 4). New York: Plenum, 1981.

Korn, S. *Temperament, vulnerability, and behavior*. Paper presented at the Louisville Temperament Conference, Louisville, Kentucky, September 1978.

Lerner, J. V. The role of temperament in psychosocial adaptation in early adolescents: A test of a "goodness of fit" model. *Journal of Genetic Psychology*, in press.

Lerner, J. V., & Lerner, R. M. Temperament and adaptation across life: Theoretical and empirical issues. In P. B. Baltes & O. G. Brim, Jr. (Eds.), *Life-span development and behavior* (Vol. 5). New York: Academic Press, in press.

Lerner, J. V., Lerner, R. M., & Zabski, S. Temperament and elementary school children's actual and rated academic abilities: A test of a "goodness of fit" model. *Journal of Child Psychology and Psychiatry*, in press.

Lerner, R. M. Nature, nurture, and dynamic interactionism. *Human Development*, 1978, 21, 1–20.

Lerner, R. M. A dynamic interactional concept of individual and social relationship development. In R. L. Burgess & T. L. Huston (Eds.), *Social exchange in developing relationships*. New York: Academic Press, 1979.

Lerner, R. M. Individual and context in developmental psychology: Conceptual and theoretical issues. In J. R. Nesselroade & A. von Eye (Eds.), *Individual development and social change: Explanatory analysis.* New York: Academic Press, in press.

Lerner, R. M., & Busch-Rossnagel, N. A. Individuals as producers of their development: Conceptual and empirical bases. In R. M. Lerner & N. A. Busch-Rossnagel (Eds.), *Individuals as producers of their development: A life-span perspective.* New York: Academic Press, 1981.

Lerner, R. M., Hultsch, D. F., & Dixon, R. A. Contextualism and the character of developmental psychology in the 1970s. *Annals of the New York Academy of Sciences,* in press.

Lerner, R. M., Palermo, M., Spiro, A., III, & Nesselroade, J. R. Assessing the dimensions of temperamental individuality across the life-span: The Dimensions Of Temperament Survey (DOTS). *Child Development,* 1982, *53,* 149–159.

Lerner, R. M., & Spanier, G. B. A dynamic interactional view of child and family development. In R. M. Lerner & G. B. Spanier (Eds.), *Child influences on marital and family interaction: A life-span perspective.* New York: Academic Press, 1978.

Lewis, M., & Lee-Painter, S. An interactional approach to the mother–infant dyad. In M. Lewis & L. A. Rosenblum (Eds.), *The effect of the infant on its caregiver.* New York: Wiley, 1974.

Looft, W. R. Socialization and personality throughout the life-span: An examination of contemporary psychological approaches. In P. B. Baltes & K. W. Schaie (Eds.), *Life-span developmental psychology: Personality and socialization.* New York: Academic Press, 1973.

Mead, G. H. *Mind, self, and society.* Chicago: University of Chicago Press, 1934.

Mischel, W. On the future of personality measurement. *American Psychologist,* 1977, *32,* 246–254.

Overton, W. F. On the assumptive bases of the nature–nurture controversy: Additive versus interactive conceptions. *Human Development,* 1973, *16,* 74–89.

Overton, W. F. Klaus Riegel: Theoretical contribution to concepts of stability and change. *Human Development,* 1978, *21,* 360–363.

Palermo, M. E. *Child temperament and contextual demands: A test of the goodness-of-fit model.* Unpublished dissertation, The Pennsylvania State University, 1982.

Pepper, S. C. *World hypotheses: A study in evidence.* Berkeley: University of California Press, 1942.

Riegel, K. F. Toward a dialectical theory of development. *Human Development,* 1975, *18,* 50–64.

Riegel, K. F. The dialectics of human development. *American Psychologist,* 1976, *31,* 689–700.

Sarbin, T. R., & Allen, V. L. Role theory. In G. Lindzey & E. Aronson (Eds.), *The handbook of social psychology* (2nd ed.). Reading, Mass.: Addison-Wesley, 1968.

Smelser, W. T. Dominance as a factor in achievement and perception in cooperative problem solving interactions. *Journal of Abnormal and Social Psychology,* 1961, *62,* 535–542.

Snyder, M. On the influence of individuals on situations. In N. Cantor & J. F. Kihlstrom (Eds.), *Cognition, social interaction, and personality.* Hillsdale, N.J.: Erlbaum, 1981.

Steinberg, L. D., & Hill, J. P. Patterns of family interaction as a function of age, the onset of puberty, and formal thinking. *Developmental Psychology,* 1978, *14,* 683–684.

Stokols, D. Group × place transactions: Some neglected issues in psychological research on settings. In D. Magnusson (Ed.), *Toward a psychology of situations: An interactional perspective.* Hillsdale, N.J.: Erlbaum, 1981.

Super, C. M., & Harkness, S. Figure, ground and gestalt: The cultural context of the active individual. In R. M. Lerner & N. A. Busch-Rossnagel (Eds.), *Individuals as producers of their development: A life-span perspective.* New York: Academic Press, 1981.

Thomas, A., & Chess, S. *Temperament and development.* New York: Bruner/Mazel, 1977.

Thomas, A., & Chess, S. *The dynamics of psychological development.* New York: Bruner/Mazel, 1980.

Thomas, A., & Chess, S. The role of temperament in the contributions of individuals to their development. In R. M. Lerner & N. A. Busch-Rossnagel (Eds.), *Individuals as producers of their development: A life-span perspective.* New York: Academic Press, 1981.

Thomas, A., Chess, S., Birch, H., Hertzig, M., & Korn, S. *Behavioral individuality in early childhood*. New York: New York University Press, 1963.

Thomas, A., Chess, S., Sillan, J., & Mendez, O. Cross-cultural study of behavior in children with special vulnerabilities to stress. In D. F. Ricks, A. Thomas, & M. Roff (Eds.), *Life history research in psychopathology*. Minneapolis: University of Minnesota Press, 1974.

White, S. H. The learning–maturation controversy: Hall to Hull. *Merrill-Palmer Quarterly*, 1968, *14*, 187–196.

Windle, M., & Lerner, R. M. *The role of temperament in the maintenance of dating relationships among young adults*. Manuscript in preparation, The Pennsylvania State University, 1982.

17

Statistical and Personal Interactions: Facets and Perspectives

MICHAEL RUTTER

In addition to the acceptance that both traits and situational effects must be taken into account in analyses of human behavior, there has been a growing body of evidence that these two different effects do not always summate in simple additive fashion; rather, under some circumstances, there may be *interactions* between persons and situations (Bem & Allen, 1974; Bem & Funder, 1978; Bowers, 1973; Endler, 1977). As a result, interactionist models of behavior have come to dominate the field (Magnusson & Endler, 1977).

Yet, at the same time, there are continuing bitter disuputes on the reality or otherwise of statistically significant interaction effects in various behavioral domains—as illustrated, for example, by the controversies aroused by Brown and Harris's (1978a) theory of the role of vulnerability factors in the genesis of depression (Brown & Harris, 1978b; Tennant & Bebbington, 1978). The disputes have tended to center around arguments on the most appropriate style of statistical analysis to test interaction effects (Everitt & Smith, 1979), but it is clear that the heart of the matter lies in disagreements about what is meant by interactions rather than about statistical techniques. Usually, interaction effects have been seen in terms of one or other of two alternative possibilities. First, there is synergistic interaction, by which the presence of one variable *potentiates* the effect of some other variable, so that the effect of the two together is greater than the sum of each in isolation (Rutter, 1979, 1981a). Second, there are ordinal or disordinal person–environment interactions, by which is meant the phenomenon of situations having *different* effects on different people as a result of those people's individual characteristics (Shields, 1980).

HUMAN DEVELOPMENT:
AN INTERACTIONAL PERSPECTIVE

Both types of interactions are known to occur, but they are far from invariable occurrences. Under many, if not most, circumstances, effects are additive and, moreover, people tend to show broadly similar responses to the same environmental stimuli. But this does not necessarily mean that an interactionist perspective is required only rarely. There are many more than two types of interactions and, although interaction effects must always be demonstrated rather than assumed, the need to look for interactions is generally applicable. Such interactions fall into two broad classes: (a) those in which there is an interplay between different independent variables in terms of effects on some dependent *outcome* variable and (b) those in which the interplay concerns the *process* of the operating mechanisms that underlie the effects on outcome. Under the first heading, we need to consider additive co-action, synergistic interaction, buffering effects, and both ordinal and disordinal interactions.

Additive Co-action

The most straightforward form of "interaction," of course, concerns additive co-actions[1] in which both person and environment variables are operative, but in which they summate in additive, rather than synergistic, fashion. According to all multivariate statistical models, this does not constitute an "interaction effect" as ordinarily understood; it merely means that two or more main effects have been found. In spite of the contemporary interest in interactionist perspectives and in the individuality or "personality" of situations, probably this constitutes the most common state of affairs. Nevertheless, it remains necessary to ask *how* the variables combine to produce their effects, and in some instances this raises questions about the mechanisms involved. For example, in our various studies of brain-damaged children, there has been the consistent finding of an additive summation or co-action between the effects of brain injury and the effects of psychosocial adversity (Rutter, 1977a). There is every reason to suppose that the association between brain injury and a markedly increased risk of psychiatric disorder represents a causal effect. This was shown, for example, by the timing and overall pattern of findings in our $2\frac{1}{4}$-year prospective study of children suffering severe head injuries resulting in a post-traumatic amnesia of 1 week or more (Rutter, Chadwick, & Shaffer, in press). Circumstantial evidence from other studies (Rutter, 1981b) also points

[1]As discussed in greater detail later in this section, the general term *additive effects* is open to misunderstanding because *additive* can be used in two quite different ways. The first, used here, refers to the situation in which the effects of two variables summate or combine without either serving to potentiate the other. Following Shields (1980), the term *co-action* is used to indicate that there is no interaction effect in statistical terms. Additive *interaction* is different in that, despite it sounding as if it does, it does *not* refer to simple summation; rather it constitutes a special form of synergistic interaction in which there is a nonmultiplicative potentiation.

to the probability that the psychosocial factors played a significant causal role in the genesis of the psychiatric disorders.

The puzzle arises from three separate aspects of the data. First, the prospective study showed that the two factors (i.e., brain injury and psychosocial adversity) operated at the same time. Second, for the most part, they served to give rise to the same kinds of disorders (those resulting from brain injury tended *not* to be different in patterns of symptomatology). Third, the evidence indicated that the main effects of brain injury were likely to be indirect, rather than direct (this was suggested, for example, by the somewhat inconsistent dose–response relationship). It seemed an obvious inference that brain injury operated by increasing children's susceptibility to life stresses and family problems. Perhaps the brain damage impaired adaptability or increased rigidity or reduced coping mechanisms. These would result in but minor sequelae provided the children were living in harmonious, well-functioning families, but could be devastating if they faced serious environmental hazards or adversities. The story seemed to make good sense but, unfortunately, it is negated by our consistent failure to find any synergetic effect.

We are left with uncertainty regarding the precise mechanisms by which brain injury leads to an increased risk of psychiatric disorder (Rutter, 1982a). If the effect is *not* usually direct and if there is no apparent effect on vulnerability to life stresses, how *does* brain damage operate in increasing the risk of psychiatric disorder? Of course, it could be that our measures tapped the wrong areas of stress—maybe they lay at school rather than at home or maybe they lay in aspects of family functioning outside the scope of our quantitative measures. Our assessment of the ways in which the families responded to the child after the accident suggests that the last may be a possibility—but it is just a suggestion. The results point to the need to adopt an interactionist perspective in order to delineate the mechanisms involved. However, it is one thing to take such a perspective and it is quite another to determine just how person–situation interactions operate in practice.

Synergistic Interaction

In other studies, we *have* found synergistic rather than additive effects. For example, in several studies (including the already mentioned head-injury study) we have employed an overall psychosocial adversity index in order to provide a convenient summary measure of home circumstances that put children at a much increased risk for psychiatric disorder (Rutter & Quinton, 1977). The index is made up of such items as gross family discord, paternal criminality, maternal psychiatric disorder, and breakup of the family. The question we asked ourselves was the extent of the risk if one, and only one, of these risk factors was present.

The results were striking and, perhaps, surprising. The presence of any one adverse factor carried with it a risk of psychiatric disorder that was no greater than if there were *no* risk factors.[2] But with two or more factors the risk went up threefold, and with three or four factors it went up further still. A synergistic interaction effect was evident by which one factor seemed to potentiate or increase the effects of others. The observed synergistic effect with chronic family adversities is important but, once more, we have to ask what does it mean and what mechanisms does it reflect. The most obvious characteristic of the one-risk-factor families was that they were rather atypical in being generally better functioning and in having many more positive features. The sample size did not allow the matter to be taken further but the results served to alert our attention to the possibly important role of protective or ameliorating factors.

A synergistic effect associated with the *number* of stress factors was also evident in our study of hospital admissions (Quinton & Rutter, 1976), as it was too in Douglas's (1975) earlier investigation. The findings showed *no* detectable long-term sequelae of one admission to hospital during the preschool years, but a substantial increase in psychological disturbance following two or more admissions. Clearly this was not a case of an additive summation of stress effects, as there was no effect to summate following one admission. At present, it is not clear just which mechanisms are involved. Presumably, the first admission in some way sensitizes the child to respond differently, and adversely, to the second admission. Whether this effect is a consequence of some alteration in the child (perhaps in terms of his altered cognitive appraisal of the admission the second time around) or, more probably, some change in the pattern of parent–child interaction remains uncertain. It may be relevant that studies of separation experiences in rhesus monkeys (Hinde & McGinnis, 1977) have shown that much of the sequelae are explicable in terms of the effects of the separation on mother–infant interaction. It is pertinent also that our own human data suggested another type of interaction effect, namely, that the effects of recurrent hospital admission tended to be greater in children from discordant or disadvantaged homes (Quinton & Rutter, 1976). The need now is to investigate the possible mechanisms involved by focusing on the changes in family interaction that may occur following the child's return home after hospital admission and also by comparing children's short-term responses to a second admission with their responses to a first hospitalization. The finding of some form of *statistical* interaction generally required the longitudinal study of processes of *personal* interactions in order to derive meaning from the finding.

Two crucial statistical points, however, need to be made with respect to tests for synergistic interactions. Both are most conveniently illustrated

---

[2]It should be noted that this method of analysis is not the same as the more conventional analysis of variance design. A significant main effect on an analysis of variance means that there is a significant effect for that variable even after other variables are statistically taken into account— it does *not* mean that there is an effect in the *absence* of all other variables (the point being examined here). This point is discussed in greater detail later in this section.

Table 1

The Role of Provoking Agents and Vulnerability Factors in Depression in Adult Women

		Vulnerability factor[a]				Totals for provoking agent	
		Present		Absent			
		Total number	Percentage depression	Total number	Percentage depression	Total number	Percentage depression
Provoking	Present	21	(43)	143	(17)	164	(19)
Agent	Absent	20	(0)	235	(2)	255	(2)
	Totals for vulnerability factor	41	(22)	378	(7)		

Note: Data are from Brown and Harris (1978a).
[a]Three or more children under the age of 14 years at home.

through reference to Brown and Harris's (1978a) study of depression in adult women. They postulated the existence of two different kinds of factors that play a role in the genesis of depression: provoking agents (i.e., severe stress events) that have an immediate effect in precipitating depressive disorders, and vulnerability factors that have *no* direct precipitating effect on their own, but rather which act as catalytic factors increasing the effect of provoking agents. It is clear that a synergistic interaction is hypothesized. The findings for one particular example of a vulnerability factor are summarized in Table 1. The first statistical point, already noted with respect to our own data, is that the testing for a "main" effect is not the same as testing for an effect of that variable when it occurs in isolation. Thus, with respect to Table 1, using log-linear methods of analysis, there is a significant main effect for the association of the vulnerability factor with depression (see Everitt & Smith, 1979; Tennant & Bebbington, 1978). Put most simply, this is based on the difference between 22% and 7% (i.e., the rates for depression in women with and without the vulnerability factor). But, in the absence of a provoking agent, there is *no* association between the vulnerability factor and depression (i.e., the rate of 0% is not higher than 2%).

The second statistical point is that most multivariate methods of analysis for snyergistic interactions test for *multiplicative* interactions, although the most straightforward hypotheses of synergistic interaction postulate what are (perhaps misleadingly) termed *additive* interactions. Once more referring to Table 1, using log-linear models to test for (multiplicative) interactive effects, no interaction is found. This is because the *ratio* between 43% and 17% does not differ significantly from that between 0% and 2%.[3] On the other hand, the

[3]This finding emphasizes another point, namely, that such testing is heavily influenced by the absolute numbers in key cells—in this case the 20 women in the bottom left-hand cell, where just one case of depression would have raised the rate of depression from 0% to 5%.

weighted least-squares procedures of Grizzle, Stormer, and Koch (1969) did show a significant additive interaction (Everitt & Smith, 1979). This is based on the absolute difference between the two pairs of *proportions* (i.e., 43% minus 0% versus 17% minus 2%).

Most of the discussions in the literature on the relative merits and demerits of additive and multiplicative interaction models (e.g., Darroch, 1974) have been based on the *statistical* properties of the two models. However, in my view, this is to miss the point of the distinction. The basic question concerns the conceptual model of the mode of operation of the postulated mechanisms. Almost always, the testing of the model cannot be settled by any one multivariate procedure. Rather, it is necessary to derive a series of predictions from the model and then to seek to falsify those predictions. For example, the Brown and Harris (1978a,b) model predicts that, even in the absence of a vulnerability factor, the presence of a provoking agent should significantly increase the likelihood of depression. Table 1 shows that it does (i.e., 17% vs. 2%). But it also predicts that the converse should not occur—that is, the presence of a vulnerability factor should not substantially increase the likelihood of depression if there is no provoking agent.[4] Again, the prediction is borne out (i.e., 0% does not exceed 2% in Table 1). However, a further prediction can be made. If vulnerability factors act only as catalytic agents, the combination of two or more vulnerability factors should not increase the rate of depression, whereas the combination of *one* vulnerability factor and a provoking agent should do so. Once more the prediction is supported. Brown and Harris (1978a) show that the first combination gives rise to a 3% rate of depression, whereas the second gives rise to a 12% rate (p. 186).

Two lessons stem from these considerations. First, care is necessary in choosing the most appropriate statistical procedure to test the hypothesized interactions. In particular, the failure to find a multiplicative interaction does *not* rule out the presence of synergistic effects. Second, under most circumstances, it will be unwise to rely on any *one* multivariate procedure to test for synergistic interactions. Such procedures are too dependent on the absolute numbers in key cells: Effects may be potentially large but statistically nonsignificant. Rather, there is a need to develop a whole series of predictions, *each* of which requires testing by the most appropriate statistical procedure.

Buffering Effects

Buffering or "neutralizing" effects represent a parallel to synergistic interactions in that they refer to the impact of one variable in terms of its alteration of

---

[4]Of course, although part of Brown and Harris's model, this prediction is not a necessary feature of synergistic interactions, which often may concern two variables, both of which have significant effects on their own.

the effects of another, but in this case the impact lies in a *reduction*, rather than a potentiation, of effects. Thus, there is a certain amount of evidence that supportive social networks serve such a role, enabling people to cope better with stressful situations (see Crockenberg, 1981; Rutter, 1981a). Also, there are a few pointers that, in adults, positive life experiences may to some extent neutralize negative events that carry threats (Tennant, Bebbington, & Hurry, 1981). However, protective factors need not necessarily involve features that appear intrinsically beneficial. For example, there is some tentative evidence to suggest that, at least under some circumstances, self-sufficient adults with rather shallow relationships and "difficult" personalities may be less likely to suffer following stress events (see Rutter, 1981a). Insofar as that proves to be the case, buffering effects would not necessarily constitute only the other side of the vulnerability coin. But, regrettably, little is known on the role of buffering effects in any age group (and next to nothing on their importance in childhood). It is a sad reflection on the research into life events and experiences that it has concentrated almost exclusively on the negative and unpleasant. The possibility of buffering or neutralizing interactive effects remains one that warrants serious study but its mention here reflects its potential importance rather than a body of evidence on demonstrated effects of this type.

Ordinal and Disordinal Interactions

Ordinal and disordinal interactions constitute the last types of interaction effects in terms of outcome to be considered. They refer to the situation in which environmental variables affect individuals of different "constitutions" to a different extent, but in the same way (i.e., ordinal interaction), or affect them in opposite ways (i.e., disordinal interaction) (see Erlenmeyer-Kimling, 1972). The terms derive from genetics in which the individual characteristics constitute the gene side of the interaction, but here ordinal and disordinal interactions refer to any circumstances in which environments have different effects on different individuals; that is, the question of whether the individual susceptibilities are genetically, prenatally, or postnatally determined is left open.

DISORDINAL INTERACTIONS

There are rather few well-established examples of disordinal interaction in the field of child development, although the phenomenon has been clearly demonstrated in genetics. For example, the Swedish and Norwegian strains of the plant goldenrod are known to differ genetically and to respond to low intensities of light in opposite ways: Low light dwarfs the Norwegian variety but makes the Swedish variety grow taller (Thoday, 1969). Martin, Maccoby, and Jacklin's (1981b) observation that maternal responsiveness increased exploration in young boys but decreased it in girls provides a parallel in the behavioral sciences. Not many other examples are available but, in large part, this may stem from both a failure to look for disordinal interactions and, more especially, a lack of good measures on the individual characteristics relevant to such disordinal interactions. This has been a problem, for example, in the attempts within the delinquency field to investigate the possibility that intensive counseling or psychotherapy may be beneficial for some individuals but yet make others worse (see Rutter & Giller, 1983). There are a variety of pointers that this may be the case. Thus, the California Community Treatment Project (Palmer, 1974) showed that, whereas "neurotic" youths did significantly better with the experimental treatment than under control conditions, "passive–conformist" or "power-oriented" youths did worse. The PICO project (Adams, 1970) similarly found that "amenable" youths (meaning those who were bright, verbal, anxious, insightful, aware of their difficulties and wanting to overcome them) did significantly better with intensive counseling, but the "non-amenables" had a poor outcome with the same type of therapy. There are too few data (and too many methodological problems) for firm conclusions on the validity of these disordinal interactions with the psychotherapy of delinquents, but the possibility of their occurrence warrants further systematic exploration.

ORDINAL GENE–ENVIRONMENT INTERACTIONS

There has been increasing interest during the last few years in ordinal gene–environment interactions by which the effects of environmental variables are increased in (or, even, are restricted to) genetically vulnerable individuals. The possibility is an important one in its suggestion that one of the ways in which genetic factors operate may be through an increase in susceptibility to nongenetic forces. For example, this seemed to apply in Hutchings and Mednick's (1974) study of criminality in Copenhagen adoptees. Rearing by a criminal adoptive father had no effect in boys whose biological father had no known crime record; that is, there was no environmental effect in the absence of a genetic predisposition. Having a criminal biological father doubled the risk of criminality in the sons when the adoptive father was not criminal, indicating a genetic effect. However, the risk was increased 3.5-fold when both the biological and adoptive fathers were criminal, showing a gene–environment interaction by which the environmental effect operated only in the group with a genetic loading. Crowe's (1974) study of the children of female offenders who had given up their babies for adoption showed a similar pattern by which the effects of adverse early experiences were evident in the genetically vulnerable adoptees but not in the control group that lacked the genetic predisposition. Bohman's data on the inheritance of alcohol abuse, derived from a cross-fostering analysis of adopted men (Cloninger, Bohman, & Sigvardsson,

1981), also showed the same kind of gene–environment interaction.[5] These findings begin to provide a possible explanation for the variations between studies in the strength of environmental effects according to the characteristics of the populations studied. But, more important, they throw much-needed light on the mechanisms involved in some genetic effects.

ORDINAL INTERACTIONS WITH PHYSICAL HAZARDS

Ordinal interactions have also been found with respect to "constitutional" variables associated with physical hazards rather than genetic predisposition. Perhaps the best documented is the finding that the effects of pre- or perinatal complications on intelligence are negligible in children living in good social circumstances (provided there is no overt neurological handicap), but are substantially greater (although still minor) in those from a severely disadvantaged background (see Sameroff & Chandler, 1975). However, the same may also apply with malnutrition, which appears to have no long-term consequences for intellectual development if the malnourishment is acute and occurs in the context of otherwise good social circumstances (Stein, Susser, Saenger, & Morolla, 1975), but which has greater effects if chronic and if associated with very poor social conditions, as is the more usual situation (Richardson, 1980). Thus, in the Jamaican study undertaken by Richardson and his colleagues, the IQ decrement associated with malnutrition in boys from a relatively advantageous social background was only 2 to 3 points, but in those from an unfavorable social background it was 7 to 9 points.

The precise mechanisms underlying these ordinal interactions remain poorly understood. However, it may be that one of the crucial factors concerns the effect of the child's state on parental behavior. Thus, Chavez, Martinez, and Yaschine (1974) found that malnourished children received less parental attention than did better-nourished children; it was thought that the weak nonspecific cries of the malnourished children were often ineffective in gaining parental attention. It is also relevant that increased parent–child interaction does much to reverse the intellectual impairments associated with malnutrition (see Cravioto & Arrieta, in press). It may be that the physical hazards associ-

[5]It should be noted that, if the data are analyzed in terms of the proportion of variance accounted for, these adoptive study findings will greatly underestimate the importance of interaction effects. This is because the very use of a cross-fostering design to separate the effects of nature and nurture means that the overlap between genetic and environmental factors is far less than that found in the general population. Because the figures on proportion of the variance accounted for are very strongly influenced by the absolute numbers in the key cells, as well as by the strength of the associations, if the "N" in the interaction cell is small, the proportion of the variance accounted for by the interaction will also be small. Under ordinary circumstances being reared by an alcoholic or criminal father represents *both* genetic and environmental influences. If there is a gene–environment interaction it is likely to account for quite a substantial proportion of the variance in real life.

ated with perinatal complications or malnutrition increase children's biological vulnerability to adverse psychosocial influences. However, it seems just as likely that the physical hazards operate through an effect on the environment itself.

Low-level exposure to lead provides other examples of ordinal interactions with physical hazards. First, levels of lead in the blood in any given environment tend to be higher in males and in blacks (see Annest, 1983; Billick, 1983; Duggan, 1983). The explanation for this difference remains obscure but presumably it may lie in individual differences in the absorption or deposition of lead in the body. Second, animal studies indicate that the behavioral consequences of increased body burdens of lead tend to be greater in the presence of malnutrition (Mahaffey & Michaelson, 1980). Third, although the evidence on this point is weaker, it may be that adverse sequelae are greater in children from a socially disadvantaged background (Yule & Lansdown, 1983).

SEX DIFFERENCES IN RESPONSE TO FAMILY DISCORD

Finally, the differences between boys and girls in their response to family discord may be cited as another example of an ordinal interaction. Considerable recent evidence has shown that marital turmoil has a greater impact on boys than on girls from both divorced and intact but discordant marriages (see Emery, 1982; Rutter, 1970, 1982b). The fact of a sex difference seems reasonably well established but its meaning remains ill-understood with various competing hypotheses put forward. It has been suggested that the difference lies less in whether there is a maladaptive response to discord than in the style of response—with girls more liable to overcontrolled behavior, which is less likely to show as overt disturbance at the time, although it may become overt later (Emery, 1982). Alternatively, it has been proposed that the meaning of discord differs for the two sexes, for example: because parents quarrel more in front of boys (Hetherington, 1980); because, when parents separate, boys are more likely to be in the custody of the parent of the opposite sex (Whitehead, 1979); because the parents have greater salience for boys or boys have a greater need to control their environment (Block, Block, & Morrison, 1981); because of sex-linked temperamental differences (Eme, 1979); or because adults respond differently to disruptive behavior in boys and girls (Maccoby & Jacklin, 1974). However, it also may be that there is a constitutionally determined greater male susceptibility to psychological stresses—a parallel, as it were, to the well-established male vulnerability to physical stresses (Rutter, 1970). At present, there is insufficient evidence for any firm conclusions on the relative merits and demerits of these hypotheses on possible mechanisms.

We need to turn now to a rather different set of interactions that are concerned with the *process* of change or of development. They are considered most conveniently in terms of transactional effects, ecological considerations, personal interactions as descriptors of the environment, interactions as selectors of environments, and interactions in terms of opportunities.

Transactional Effects

Transactional effects differ from all the interaction effects considered thus far in that it is not a question of one variable potentiating, reducing, or altering the effect of some other variable on outcome, but rather a matter of one variable *changing* the other.

EFFECT OF THE INDIVIDUAL ON THE ENVIRONMENT

This may occur in terms of the effect of individuals on their environment, as shown, for example, in Dunn and Kendrick's (1982) study of the effects of the birth of a sibling. The arrival of a second child in the family was found to result in changes in the mother's interaction with the *first*born. Mothers tended to become more critical and demanding and also tended to spend less time with the older child. Thus, it was not just that the firstborn had to cope with an addition to the family circle but also that his own relationship with his parents was no longer the same. Obviously, the detection of this type of transactional effect requires some form of longitudinal study of altering patterns over time.

A somewhat different form of transactional effect was evident in our study of the role of temperamental characteristics in the impact of a mentally ill parent on the children (Rutter, 1978). Much of the effect of the ill parent seemed to be mediated through the discord and disruption that accompanied the parental mental disorder (Quinton & Rutter, in press a; Rutter, 1970, 1971). However, this effect did not impinge equally on all the children in the family. Children with adverse temperamental characteristics were twice as likely as other children to be the target of parental criticism (exact test; $p = .054$). As a result, although "objectively" in the same discordant family environment as the temperamentally easy children, the "effective" environment for those with difficult temperaments was different in that they were more likely to be personally involved in the discord and disharmony. The child with adverse personality features is more likely to be the butt or scapegoat in a quarrelsome family; conversely, the easy, adaptable child tends to be protected even in a stressful environment simply because much of the hostility and discord is focused on other members of the family. Hetherington's (1980) observation that parents with a discordant marriage were more likely to quarrel in front of their sons than their daughters suggests a similar transactional effect, as does the observation that, when they reached adult life, Harlow and Suomi's monkeys subjected to total social isolation in infancy were more likely to abuse and kill their male than their female offspring (Ruppenthal, Arling, Harlow, Sackett, & Suomi, 1976).

Another example is provided by the findings from our study of children with mild head injuries. As found also by other investigators, our results showed that the children who suffered head injuries were behaviorally different from other children *before* their accident in terms of being more overactive, impulsive, daring, and disobedient (Rutter, Chadwick, & Shaffer; in press). Not surprisingly, their tendency to engage in risky behavior led to their having different life experiences—with the consequence of head injuries stemming from falling off roofs or out of trees and the like. The brain damage suffered in the head injury might lead to an increase in disruptive behavior, but the head injury itself stemmed in part from the children's prior behavioral characteristics.

The notion of transaction as one variable increasing the frequency of another variable reduces a dynamic concept to an operationally defined statistical relationship (Rutter, 1977b). That is necessary if we are to test in rigorous fashion the assumptions that underlie transactional models of development (an essential step if such models are to be more than a trendy posture or position). But, equally, it is crucial that we do not lose sight of the essential feature of the model, namely, the suggestion that interactions are reciprocal and changing, with one person's reaction to another altering the other person's behavior, which in turn alters the first's reaction. In short, it is the process of change over time that has to be studied. That was provided over the time scale of months in Dunn and Kendrick's study of the effects on the family of the birth of a second child. Patterson's (1977, 1981, 1982) study of cycles of hostile or coercive interchanges in the families of aggressive boys constitutes a rather different example over the time scale of minutes. There are numerous conceptual and practical difficulties in both the recording and analysis of such moment-by-moment sequential data (Martin, Maccoby, Baran, & Jacklin, 1981a) but they constitute essential elements in the testing of transactional concepts.

INDIVIDUAL EFFECTS REGARDING THE MEANING
OF THE ENVIRONMENT

A rather different type of transactional effect concerns the influence of individual characteristics in the determination of the *meaning* of the environment. For example, although the samples studied have been small, there is some indication that deaf children reared by deaf parents show a more positive social development than those reared by hearing parents (Meadow, 1968, 1975). Presumably, the reverse would be the case for hearing children. Why it may be better for deaf children to be brought up by deaf parents is not known with any certainty but perhaps it may be because deaf parents are more accepting of a deaf child or that they communicate better and earlier by means of signs and gestures. In that respect the deaf parents probably provide an environment that is "effectively" more stimulating, although "objectively," at least to a hearing child, it would be lacking in linguistic stimulation. The child's handicaps mean that the parents' deficits become assets.

The matter of the meaning of the environment also raises another issue, the role of people's perceptions of the environment. At one time, it was sometimes assumed that the environment could be reduced to measures of the "behavior" of objects and persons in the surround as they impinged on the individual. Of course, these do indeed constitute key features of the environment. But, under some circumstances, people's beliefs, attitudes, or perceptions of the environment may be as important as the objective environment itself. For example, this is apparent in the experimental studies designed to determine whether adults behave differently with male and with female infants because baby boys and girls themselves behave differently and, therefore, present the adults with different "stimuli" or because their value structure means that they "should" treat boys and girls differently. The differentiation was made possible by getting adults to play with ambiguously dressed babies randomly assigned male or female names. In that way, it could be determined whether the adult behavior varied according to the true (but nonperceived) or the perceived (but false) sex of the infant (see, e.g., Bell & Carver, 1980; Smith & Lloyd, 1978). The results have tended to support both effects; that is, parents behave in the ways that they do in part because of their own sex-related perceptions and preconceptions and in part as a response to actual differences in the behavior of male and female infants.

Ecological Considerations

The question of the meaning of the environment also raises the issue of the need to adopt an ecological perspective, that is, that the influence of any environmental variable must be considered in terms of the social context within which it operates (Bronfenbrenner, 1979). In particular, personal relationships have to be considered in terms of a *network* of interactions (Hinde, 1979, 1980). The behavior of one individual to another is affected by the relationships of each with others; dyadic interaction will not be the same if that dyad is part of a larger group as it is if the dyadic interaction occurs in isolation. Moreover, such networks of relationships will themselves be influenced by external environmental circumstances of different kinds.

These issues were evident at a molecular level in the demonstrations by Clarke-Stewart (1978) and by Parke (1978) that a mother's interaction with her child is influenced by whether or not the father is also present. These findings reflect a statistical interaction as ordinarily understood. But there may be other social context effects of a somewhat different kind. For example, in our own data from the epidemiological studies in inner London and the Isle of Wight (Rutter & Quinton, 1977), we found that emotional disorder in London women was strongly associated with social class (as also found by other investigators), whereas that in Isle of Wight women was not. Whether that implies that low social class has a different meaning in the metropolis or that low social class operates as a vulnerability factor increasing the risk of disorder only in the presence of adversities or hazards that are much commoner in London remains uncertain. What is apparent is that what seems to constitute the same variable has rather different effects in two different environments; the explanation for that difference has yet to be identified.

The social context effect was also evident in West's (1982) finding that boys' delinquent behavior diminished when their families moved out of London [similar effects of moves out of the city were evident in Buikhuisen & Hoekstra's (1974) study]. The West finding was not an artifact of police practices in that the effect applied with self-reported data; nor was it a function of differences between the families that stay in London and those that move out, as West had extensive systematic family measures which were taken into account in testing for the change in delinquent activities following the geographical move. Whether the drop in delinquency means that family interactions changed with the alteration in social context, that the drop reflected a difference in the opportunities for delinquent behavior, or that there was a change in peer-group pressures cannot be determined from the data. What is clear, however, is that in some way the move from one geographical area to another had a substantial impact on the boys' behavior.

An example of a somewhat different ecological effect is provided by our study of inner London secondary schools (Rutter, Maughan, Mortimore, Ouston, & Smith, 1979). When comparing schools in terms of some "outcome" variable, it is always necessary to take into account the characteristics of the student population "intake" to the schools. Only by controlling for the characteristics of the pupils (and of their backgrounds) at the time they entered the schools is it possible to differentiate school effects from pupil effects. However, our findings show that the particular means used to control for intake are important, because pupil variables also constitute features of the schools. Thus, we found (as have numerous others) that boys of lower IQ were more likely to become delinquent. Accordingly, we used a log-linear modeling technique to control for IQ differences between the intakes to different schools. After these controls had been introduced, substantial differences between schools in delinquency rates still remained—demonstrating a significant school effect above and beyond that arising artifactually from differences in the types of children admitted to the schools studied. But that was not the whole story, because the delinquency rates of schools (after adjusting for individual characteristics at intake) were found to correlate highly with the overall proportions of intelligent and less intelligent children in the schools. In other words, not only did the individual child's *own* IQ predict the likelihood of his becoming delinquent but so also did the IQs of the *other* children in the same school. That is to say, the overall mix or balance of children in the school created some kind of schoolwide group effect. One child's individual or personal characteristics constituted part of other children's environmental features.

Personal Interactions as Descriptors of the Environment

In some situations, the personal interactions themselves constitute the key elements that define the environment. For example, this is the case with the various animal studies showing that *active* experiences are more potent than *passive* experiences as facilitators of cognitive development (Hunt, 1979; Rutter, 1981c; Thompson & Grusec, 1970). For example, Held and his colleagues demonstrated this with respect to vision in both cats and monkeys (e.g., Held & Bauer, 1967). Animals whose visual experience was the result of their own active movements showed superior judgments of distance and space than those whose visual experience was the result of their being passively transported. It was the experience of active person–environment interactions that constituted the crucial features of the environment.

Similar conclusions derive from animal studies of attachment. Inanimate objects of various kinds can give rise to strong selective attachments and also the presence of these inanimate objects can reduce anxiety in stress situations (see Rutter, 1981b). On the face of it, these attachments to objects seem very similar to infants' attachments to parent figures. Yet the research findings are consistent in showing that animals reared with surrogates show the same severe social deficits found with animals reared in total isolation, but not found with those reared with their mothers. The attachments to inanimate objects do not serve the same long-term functions in social development served by parent–infant attachment. The studies by Levine (1982) and his colleagues also indicate that the physiological consequences of separation from a surrogate are different from separation from a parent. Rearing with a mobile surrogate seems marginally "better" than rearing with a stationary object, rearing with dogs is associated with still fewer deficits (Mason, 1978), and rearing with peers is most near rearing with the mother. The implication is that it may be the *reciprocity* of personal interactions that most crucially differentiates attachment to a parent from attachment to an inanimate object.

Human studies, too, emphasize the importance of active experiences and reciprocal interactions. For example, the recent report by the late Jack Tizard and his colleagues (1982) indicated, from both naturalistic and experimental data, that children (most of whom were from socially disadvantaged backgrounds) who regularly read to their parents made better progress in reading than those who did not do so. Note that it was the *children* who did the reading and not the parents. The suggestion is that it is active experiences that count most.

But the human data also point to the importance of the *quality*, as well as the amount, of personal interactions. Thus, Barbara Tizard (1975) showed that children reared in residential nurseries experienced much interaction with their caretakers: There were plenty of talk and play, an ample provision of toys and books, and frequent reading aloud to the children. Probably as a consequence, comparisons with ordinary family-reared children showed no intellectual impairment in the institutional group. However, the staff was discouraged from forming close personal relationships with the children and there were frequent changes in caretakers—so that by the age of 5 it is likely that the children will have had some 50 parent figures looking after them. Perhaps as a result of this extreme discontinuity in relationships, the children who spent their early years in an institution showed marked sociobehavioral differences from other children both in infancy and when followed up at age 8 years (Tizard & Hodges, 1978). Roy (1983) found an almost identical pattern in her comparison of institution-reared and family-fostered children, the latter group being much more like ordinary children brought up by their biological parents. Our own long-term follow-up into adult life of institution-reared females (Rutter, Quinton, & Liddle, 1983) tells much the same story. In terms of social functioning in the early to mid-twenties the institution group fared much worse than their controls, but most strikingly those admitted to institutions in infancy who remained there throughout the whole of their childhoods did rather worse than those who returned to discordant, quarrelsome, chaotic families. The inference seems to be that *continuity* in early (and possibly also, later) parent–child relationships constitutes a key feature of children's experiences with respect to social development. Once more, it is the quality of person–environment interactions that define the environment.

Interactions as Selectors of Environments

In this chapter I have moved from statistical-type interactions to personal interactions, and now I move to another type of interaction, namely, that between experiences, in order to indicate two of the more important ways in which interactions underlie indirect continuities in development (Rutter, 1983). Our study of institution-reared women (Rutter, Quinton, & Liddle, 1983) provides a convenient example of interactions that reflect selections of

Table 2

Institutional Rearing, Marital Support, and Poor Parenting

	Institution-reared women		Comparison group		Total	
	Total number	Poor parenting no. (%)	Total number	Poor parenting no. (%)	Total number	Poor parenting no. (%)
Marital support	15	1 (6.7)	20	1 (5.0)	35	2 (5.7)
Lack of support	26	17/65.4	7	2/28.6	33	19/57.6
Total	41	18/43.9	27	3/11.1		

Note: Data are from Rutter, Quinton, and Liddle (1983).

Table 3
Linear Logistic Analysis of Table 2

Model fitted	df	Deviance	Reduction in deviance	df	Significance
Initial Model Constant[a]	7	30.54			
Group (i.e., institution versus comparison)	6	21.54	9.00	1	<.01
Marital support	6	6.79	23.75	1	<.001
Group plus marital support	5	4.19	26.35	2	<.001

Note: From Rutter *et al.* (1983).

[a]The analysis in Rutter *et al.* (1982) includes social circumstances, but that variable has been omitted here in order to simplify the argument.

environments. The dependent variable in this case concerns an overall measure of parenting obtained when the women were aged 21 to 27 years and, hence, the sample is restricted to the subgroup with children at home. The independent variables concern the fact of institution rearing (that group is contrasted with that of girls from the same general area in inner London reared by their own biological parents) and the presence of marital support (defined in terms of the presence of a nondeviant spouse with whom there is a good relationship). The findings are summarized in Table 2, and Table 3 gives the linear logistic analysis of the same data.

It is clear that individuals from the institution-reared group were much more likely to show poor parenting (43.9% versus 11.1%) but also that poor parenting was much more likely when marital support was lacking (57.6% versus 5.7%). Not surprisingly, therefore, the statistical analysis shows highly significant main effects for both variables, that for marital support being greater (because, in effect, the difference between 57.6% and 5.7% was greater than that between 43.9% and 11.1%). The sum of these two effects[6] left little variance unexplained so that, statistically speaking, there was no need to search for interaction effects as they could not provide a significant contribution to the model.

But in conceptual, as distinct from statistical,[7] terms the data provided obvious evidence of at least one form, if not two forms, of interaction. Most strikingly, it was apparent that the individuals in the institution-reared group

[6]Group plus marital support reflects the sum of the two main effects and not an interaction between them. The reduction in deviance (i.e., 26.35) is less than the arithmetical sum of the two considered separately (i.e., 23.75 + 9.00 = 32.75) because of overlap between them.

[7]Of course, this is not to suggest that the mathematical answer differs from the conceptual answer, or that the mathematical description contradicts the conceptual view. Rather, the point is that person–situation interactions may carry a somewhat different meaning from statistical interaction effects; moreover, even in statistical terms there is more than one variety of interaction effect. In any statistical analysis one gets answers to the questions posed; accordingly it is crucial to pose the appropriate question and to choose the statistic that deals with that question.

were much more likely to lack marital support (26 out of 41, or 63.4%, versus 7 out of 27, or 25.9%). This was because they were significantly more likely to be without any kind of spouse at follow-up (22% versus 0%) and because they were significantly more likely to marry men with problems (such as criminality or psychiatric disorder) with whom they had a poor relationship. The nature of the variables and the timing of the association justify the inference that the experience of an institutional rearing (or factors with which it was associated) made it more likely that the women would land up with unsatisfactory spouses who would fail to provide support.[8] In short, to an important extent, one independent variable (institution rearing) "caused" the other (lack of marital support). The other possible interaction concerns the difference between the groups in the proportion who exhibited poor parenting when there was lack of marital support (65.4% versus 28.6%); strikingly, they did not differ when there was support (6.7% versus 5.0%). The implication is that the institution rearing predisposed to poor parenting both because it led to a lack of marital support *and* because it left the women without the necessary "skills" or "resources" to cope with parenting when they lacked marital support. Necessarily, that inference is less secure simply because of the small number (7) in the cell on which the figure of 28.6% is based. However, there are a variety of reasons for suggesting that that hypothesis is likely to be correct.

The points here are that, on the one hand, knowledge of the nature of the variables (outside the data in the table) suggests the likely form of the causal links and, on the other, that at least the first type of interaction postulated is not of a kind that is tested for in the usual mutlivariate statistical analysis.[9] The composite analyses are necessary to test the significance of the findings (multiple univariate analyses are less satisfactory both because of the overlap between variables and because of the dangers of spuriously significant findings when multiple comparisons are being made). Nevertheless, the interactionist hypotheses have to stem from the concepts being investigated in the study (and not post hoc from the second-order interactions deriving from multivariate

[8]This study provides several other examples of the same type of interaction that serves to reflect continuities in the developmental process, as well as changes in behavior (see Quinton, Rutter, & Liddle, 1983; Quinton & Rutter, 1983b). Their ubiquity emphasizes the importance of undertaking statistical analyses designed to test for their presence.

[9]But that is not to say that statistical tests *could* not be used to test for the postulated interaction; it is just that the postulate concerns an "interaction" that differs from that usually implied in a statistical "interaction effect." The apparent confusion arises from two sources. First, statistical interaction effects generally refer to the effect of one independent variable in its alteration of the effect of a second independent variable on some dependent variable. The postulate that institutional rearing decreases the likelihood of marital support does not deal with an interaction effect of that type; rather it concerns an "association" between two independent variables, which, in statistical terms, is quite different. Second, although linear logistic models do not deal with possible associations between independent variables (because they focus on the variance in the dependent variable), other forms of analysis (such as log-linear models) can take those into account.

analyses) and, moreover, in many cases an adequate understanding of the relationships between variables demands the (somewhat old-fashioned) recourse to examination of all the relevant two-by-two contingency tables that apply to those hypotheses.

Interactions in Terms of Opportunities

A related type of interaction between experiences, one that also influences indirect continuities in development, concerns the way in which events or happenings influence later experiences or accomplishments by means of the opening up or closing down of opportunities. Our study of the first year of employment (Rutter, Gray, Maughan, & Smith, 1982), based on the study of 12 inner London secondary schools (Rutter et al., 1979), well illustrates this process. Two examples from the findings illustrate the manner in which these types of interactions may either enhance disadvantage or serve to translate deficits into assets. The first concerns possible school influences on employment (Gray, Smith, & Rutter, 1980). We found major school effects on attendance; these, in turn, were associated with major variations in the likelihood of the pupils leaving school before taking the usual public examinations at 16 years of age. Necessarily, this leaving early meant that the young people failed to gain any formal educational qualifications; the lack of qualifications was then associated with a high likelihood of landing up in an unskilled job. There was no school effect on employment that was independent of these other variables but, of course, the indirect effects were considerable in terms of the links between attendance, early leaving of school, lack of educational qualifications, and unskilled work.

The second sequence provides a more interesting, and perhaps surprising, example in that the chain of associations led to a *reversal* of the outcome expected in terms of the initial set of predictors in spite of the lack, at any stage, of the (multiplicative) statistical interactions identifiable in the usual multivariate analyses. The issue concerned the comparison of the educational progress and employment of blacks and white youngsters attending the 12 inner London secondary schools used in our schools study (Rutter et al., 1979). At age 10 years, before entering secondary schools, the black children appeared at a considerable disadvantage compared with the whites. As a group they were, on average, more than 10 points lower in IQ, with substantially worse reading attainments. Moreover, they were nearly twice as likely to come from families with at least four children (a well-established risk factor for poor educational attainments). They did not differ substantially from the white group in social class distribution (both were predominantly working class, with a third of the family breadwinners in semiskilled or unskilled work), but earlier studies had shown that black children tended to live in worse home conditions (Rutter, Yule, Morton, & Bagley, 1975). An unpromising start, since in this group as a whole, as in others, low IQ and poor reading skills were associated with a worse employment outcome. The findings at 14 years were almost as discouraging, although the gap between blacks and whites on reading was less than that for IQ. But, the black young people left school with equally good exam qualifications, a much higher proportion went on to some form of further education, and their employment was closely comparable to that of the white group. This important turnabout occurred because the young blacks showed a much greater "persistence" in education. Their school attendance was substantially better, far fewer left school early, considerably more stayed on into the sixth form (i.e., beyond the period of compulsory schooling), and, as a consequence, more blacks improved their examination performance by retaking exams or by taking more advanced exams. In turn, their exam credentials opened up job opportunities for them. The net effect was the transformation of deficit into asset. This occurred in spite of the fact that each of the variables that predicted outcome in the white group did so in a generally comparable fashion in the black group; that among those taking exams the blacks did somewhat worse than whites at each stage (considered in isolation); and that none of the multivariate analyses showed significant interaction effects relevant to black–white comparisons. Nevertheless, in conceptual, rather than statistical, terms there had been a series of interactions between variables that led to long-term change through a process of short-term continuities.[10]

Conclusions

Person–environment interactions take many forms and reflect a variety of psychological mechanisms. In this chapter I have considered some examples of such interactions in terms of five types in which there is an interplay between independent variables in terms of their effects on *outcome*—namely, additive co-action, synergistic interaction (both additive and multiplicative), buffering effects, and ordinal and disordinal interactions—and five types in which the interplay concerns the *process* of operating mechanisms—namely, transactional effects, ecological considerations, personal interactions as descriptors of the environment, interactions as selectors of environments, and interactions in terms of opportunities. The list is not intended to be exhaustive with respect to all possible interactions; others may prefer to classify interactions in alternative ways, and there is room for disagreement on just which processes should

---

[10]The story is an encouraging one but a cautionary note is needed with respect to the long-term implications for the position of blacks in the United Kingdom. The sample did not include pupils at independent or state-selective schools (the vast majority of whom were white) and, as far more of them went on to higher education and were likely to take higher status jobs, the findings for these comprehensive schools do *not* mean that the disadvantages of blacks have been righted in society as a whole. Moreover, there is evidence (from other studies) that covert discrimination is leading to much higher rates of unemployment in blacks.

be included under person–environment interactions. I should emphasize that I am *not* suggesting that the 10 processes that I have discussed should be grouped together under a general term of "interactions" or "interaction effects." To the contrary, my argument is that the processes are heterogeneous and should not be pooled under any umbrella category. Rather, it is preferable to examine each in terms of its own features.

The issue of the classification of interactive processes is peripheral to my main argument, which has five interlinked elements. First, personal interactions are not synonymous with statistical interaction effects. Most of the interactions that I have considered would not be detectable in terms of the conventional testing for multiplicative interactions in multivariate analyses. Second, interactions and transactions do not constitute a perspective, model, or posture to be adopted when interpreting statistical analyses or when describing developmental processes. Rather, the interactionist perspective should give rise to quite specific hypotheses on the particular types of interactions that are hypothesized to be operating. Unless such hypotheses can be formulated and translated into testable operationalized predictions, the interactionist perspective will not lead to a better understanding of developmental processes. Third, there is a wide variety of interaction hypotheses which incorporate a disparate range of mechanisms. Few of these can be detected (or disproven) by any one statistical procedure. Rather, the art, as well as the science, of research into interactions lies in the ingenuity applied to the testing of the hypotheses. Fourth, because interactions can take many forms and cannot be examined satisfactorily through any one overall multivariate analysis, there is a considerable danger that spurious interactions will be detected as a consequence of looking at the data in numerous alternative combinations and permutations. Statistical procedures can be helpful in avoiding such artifactual conclusions, but, as in the rest of science, replication provides the most important test. Last, the identification of some form of interaction rarely provides information on the mechanisms that underlie the interaction. The finding of an interactive effect, therefore, constitutes not the end of the search but rather the beginning for a further set of investigations designed to test hypotheses on processes.

Acknowledgment

I am most grateful to Graham Dunn for helpful comments on an earlier version of this chapter.

References

Adams, S. The PICO Project. In N. Johnston, L. Savitz, & M. E. Wolfgang (Eds.), *The sociology of punishment and correction.* New York: Wiley, 1970.

Annest, J. L. Trends in the blood lead levels of the USA population. In M. Rutter & R. R. Jones (Eds.), *Lead versus health: Sources and effects of low level lead exposure.* Chichester: Wiley, 1983.

Bell, N. J., & Carver, W. A re-evaluation of gender label effects: Expectant mothers' responses to infants. *Child Development,* 1980, *51,* 925–927.

Bem, D. J., & Allen, A. On predicting some of the people some of the time: The search for cross-situational consistencies in behavior. *Psychological Review,* 1974, *81,* 506–520.

Bem, D. J., & Funder, D. C. Predicting more of the people more of the time: Assessing the personality of situations. *Psychological Review,* 1978, *85,* 485–501.

Billick, I. H. Sources of lead in the environment. In M. Rutter & R. R. Jones (Eds.), *Lead versus health: Sources and effects of low level lead exposure.* Chichester: Wiley, 1983.

Block, J. H., Block, J., & Morrison, A. Parental agreement–disagreement on childrearing orientations and gender-related personality correlates in children. *Child Development,* 1981, *52,* 965–974.

Bowers, K. S. Situationism in psychology: An analysis and a critique. *Psychological Review,* 1973, *80,* 307–336.

Bronfenbrenner, U. *The ecology of human development: Experiments by nature and design.* Cambridge, Mass.: Harvard University Press, 1979.

Brown, G. W., & Harris, T. *Social origins of depression.* London: Tavistock, 1978. (a).

Brown, G. W., & Harris, T. Social origins of depression: A reply. *Psychological Medicine,* 1978, *8,* 577–588. (b)

Buikhuisen, W., & Hoekstra, H. A. Factors related to recidivism. *British Journal of Criminology,* 1974, *14,* 63–69.

Chavez, A., Martinez, C., & Yaschine, T. The importance of nutrition and stimuli on child mental and social development. In J. Cravioto, L. Hambraeus, & B. Vahlquist (Eds.), *Early malnutrition and mental development* (Symposia of the Swedish Nutrition Foundation). Stockholm: Almquist and Wilksell, 1974.

Clarke-Stewart, K. A. And daddy makes three: The father's impact on mother and young child. *Child Development,* 1978, *49,* 446–478.

Cloninger, C. R., Bohman, M., & Sigvardsson, S. Inheritance of alcohol abuse: Cross-fostering analysis of adopted men. *Archives of General Psychiatry,* 1981, *38,* 861–868.

Cravioto, J., & Arrieta, R. Malnutrition in childhood. In M. Rutter (Ed.), *Developmental neuropsychiatry.* New York: Guilford Press, in press.

Crockenberg, S. Infant irritability, mother responsiveness, and social support influences on the security of infant–mother attachment. *Child Development,* 1981, *52,* 857–865.

Crowe, R. R. An adoption study of antisocial personality. *Archives of General Psychiatry,* 1974, *31,* 785–791.

Darroch, J. N. Multiplicative and additive interaction in contingency tables. *Biometrika,* 1974, *61,* 207–214.

Douglas, J. W. B. Early hospital admissions and later disturbances of behavior and learning. *Developmental Medicine and Child Neurology,* 1975, *17,* 456–480.

Duggan, M. J. Lead in dust as a source of children's body lead levels. In M. Rutter & R. R. Jones (Eds.), *Lead versus health: Sources and effects of low level lead exposure.* Chichester: Wiley, 1983.

Dunn, J., & Kendrick, C. *Siblings: Love, envy and understanding.* Cambridge, Mass.: Harvard University Press, 1982. (London: Grant McIntyre).

Eme, R. F. Sex differences in childhood psychopathology: A review. *Psychological Bulletin,* 1979, *86,* 574–595.

Emery, R. E. Interparental conflict and the children of discord and divorce. *Psychological Bulletin,* 1982, *92,* 310–330.

Endler, N. S. The role of person by situation interactions in personality theory. In I. C. Uzgiris & F. Weizmann (Eds.), *The structuring of experience.* New York: Plenum, 1977.

Erlenmeyer-Kimling, L. Gene–environment interactions and the variability of behavior. In L. Ehrman, G. Omenn, & E. Caspari (Eds.), *Genetics, environment, and behavior: Implications for educational policy.* New York: Academic Press, 1972. Pp. 181–208.

Everitt, B. S., & Smith, A. M. R. Interactions in contingency tables: A brief discussion of alternative definitions. *Psychological Medicine*, 1979, 9, 581–584.

Gray, G., Smith, A., & Rutter, M. School attendance and the first year of employment. In L. Hersov & I. Berg (Eds.), *Out of school: Modern perspectives in truancy and school refusal.* Chichester: Wiley, 1980. Pp. 343–370.

Grizzle, J. E., Stormer, C. F., & Koch, G. G. Analysis of categorical data by linear models. *Biometrics*, 1969, 25, 489–504.

Held, R., & Bauer, J. A. Visually guided reaching in infant monkeys after restricted rearing. *Science*, 1967, 155, 718–720.

Hetherington, E. M. Children and divorce. In R. Henderson (Ed.), *Parent–child interaction: Theory, research and prospect.* New York: Academic Press, 1980.

Hinde, R. A. *Towards understanding relationships.* London: Academic Press, 1979.

Hinde, R. A. Family influences. In M. Rutter (Ed.), *Scientific foundations of developmental psychiatry.* London: Heinemann Medical, 1980. Pp. 47–66.

Hinde, R. A., & McGinnis, L. Some factors influencing the effect of temporary mother–infant separation: Some experiments with rhesus monkeys. *Psychological Medicine*, 1977, 7, 197–212.

Hunt, J. McV. Psychological development: Early experience. *Annual Review of Psychology*, 1979, 30, 103–143.

Hutchings, B., & Mednick, S. A. Registered criminality in the adoptive and biological parents of registered male adoptees. In S. A. Mednick *et al.* (Eds.), *Genetics, environment and psychopathology.* Amsterdam: North-Holland, 1974.

Levine, S. Comparative and psychobiological perspectives on development. In W. A. Collins (Ed.), *The concept of development: Minnesota Symposia on Child Psychology* (Vol. 15). Hillsdale, N.J.: Erlbaum, 1982.

Maccoby, E. E., & Jacklin, C. N. *Psychology of sex differences.* Stanford, Calif.: Stanford University Press, 1974.

Magnusson, D., & Endler, N. S. Interactional psychology: Present status and future prospects. In D. Magnusson & N. S. Endler (Eds.), *Personality at the crossroads: Current issues in interactional psychology.* Hillsdale, N.J.: Erlbaum, 1977.

Mahaffey, K., & Michaelson, I. A. Interaction between lead and nutrition. In H. L. Needleman (Ed.), *Low level lead exposure: The clinical implications of current research.* New York: Raven, 1980.

Martin, J. A., Maccoby, E. E., Baran, K. E., & Jacklin, C. N. The sequential analysis of mother–child interaction at 18 months: A comparison of microanalytic methods. *Developmental Psychology*, 1981, 17, 146–157. (a)

Martin, J. A., Maccoby, E. E., & Jacklin, C. N. Mothers' responsiveness to interactive bidding and nonbidding in boys and girls. *Child Development*, 1981, 52, 1064–1067. (b)

Mason, W. A. Social experience in primate cognitive development. In B.-M. Burghardt & M. Bekoff (Eds.), *The development of behavior: Comparative and evolutionary aspects.* New York: Garland, 1978.

Meadow, K. P. Toward a developmental understanding of deafness. *Journal on the Rehabilitation of the Deaf*, 1968, 2, 1–18.

Meadow, K. P. The development of deaf children. In E. M. Hetherington (Ed.), *Review of child development research* (Vol. 5). Chicago: University of Chicago Press, 1975.

Palmer, T. B. The Youth Authority's community treatment project. *Federal Probation*, 1974, 38, 3–14.

Parke, R. D. Parent–infant interaction: Progress, paradigms and problems. In G. P. Sackett (Ed.), *Observing behavior* (Vol. 1): *Theory and applications in mental retardation.* Baltimore: University Park Press, 1978.

Patterson, G. R. Accelerating stimuli for two classes of coercive behaviors. *Journal of Abnormal Child Psychology*, 1977, 5, 335–350.

Patterson, G. R. Mothers: The unacknowledged victims. *Monographs of the Society for Research in Child Development,* 1981, 46(No. 5), 1–63.

Patterson, G. R. *Coercive family process.* Eugene, Ore.: Castalia Publishing, 1982.

Quinton, D., & Rutter, M. Early hospital admissions and later disturbances of behaviour: An attempted replication of Douglas' findings. *Developmental Medicine and Child Neurology,* 1976, *18,* 447–459.

Quinton, D., & Rutter, M. Family pathology and child disorder: A four year prospective study. In A. R. Nicol (Ed.), *Practical lessons from longitudinal studies.* Chichester: Wiley, 1983 (in press). (a)

Quinton, D., & Rutter, M. Parenting behaviour of mothers raised 'in care.' In A. R. Nicol (Ed.), *Practical lessons from longitudinal studies.* Chichester: Wiley, 1983 (in press). (b)

Quinton, D., Rutter, M., & Liddle, C. Institutional rearing, parenting difficulties, and marital support. *Psychological Medicine,* 1983 (in press).

Richardson, S. A. The long range consequences on malnutrition in infancy: A study of children in Jamaica, West Indies. In B. Wharton (Ed.), *Topics in paediatrics* (Vol. 2): *Nutrition in childhood.* London: Pitman Medical, 1980.

Roy, P. *Is continuity enough? Substitute care and socialization.* Paper presented at the Spring Scientific Meeting, Child and Adolescent Psychiatry Specialist Section, Royal College of Psychiatrists, London, March 1983.

Ruppenthal, G. C., Arling, G. L., Harlow, H. F., Sackett, G. P., & Suomi, S. J. A 10-year perspective of motherless–mother monkey behavior. *Journal of Abnormal Psychology,* 1976, *85,* 341–349.

Rutter, M. Sex differences in children's responses to family stress. In E. J. Anthony & C. Koupernik (Eds.), *The child in his family.* New York: Wiley, 1970. Pp. 165–196.

Rutter, M. Parent–child separation: Psychological effects on the children. *Journal of Child Psychology and Psychiatry,* 1971, *12,* 233–260.

Rutter, M. Brain damage syndromes in childhood: Concepts and findings. *Journal of Child Psychology and Psychiatry,* 1977, *18,* 1–21. (a)

Rutter, M. Prospective studies to investigate behavioral change. In J. S. Strauss, H. M. Babigian, & M. Roff (Eds.), *The origins and course of psychopathology.* New York: Plenum, 1977. (b)

Rutter, M. Family, area and school influences in the genesis of conduct disorders. In L. Hersov & M. Berger (Eds.), *Aggression and anti-social behaviour in childhood and adolescence.* Oxford: Pergamon Press, 1978.

Rutter, M. Protective factors in children's responses to stress and disadvantage. In M. W. Kent & J. E. Rolf (Eds.), *Primary prevention of psychopathology* (Vol. 3): *Social competence in children.* Hanover, N.H.: University Press of New England, 1979.

Rutter, M. Stress, coping and development: Some issues and some questions. *Journal of Child Psychology and Psychiatry,* 1981, *22,* 323–356. (a)

Rutter, M. Psychological sequelae of brain damage in childhood. *American Journal of Psychiatry,* 1981, *138,* 1533–1544. (b)

Rutter, M. *Maternal deprivation reassessed* (2nd ed.). Harmondsworth, Middlesex: Penguin Books, 1981. (c)

Rutter, M. Developmental neuropsychiatry: Concepts, issues and prospects. *Journal of Clinical Neuropsychology,* 1982, *4,* 91–115. (a)

Rutter, M. Epidemiological–longitudinal approaches to the study of development. In W. A. Collins (Ed.), *The concept of development: Minnesota Symposia on Child Psychology* (Vol. 15). Hillsdale, N.J.: Erlbaum, 1982. (b)

Rutter, M. Continuities and discontinuities in socio-emotional development: Empirical and conceptual perspectives. In R. Emde & R. Harmon (Eds.), *Continuities and discontinuities in development.* New York: Plenum, in press.

Rutter, M., Chadwick, O., & Shaffer, D. Head injury. In M. Rutter (Ed.), *Developmental neuropsychiatry.* New York: Guilford Press, in press.

Rutter, M., & Giller, H. *Juvenile delinquency: Trends and perspectives.* Harmondsworth, Middlesex: Penguin Books, 1983.

Rutter, M., Gray, G., Maughan, B., & Smith, A. *School experiences and achievements and the first year of employment.* Final Report to the Department of Education and Science, London, 1982.

Rutter, M., Maughan, B., Mortimore, P., Ouston, J., & Smith, A. *Fifteen thousand hours: Secondary schools and their effects on children.* London: Open Books, 1979. (Cambridge, Mass.: Harvard University Press, 1979).

Rutter, M., & Quinton, D. Psychiatric disorder—Ecological factors and concepts of causation. In H. McGurk (Ed.), *Ecological factors in human development.* Amsterdam: North-Holland, 1977.

Rutter, M., Quinton, D., & Liddle, C. Parenting in two generations: Looking backwards and looking forwards. In N. Madge (Ed.), *Families at risk.* London: Heinemann Educational, 1983.

Rutter, M., Yule, B., Morton, J., & Bagley, C. Children of West Indian immigrants. III. Home circumstances and family patterns. *Journal of Child Psychology and Psychiatry,* 1975, *16,* 105–123.

Sameroff, A. J., & Chandler, M. J. Reproductive risk and the continuum of caretaking casualty. In F. Horowitz (Ed.), *Review of child development research* (Vol. 4). Chicago: University of Chicago Press, 1975.

Shields, J. Genetics and mental development. In M. Rutter (Ed.), *Scientific foundations of developmental psychiatry.* London: Heinemann Medical, 1980. Pp. 8–24.

Smith, C., & Lloyd, B. Maternal behavior and perceived sex of infant: Revisited. *Child Development,* 1978, *49,* 1263–1265.

Stein, Z., Susser, M., Saenger, G., & Marolla, F. *Famine and human development.* New York: Oxford University Press, 1975.

Tennant, C., & Bebbington, P. The social causation of depression: A critique of the work of Brown and his colleagues. *Psychological Medicine,* 1978, *8,* 565–576.

Tennant, C., Bebbington, P., & Hurry, J. The short-term outcome of neurotic disorders in the community: The relation of remission to clinical factors and to 'neutralizing' life events. *British Journal of Psychiatry,* 1981, *139,* 213–220.

Thoday, J. M. Limitations to genetic comparison of populations. In G. A. Harrison & J. Peel (Eds.), *Biosocial aspects of race (Journal of Biosocial Science,* Suppl. No. 1). Oxford: Blackwell Scientific, 1969. Pp. 3–14.

Thompson, W. R., & Grusec, J. E. Studies of early experience. In P. H. Mussen (Ed.), *Carmichael's manual of child psychology.* New York: Wiley, 1970. Pp. 565–654.

Tizard, B. Varieties of residential nursery experience. In J. Tizard, I. Sinclair, & R. V. G. Clarke (Eds.), *Varieties of residential experience.* London: Routledge & Kegan Paul, 1975.

Tizard, B., & Hodges, J. The effect of early institutional rearing on the development of eight-year-old children. *Journal of Child Psychology and Psychiatry,* 1978, *19,* 99–118.

Tizard, J., Schofield, W. N., & Hewison, J. Collaboration between teachers and parents in assisting children's reading. *British Journal of Educational Psychology,* 1982, *52,* 1–15.

West, D. J. *Delinquency careers: The first fifteen years.* London: Heinemann Educational, 1982.

Whitehead, L. Sex differences in children's responses to family stress: A re-evaluation. *Journal of Child Psychology and Psychiatry,* 1979, *20,* 247–254.

Yule, W. & Lansdown, R. *The London blood lead studies.* Paper presented at the Annual Conference, British Psychological Society. York, April 1983.

18

The Stability of Change: Psychosocial Development from Adolescence to Young Adulthood[1]

RICHARD JESSOR

A fundamental challenge for conceptualizations of psychological development has been to make provision for both continuity and change (Bloom, 1964). Although often posed as an irreconcilable antinomy requiring theorists to cast their lot on one side or the other, continuity and change are best seen as two aspects of a single dialectical process. In that process—whether called psychosocial development, personal growth, or individual maturation—the occurrence of even major transformations of individuality do not preclude conservation of the past; the latter can readily be seen, for example, in the timing of the transformation, in its contours and scope, and in its meaning for the person. In short, even when psychosocial change is pervasive and radical, it tends to be neither adventitious nor arbitrary but, rather, consequential—a predictable and systematic outcome of what has gone before.

In emphasizing the stability of change, our intent in this chapter is to illuminate the continuities that accompany, underlie, or account for change. The perspective adopted is one that recognizes and makes room for sharp directional shifts and novel emergents in development while seeking also to trace the psychosocial threads that are being raveled out through time.

Although change is ineluctable, most psychological research has been framed in a way that precludes not only its analysis but, more important, its very observation. Even in the developmental literature, the study of change has

[1]This chapter is a report of research supported by NIAAA Grant No. AA03745, R. Jessor, principal investigator, and is a report from the Research Program on Problem Behavior in the Institute of Behavioral Science, University of Colorado.

321

HUMAN DEVELOPMENT:
AN INTERACTIONAL PERSPECTIVE

remained elusive, a casualty of the commitment to cross-sectional design and of the traditional foreshortening required by the laboratory experiment. Happily, there has been a reemergence of interest in naturalistic observation of life-span development and an increased reliance upon longitudinal or panel designs. These trends promise to restore the study of change—especially longer-term change over significant portions of the life trajectory—to a central place in psychosocial research.

This chapter, a report from a longitudinal study that has followed cohorts of adolescents and youths over a 12-year time period well into young adulthood, has several aims. The first is to add to the store of empirical knowledge about the magnitude and direction of psychosocial change among youth during the decade of the 1970s. Toward this end, we have plotted developmental curves for a number of personality, perceived environment, and behavior attributes; they provide descriptive information about the "natural" course of growth and change among our participants. The second aim is to show that, while such change is significant and pervasive, it is also systematic and predictable, that is, stable. Toward this end, three types of analyses are presented: stability coefficients across a 6- or 7-year time interval for the measures of a set of psychosocial attributes; prediction, across that same time interval, of *differential* change on the basis of an antecedent psychosocial profile; and prediction of variation in the timing of a major developmental transition, becoming a nonvirgin, from prior personality, perceived environment, and behavioral characteristics.

A third aim of the chapter is more general, namely, to show the usefulness of the dimension of *psychosocial conventionality–unconventionality* in accounting for the course of psychosocial development—at least for this portion of the life span, among our particular samples, over this historical period. And the final aim is also a general one, to demonstrate the value of considering *both* person and environment characteristics in any attempt to gain a grasp on the developmental process.

A Prospective Study of Problem Behavior and Psychosocial Development

An overview of the larger, longitudinal study will be helpful as context for the later analyses (for more detail, see Jessor & Jessor, in press). The research has been carried out in two separate phases, each of them longitudinal. The first phase has already been reported in a number of papers and in a recent book (Jessor & Jessor, 1977). It involved cohorts of seventh-, eighth-, and ninth-grade students, both male and female, who were followed across four annual testings from 1969 to 1972; it also involved male and female cohorts drawn from the freshman class in the college of arts and sciences of a major university who were followed for four successive years from 1970 to 1973.

In its initial phase, the research was concerned with the early and late years of adolescence and with the life tasks and transitions that mark its course. The central focus was on problem behavior, for example, marijuana involvement, excessive alcohol use, precocious sexual activity, and delinquent-type behavior, and on the role such behavior plays in the normal process of psychosocial growth and development. A major aim of the research was to test the usefulness of an explanatory framework—problem-behavior theory—that relies upon both personality and environmental concepts in accounting for variation in problem behavior in youth.

After the initial longitudinal phase was completed, 1972 for the junior high school cohorts and 1973 for the college cohorts, there was a hiatus in the research during which there was no contact with any of the participants. In 1979, the second phase of the research, the Young Adult Follow-Up Study, began. Contact with all of the participants was renewed after extensive efforts to locate their whereabouts. The seventh-, eighth-, and ninth-graders ($N = 432$) had reached the ages of 23, 24, and 25, and the college youth ($N = 205$) had reached the age of 28. Of the 634 former participants available from the initial phase (three had died in the interim), fully 596 resumed participation in the research, a follow-up retention rate of 94%. That percentage is all the more noteworthy given the total absence of contact in the intervening 6 or 7 years and the fact that renewed participation meant filling out a 65-page questionnaire that required an average time of 2.5 hr and, for many, took as long as 5 hr to complete.

Another wave of data was collected in 1981, thereby providing two data points within young adulthood to connect with the four data points yielded by the initial adolescence/early youth phase. Retention between the 1981 and the 1979 waves was 96%. Thus, the overall retention rate across all six data points and across the 12-year time span is 90%. Since much of it is still to be analyzed, the 1981 data will not be dealt with in this chapter.

In its follow-up phase, the research continued its concern with problem behavior, including their personality and environmental correlates, and with psychosocial development in general. But it also began an exploration of several new areas reflecting the life tasks of young adulthood: marriage or entering into committed relationships, childrearing, work and career, leisure interests, stable friendship networks, etc. Although each phase of the research can be seen as a separate, self-contained, longitudinal study of a stage of the life trajectory, it is when the two phases are taken together that they make possible the exploration of developmental issues of the sort this paper is concerned with. These include tracing the linkages or continuities *between* life stages, here between adolescence/youth and young adulthood; examining the predictability of young adult outcomes from antecedent information gathered in adolescence; and identifying possible adolescent "risk factors" that can signal the likelihood of problems in behavior and adjustment later on in life.

Psychosocial Change from Adolescence to Young Adulthood

The developmental span covered by the research design, from the youngest cohort aged 13 in 1969 to the oldest cohort aged 30 in 1981, is a substantial one, including nearly all of the second and third decades of life. More important, it is an age range in which personal psychosocial growth and change are known to be rapid and pervasive. In addition, it is a period within which the environmental contexts of daily life shift markedly, especially in relation to school, home, and parental involvement. Thus, the younger cohorts had moved from junior high school to senior high school during the initial phase, and most of those participants were beyond their school years and out into the world of work by the time of the second phase (ages 23–25). The freshman cohort had moved through college or had dropped out during the initial phase, and those participants were for the most part beyond further education and much involved with family roles and careers by the second phase. Finally, the historical period of the research, 1969–1981, was one by the end of which major societal change was apparent, including the damping of youthful protest, the broad accommodation to new patterns of sexual relationships and drug use, and the increased preoccupation of young people with economic well-being and societal acceptance. Given the nature of these three different arenas of change—personal, environmental, and historical—it would be reasonable to expect that change could be a predominant characteristic of the psychosocial trajectories plotted across the data points between 1969 and 1979.

In the trajectories presented here, the effort has been made to select a set

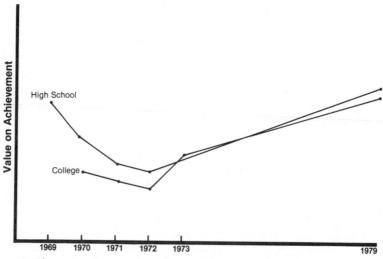

Figure 1. *Change in value on achievement over time.*

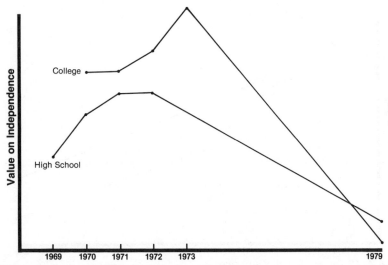

Figure 2. *Change in value on independence over time.*

that would map all three systems of problem-behavior theory: personality, the perceived environment, and behavior. The first six figures deal with value on achievement, value on independence, social criticism, alienation, tolerance of deviance, and religiosity; all are from the personality system. The next two figures deal with perceived friends' approval of drug use and perceived friends models for drug use; both are from the proximal structure of the perceived environment system. Of the next two figures, and last of this group, the one plotting deviant behavior is from the problem-behavior structure, and the one

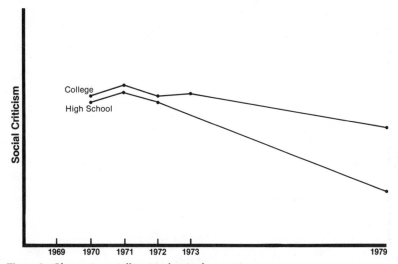

Figure 3. *Change in socially critical attitude over time.*

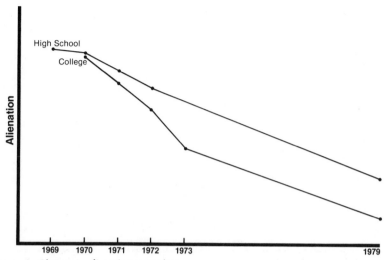

Figure 4. *Change in alienation over time.*

plotting church attendance is from the conventional-behavior structure of the behavior system. Each figure includes the curves for the high school sample and for the college sample with the sexes combined. (In general, we have found that developmental change for each sex is essentially parallel to that for the other sex within both the high school and college samples.)

Although the trajectories bear detailed consideration, especially in regard to the measures involved, the number of items in each measure, and the degree to which the measures are identical or may differ somewhat at the different points

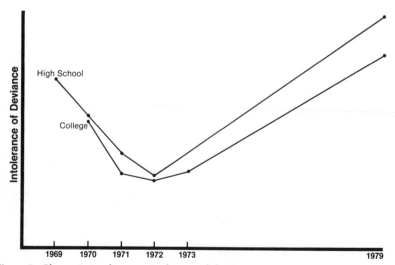

Figure 5. *Change in intolerant attitude toward deviance over time.*

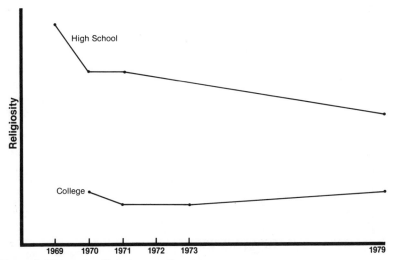

Figure 6. *Change in religiosity over time.*

of time, our purpose here will be served by taking note of the most obvious trends and by remarking on their implications within the framework of problem-behavior theory. The key concern, of course, is with the extent and direction of developmental change between adolescence/early youth, on the one hand, and young adulthood on the other, that is, between the 1972/1973 and the 1979 data points. Over that time period, the high school cohorts went from ages 16, 17, and 18 to ages 23, 24, and 25, and the college sample went from age 22 to age 28.

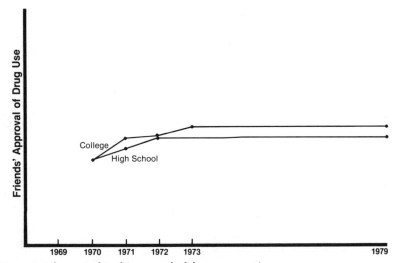

Figure 7. *Change in friends' approval of drug use over time.*

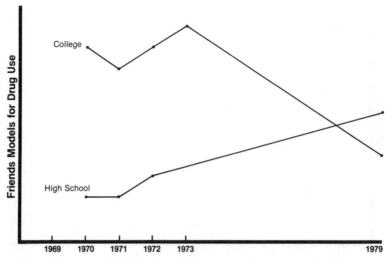

Figure 8. *Change in friends models for drug use over time.*

With respect to the personality system measures, there was an increase in value on achievement, a decrease in value on independence, a decrease in social criticism, a decrease in alienation, an increase in *in*tolerance of deviance, and a decrease (high school sample) or no change (college sample) in religiosity. Wherever change occurred across the 1972/1973 versus 1979 data points it was significant at the .001 level for both the high school and college samples, the only exception being religiosity. More important, every one of the significant changes is in the direction of conformity proneness according to problem-

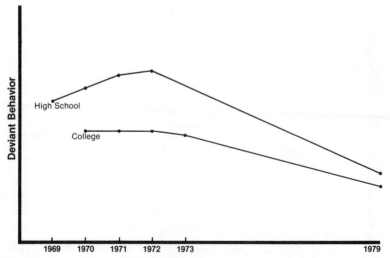

Figure 9. *Change in deviant behavior over time.*

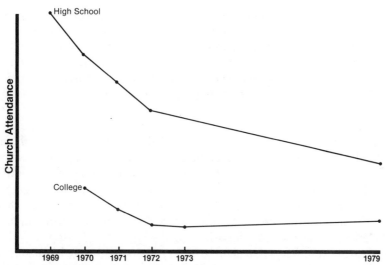

Figure 10. *Change in church attendance over time.*

behavior theory (again excepting religiosity for the high school sample). That is to say, the course of personality development across the developmental and historical interval examined is theoretically away from involvement in problem behavior and toward commitment to conventional behavior.

Most important, and in some cases striking, is that this developmental trend between 1972/1973 and 1979 is an actual *reversal* on several measures of the prior developmental trend that obtained between 1969 and 1972 for the high school and between 1970 and 1973 for the college samples. Thus, value on achievement, which was declining in the initial phase of the research, has shown an increase in the second phase; value on independence, which was increasing in the earlier phase, has now declined; and *in*tolerance of deviance, which was previously declining, has now increased beyond even its earliest and formerly highest level. Those earlier directions of change were all theoretically deviance-prone; it is that direction that has actually been reversed with development into young adulthood. The decline of social criticism and the continuing decline in alienation, although not clear reversals, buttress this evident shift toward conventionality. It is only the continuing decline in religiosity for the high school sample that is discrepant from this overall pattern of personality change (for the college youth, religiosity levels off rather than declining).

Turning to the two measures of the proximal structure of the perceived environment, we can see that perceived friends' approval of drug use has leveled off in the 1972/1973–1979 interval after consistently increasing in the prior period, and perceived friends models for drug use has decreased significantly for the college sample while continuing its increase for the high school youth. The very different trends for the two samples on this latter measure is unusual in our data; what it may reflect is a major difference in the extent of social environment shift that takes place after the college years in comparison to that after the high school years. In any event, it is only for the high school sample and only on that measure that deviance proneness can be said, theoretically, to be increasing. For the college sample, the trend on this perceived environment measure is again a reversal of the preceding trend, a phenomenon seen earlier on several of the personality measures, and the change is in the conformity-prone direction.

Change on the measure of self-reported deviant behavior shows exactly the developmental character that would be theoretically consonant with the main changes already noted for the personality and perceived environment variables. There is a significant decline in deviance between adolescence/youth and young adulthood for both samples and, especially for the high school sample, a reversal of the trend seen in the previous period. On church attendance, there is a slight nonsignificant increase for the college youth and a continuing decline (paralleling their decline on religiosity) for the high school sample.

It is clear, in summary, that significant psychosocial change has taken place between adolescence and young adulthood. Although change was not unexpected, given the life stages being dealt with and the period in history during which the data were collected, these descriptive findings add significantly to our empirical knowledge about development, at least in these cohorts. What is especially intriguing about the data is that *the main direction of change is toward greater conventionality* and away from problem-behavior proneness. This reversal of the main direction of change that was shown on these very same measures during adolescence suggests a rather strong contrast between adolescence as a deviance-prone life stage and young adulthood as a conformity-prone stage of life for these cohorts. What is also intriguing is the theoretical consonance that is evident in the developmental changes occurring in each of the three theoretical systems: personality, the perceived environment, and behavior.

Although this empirical documentation of psychosocial change over time shows it to be significant and pervasive, it is not possible to determine whether such change is an invariant function of development, a reflection of the particular historical period involved, or an interaction between cohort and development. The key purpose of documenting these group changes, beyond their intrinsic interest, is to permit the analyses of continuity and stability that follow.

The Temporal Stability of Changing Psychosocial Attributes

The degree to which there is continuity or stability in change can be observed through several different windows. The first of these involves a traditional perspective on the question of stability, the reliance upon correlations between measures of the same variable taken at two different times, that is, stability correlations. Such correlations can yield evidence that, even in the context of such overall group change as was shown earlier, the amount and direction of individual change over time are neither arbitrary nor unsystematic. They indicate the degree to which the *relative* position of individual participants on a particular measure remains invariant over time despite the change in the mean for the group as a whole. Thus, they represent one kind of stability that can be identified during the process of change, namely, the stability of individual differences. Related inquiries have been presented by Dusek and Flaherty (1981) and, for preadolescents, by Backteman and Magnusson (1981).

Stability coefficients for a set of the psychosocial variables included in problem-behavior theory are presented in Table 1. These data are relatively unique: They cover rather different birth cohorts, the high school and college samples; they involve a rather long time interval; they focus on the little-studied developmental period between adolescence and young adulthood; and they include measures of personality and of the perceived environment as well as of behavior.

The data in Table 1 are raw correlations between the 1972 or 1973 measure and the 1979 measure of each variable. Such correlations are obviously attenuated by the unreliability of the measures and are therefore conservative estimates of stability over time. Correcting for attenuation yields the correlations shown in parentheses for the multi-item scales whose internal reliability can be determined.

The overriding impression to be gained from the data in Table 1 is that there is considerable stability across time for nearly all of the measures drawn from problem-behavior theory. In nearly all cases, the correlations are statistically significant, and, in a number of instances, they are substantial in magnitude. When it is kept in mind that the time interval involved—6 or 7 years—is a very long one, that this portion of the life trajectory is considered to be one of major growth and transformation, that the environmental context of life during this period is itself likely to have changed markedly, and that the general social and historical background has also shifted, the stability represented by these correlations is even more impressive. In relation to the psychosocial change that was demonstrated at the group level in the preceding section, it is clear from these correlations that there is nevertheless considerable consistency and stability within that process of change. The position of individual practicipants relative to the distribution of scores tends to be conserved under change over time. Thus, while the general direction of psychosocial change has been toward greater conventionality, those who were initially least conventional remain less conventional as young adults and those who were initially most conventional remain more conventional relative to the rest of the participants.

There are, in addition to this key conclusion about stability, several other aspects of the data in Table 1 that are worth noting. First, the magnitude of the

Table 1
Stability Coefficients between the 1972/1973 and the 1979 Psychosocial Measures in Both the High School and College Samples—Young Adult Follow-Up Study

Measure	High school sample		College sample	
	Males (N = 172)	Females (N = 231)	Males (N = 86)	Females (N = 106)
Personality System				
Value on achievement	.08 (.12)[a]	.10* (.15)	.37**** (.54)	.31**** (.53)
Value on independence	.22*** (.59)	.23**** (.74)	.09 (.25)	.10 (.33)
Value on affection	.25**** (.42)	.22**** (.36)	.35**** (.45)	.24*** (.37)
Expectation for achievement	.24**** (.32)	.12** (.15)	.21** (.36)	.15* (.22)
Expectation for independence	.22**** (.43)	.10* (.29)	.06 (.19)	.21** (.93)
Expectation for affection	.29**** (.46)	.22**** (.32)	.34**** (.51)	.27**** (.41)
Self-esteem	.46**** (.66)	.42**** (.60)	.59**** (.80)	.46**** (.65)
Internal–external control—political	.32**** (.68)	.25**** (.46)	.30*** (.44)	.34**** (.64)
Internal–external control—general	.15** (.38)	.02 (.05)	.26*** (.55)	.37**** (.70)
Social criticism	.24**** (.47)	.29**** (.52)	.52**** (.72)	.46**** (.63)
Alienation	.37**** (.57)	.42**** (.62)	.50**** (.70)	.42**** (.58)
Tolerance of deviance	.33**** (.41)	.37**** (.47)	.42**** (.57)	.52**** (.66)
Religiosity	.53**** (.61)	.45**** (.51)	.65**** (.80)	.73**** (.89)
Sex-role attitude	—[b]	—[b]	.60**** (.77)	.36**** (.46)
Perceived Environment System				
Relative parent versus peer influence	.12* (.17)	.23**** (.32)	.31**** (.44)	.30**** (.45)
Parental approval of drug use	.20***	.27****	.43****	.32****
Friends' approval of drug use	.27****	.21****	.35****	.54****
Friends models for drug use	.28****	.20****	.44****	.42****
Behavior System				
Deviant behavior/past year	.30**** (.47)	.29**** (.45)	.33**** (.67)	.20** (.35)
Church attendance/past year	.40****	.42****	.60****	.33****

[a] Correlations in parentheses have been corrected for attenuation for those measures that are multiple-item scales for which the reliability can be ascertained.
[b] The sex-role measure was not available in 1972 for the high school sample.
*p ≤ .10.
**p ≤ .05.
***p ≤ .01.
****p ≤ .001.

stability coefficients tends to be somewhat higher for the college sample than for the high school sample, suggesting, perhaps, that there is greater stability across a later portion of the developmental trajectory than across an earlier portion (see Schuerger, Tait, & Tavernelli, 1982, for similar findings with other personality questionnaires). This finding would, of course, be consonant with most theories of individual development. Such an inference needs to be held tentatively since the two samples in the present study were drawn from quite different populations and differ on other attributes besides age. Second, stability seems greater for the major attitudinal-type variables than for the others, for example, self-esteem, social criticism, alienation, tolerance of deviance, religiosity, and sex-role orientation. Although this may be an artifact of their generally greater length and reliability as scales, it may also imply that consistency is greater for more generalized cognitive orientations. Third, it is of interest to note that in the two cases where we have direct parallels between a personality measure and a behavior measure—between religiosity and church attendance as one example, and between tolerance of deviance and deviant behavior as another—there is greater temporal stability for the *personality* measure than there is for the behavior measure. Finally, it is worth emphasizing that there is significant stability on measures from all three systems of problem-behavior theory: personality, the perceived environment, and behavior. In short, these coefficients, taken together, would seem to suggest the stability of *individuality* across a significant segment of the life span.

The Prediction of Differential Psychosocial Change

There is yet another window that provides a quite different vantage point from which to view the stability of change. Given that psychosocial change has been demonstrated for our samples as a whole over the 1972/1973–1979 time interval, and given that the individuals in those samples have maintained their relative positions to a significant degree, the question that remains is whether there has been *differential* change during that interval and, if so, whether it is systematically linked to antecedent characteristics. Insofar as a pattern of prior characteristics can be shown to be related to variation in the amount, magnitude, or rate of developmental change, there is another evidential basis for the stability of change.

Awareness of the overall shift in our longitudinal data from deviance-proneness in adolescence to conformity-proneness in young adulthood, and awareness of the popular characterizations of youth at the end of the 1970s as having become much more conventional than before, led us to ask whether the shift toward conventionality was a generalized phenomenon, or whether there are segments of youth among whom the shift is greater or more pronounced than it is in other segments. What about those adolescents or youth, for example, who were the least conventional, the most radical: Have they, at least, held on to that position, or have they, too, gotten caught up in the pendulum swing toward conventionality?

The approach we took to answering that question was to devise an Index of Conventionality to summarize the personality and perceived environment profile for each participant at the end of the initial phase of the research, 1972 for the high school sample and 1973 for the college sample. By trichotomizing that antecedent index, it was possible to establish three 1972/1973 groups in each sample: a group that was highly conventional (High); a group that was medium in conventionality (Medium); and a group that was low in conventionality, that is, our most unconventional participants (Low). It then became possible to plot the trajectories of psychosocial change between 1972/1973 and 1979 for the High, the Medium, and the Low groups separately. Different developmental trajectories for the three groups would implicate the role played by the antecedent pattern of conventionality and thus would provide support for the predictability, consistency, or stability of differential change.

Before turning to those trajectories, it is necessary to say something more about the Index of Conventionality. The index includes four measures from the personality system (social criticism, sex-role attitude [available for the college sample only], religiosity, and tolerance of deviance) and four measures from the perceived environment system (friends models for drugs, friends' approval of drugs, friends models for religion, and perceived friends' strictness). Initially, a separate, four-item Personality Conventionality Index and a separate, four-item Environmental Conventionality Index were developed. Exploration of the relation of these two indexes to a number of criterion measures showed them to have very similar patterns, and the correlation between the two indexes was better than .5 in both samples for both sexes. It seemed preferable, therefore, to combine the eight measures into a single Index of Conventionality that would map both the personality and the perceived environment domains and yield a broader, more comprehensive, and more reliable appraisal of conventionality at the end of the initial phase of the research. The Index thus represents the joint influence of personality and perceived environment aspects of conventionality, that is, the degree to which both personal dispositions and contextual supports and opportunities constitute a coherent constellation promoting conformity-proneness or controlling against deviance-proneness.

Although constructed as an index rather than a scale, the Index of Conventionality has very good psychometric properties, with alpha reliability of .74 and .76 and a nearly optimal homogeneity ratio of .29 and .29 for the high school sample and the college sample, respectively, sexes combined. There is also abundant support for the construct validity of the combined Index of Conventionality in relation to a large number of the 1972/1973 cross-sectional criterion measures and the 1979 longitudinal criterion measures.

It is possible now to turn to an examination of the relation between antecedent conventionality, as classified by the index, and variation in the course of subsequent psychosocial development. The developmental trajectories for the High, Medium, and Low conventionality groups on the measure of attitudinal tolerance of deviance are presented for the high school and college samples separately in Figure 11.

The findings apparent in Figure 11 are interesting and provide clear evidence of *differential* developmental change linked to variation in antecedent person–environment conventionality. Considering the trajectories for the high school sample first, we can see that the High conventionality group was most intolerant of deviance in 1972 (as expected, since that measure is actually a component of the index) and it has remained very intolerant to 1979; there is *no* significant developmental change for this group on this measure. By contrast, the Low conventionality group which was least *in*tolerant of deviance in 1972 *has* changed significantly by 1979, *in the direction of greater intolerance.* The same direction of significant change is true also for the Medium conventionality group. Although all three groups have retained their relative position in the distribution—as we would have expected from what was learned from the stability coefficients—the Low and Medium groups have both changed significantly and have converged on the High group, which has remained static. Exactly the same pattern can be seen for the three conventionality groups in the college sample, providing, thereby, an independent replication of this important finding. Thus, the data in Figure 11 offer evidence for another kind of stability of change: Differential developmental change has been shown to be a function of variation in the pattern of its psychosocial precursors.

Equally interesting in Figure 11 is the content of the findings. It is apparent that there is a *return* to conventionality by those youth who in 1972/1973 were the least conventional or the most radical. Rather than holding on to their unconventionality into young adulthood, they show a course of development

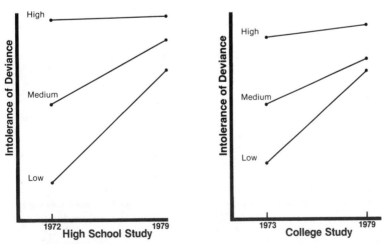

Figure 11. *Differential change in intolerant attitude toward deviance over time.*

toward the position of the High conventional group as an asymptote, and the slopes of their curves are the steepest of the three groups in each sample. It is important to emphasize what the curves in Figure 11 do *not* show. They do not show a convergence of both extreme groups—the High group and the Low group—toward the Medium group, an outcome that might have raised the possible interpretation of regression toward the mean.

Further evidence for a "return to conventionality" is apparent in Figure 12 for the measure of social criticism. In the high school sample, all three conventionality groups show a significant developmental decline on this measure, but again the rate of decline is greatest for the Low conventionality group, and all three groups have converged by 1979 in a similar position of low social criticism. In the college sample, the High conventional group does not show significant developmental change, but the other two groups, in converging upon it by 1979, do.

In Figure 13, the developmental trajectories for the three conventionality groups are presented for a perceived environment measure, friends models for drug use, and, in Figure 14, for a behavior measure, deviant behavior. With the exception of the high school sample curves on friends models for drug use, these additional data are fully consonant with those already discussed.

What has been shown in these figures is that the preexisting pattern of person-perceived environment attributes has systematic implications for the course of subsequent development. Developmental change is differential depending on the pattern of psychosocial attributes that antedates it—in this case, on the degree of conventionality.

What has also been shown is something of more general societal interest: With aging, with the assumption of new tasks and obligations, with exposure

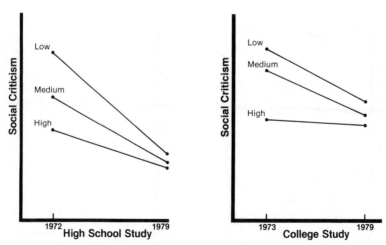

Figure 12. *Differential change in socially critical attitude over time.*

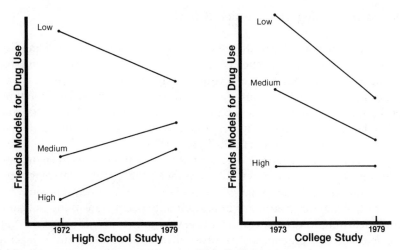

Figure 13. *Differential change in friends models for drug use over time.*

to new environmental contexts, with sociohistorical change, or with some interaction of all of these, there seems to have been a return to conventionality among youth from the late 1960s and early 1970s. Although this generalization cannot apply, of course, to all of the unconventional youths of the last decade, and although our samples may not have included the really radical youth of that period, the overall trend is clear. Even those in our samples who represented the least conventional positions as adolescents or youth seem to have become assimilated to or homogenized with those who were and who remained most conventional as they have entered into and proceeded through young adulthood.

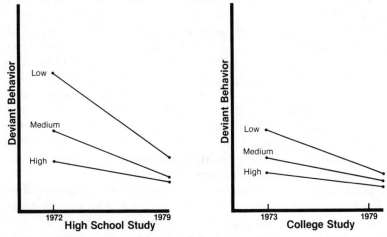

Figure 14. *Differential change in deviant behavior over time.*

Predicting the Timing of Transition Behavior

A final window on the stability of change looks toward the predictability of the emergence of certain new behaviors that serve as developmental milestones along the path from adolescence to young adulthood. Our focus, here, is on the timing of initial sexual intercourse and the degree to which variation in time of onset is signaled by an antecedent pattern of differential "readiness" for transition. Similar analyses have been carried out for the onset of drinking (Jessor & Jessor, 1975) and of marijuana use (Jessor, 1976).

In problem-behavior theory, a pattern of person and perceived environment variables is specified as theoretically deviance-prone, that is, as representing the dispositional and contextual likelihood of normative transgression. Since many of the behaviors that mark important adolescent transitions—beginning to drink, learning to drive a car, having sexual intercourse for the first time— are normatively age-graded, that is, proscribed for those who are younger and permitted or even prescribed for those who are older, the notion of deviance-proneness can be applied to the likelihood of transgressing regulatory *age* norms. Under these circumstances, the pattern of person–environment variables is interpreted as representing *transition-proneness,* the likelihood of engaging in transition-marking behavior, a key aspect of developmental change.

The availability of longitudinal data on sexual experience for our participants makes it possible to explore the predictability of the onset of nonvirginity over an extended period of time. We were able to establish, for the high school sample (the college sample will not be considered here), that there were 142 males and 204 females who were virgins as of the 1970 testing, and that 93% of them had made the transition to nonvirginity by the 1979 testing. We were also able to establish the period of time within that 9-year interval when the transition took place. On this basis, it was possible to order all of the participants along a dimension of earliness–lateness of initial sexual intercourse. Six time-of-onset groups were formed: 1970–1971 (5 males and 27 females); 1971–1972 (20 males and 43 females); 1972–1973 (40 males and 50 females); 1974–1975 (38 males and 32 females); 1976–1979 (27 males and 36 females); and finally, of course, the *no onset* group of those who were still virgins in 1979 (12 males and 16 females). These six groups varying in earliness–lateness of the onset of nonvirginity constitute the criterion measure for developmental change. To the extent that the criterion measure is predictable from the 1970 pattern of psychosocial transition-proneness *when all of these participants were still virgins,* there will be further support for the stability of change, in this case behavioral change.

The key question to be answered is whether the 1970 psychosocial predictors already vary in a systematic way that signals and is consonant with the earliness–lateness of the subsequent transition to nonvirginity. The data, although not presented here (see Jessor, Costa, Jessor, & Donovan, 1983, for details), provide considerable evidence that that is precisely the case. The earlier onset groups show theoretically greater proneness to engage in age-graded, transition-marking behavior—in this case, sexual intercourse—than the later onset groups. In several instances, for example, for the females on the independence–achievement value discrepancy, the groups are perfectly ordered in the theoretically expected direction. In other instances full ordering is not attained, but the earlier onset groups have mean scores that are theoretically more transition-prone than those of the later onset groups, or else the largest mean difference obtains between the earliest onset group and the no onset group, for example, for the males on social criticism. The F ratios are significant for a larger-than-chance number of the psychosocial predictor measures examined (12 out of 27 for the males, and 18 out of 27 for the females); in every one of those cases the directionality is as theoretically expected, and on 11 out of the 27 measures the significant F ratio is replicated across the two sexes.

The content of these findings is of special interest to summarize. Earlier onset of nonvirginity, as contrasted with later onset, is associated with transition-prone characteristics in all three of the systems of problem-behavior theory. In the personality system, these include greater value on independence, lower value on academic achievement, greater independence–achievement value discrepancy, higher expectations for independence, lower expectations for academic achievement, greater social criticism, lower intolerance of deviance, less religiosity, and greater positive-as-against-negative reasons for drug use; in the perceived environment system, less parental support, less parent–friends compatibility, greater friends-relative-to-parents influence, more parent and friends approval for problem behavior, and more friends models for problem behavior; in the behavior system, more actual involvement in other problem behaviors and less involvement in conventional behavior. This antecedent, theoretically coherent pattern of variation in overall transition-proneness *in 1970* has been shown to be consonant with the variation in time of onset of nonvirginity over the succeeding, 9-year interval.

To assess the degree to which the multivariate pattern of the 1970 psychosocial measures can account for variation in subsequent time of onset of initial intercourse, multiple regression analyses were carried out. The time-of-onset criterion was successively regressed against sets of selected measures in the various theoretical systems of problem-behavior theory. The multiple correlations for the set of personality system measures are $R = .39$ for males and .37 for females. The multiple correlations for the perceived environment measures are higher, due largely to the proximal structure measures: $R = .51$ for males and .44 for females (see Jessor, 1981). When the personality set and the perceived environment set are aggregated, there is a further increase in the multiple correlations: $R = .60$ for males and .54 for females. Thus, the 1970 personality–environment predictors, taken together, account for about a third of the variance in the timing of initial sexual intercourse over the subsequent 9-year interval. The fact that variation in the timing of such a major developmental change can be signaled by antecedent psychosocial patterns adds further conviction about the stability of change.

Conclusions

This chapter began with a focus on one of the enduring concerns of developmental theory—how to provide an account for both continuity and change. The resolution of this dilemma, it was argued, might be found by seeking the continuities within change, that is, its predictability or stability. After documenting the occurrence of significant psychosocial change between the stage of adolescence/youth and the stage of young adulthood, the attempt was made to bring to bear multiple, independent lines of evidence in support of the stability of that change. The evidence, though diverse, appears to be coherent and to illuminate the developmental continuities that obtain in the process of growth into young adulthood. Stability and change seem best considered as two aspects of a single, dialectical process. Thought of in this way, there is clearly room for major shifts, pervasive transformations, and even radical innovations in development without the requirement for a disjunction from what has gone before.

The dimension of conventionality—unconventionality emerges from these analyses as one of central importance for development during this portion of the life trajectory at least. Its relevance to the direction that developmental change has taken in these samples over this historical period is very apparent, as is its role in the prediction of differential psychosocial change and of the timing of transition behavior. Since the dimension is an elliptical summary of the variables representing transition-proneness in problem-behavior theory, its demonstrable relevance provides indirect support for the developmental formulations of that theory.

A further aspect of the formulations of problem-behavior theory that has received support in these explorations is its emphasis on *both* personality and the perceived environment as sources of variance in behavior and development. In the prediction of differential developmental change, the Index of Conventionality represented a successful composition of measures from both explanatory domains. And the joint role of person and environment predictors in forecasting the onset of nonvirginity was shown to be more successful than reliance on either set alone would have been.

Finally, the indispensable role of longitudinal design in the proper study of psychosocial development should be emphasized. Without it, the contours of change would continue to remain elusive, and the stability of change would continue to go largely unnoticed.

Acknowledgments

Preparation of this chapter would have been impossible without the ideas, the assistance, and the collegiality of my collaborators on the project: Frances Costa, John Donovan, and Lee Jessor.

References

Backteman, G., & Magnusson, D. Longitudinal stability of personality characteristics. *Journal of Personality,* 1981, *49,* 148–160.

Bloom, B. S. *Stability and change in human characteristics.* New York: Wiley, 1964.

Dusek, J. B., & Flaherty, J. F. The development of the self-concept during the adolescent years. *Monographs of the Society for Research in Child Development,* 1981, *46*(4, Serial No. 191).

Jessor, R. Predicting time of onset of marijuana use: A developmental study of high school youth. *Journal of Consulting and Clinical Psychology,* 1976, *44,* 125–134.

Jessor, R. The perceived environment in psychological theory and research. In D. Magnusson (Ed.), *Toward a psychology of situations: An interactional perspective.* Hillsdale, N. J.: Erlbaum, 1981.

Jessor, R., Costa, F., Jessor, L., & Donovan, J. E. Time of first intercourse: A prospective study. *Journal of Personality and Social Psychology,* 1983, *44,* 608–626.

Jessor, R., & Jessor, S. L. Adolescent development and the onset of drinking: A longitudinal study. *Journal of Studies on Alcohol,* 1975, *36,* 27–51.

Jessor, R., & Jessor, S. L. *Problem behavior and psychosocial development: A longitudinal study of youth.* New York: Academic Press, 1977.

Jessor, R., & Jessor, S. L. Adolescence to young adulthood: A twelve-year prospective study of problem behavior and psychosocial development. In S. A. Mednick & M. Harway (Eds.), *Longitudinal research in the United States.* New York: Praeger, in press.

Schuerger, J. M., Tait, E., & Tavernelli, M. Temporal stability of personality by questionnaire. *Journal of Personality and Social Psychology,* 1982, *43,* 176–182.

19

Childhood Environment
and Maturity of Defense
Mechanisms[1]

GEORGE E. VAILLANT

There is accumulating evidence that differences in unconscious coping styles or defenses make a major contribution to individual differences in response to stressful environmental stimuli (Vaillant, 1977). Such involuntary coping styles or ego mechanisms of defense (A. Freud, 1937) refer to largely unconscious regulatory mechanisms that allow individuals to minimize sudden changes in internal and external environments by altering how such changes are perceived.

As in the case of physiological homeostatic mechanisms, deployment of ego mechanisms of defense is largely based on processes that evolve for the most part outside of voluntary control and are as distinct from the conscious coping strategies outlined by Lazarus (1966) or Caplan (1981) as antibodies and immune mechanisms are distinct from the administration of antibiotics. In some ways defense mechanisms are the psychological counterpart to immune mechanisms. Presented with the same infectious challenge, individuals will differ greatly in their response. Due to differences in immunological competence, some individuals will die and others will not even grow ill from the same inoculation of live bacilli. Recently, however, evidence is growing that immunological competence is very sensitive to environmental change. This chapter is an effort to study the similar interaction between environment and mechanisms of defense. How susceptible are a person's characteristic mechanisms of defense to the effects of the environment?

[1]This work was supported by Research Grants K05-MH00364-01 and MH 32885-04 from the National Institute of Mental Health.

HUMAN DEVELOPMENT:
AN INTERACTIONAL PERSPECTIVE

Ego Mechanisms of Defense: A Definition

The use of ego mechanisms of defense usually alters the individual's perception of both internal and external reality, and such use often compromises other facets of cognition. Awareness of instinctual "wishes" is usually diminished; alternative, sometimes antithetical, wishes may be passionately adhered to. Ego mechanisms of defense imply integrated, dynamic psychological processes; they are not under conscious control.

Some inferred purposes of ego mechanisms of defense are (a) to keep affects within bearable limits during sudden alterations in one's emotional life (e.g., following acute object loss or during sudden awareness of heightened intimacy with or dependence upon a taboo person); (b) to restore psychological homeostasis by postponing or deflecting sudden increases in biological drives (e.g., heightened sexual awareness and aggression during adolescence); (c) to attain a time out to master changes in life image that cannot be immediately integrated (e.g., puberty, major surgery, or promotion); (d) to handle unresolved conflicts with important people living or dead from whom one cannot bear to take leave; and (e) to resolve cognitive dissonance.

In the psychosomatic literature (e.g., Hackett & Cassem, 1974), defense mechanisms are sometimes grouped together as *denial* mechanisms. For the period 1905–1926, Sigmund Freud subsumed all defense mechanisms under the umbrella term *repression*. In this chapter, however, conventional psychoanalytic nomenclature will be employed; this nomenclature recognizes a large number of differentiated ego mechanisms of defense (A. Freud, 1937). Defense mechanisms will be discussed as they are manifested in external behaviors, or via sustained modification of mental ideation. But defenses are easier to talk about than to validate consensually. Defenses cannot be directly visualized; rather, they are appreciated by their systematic distortion of those events that we can see.

This book addresses many facets of development from the perspective of person–environment interaction. Such interactions are usually viewed in a time frame that varies from a few minutes to a few months. In discussing defense mechanisms, I have chosen a time frame of three decades. My chapter on defenses may be viewed as analogous to the use of aerial photography in archeology. Much of the fine detail of person–environment interaction will not be visible, but certain telltale landmarks may become apparent that might have been obscured by closer scrutiny.

My research strategy has been dictated by the limitations inherent in harvesting multidecade prospective studies of two socially very diverse groups of men. The first of these two groups I shall identify as the College sample; it is a study of 268 gifted college men followed from age 18 until age 60 (Heath, 1946; Vaillant, 1977). The second cohort I shall identify as the Core City sample; it is a study of 456 socially and intellectually disadvantaged men followed from age 14 until age 47 (Glueck & Glueck, 1950; Vaillant &

Vaillant, 1981). I have used global childhood measures to assess individual and environmental differences in the childhoods of these men; these differences in turn have been correlated with the outcome of the men 35 years later in terms of physical health, objective mental health, delinquency, alcoholism, and defense mechanisms.

It seems clear that people who deploy "mature," "coping," or "healthy" ego mechanisms of defense are happier, age more successfully, enjoy better mental health, and achieve more gratifying personal relationships than individuals who use immature or "pathological" defense mechanisms. Previously, I have suggested (Vaillant, 1976, 1977) that relative "maturity"—rather than "pathology"—predicts which defenses lead to health and which to disease. Certainly, choice of defense mechanisms differentiates individuals in terms of the effect that deleterious environments and situations exert upon the individual. But what determines choice of defense?

This chapter will use fresh data to address a puzzling phenomenon that emerged in prior work on the College sample (Vaillant, 1977). Quality of childhood environment significantly predicted adult mental health and successful personal relationships. Maturity of adult defense mechanisms was also very highly correlated with both adult mental health and adult personal relationships. But quality of childhood environment only weakly predicted adult defense mechanisms. Did that mean that defenses reflect "person" more than "situation"?

Table 1

A Theoretical Hierarchy of Defenses and Their Individual Correlation with Objective Mental Health[a]

I. Mature defenses	
Suppression	.57
Anticipation	.34
Altruism	.10
Sublimation	.04
Humor	Not rated
II. Neurotic defenses	
Repression	.04
Reaction formation	−.13
Intellectualization	−.14
Displacement	−.16
III. Immature defenses	
Passive aggression (masochism)	−.19
Hyponchondriasis	−.23
Dissociation (neurotic denial)	−.24
Schizoid fantasy	−.28
Acting out	−.37
Projection	−.41

[a]The Adult Adjustment Scale (Vaillant, 1975) was based on objective behavioral assessment and appeared to be both a valid and a reliable measure.

Previous empirical work on the College sample suggested the hierarchy of defenses depicted in Table 1. A decade earlier, longitudinal studies by Norma Haan (1977) on the Berkeley Growth Study and, more recently, Battista (1982), using a very different sample and a cross-sectional design, arrived at very similar hierarchies. The definitions of the individual defenses are provided elsewhere (Vaillant, 1971) as is the empirical rationale for equating "maturity" of defenses with psychopathology (Vaillant, 1976).

Deployment of mature defenses was positively correlated with successful adaptations of all kinds—not just different facets of mental health but also with variables as diverse as physical health and unemployment. Deployment of immature defenses was negatively correlated with successful adaptation (e.g., warm human relationships, upward social mobility). The relative frequency with which subjects used neurotic defenses correlated with few adaptations of any kind.

Empirical Validation

Table 2 illustrates that the relative immaturity of defenses in the College sample correlated well with deterioration of physical health over the next 7 years. In addition, maturity of defenses was identified between ages 20 and 35 for those 86 men then in excellent health. Results suggested that maturity of defenses could also predict physical health over the next two decades. The implication is that how the ego deals with stressful conflictual situations affects physical as well as psychological well-being.

Could the findings be replicated in a different sample? The 456 men from the Core City sample provided an extraordinary research opportunity to cross validate findings from the College sample. The Gluecks (1950) had selected the Core City men during 1940 and 1945 in an interdisciplinary research effort to unravel juvenile delinquency. The Core City men were born between 1926 and 1932 and the mean age when their childhoods were assessed was 14 ± 2 years. In terms of IQ, ethnicity, and residence in high-crime neighborhoods, the Core

Table 2

Association of Maturity of Defenses and Subsequent Physical Health of the College Sample

	Maturity of defenses; 1940–1967 (%)		
Health in 1974	Mature (N = 25)	Intermediate (N = 39)	Immature (N = 31)
Excellent	80	67	32
Minor problems	16	18	26
Chronic illness	4	10	10
Disability	0	0	22
Dead	0	5	10

City sample had been carefully matched with 500 Boston delinquents who had been remanded to reform school. Their average IQ was 95 ± 12 and they attended the same inner city schools as delinquents. Not only were almost all of the Core City men from blue-collar homes, but 31% of their parents met the criteria for Hollingshead and Redlich's (1958) social class V (e.g., an unskilled worker living in derelict housing with nine or fewer grades of education). Only 33% of the Core City parents had attended high school.

Although there were no blacks in the study, one or more of the parents of 61% of the boys had been born in a foreign country. Thus, one of the important independent variables was the effect of different cultures on the men's adult outcomes. In actual fact, ethnicity predicted alcoholism but no other major adult outcome variable.

Forty-eight percent of the boys had been graduated from high school. Although they had been chosen for nondelinquency, 19% of the sample would later spend some time in jail and 7% would meet Robins' (1966) criteria for sociopathy. In other words, although they had been chosen as a control group for severely delinquent youth, the Core City men did not represent a particularly nondelinquent sample.

The boys, their parents, and their teachers were individually interviewed. For all first-degree relatives, public records were searched for evidence of alcoholism, criminal behavior, and mental illness. A total of 80–85% of subjects were reinterviewed at ages 25, 31, and 47. Attrition has been modest; no subject was completely lost. Nineteen subjects withdrew from the study and many data were missing for another 15; but, excluding the 30 men who died, attrition was kept at 7%. After 35 years, due to death and withdrawal, the original sample of Core City men had been reduced from 456 to 392. By age 47, the Core City men had achieved considerable upward social mobility, but upward social mobility was less and social deviance greater for those 64 men for whom our records are less complete than for the other (completely studied) 392 men.

In order for raters to determine maturity of defenses, only the most complete and clinically rich interviews could be used. These restrictions further reduced the sample to 305. When we compared these 305 men to the excluded 151, besides differences in mortality, there was significant bias in only one area. Attrition was more common among men from multiproblem families, who in youth and adult life were most antisocial and who, in adult life, were the most severely mentally ill. Premorbidly, the men rated on defenses did not differ from those not so rated in terms of IQ, ethnicity, childhood emotional problems, or environmental strengths. Since the comparisons and conclusions of this chapter are based upon comparison among the individuals remaining in the study, these limitations should not seriously prejudice the findings.

To rate defenses, raters kept blind to childhood and other adult data were given a 20- to 30-page summary of the 2-hr interview at age 47. These research interviews were semistructured and were designed to focus on difficulties in the individual's relationships, physical health, and work and to elucidate the behaviors by which the individuals had coped with these difficulties. They were recorded by notes and not tape-recorded. Numerous direct quotes were included in the interview protocols but the methodology manifested both the limitations and the advantages of journalism. Interview reports were *not* written to focus on defensive style but rather to focus upon objective behavior on which to base assessment of capacity to work and to love.

Blind raters were given uniform definitions of defenses and trained on protocols that had been rated by many others. In each of the research interviews raters were then asked to note all possible instances of defensive style. Attention was paid to concrete behaviors, to character style, and to the specific vicissitudes of the interview. Each instance of possible defense utilization was weighted equally. In rating defenses our strategy was to achieve rater reliability of maturity of defenses through redundancy rather than through absolutely reliable identification of any given example of defense.

Depending on the nature of the interviewee, 3–10 different defenses from Table 1 were noted for each individual and 10–30 instances of defensive behaviors were noted. In order to control for variation of this magnitude the following strategy was adopted to quantify maturity of defenses. Raters blind to other ratings assigned each subject 1–5 points for the tendency to deploy

Table 3

Major Use of 15 Defense Mechanisms by Core City Men at Extremes of Mental Health

	Mental health ratings (%)	
Type of defense	Low, 0–69 (N = 77)	High, 85–100 (N = 70)
I. Mature		
Anticipation	0	14
Suppression	4	61
Altruism	1	37
Sublimation	0	17
Humor	0	11
II. Neurotic		
Intellectualization	48	44
Repression	16	7
Reaction formation	7	10
Displacement	36	44
III. Immature		
Passive aggression	35	1
Hypochondriasis	18	0
Acting out	4	0
Dissociation	51	13
Projection	30	0
Schizoid fantasy	17	0

Table 4

Maturity of Defenses as a Discriminator between Other Facets of Adult Outcomes Assessed by Independent Raters

	Maturity of defenses of core city men (%)	
	Top quartile (N = 69)	Bottom quartile (N = 72)
HSRS (85–100), top quartile	71	1
Psychosocial maturity ("generative")	70	4
Income > $20,000 per year (1978)	43	7
Social adjustment,[a] top quartile	38	6
Social class I–III	75	25
HSRS (0–65), bottom quartile	0	54
5+ Symptoms of sociopathy	3	21
Unemployed 4+ years	4	44
Social adjustment, bottom quartile[a]	3	50
Never married[b]	0	22
Social class V	1	21

[a]Marital relations are excluded.

[b]In this cultural group, it is likely that many men with a well-established homosexual orientation withdrew from the study and refused reinterview.

each of the three categories of defenses: mature, neurotic, and immature. To control for variation in the total number of identified defenses, ratings (1 = lowest, 5 = highest) were based on the relative distribution of defense use among the three categories and it was required that the three 1–5 ratings sum to 8. Relative maturity of overall defensive style was then estimated by subtracting the rating for mature defenses (ratings of 1–5) from the rating for immature defenses (ratings of 1–5) producing a 9-point range. (Five was added to the final score so that all numbers were positive.) Thus, a score of 1 equaled the most mature and 9 equaled the least mature overall defensive style. Rater agreement ($r = .83$) was within acceptable limits, and, despite the subjectivity inherent in rating defenses, the ratings on only 23 men differed by more than 2 on the 9-point scale. The raters of defensive maturity were kept blind to all other ratings but undoubtedly there were some halo effects.

Table 3 confirms for the Core City sample what Table 1 suggested for the College sample. Namely, mature defenses characterized those men who received the highest mental health ratings on the highly reliable Health–Sickness Rating Scale, HSRS (Luborsky & Bachrach, 1974), and immature defenses characterized those men independently rated as psychiatrically disabled. Utilization of predominantly mature defenses also identified Core City individuals who by a wide variety of other outcome measures manifested positive mental health. The measures given in Table 4 are as diverse as earned income, social class, sociopathy (Robins, 1966), objective social adjustment, and an estimate of Eriksonian psychosocial maturity (Erikson, 1950; Vaillant & Milofsky, 1980), but all are dramatically associated with maturity of defensive style. Social adjustment was assessed in terms of relationships with family of origin, children, workmates, and friends. Table 4 also suggests that those Core City men who employed largely immature defenses were those who by external evidence met the criteria for personality disorder.

The Failure of Childhood Environment to Predict Adult Mechanisms of Defense

Longitudinal studies produce many surprises and not everything in childhood shapes our lives indefinitely. Many variables from both the College and Core City study did not predict mental health in middle life. These variables included fingernail-biting, loss of parents, breastfeeding, and age of toilet training in the College sample and parental social class and belonging to a multiproblem family in the Core City study (Vaillant & Vaillant, 1981).

The most powerful single predictor of adult mental health was the Childhood Environmental Strengths Scale (Vaillant, 1974, 1977). This 20-point scale of environmental strengths was a composite variable that reflected what went well in these men's lives as children and adolescents. It significantly predicted almost every facet of adult mental health, for example, midlife physical health, capacity to play, capacity for warm human relationships, and overall mental health. But the scale did not significantly predict maturity of defenses.

Premorbid Predictors of Maturity of Defenses

Table 5 addresses the central argument of this Chapter. Multiple regression was used to examine the relative contribution of the premorbid variables to HSRS scores and to the maturity of defenses. The hypothesis generated by the study of College men is that extrinsic situational childhood variables would be more important in affecting adult mental health but that endogenous variables would be more important in determining maturity of defenses. The two variables most significantly correlated with adult defenses were IQ (which in this socially and educationally disadvantaged population must have measured ego qualities other than simple cognitive competence) and a "feeling of adequacy." Although the amount of variance explained in Table 5 is small, and beta weights are enormously susceptible to the vagaries of variable choice and statistical distribution, the implication of Table 5 is that, if theoretically intrinsic childhood variables are controlled, then childhood environmental differences contribute little to differences in maturity of midlife defenses. Con-

Table 5

Use of Multiple Regression to Assess the Relative Importance of Childhood Variables upon Adult Mental Health and Maturity of Defenses

Childhood variables	Maturity of defenses		HSRS	
	Independent variance explained (%)	Beta weight	Independent variance explained (%)	Beta weight
Intrinsic variables (entered first)				
IQ	2.4	.12	2.6	.10
Feels adequate	3.2	.17	2.8	.14
Not restless	1.1	.11	0.6	.05
Extrinsic variables (entered second)				
Parental delinquency	2.1	−.16	1.2	−.12
Childhood environmental strengths	0.2	.03	2.4	.19
Childhood environmental weaknesses	0.0	−.07	0.5	−.09
Parental social class	0.0	.01	0.1	.04

versely, both the beta weights and the significant contribution of childhood environmental strengths to mental health—*after* all the hypothesized intrinsic variables were entered—suggest different partial etiologies for mental health and for defensive competence.

The fact that premorbid variables contributing to maturity of defenses appeared to have more to do with nature than nurture, more to do with person than with situation, may help to explain the riddle of "invulnerability" among children and why parental social class and multiproblem family membership proved such poor long-range predictors of adult outcome.

The problems in this analysis are many, and at best the findings can only be considered suggestive. Indeed, there are at least five caveats to the conclusions. First, the study's major variables are global and each confound person and situation. Second, attrition probably minimized the association between multiproblem childhood and immature adult defenses because attrition selectively excluded the most antisocial and self-destructive adults—characteristics correlated with disorganized childhoods. Third, the variables of "feeling of adequacy" and "restlessness" were chosen after the fact. By this I mean that, of over 100 variables selected and measured by the Gluecks in 1945, these two were chosen for detailed analysis only because of their observed post hoc correlation with defenses. Fourth, most of the variance of maturity of defenses is "unexplained." Last, long-term follow-up examines interactions only after the fact; experimental manipulation to "prove" causation was not possible. Microscopic analysis in more highly controlled experimental settings is necessary for real understanding.

Conclusion

In summary, the justification for sharing these data is heuristic. The study does illustrate the importance of measuring ego mechanisms of defense as independent "person" variables and illustrates many of the advantages and disadvantages of longitudinal study for studying person–situation interactions. However, if we are ever to understand what accounts for the enormous interindividual differences in maturity of defenses, far more research is needed.

References

Battista, J. R. Empirical test of Vaillant's hierarchy of ego functions. *American Journal of Psychiatry*, 1982, *139*, 356–357.

Caplan, G. Mastery of stress: Psychosocial aspects. *American Journal of Psychiatry*, 1981, *138*, 413–417.

Erikson, E. *Childhood and society*. New York: Norton, 1950.

Freud, A. *Ego mechanisms of defense*. London: Hogarth, 1937.

Glueck, S., & Glueck, E. *Unravelling juvenile delinquency*. New York: Commonwealth Fund, 1950.

Haan, N. *Coping and defending*. New York: Academic Press, 1977.

Hackett, T. P., & Cassem, N. H. Development of a quantitative rating scale to assess denial. *Journal of Psychosomatic Research*, 1974, *18*, 93–100.

Heath, C. W. *What people are*. Cambridge, Mass.: Harvard University Press, 1946.

Hollingshead, A. B., & Redlich, F. C. *Social class and mental illness*. New York: Wiley, 1958.

Lazarus, R. S. *Psychological stress and the coping process*. New York: McGraw-Hill, 1966.

Luborsky, L., & Bachrach, H. Factors influencing clinicians' judgements of mental health. *Archives of General Psychiatry*, 1974, *31*, 292–299.

Robins, L. N. *Deviant children grown up: A sociological and psychiatric study of sociopathic personality*. Baltimore, Md.: Williams & Wilkins, 1966.

Vaillant, G. E. Theoretical hierarchy of adaptive ego mechanisms. *Archives of General Psychiatry*, 1971, *24*, 107–118.

Vaillant, G. E. The natural history of male psychological health. II. Some antecedents of healthy adult adjustment. *Archives of General Psychiatry*, 1974, *31*, 15–22.

Vaillant, G. E. The natural history of male psychological health. III. Empirical dimensions of mental health. *Archives of General Psychiatry*, 1975, *32*, 420–426.

Vaillant, G. E. Natural history of male psychological health. V. The relation of choice of ego mechanisms of defense to adult adjustment. *Archives of General Psychiatry*, 1976, *33*, 535–545.

Vaillant, G. E. *Adaptation to life*. Boston, Mass.: Little, Brown, 1977.

Vaillant, G. E., Gale, L., & Milofsky, E. S. Natural history of male alcoholism. II. The relationship between different diagnostic dimensions. *Journal of Studies in Alcoholism*, 1982, *43*, 216–232.

Vaillant, G. E., & Milofsky, E. S. Natural history of male psychological health. IX. Empirical evidence for Erikson's model of the life cycle. *American Journal of Psychiatry*, 1980, *137*, 1348–1359.

20

Low School Achievement
and Aggressive Behavior in
Adolescent Boys[1]

DAN OLWEUS

It has been repeatedly demonstrated that school children (particularly boys) characterized by delinquent behavior, conduct problems, or aggression tend to be below average in educational achievement (see, e.g., Carlsson, 1972; Douglas, Ross, & Simpson, 1968; Hirschi & Hindelang, 1977; Rutter, 1974). However, relatively little precise information is available on the mechanisms implicated in this association.

If a study of the causal dynamics involved contains measures of the relevant variables at only one point in time, it is in most cases difficult to choose with some certainty between different causal hypothesis. The situation is clearly better if the study has a panel design with measures for each of the variables at two or more time points. Specifically, cross-lagged, cross-variable relationships, within the context of a structural equation model, are of particular interest in a comparison of competing causal explanations. The design of the study becomes even more attractive if potentially important causally prior variables can be included in the analyses. Addition of such variables permits exploring the possibility that obtained cross-lagged relationships are wholly or partially spurious, a consequence of common antecedents. Results from a study on 444 adolescent boys, using this design, will be reported in this chapter.

[1]The research reported in this chapter was supported by grants from the Bank of Sweden Tercentenary Foundation. Earlier phases of the research were supported by grants from the Swedish Council for Social Research and the Norwegian Research Council for Science and the Humanities.

353

HUMAN DEVELOPMENT:
AN INTERACTIONAL PERSPECTIVE

Basic Variables

An average of certain school grades in grades 6 and 9 was used as a measure of school achievement in this study. Thus, low school achievement was defined in absolute terms (see Rutter, 1974), not in terms of achievement relative to intelligence (e.g., Stattin, 1979; Svensson, 1971). It should be noted that it is mainly achievement measured in absolute terms that has been used as a prediction of later antisocial behavior and as a variable in theories of delinquency (e.g., Carlsson, 1972; Hirschi & Hindelang, 1977). Intelligence level has been found to be (negatively) related to antisocial behavior in many studies, but it is usually believed that a possible effect of intelligence on such behavior is largely indirect, via school performance (Hirschi & Hindelang, 1977). In keeping with this, the relationship of delinquency with intelligence should, by and large, be weaker than with measures of school achievement. Also, school grades in all probability change more easily than intelligence scores, which makes them better suited as a possible cause or effect in a panel design. In sum, school grades as a reflection of school achievement are a relevant variable to use in the present causal context.

Peer ratings of aggressive behavior, collected in grade 6 and 9, were employed as a measure of antisocial or conduct problem behavior in this study. As defined here, the peer ratings reflected largely negative, destructive aggression. Aggressive behavior of this kind can be considered part of a generally antisocial reaction pattern (Olweus, 1978) and has been found to predict later criminal behavior (Farrington, 1978; Magnusson, Dunér, & Stattin, in preparation; Pulkkinen, in press; Robins, 1978).

In addition to the two key variables just mentioned, data on the boys' attitudes to school and schoolwork were included in the analyses. These data had also been collected during the spring term of grades 6 and 9 through a four-item scale of an inventory. It was assumed that this variable might help increase our understanding of the mechanisms involved. Furthermore, there was information on five potentially important antecedent variables such as divorce, parents' ages, and the family's socioeconomic conditions.

Possible Hypotheses

In a panel study of school grades and aggressive behavior, measured at two time points, several competing hypotheses can be compared:

1. One view of the causal dynamics frequently expressed by researchers, school personnel, and lay people alike is roughly as follows. Poor school results, manifested in low grades, create feelings of frustration, failure, and reduced self-esteem, which in turn leads to compensatory reactions in the form of disruptiveness and aggressive behavior (and delinquency). The low achiever is a "loser in the system" and responds by becoming aggressive to peers and to

teachers who attempt to enforce the norms of the school systems. These processes are assumed to be operative in particular during the last three or four years of compulsory schooling (in grades 6 through 9) when pressures for academic achievement are gradually increasing. The formulation just described is a one-way causal hypothesis that can be schematized as follows: Poor grades at Time 1 lead to an increase in aggressive behavior at Time 2 while aggressive behavior (or characteristics associated with such behavior) at Time 1 does not influence grades at Time 2. I call this formulation the *Poor Grades–Aggression Hypothesis*.

2. The opposite hypothesis is that aggressive behavior at Time 1 leads to poor grades at Time 2 while poor grades at Time 1 do not influence aggressive behavior at Time 2. This hypothesis may be elaborated to mean that attitudes and behavior patterns associated with a high level of habitual aggression at Time 1 will gradually lead to a reduced interest in schoolwork, with poor grades as a result. Such behavior patterns may also imply a deliberate rejection of the whole school system, including work for good grades. In addition, it is possible that persistently aggressive and oppositional behavior on the part of a student may elicit a negative attitude in the teachers, who react by giving poor grades. These processes (and possibly others of the same kind) could work alone or in combination. This view is designated as the *Aggression–Poor Grades Hypothesis*.

3. A third hypothesis is that grades and aggressive behavior influence each other over time in a reciprocal way. This two-way causal hypothesis states that both kinds of processes described in the first and second hypotheses are operative. One of the causal influences may be clearly dominant over the other or they may be of approximately the same strength. This alternative is called the *Reciprocal Causation Hypothesis*.

4. A final possibility to be considered is that one or both of the cross-lagged relationships are spurious, a function of common causally prior variables. Exploration of the *Spurious Relationship Hypothesis* thus requires inclusion of potentially relevant antecedent variables in the causal model. If a previously significant cross-lagged coefficient then disappears, the relationship was spurious. If, however, one or both cross-lagged coefficients remain significant, though perhaps reduced in size, one of the first three hypotheses may be correct. But, of course, there is always the possibility that what appears to be a causal influence will turn out to be a spurious relationship, if other relevant antecedent variables were added.

In the preceding formulations, only one end of the scales—poor grades and aggressive behavior—has been used. Implied is, of course, also the opposite, that good grades lead to nonaggressive behavior, and vice versa. As far as I know, a panel analysis of the possible causal relationships between school grades and aggressive behavior has not been carried out before. This is surprising, in view of the popularity of the Poor Grades–Aggression Hypothesis.

The preceding hypotheses and associated empirical analyses are certainly of interest from the perspective of this book. Generally, the empirical results will provide information on what affects what and the magnitude of such effects, if causal influences are operative (Hypotheses 1–3). They will also give suggestions about the processes involved. From an interactional viewpoint, the third hypothesis is particularly interesting since an assumption of reciprocal causation is a key element in an interactional framework (e.g., Magnusson & Endler, 1977, p. 4). Naturally, if the empirical analyses support the Spurious Relationship Hypothesis, this would also be of considerable interest since such a result runs counter to common belief.

Methods

In evaluating the four hypotheses, two methods of panel analysis were used: cross-lagged correlation and the linear structural relationships method (LISREL V, Jöreskog & Sörbom, 1981). The latter technique, which is based on maximum likelihood estimation, permits the identification and estimation of correlations (covariances) between errors of measurement in different variables. Main emphasis will be placed on results obtained with the most sophisticated method, LISREL.

The data were also analyzed by path analysis, on raw and attenuation-corrected correlation coefficients, but this will not be reported on here. By and large, the results were fairly similar to those obtained in the LISREL analyses. I relate here only summary information on procedure, variables, and statistical analyses. A more detailed description will be published in the future.

FRAGMENTS ABOUT PROCEDURE

The *subjects* of this study were 444 boys aged 13 at Time 1 (grade 6) and 16 at Time 2 (grade 9) (Olweus, 1978). *Grades* in Swedish, Mathematics, and English and the mean grade for remaining theoretical subjects (Rest) were averaged. To avoid negative correlations, the lowest grade was given a score of 5 and the highest a score of 1. Thus, high values signify poor grades. For the LISREL analyses, two indicators were formed consisting of Swedish and English, on the one hand, and Mathematics and Rest on the other.

The extent to which the boys had *a negative attitude to school* and school-work was measured by a four-item scale, being part of a larger inventory. In the LISREL analysis, the items were grouped into two indicators.

Peer ratings were used to obtain information about the boys' levels of interpersonal *aggressive behavior*. Three seven-point scales were combined into a composite measure: Starts Fights (unprovoked physical aggression against peers), Verbal Protest (verbal aggression against teachers), and Verbal Hurt (verbal aggression against peers). In each class, four to six randomly chosen boys independently rated all boys in the class. The average of the ratings on a particular variable was used as a boy's value on that variable. Each of the three variables was employed as a separate indicator in the LISREL analyses. For more information on this rating procedure, see Olweus (1977, 1978, 1980).

In the most complete analysis, five additional variables were included. One was an average of the mother's and father's ages. Another was a composite of two measures of the family's socioeconomic status: occupational prestige (three levels) and income. High values on these variables represented young age and low social status, respectively. In the LISREL analyses, each variable in the composites was used as an indicator. The last three variables consisted of only one variable each (with an assumed reliability of 1.00): if the boy had experienced a divorce in his family (yes = 1, no = 0), if he was born out of wedlock (yes = 1, no = 0), and if he was a middle child (yes = 1, all other positions = 0). Information on the last three variables was collected from official registers.

Results

OVERVIEW OF DATA

Let us first take a look at the pattern of raw correlations for the panel variables shown in Figure 1. The associates between the three variables at grade 6 were fairly weak, varying between .195 and .266. (A correlation of .093 is significant at the 5% level.) At grade 9, the relationships had grown stronger (from .288 to .360). As with the variables for grade 6, the highest correlation was between Poor Grades and Negative Attitude to School. The stability correlations were of substantial magnitude, both for Aggressive Behavior and, in particular, Poor Grades. The stability of Negative Attitude was only moderate.

The cross-lagged correlations were in general slightly lower or of approximately the same size as the within-time (synchronous) correlations at grade 6. An exception was the correlation between Aggressive Behavior at grade 6 and Poor Grades at grade 9 (.252), which was somewhat higher than the corresponding within-time coefficient (.195). In summary, the expected within-time correlations between grades, attitude to school, and aggressive behavior showed up in the data.

CROSS-LAGGED CORRELATION

When using the cross-lagged correlation technique (see, e.g., Cook & Campbell, 1979) for inferring causal predominance, the difference between the cross-lagged correlation coefficients is of central importance. With the present

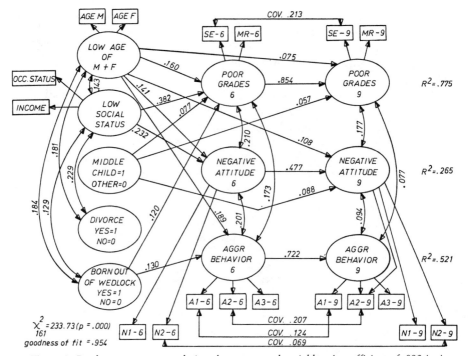

Figure 1. *Product–moment correlations between panel variables. A coefficient of .093 is significant at the .05 level (N = 444).*

data, none of the three pairs of differences was significant, although the Aggressive Behavior 6–Poor Grades 9 versus Poor Grades 6–Aggressive Behavior 9 difference approached significance ($p < .10$). With all cross-lagged coefficients significant but no significant differences between them, one might be tempted to infer that all three variables influence each other reciprocally and with about the same strength. Such a conclusion would thus be in agreement with the Reciprocal Causation Hypothesis (No. 3).

Another possibility is to conclude that the approximately equal cross-lagged correlations for each pair of variables signify the influence of a common causal factor. This would be consistent with the Spurious Relationship Hypothesis (No. 4). There are, however, serious problems with the cross-lagged correlation technique as a method of causal analysis (see, e.g., Rogosa, 1979, 1980). A better approach is to use a structural equation model such as path analysis or LISREL (Jöreskog & Sörbom, 1981). As mentioned, only LISREL analyses will be presented here.

LISREL ANALYSIS OF PANEL DATA

The capability of the LISREL technique to handle models with correlated errors is a major advantage over conventional path analysis. Another feature is that it includes a measurement model in which several fallible variables are used as indicators of a latent variable or construct. In models comprising such variables, the structural coefficients express the relationships between the latent, errorfree, rather than fallible, variables (which is similar to path analysis on attenuation-corrected correlations).

The structural equation model for two-wave panel data implies direct causal paths from each grade-6 variable on itself at grade 9 (continuity) as well as direct cross-lagged influences. With regard to the synchronous relationships, there is in the present case (as is frequent) no logical basis for assigning causal priority to one variable over the other(s). Accordingly, these relationships are left unanalyzed. They are designated by the curved, double-headed arrows in Figure 2. It should be noted that the presence of unanalyzed relationships at grade 6 does not affect the estimation of direct effects in the model.

In specifying the LISREL model, errors of measurement were allowed to correlate for identical indicators at different time points (such as Starts Fights at grade 6 and at grade 9). Parameters found to be nonsignificant (at the 5% level) were set to zero and new estimates were obtained for the modified model.

The goodness of fit index was .969 and χ^2 was 102.30 ($p < .001$) with 62 degrees of freedom. The modification indexes (Jöreskog & Sörbom, 1981) showed that additional changes in the model would lead to only minor improvements in fit.

In Figure 2 all three coefficients representing the stability of the variables over time are very significant and two are quite high, those for Poor Grades and Aggressive Behavior. Of the cross-lagged coefficients, three are significant. They are all of quite modest size.

The analysis also showed that errors of measurement were significantly correlated for four of the indicator variables. In the figure, covariances are inserted at the double-headed arrows connecting the indicators with correlated errors. In addition, the modification index showed that the second indicator of

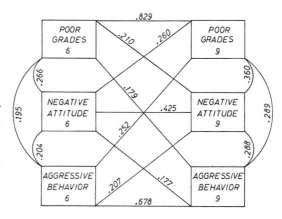

Figure 2. *LISREL analysis of panel variables (N = 444). Reported coefficients are standardized. SE, Average of Swedish and English; MR, Average of Mathematics and Rest; N1, N2, Indicators of Negative Attitude; A1, Starts Fights; A2, Verbal Protests; A3, Verbal Hurt.*

Aggressive Behavior at grade 9, Verbal Protest, had a small loading on Negative Attitude 9, and this was incorporated in the model (and shown in the figure).

The results give no support at all to the Poor Grades–Aggression Hypothesis: The coefficient from Poor Grades 6 to Aggressive Behavior 9 is zero. The small path from Aggressive Behavior 6 to Poor Grades 9 points to an influence in the opposite direction, in line with the Aggression–Poor Grades hypothesis. In addition, a negative attitude to school at grade 9 is weakly determined by Aggressive Behavior 6 as well as by Poor Grades 6. However, the major "influence" on this variable, as on the other two grade-9 variables, comes from the variable itself, measured 3 years earlier. The conclusion derived from this analysis would differ considerably from those reached with the cross-lagged correlation technique.

LISREL ANALYSIS INCLUDING ANTECEDENT VARIABLES

To test the Spurious Relationship Hypothesis, the possibility that a significant relationship is due to one or more common antecedent causes, the five demographic and familial variables were included in the analysis. In relation to the panel variables, the five additional variables were all considered as antecedents. Since there were no convincing grounds for making distinctions among the new variables in terms of causal priority, they were all given the same position in the causal sequence. Thus, the relationships between these variables were left unanalyzed. In other respects, the model was the same as that specified for the panel variables (Fig. 2).

The solution shown in Figure 3 had a χ^2 value of 233.73, $p < .001$, and the goodness of fit index was .954. Since the modification indexes showed that further modifications of the model would result in only minor changes in fit, the specified model was considered final. With the five antecedent variables added, all three cross-lagged relationships from the earlier analysis disappeared. Thus, the data are consistent with the Spurious Relationship Hypothesis. What appeared to be real, though weak, cross-lagged relationships were a function of common antecedent variables, to the extent that the previously significant relationships became nonsignificant. With the present sample size, one can conclude that if there are still non-zero, cross-lagged relationships in the population, they are so small as to be of no practical or theoretical interest.

The factors most responsible for the reduction of the cross-lagged coefficients were Social Status, Mother's and Father's Ages, and Born Out of Wedlock. The family's social status had a marked effect on Poor Grades and, to a lesser extent, on Negative Attitude 6. These effects are likely to be, in part, a reflection of class differences in intelligence. Class-related differences in parental emphasis on school achievement very probably also play a role. In agreement with previous findings (Olweus, 1978, 1980), there was no association between the family's socioeconomic conditions and the boy's level of aggressive behavior, neither in grade 6 nor in grade 9.

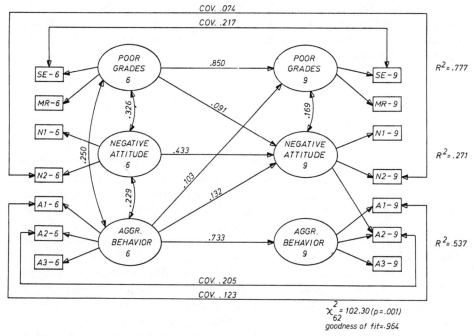

Figure 3. *LISREL analysis of background and panel variables (N = 444) using standardized coefficients. The abbreviations are defined in Figure 2.*

Some of the background variables had direct effects on the variables measured at grade 9. In the case of Being a Middle Child, there were only direct effects, on Poor Grades 9 and Negative Attitude 9. However, Mother's and Father's Ages had both direct and indirect effects on the same grade-9 variables. These effects were all fairly small.

When the cross-lagged relationships disappeared, the residual correlations between Negative Attitude 9 and Aggressive Behavior 9 and Poor Grades 9 and Aggressive Behavior 9 became significant. The size of the coefficients, however, were quite modest (.094 and .077). The corresponding correlation between Poor Grades 9 and Negative Attitude 9 (.177) was significant in the panel analysis.

The amount of variance "explained" in the grade-6 variables varied between 6.0% (Aggressive Behavior 6) and 23.5% (Poor Grades 6). The figures for the grade-9 variables were much higher: 26.5% for Negative Attitude 9, 52.1% for Aggressive Behavior 9, and 77.5% for Poor Grades 9. This increase is in large measure a reflection of the "effect" of each grade-6 variable on itself at grade 9.

The present LISREL analysis showed, in agreement with the previous panel result, that there was a small but significant loading of the second Aggressive Behavior indicator at grade 9, Verbal Protest, on the latent variable Negative

Attitude 9 (.138). This is understandable in that both can be considered to involve verbal opposition. The correlations between errors of measurement identified in the LISREL panel analysis remained very much the same in the present, more complete analysis.

Discussion

METHODOLOGICAL ASSUMPTIONS

Use of LISREL presupposes joint, multivariate normal distributions of the variables, and the relations among them should be linear and additive. These assumptions were not specifically tested in the present study, but the distributions of the panel variables were unimodal and normal, and the bivariate relations were essentially linear. A number of regression analyses failed to detect significant two-way interactions. In sum, the data showed no gross departures from assumptions.

The regression (path) coefficients of the structural equation are the same for all individuals in the sample studied. This means that the relevant set of causal variables is assumed to operate in the same way for all individuals, irrespectie of their values on the independent variables in question. This may be a false model of reality. It might be, to take an example with only one independent variable, that poor grades in the majority of cases lead to aggressive behavior, while the association of average and good grades with aggression is close to zero. For the group as a whole, then, there will be a modest positive correlation between poor grades and aggressive behavior. The regression coefficient, which is a kind of average, of course does not reveal that the relationships are distinctly different for different levels of the independent variable. Several ANCOVA analyses were performed to investigate such a possibility. The result was that there is little indication that different mechanisms are operative at different levels of the independent variable (but, if there is a trend, it would seem to implicate the effects of aggressive behavior on poor grades, and not vice versa). Actually, if the relationship between the causal and effect variables is strictly linear (above), this suggests that the causal mechanism is the same for individuals at different levels of the independent and dependent variables. However, inspection of the bivariate plot may not be a sensitive enough way of detecting moderate deviations from linearity, in particular if the correlation is relatively weak.

The preceding models imply that indirect effects of a grade-6 variable on a later variable cannot take place via another variable measured at grade 6. The presence of such indirect effects could, however, be inferred from the pattern of cross-lagged relationships. If, for instance, poor grades affected the boy's attitude to school, which in turn increased his level of aggressive behavior, one would have expected significant cross-lagged coefficients from Poor Grades 6 to both Negative Attitude 9 and Aggressive Behavior 9, and possibly also from Negative Attitude 6 to Aggressive Behavior 9. The coefficient from Poor Grades 6 to Negative Attitude 9 would presumably have been stronger than the one leading to Aggressive Behavior 9.

SUBSTANTIVE RESULTS

The empirical results from the complete LISREL analysis gave no support at all for the popular Poor Grades–Aggression Hypothesis. The less common Aggression–Poor Grades and Reciprocal Causation Hypotheses were not supported either. Rather, the cross-lagged relationships could be accounted for by the influence of a set of common antecedent factors such as Social Status, Mother's and Father's Ages, and Born Out of Wedlock.

In summary, the results were clearly in agreement with the Spurious Relationship Hypothesis. As is evident from Figure 2, the panel variables, in particular Poor Grades and Aggressive Behavior, showed considerable stability over time (see Olweus, 1977, 1979). Thus, the relative level a boy had reached on these dimensions at grade 6 tended to remain fairly constant over the 3 years from grades 6 to 9, and the changes that occurred during this period were not appreciably influenced by the other variables in the panel system.

One insight to be gained from this study is that analyses that are restricted only to panel variables may give misleading results. If the antecedent variables had not been included in the present models, the substantive conclusions would have been different, to the effect that there were several one-way cross-lagged influences in the system (Fig. 2). This insight should obviously be of interest from the perspective of an interactional framework. Thus, what appear to be one-way or reciprocal causal effects in a panel system may well turn out to be spurious relationships on closer analysis, including antecedent variables and using adequate methods of analysis.

Also, in the present study it would have been desirable to have data on other variables, such as certain childrearing dimensions that have proved to be important determinants of aggressive behavior in earlier investigations (Olweus, 1980). Data on these dimensions were available only for a subset of the subjects that will be studied in separate analyses. It would also have been of value, for example, to have direct information on the boys' levels of intelligence. (The correlation between average grade level at grade 6 and intelligence test scores is typically around .65–.70 in large Swedish samples, probably .75–.80 after correction for attenuation [Svensson, 1971].)

Looking at the grade-6 variables in Figure 3, there were positive, though fairly weak, residual correlations (.173–.210) among them. This might lead to the suggestion that poor achievement in earlier grades had a causal influence on Aggressive Behavior 6 and Negative Attitude 6. Since grades were available for grade 2 as well as grade 4 (for the majority of subjects), it was possible to get an impression of the reasonableness of this suggestion. The correlation of grade-2 grades with Aggressive Behavior 6 was $-.006$, and $.094$ with Negative Attitude 6. Corresponding figures for average grades at grade 4 were $.157$ and $.175$. The first coefficients are close to zero and the latter ones are almost certain to disappear if the grade-4 grades were to be included in a causal model. Thus, these data no more than the earlier ones supported the idea that poor grades have a causal influence on aggressive behavior or the boys' attitudes to school.

The residual correlation between Poor Grades 6 and Negative Attitude 6 is obviously a function of common antecedent factors that are not measured in the present study. It is possible that intelligence level is one such variable, but factors related to parental support of school achievement may also be involved. However, what remains to be accounted for is only a fairly weak association.

With regard to the residual associations with Aggressive Behavior 6, intelligence level is not likely to play an important role. On the basis of the pattern of paths from antecedent variables that connect Aggressive Behavior 6 with the other two grade-6 variables, it seems more plausible that childrearing factors and the quality of the parent–child relationship are implied. The separate analyses on the subgroup referred to above may provide valuable clues in this regard. Inclusion of such variables in the model will also result in a considerably higher proportion of variance explained in Aggressive Behavior 6.

The residual correlation between Poor Grades 9 and Negative Attitude 9 $(.177)$ may be due to omitted antecedent factors that operate via the grade-6 variables or, like Mother's and Father's Ages, also directly on the variables at grade 9. Furthermore, it is possible that the association is a consequence of variables that exert their effects during the period from grades 6 to 9. Analyses utilizing additional information available for a substantial portion of the subjects may be of value in this context.

The main substantive conclusion from the present study is that there was no support of the Poor Grades–Aggression Hypothesis. This popular view can thus be considered a myth, at least so far as the present Swedish data are concerned. In 1973 I maintained (Olweus, 1973; 1978, pp. 162–165), on the basis of the total pattern of largely simultaneous relationships, that there was little or no evidence for the idea that highly aggressive behavior in the form of bullying at grade 6 was a consequence of failures at school. This conclusion has now been confirmed and extended to the period from grades 6 to 9.

It should be noted that, in the present study, only one aspect of antisocial behavior (aggression) was included. Though a substantial association between aggressive behavior in school and later criminality has been reported in several investigations (e.g., Farrington, 1978; Magnusson, *et al.*, in preparation), it is possible that the relationship of poor grades to more serious antisocial behavior is somewhat different from that found for aggression. This will be explored in future analyses.

Acknowledgments

I thank Dag Sörbom and Olav Næss for assistance with the statistical analyses and data processing.

References

Carlsson, G. *Unga lagöverträdare II.* Statens offentliga utredningar 1972:76. Stockholm: 1972.
Cook, T. D., & Campbell, D. T. *Quasi-experimentation. Design and analysis issues for field settings.* Chicago: Rand McNally, 1979.
Douglas, J. W. B., Ross, J. M., & Simpson, H. R. *All our future.* London: Davies, 1968.
Farrington, D. P. The family backgrounds of aggressive youths. In L. A. Hersov, M. Berger, & D. Schaffer (Eds.), *Aggression and anti-social behavior in childhood and adolescence.* Oxford: Pergamon Press, 1978.
Hirschi, T., & Hindelang, M. J. Intelligence and delinquency: A revisionist review. *American Sociological Review,* 1977, *42,* 571–587.
Jöreskog, K. G., & Sörbom, D. LISREL V. Analysis of linear structural relationships by maximum likelihood and least squares methods. *Research reports from the department of statistics,* University of Uppsala, Sweden, No. 81-8, 1981.
Magnusson, D., Dunér, A., & Stattin, H. *Aggression and criminality in a longitudinal perspective.* Manuscript in preparation.
Magnusson, D., & Endler, N. S. Interactional psychology: Present status and future prospects. In D. Magnusson & N. Endler (Eds.), *Personality at the cross-roads: Current issues in interactional psychology.* New York: Wiley, 1977.
Olweus, D. *Hackkycklingar och översittare, Forskning om skolmobbning.* Stockholm: Almqvist & Wiksell, 1973.
Olweus, D. Aggression and peer acceptance in adolescent boys: Two short-term longitudinal studies of ratings. *Child Development,* 1977, *48,* 1301–1313.
Olweus, D. *Aggression in the schools: Bullies and whipping boys.* Washington, D.C.: Hemisphere, 1978.
Olweus, D. Stability of aggressive reaction patterns in males: A review. *Psychological Bulletin,* 1979, *86,* 852–875.
Olweus, D. Familial and temperamental determinants of aggressive behavior in adolescent boys: A causal analysis. *Developmental Psychology,* 1980, *16,* 644–660.
Pulkkinen, L. Search for alternatives to aggression in Finland. In A. P. Goldstein & M. Segall (Eds.), *Aggression in global perspective.* New York: Pergamon, in press.
Robins, L. Sturdy childhood predictors of adult antisocial behavior: Replications from longitudinal studies: *Psychological Medicine,* 1978, *8,* 611–622.
Rogosa, D. Causal models in longitudinal research: Rationale, formulation, and interpretation. In J. R. Nesselroade & P. B. Baltes (Eds.), *Longitudinal research in the study of behavior and development.* New York: Academic Press, 1979.
Rogosa, D. A critique of cross-lagged correlation. *Psychological Bulletin,* 1980, *88,* 245–258.
Rutter, M. Emotional disorder and educational underachievement. *Archives of Disease in Childhood,* 1974, *49,* 249–256.
Stattin, H. *Juvenile delinquency and changes in relative achievement: A longitudinal analysis.* Report from the Department of Psychology, University of Stockholm, No. 30, 1979 (summary in English).
Svensson, A. *Relative achievement.* Stockholm: Almqvist & Wiksell, 1971.

VI

Uses of Interactional
Perspective:
Conceptual and
Methodological Issues

In the final chapter we concentrate upon a number of implications that are associated with the interactional perspective. The implications are discussed at a programmatic level with few suggestions of concrete solutions to specific problems. Conceptual distinctions and implications, as well as methodological suggestions that can be derived from the interactional point of view, are presented. This approach provides a common frame of reference and unit of analysis for research. We compare the person-centered approach to research (consistent with the interactional perspective) with the more common variable-centered approach; we then point out some of the consequences of these contrasting strategies.

The interactional perspective has important implications for the problem of stability and consistency of behaviors, a central issue in psychology in recent years. We make the distinction between the prediction of behavior and the lawfulness of processes, and we argue that too much attention has been devoted to studying and conceptualizing the former. Temporal consistency is also discussed, along with factors determining the size of coefficients for the stability of rank orders.

The interactional approach also suggests certain directions to take in the collection and treatment of data. In particular, we emphasize the importance of systematic observation and description in real-life situations in connection with data collection. We also stress the importance of longitudinal research for understanding the lawfulness of developmental process. Similarly, we urge that time and attention be devoted to systematic conceptual analysis and empirical

HUMAN DEVELOPMENT:
AN INTERACTIONAL PERSPECTIVE

research on environments, which have not received the attention that they deserve.

Finally, we summarize an interactional view for understanding stress, maladaption, and behavioral disorders from the person–environment interaction perspective. The model posits that maladaptive behavior is a joint function of vulnerability (biological and psychological) of the individual and the strength of the environmental provocation. This model of vulnerability may help explain individual differences in stress and maladaptation. We end by offering some suggestions concerning the question of why some individuals seem not to manifest maladaptive behavior despite having lived under strongly adverse conditions as children.

21

Implications and Applications of an Interactional Perspective for Human Development

DAVID MAGNUSSON   VERNON L. ALLEN

The goal of this book has been to examine human development from the framework of person–environment interaction. We believe that the interactional perspective can serve a useful heuristic purpose by stimulating new approaches to the formulations of research problems and by offering more satisfactory theoretical interpretations of research findings in the area of human development. A number of implications and applications of the person–environment interaction approach will be discussed in this chapter.

When we analyze the implications of an interactional perspective and suggest what we believe are fruitful directions of further research on human development, it does not, of course, mean that we are critical to everything that has been done earlier or that we should abandon the methods and strategies used before. We have had too much of traveling from one ditch to the other in the history of psychology. To make progress, however, we always have to analyze the way we do things now, in order to see what we can do better.

As stated in Chapter 1, researchers with different approaches to psychological theory have agreed about the main formulations in what has been designated as an interactional perspective. However, it is an interesting and somewhat distressing fact that these theoretical formulations have very little impact on actual empirical research, though they have been stated forcefully and for a long time (Magnusson, 1983). Because the implications are far-reaching for research strategies, for models of measurement, for relevant types of data, and

HUMAN DEVELOPMENT:
AN INTERACTIONAL PERSPECTIVE

for appropriate methods of data collection, we want to draw attention to some of these implications again and emphasize their importance, though much of it has been said before.

General Implications

Before turning to some of the implications and applications, there are some general observations that deserve to be made explicit at this point.

As we said in the first chapter, the person–environment interaction process is an open system that consists of a dynamic process in which mutual influence and change are taking place continuously. Even though we conceptualize an individual's functioning during the course of development from the perspective of a total system, this does not mean that a particular research study can be expected to give attention to all the important components that comprise the system. For most investigators this would be an unrealistic condition.

Our point is that an interactional perspective forms a psychologically realistic, fruitful frame of reference for the identification and formulation of relevant and important problems to be analyzed, and for the planning and carrying through of empirical research on these specific problems. As emphasized in Chapter 1, it also serves as a common frame of reference for the interpretation of the results, thereby making possible accumulation of knowledge. Each of the chapters in this book has reported theory or empirical research dealing with particular portions of the many issues that are suggested when human development is viewed from the interactional perspective.

Another broad implication that can be derived from the interactional model concerns the importance of the relationship existing among different levels of systems in the design and interpretation of research on human development. The process of person–environment interaction is a system, as we have noted; but it must also be remembered that this system is embedded within a hierarchy of other systems, some of which are at a higher, and others at a lower, level than the person–environment interaction system itself. In designing research to answer questions about some aspect of human functioning within the person–environment interaction system, it will often be necessary to refer to factors in other systems. Long ago, Wundt realized that mental processes could only be understood by knowing more about phenomena at higher cultural and social levels, hence his 10 volumes on "Volkpsychologie" (Boring, 1950). Thus, a satisfactory interpretation of some aspect of functioning in the person–environment system may be achieved only by resorting to factors that appear in systems at other levels; for example, socially maladjusted behavior of teenagers may be explicable by information from systems at lower (biological factors) or higher (social norms of the group) levels.

The person–environment interaction perspective implies, therefore, that when studying a problem we need to know as much as possible about the degree and frequency of penetration from other systems at different levels into the system being studied. In Bronfenbrenner's (1979a) recent book, excellent examples are presented which indicate that significant influences are exerted across different levels of the ecology.

Units of Analysis

A recurring discussion throughout the history of psychology has centered around the issue of what should be used as the basic unit of analysis for purposes of theory construction and research. A variety of units have been proposed at one time or another, such as trait, sentiment, stimulus–response, instinct, and situation, among others. These units of analysis can be seen as varying along the two basic dimensions of the *kind* of unit and the *size* of unit. Many apparent disagreements concerning empirical findings and interpretation of results can be resolved to a basic disagreement among researchers about the appropriateness of the kind or size of the unit of analysis used in different investigations.

The person–environment interaction perspective has some implications about the appropriate unit of analysis that should be used in studying the psychological functioning of individuals. First of all, this approach emphasizes that the person and the environment are not separable entities, but that they form an indivisible whole—an ongoing system. As such, the appropriate unit of analysis should be neither the person (or a particular element within the person) taken alone nor the situation (or elements within it) taken alone; instead, the person-in-the-situation should be considered to be the meaningful unit for use in the description, analysis, and interpretation of various aspects of an individual's psychological functioning.

Researchers find it easy to concur with this admonition at the verbal level, but often tend to ignore its implications at the concrete level when planning and designing their empirical studies. Giving serious consideration to the implications of person–situation interaction as the basic unit of analysis would require that more careful thought be given to the nature of the environmental context within which behavior is observed, and to the development of sensitive instruments for collecting the kinds of data that will be appropriate for this unit of analysis.

A crucial feature of the person–environment interaction is that it is an ongoing process with a trajectory that extends over time, and that changes are taking place in the structure of the processes operating in the system. Applying this unit of analysis to research on developmental problems means that we must study a series or a sequence of person–environment units that are in a constant state of change as they extend across widely separated points in time. The essential unit of analysis, then, is part of a recursive process, and beginning and ending points can only be demarcated arbitrarily.

Person versus Variable Approaches to
Developmental Research

It is fair to say that psychological research has been dominated by what can be called a *variable* or dimensional approach to the study of personality and development. The goals of this approach are (*a*) to discover the important psychological dimensions required to explain individuals' behavior and (*b*) to uncover the general laws or principles that govern the relationship between those variables that have relevance to the researcher's theoretical model. It is the nature of the relationship among the variables that is the object of interest in this approach; the person, per se, is important as the means of providing measures for the variables. Since variables take on meaning only as quantitative dimensions when they are observed across individuals, this approach does not provide a representation of the complex organization that describes any particular person. Nor is the configuration of relationships for different individuals the goal of such research. Such a strong focus on variables, to the neglect of the person, led Carlsson (1971) to lament, "Where is the person in personality research?"

When assigning a label to a variable that represents a psychological dimension in terms of hypothetical constructs or intervening variables, we should be very careful about the risk of reification of the construct. The real nature of the phenomenon under observation should be kept clearly in mind at all times. There are no entities such as aggressiveness, intelligence, and paranoia that steer the person in different directions and that operate in isolation from the person as a whole. The reality is the person as a totality, who views the external world from a certain perspective and who functions as an ongoing system.

Different aspects of the individual's total functioning can be emphasized more than others at particular times. And some aspect of the person's total functioning can be labeled as a variable. But, of course, the person also displays many other characteristics at the same time as well. Simply stated, a person is not merely the sum of separate entities, and our theories should provide for the conceptualization of the person as an integrated totality.

The *person-centered* approach to research (in contrast to the variable-centered approach) takes a holistic and dynamic view; the person is conceptualized as an integrated totality rather than as a summation of variables. The goal of this approach is to gain a better understanding of specific individuals by trying to discover the distinctive configuration or pattern of organization of psychological functions that will satisfactorily characterize each person. Moreover, it must be remembered that the total pattern of factors that determine an individual's behavior is in a constant state of transition over time. By using appropriate models for the total person as a frame of reference for our research we can avoid the fragmentation and the neglect of process and organization, which is a limitation of the variable-centered approach.

The person-centered approach has the aim of understanding psychological continuity and the lawfulness of processes. Viewing the relationship among various behaviors from the perspective of the person as a system—instead of viewing the relationship among the variables only—underlines the importance of the concept of *functional equivalence* in behavior (see, e.g., Baltes, Reese, & Lipsitt, 1980; Loevinger, 1965). That is, for a particular person, it is very clear that there is a strong degree of interdependence and substitutibility among one's total repertoire of responses. Several identical behaviors may have radically different meaning to the individual because different mediating factors account for each of them. Likewise, extremely different behaviors may be produced by the same mediating factor. The person-centered approach is particularly important for the study of development because of the high degree of substitutibility, as well as interdependence, that exists among the various factors which operate within the person and which undergo transformation across age periods (see, e.g., Emmerich, 1964, 1968; Kagan, 1971; McCall 1977; Moss & Susman, 1980; Meyer, Rösler, & Probst, Chapter 14 in this volume).

To use the person-centered approach or the variable-centered approach to developmental research is more than just a theoretical problem; there are serious consequences that can be derived from them for methodology and research strategy in developmental research. Critics of the person-centered approach acknowledge that it may be appropriate for case studies of individuals, but claim that it does not permit the same degree of generalization as is possible in the variable-centered approach. But it should be stressed that the person-centered approach is not limited to being used for case studies only. On the contrary, in principle (and practice), generalizations can be made with the same degree of effectiveness when using this approach as when using the variable-centered strategy. Individuals can readily be categorized into subgroups (or sub-subgroups) on the basis of pattern similarity. By using these homogeneous subgroups of persons, comparisons can be made across different categories of persons and generalizations can be made to the appropriate population. The great advantage of the person-centered approach in this case is that generalizations refer to persons rather than to variables.

The distinctions we have discussed earlier between the variable-centered and the person-centered approaches are similar to the distinctions drawn between the idiographic and nomothetic approaches in personality research (Allport, 1937; see Lamiell, 1982, and Pervin, in press, for recent reviews of this issue). A great deal of controversy has been associated with this issue for many years. Both approaches are valuable, of course, when they are used appropriately and when attempting to answer certain kinds of research questions. Our emphasis on a holistic dynamic view does not, of course, imply that we should abandon the variable construct or stop measuring variables. Our main point is that when studying certain aspects of human functioning in terms of variables, we should keep in mind the nature of the phenomena that are of basic interest and realize that these phenomena are parts of a process taking place in an open system.

Prediction of Behavior versus Lawfulness of Processes

One of the most common concepts in psychology is the concept of "prediction of behavior." It has often been stated as the ultimate goal of psychology as a science. The formulation of this goal of psychological theorizing and research is associated with a mechanistic model of man (see p. 6). Connected with this view are the concepts of cause–effect relations, independent–dependent variable, and predictor–criterion relations. When motivated by the goal of prediction, the concern of research is often one variable at a time, in which cause and effect are studied as a one-directional relation between an independent and a dependent variable. When more than one variable is included, the relations are most often studied in terms of additive, linear effects. The development and extensive use of sophisticated multiple regression techniques for maximizing predictive power with respect to a criterion variable also reflects this tradition.

This view of psychological theorizing and research is reflected in the operationalization of psychological concepts, the choice of variables for study, the treatment of data, the interpretation of empirical results, and so forth. It has been a dominant view in most fields of psychology. The best example is the S–R tradition in experimental psychology; many examples can also be found, however, in developmental psychology. As discussed in a previous section, much of the research on stability of behavior, for example, has been concerned with the stability of single variables, which makes it possible to predict the behavior of a person from one age to another. The goal of predicting behavior seems to have been the central aim in this corpus of research.

The chapters in this volume illustrate the dynamic nature of the person–environment interaction as it is manifested across several different areas of human behavior during development. Among other consequences of the interactional perspective, the traditional distinction between dependent and independent variables becomes less unambiguous, in the sense of identifying a simple and unidirectional sequence of cause and effect for any two factors.

It is our opinion that too much weight has been placed on prediction as a goal in psychology and a strong prediction as a criterion of success. It seems sometimes that the scientific status of psychology is dependent upon its ability to predict behavior with a high degree of certainty. The better the prediction, the higher the scientific quality. An interactional view emphasizes the process character of development and leads to an interest in lawfulness and continuity of the process of person–environment interaction. In line with that view, the ultimate goal of psychological theory and empirical research is to understand and explain the *lawfulness* of the processes underlying individual functioning and the continuous change taking place in these processes during the course of development.

An emphasis on lawfulness instead of prediction is commonly accepted as a scientific approach in other disciplines; meteorology is a good example. Interestingly, the nature of meteorological phenomena bears a striking resemblance to the phenomena of concern in psychology. Weather is best described by a process model: Many factors are involved, they operate in a continuous and bidirectional interaction, and they interact in a nonlinear way. Though a great deal is known about the effective factors associated with a certain change in the weather and about the way each factor operates (i.e., about the lawfulness of the process), meteorologists cannot predict weather with a very high degree of certainty. However, this fact has not diminished their status in the scientific community.

In order to avoid misunderstanding our position, a rather self-evident point should be stressed. Of course, there is no contradiction between prediction of behavior and understanding of lawfulness of psychological processes. Obviously prediction of outcomes is an important element in the research process in which hypotheses about direct relations between single factors or combinations of factors are tested, for example, in laboratory research. What we suggest is that too much emphasis has been placed on prediction even in research where it is not motivated or is wrong. This point is particularly valid when we are interested in and investigate developmental processes over long periods of time (cf. Baltes, Reese, & Lipsitt, 1980).

Of course, an emphasis on lawfulness and continuity of behavior rather than on stability and prediction in developmental research does not mean that stability in the traditional sense of rank order stability does not exist. Expressed in coefficients for rank order stability, some variables do seem to be highly stable across time. The degree of stability of a given aspect of behavior depends upon several factors, such as (*a*) the nature of the variable being examined (physiological variables, cognitive processes, social behavior); (*b*) the types of data used to measure the variable under consideration (i.e., self-ratings, ratings by others, standardized tests, objective instruments such as measures of skin conductance, etc.); (*c*) the heterogeneity of the sample of individuals being studied; (*d*) the homogeneity and stability characterizing the environmental conditions that exist during the time period in which the behavior is observed; (*e*) the age of individuals when the data were first collected; and (*f*) the length of the time period involved in the measures of stability.

Stability Coefficients as Indicators of Temporal Consistency

The empirical basis for discussions of temporal consistency is very often coefficients that express the stability of rank orders for the specific function under consideration across time (see, e.g., Olweus, 1979, who presents a comprehensive review of research on stability of aggression, and Backteman & Magnusson, 1981, who discuss stability of person characteristics). Here we will discuss some factors associated with the environment and persons that must be considered in the interpretation of stability coefficients.

ENVIRONMENTAL FACTORS AND STABILITY COEFFICIENTS

A basic assumption in an interactional view of development is that the process of learning and maturation by which an individual acquires his way of functioning is highly influenced by the physical and social properties of that environment. The direction an individual's development takes and the changes that occur in the course of development will then depend to some extent upon the type of environment he or she encounters. These circumstances have obvious consequences for the interpretation of stability coefficients.

Given the assumption about the influence of environmental conditions on individual development, the size of coefficients for the stability of rank orders of a sample of individuals for a certain type of behavior will depend upon (a) the type of behavior and the degree to which it is influenced by environmental forces; (b) the heterogeneity of the environments across individuals; and (c) whether individuals have remained in their original environments. Therefore, stability coefficients reflect only the relative stability of rank orders of individuals for a particular behavior under certain (as a rule, rather stable) conditions. Stability coefficients cannot be interpreted as indicators of the extent to which different directions of individual development are possible or the potentialities for change in individual development due to environmental influence.

STABILITY COEFFICIENTS AND
INTERINDIVIDUAL DIFFERENCES
IN TRANSITION TO NEW STATES

In Chapter 1 we made the statement that individuals are in constant transition into new biological and psychological states. The concepts of critical periods, readiness, and optimal stimulation are important aspects of this transition process and have implications for the interpretation of growth curves that reflect individual development (see, e.g., Loevinger, 1966).

Growth curves for different biological and psychological functions differ with respect to the age of the onset, level, and general form. For the present discussion the essential fact is that there are interindividual differences in these respects, which have various methodological implications for developmental research. Implications for the interpretation of stability coefficients will be briefly discussed here (see Magnusson, 1983 for a more comprehensive discussion, and Magnusson & Stattin, 1983, for an empirical illustration).

In Figure 1 growth curves for four individuals A, B, C, and D are shown for a certain function during a critical period of development. (The growth curve for the weight of the thymus gland typically take this form, as described by Tanner, 1978.) The case assumes that the growth curves are similar for all individuals, that is, that individuals follow the same course of development

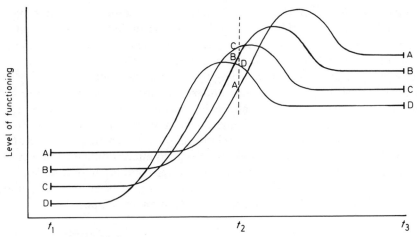

Figure 1. *Developmental curves for four individuals (A, B, C, and D) showing a certain person factor.*

during the transition period. In this sense, individual development in this case is assumed to be totally lawful and predictable. The example in Figure 1 also assumes that there are interindividual differences in the onset of the transition period and that it is inversely related to the individuals' level of functioning.

The figure clearly demonstrates the following implications for the interpretation of stability coefficients as indicators of temporal consistency in individual development.

First, though the individuals pass through the transition period in the same way, the stability coefficients may be very low and even approach zero. At age t_1 the rank order of the individuals is A, B, C, and D. At age t_2, it is C, B, D, and A. A coefficient for this function covering the time interval t_1-t_2 would certainly be interpreted by many researchers as an indication in general terms of no consistency at all in the development of this function.

Second, the size of stability coefficients depends not only on the length of the time interval and the age at the first data collection; it also depends upon where during the transition period the data are collected. Figure 1 illustrates that coefficients covering the time before and after a transition period may be higher than coefficients covering a shorter period of time, when at least one of the data collections occurs during the transition period.

Figure 1 represents one possible case. The main conclusions drawn here are equally valid also for other possible cases, for example, when one assumes that the age of onset for the transition of a certain factor is related to the final level. An example of this case can be found in studies of growth curves for height (see Garn, 1980).

The general conclusion is that stability coefficients as indicators of individual development must be interpreted with great caution. It must always be kept in mind that stability coefficients do not express anything other than *the relative stability of rank orders.* Low stability coefficients cannot be interpreted as indicators of low temporal consistency in individual development, and they cannot be used as evidence against personality constructs. What has been pointed to as limitations in the interpretation of stability coefficients, and the warnings against too far-reaching use of them without the necessary theoretical analysis of the phenomena underlying data, can be extended to hold for the use of linear regression models in general in studying individual development. For example, there is always a risk in interpreting correlation coefficients as indicators of cause–effect relationships. As a general point we want to emphasize the risk of concentration of one-sided interest on data and methods for data analyses. We have to remind ourselves continually that no sophisticated methods for data analysis can save data that have been collected without analysis of the psychological phenomena that data are supposed to represent.

Limitations of Cross-Sectional Research

The shortcomings of a cross-sectional approach to the study of individual development have been dealt with in detail by others and will not be repeated here. Only a few points that are well illustrated by the discussion and Figure 1 in the previous section will be touched upon.

Figure 1 illustrates that, in any matrix of data where a variable is under transition and where individual differences exist with respect to the onset of the critical period, part of the variance will depend on interindividual differences in this respect. The extent to which this is the case will depend upon the stage of the transition at which data are collected. Thus, the variance in a matrix of data for a function under transition will depend upon different sources, among which will be interindividual differences in the age of the onset.

The foregoing implies that all matrices of coefficients for the correlation between functions, where at least one is under transition and where interindividual differences in the age of the onset exist, will be influenced to some extent (and as a rule to an unknown extent) by interindividual differences in this respect.

These conclusions emphasize the need for exercising great caution when planning, performing, and interpreting developmental research in a cross-sectional perspective. Obviously, such research must be based on careful theoretical analysis about the functions and processes involved before the results can be interpreted in a meaningful way.

A Plea for Longitudinal Research

The discussion of the characteristics of development in the perspective of person–environment interaction in Chapter 1, and the discussion and illustration of limitations of linear regression models and of a cross-sectional approach in developmental research in the previous sections of this chapter, lead to the conclusion that we need to observe the phenomena under consideration across time for the same individuals. That is, we need more longitudinal research in order to understand important aspects of individual development (cf. McCall, 1977). Since longitudinal research has become "à la mode," it has become popular to designate even rather short-term observations by this title. For longitudinal studies to be effective, it is necessary (a) that they cover the total critical periods of development for the function(s) under consideration and (b) that observations are made so frequently during the crucial stages of development that important transitions are not missed (Magnusson & Stattin, 1983). This means in most cases that longitudinal studies must continue over rather long periods of time. This, in turn, implies the need for careful theoretical and methodological planning (see Magnusson, 1981).

PROSPECTIVE VERSUS RETROSPECTIVE APPROACHES

Access to data from longitudinal studies permits both prospective and retrospective analyses of developmental problems. Both approaches are valuable and should be used; the one cannot replace the other. Which is the more effective for the treatment of a certain problem depends, of course, on the type of problem. Sometimes the simultaneous application of both types of analyses can be fruitful.

Here it might be worth commenting upon the very common criticisms against the retrospective approach per se for studying developmental problems. The critique seems to be based on a lack of distinction between retrospective *data* and use of retrospective *analysis* of longitudinal data. (The retrospective approach to analysis means, for example, that individuals who are grouped on the basis of a certain criterion at a certain point in time are compared on measures for relevant variables referring to an earlier point in time.) Retrospective studies have seldom had access to data that were collected at the appropriate time. Instead, they tend to rely upon retrospective data, that is, data collected at the time of the analysis. Data of this type often have obvious and sometimes devastating deficiences, and the critique that can be directed against them has erroneously been directed toward the retrospective approach per se. As already stated, however, both the prospective and the retrospective approaches are effective when applied to relevant problems in an appropriate way.

Data Collection and Treatment

We made a distinction in the first chapter between the dynamic *process* occurring in person–environment interaction, on the one hand, and the *product or outcome* on the other. Data concerning products or outcomes are relatively easy to obtain and are commonly used in traditional mechanistic research. Often the pertinent responses need to be obtained only once at the end of a long sequence of behavior, and a single measure often serves as a satisfactory summary index of a large amount of interactional processes that have occurred at an earlier period of time. For example, a single measure can be used as an index of the productivity of a work team without making reference to the prior interactions (among persons and between each person and relevant situational elements) that are the determinants of the final out-come of product.

DATA TREATMENT

Many sophisticated techniques have been developed for the analyses of outcome data: analysis of variance, cluster analyses, regression analysis, multi-dimensional scaling in general, and so forth. The development of such techniques has meant much to the development of traditional research concerned with outcomes or products of prior processes.

Following the implications of an interactional perspective would, however, also lead us to be interested in studying the ongoing process itself. To follow through the methodological implications of the interactional view to the stage of treatment of data makes it clear that techniques are needed that are based on assumptions more congruent with a process model of behavior. For further progress to take place in research on development from the perspective of person–environment interaction, there is an urgent need for analytic techniques that are consistent with the assumptions of person–environment interaction as a dynamic process.

In a person approach the aim is to understand the functioning of the total individual by studying the distinctive configuration of psychological and biological functions that will characterize each person as a basis for understanding the lawful patterning of developmental change (see, e.g., Loevinger, 1965). This view leads to demands for a complement to the linear regression methods and models that are so frequently used for data treatment in a variable approach. The appropriate methods are those by which individuals can be grouped and studied on the basis of their characteristic configurations of crucial factors as a basis for generalizations. An important task for further research is the development and application of appropriate methods and models for data treatment in this perspective (see Bergman & Magnusson, 1983).

DATA COLLECTION

The basis for meaningful results in any empirical research is the kind of data that are collected, and their appropriateness to the problem under consideration. Effective methods for analysis are necessary in order to use good data efficaciously. But there are no methods for data treatment sophisticated enough to overcome the deficiencies inherent in the original data. The quality of the data determines the upper limit of the quality of the final results.

Naturally, developmental research relies on the traditional arsenal of methods for data collection available in psychology. With regard to the specific character of the person–environment interaction, we want to emphasize the importance of *systematic observations and description* in real-life situations as a relevant method for data collection. A good example of this kind of research is presented by Radke-Yarrow and Kuczynski in Chapter 3. Although methods of observation and description are commonly used in other sciences that deal with similar problems (e.g., biology, ethology), these obvious and available techniques have been relatively neglected in psychology. The lack of generalizability and the inconsistency of results of much research in psychology can be explained by the fact that it has been conducted by experiments in laboratory settings without preceding systematic observation of the phenomena under consideration in real-life situations. Systematic observation has been used more in developmental research than in other fields of psychology, but it is still not used to the limits of its potentialities in developmental research (see, e.g., Wohlwill, 1970). In this case we have much to learn from our colleagues in anthropology, astronomy, ethology, biology, and so forth.

Analysis of Environments

From what has been said in previous chapters in this book about person–environment interaction, the importance of the characteristics of the environment for development in that perspective should be clear. In order to deal with the environment in a scientific way in theorizing and in empirical research, one basic requirement is effective conceptualization, dimensionalization, and categorization of actual and perceived environments at the different levels of analysis that are operating on the environmental side in the person–environment interaction. This is needed for planning effective research on individual development and for interpreting the results of such research in a meaningful way.

Though the interest in theorizing and empirical research on the environment increased conspicuously during the 1970s, the following statement by Bronfenbrenner (1979b) well describe the present situation with respect to our knowledge about environments: "We know much more about children than about the environments in which they live or the processes through which these environments affect the course of development . . . in sum, we still lack a specific taxonomy for analyzing settings in terms of developmentally relevant parameters or for assessing development in terms of environmentally relevant outcomes [p. 844]."

It is an interesting and noteworthy fact that we lack a comprehensive system of concepts about the environment, a "scientific language" for dealing with the environment in a systematic way in theoretical analyses and empirical research on development in the person—environment perspective (Magnusson, 1982). This is the case in spite of the strong formulations about the crucial role of the environmental context for understanding human behavior that have been made for many decades (see p. 10).

Therefore, it is one of the most urgent tasks for developmental research to devote time and other resources to systematic conceptual analyses and empirical research on environments. The operating factors in both actual and perceived environments and their interrelationship at various levels of analyses must be investigated. This field of research is a promising and fruitful one, though some researchers have expressed doubts about the possibility of arriving at meaningful taxonomies of environments and situations (e.g., Block & Block, 1981; Pervin, 1981). There is a strong need for systematic analyses of environments. Moreover, it is certainly possible to analyze environments and situations in a suitable way (cf. Wohlwill, Chapter 6). As long as order and regularity exist in the physical and social environments (and in the cognitive representations of these environments in the minds of the individuals living in them), it is a scientific challenge to map these regularities and express them in relevant terms. The result of such analyses will help to promote real progress in research on human development. This is particularly true in development, as seen in the perspective of person—environment interaction. That systematic analyses of the environment implies many difficult conceptual and methodological problems should not prevent us from setting to work.

An Interactional Model of Maladaptation, Stress, and Behavioral Disorders

Of particular interest in individual development is the genesis of maladaptive reactions such as stress and anxiety reactions, criminality, mental illness, alcohol abuse, etc. An interactional view implies that maladaptive behavior is not determined by either person *or* environmental factors (whether in a contemporaneous or developmental perspective). Rather, maladaptive behavior is seen as being the joint outcome of both person and environment factors (Magnusson, 1982). The general model is illustrated in Figure 2. For a particular person the degree of maladaptive behavior is determined by the relation between his biological—psychological vulnerability to the condition at hand and the intensity of the environmental provocation.

It should be understood that the model presented in Figure 2 can be investigated in terms of a combination of a single factor from the person and a single factor from the environment, for example, the probability of alcohol abuse is the joint function of genetic propensity in the individual and easy access to alcohol in the society. Of course, in actual cases alcohol abuse is (like other

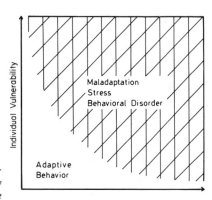

Figure 2. *Maladaptive behavior, stress, and behavioral disorders as a joint outcome of vulnerability in the individual and provocativeness in the environment.*

forms of maladaptive behavior) the joint effect of multiple factors from both the person and the environment dimensions.

The model implies that maladaptive behaviors will be learned and manifested in some proportion to the provocativeness of the environment, given similar predispositions of persons. Thus, a certain maladaptive behavior (e.g., stress reactions, crime, alcohol abuse) occurs in some situations but not in others. And even though two persons have the same predispositional vulnerability for excessive use of alcohol (learned or inherited), one of them may become an alcoholic due to encountering situations with a high degree of provocativeness for the behavior while the other person may become an abstainer because of lack of opportunity to use alcohol. The same difference among individuals may be found for other maladaptive behaviors, for example, crime or schizophrenia (Garmezy, 1976; Zubin & Spring, 1977).

The curves drawn in Figure 2 are suggestive and arbitrary. The slope of the curve reflecting the relation between personal vulnerability and environmental provocativeness that leads to maladaptive behavior is not invariant, however. Its slope will change across different variables for a given environmental condition (heat, crowding, achievement situations, etc.); it will also vary across situations for a given person variable (extreme secretion of adrenalin, strong emotional reactions). Hence, the slope of the curve will be unique for each combination of person–situation variables.

In line with our emphasis on development taken in this book, it is obvious that the person–environment system model of vulnerability will become more complex when the temporal dimension is added. From the developmental perspective, it would be expected that the slope of the curve for any combination of person variable and environmental condition would differ depending upon the age of the individual. Through the course of development the particular shape of the curve for a person will be transformed as a function of changes in the person–environment factors. For example, if the individual possesses biological characteristics that are less susceptible to environmental provocativeness as he or she becomes older, then the shape of the curve would change as indicated in the example shown in Figure 3.

From a developmental point of view, both psychological and biological vulnerability can be inherited and/or learned. Individual vulnerability can be restricted to specific types of reactions (skin or heart reactions, etc.) or be so general as to include the total organism. Environmental vulnerability can be restricted to specific situations for a person (phobic situations, for example) or include almost all types of environments. The effective environmental factors may be physical, social, cultural, or psychological and may operate independently or in conjunction with each other.

Individuals may be born with specific or general vulnerability: Thus, there are biological differences in vulnerability among individuals from the beginning. For example, empirical evidence suggests that a sex difference in vulnerability may exist as a function of stage of development (Bergman, 1981; Werner & Smith, 1982).

When dealing with the genesis and contemporaneous expression of maladaptive behavior, a crucial question arises: When an environmental factor is significantly associated with a certain kind of maladaptive behavior (e.g., poor environmental conditions and crime), how do we explain the fact that most individuals reared under such conditions do *not* show the maladaptive behavior? This brings up the interesting and important issue of individual's norms, values, and goals as moderating factors in the person—environment interaction process. Some persons who have been highly successful in society, politics, business, and science lived as children under extremely adverse conditions that are presumably conducive to a wide range of maladaptive behaviors (e.g., criminality, alcohol abuse, mental illness). A great deal of research has investi-

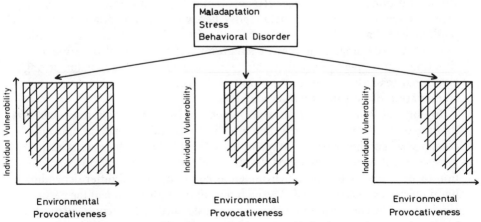

Figure 3. *An illustration of developmental changes in maladaptive reactions as a function of vulnerability in the individual and provocativeness in the environment.*

gated the factors that are associated with maladaptive behavior. More attention needs to be directed toward the systematic investigation of why most individuals from environments that are considered to be highly unfavorable nevertheless develop into well-adapted adults. Only one comment on this general issue will be offered here.

Most previous research on the relation between children's upbringing and maladaptive or antisocial behavior has investigated external factors in the home environment (i.e., socioeconomic status, parents' income and education, etc.). A negative relation is typically found between these external factors and an individual's tendency to engage in antisocial behavior. Longitudinal studies indicate that the important factors associated with maladaptive and antisocial behavior may be internal factors in the family, such as family norms, values, and social relations (see, e.g., Dunér & Magnusson, 1979; Werner & Smith, 1982). When these factors are favorable for positive development, then adverse external environmental conditions seem to have a negligible effect. The complex person–environment interaction includes the opportunity for learning norms and values, relationships among family members, and parental expectations, as well as hereditary influences and other factors. The extent to which these various factors that comprise the dynamic person–environment interaction are cause or effect, and how they operate within the total social interaction process, is still unclear. Further research on this important area is urgently needed, taking into account the fact that an individual develops in a process in which both he and his environment as one total system are under constant dynamic change.

In conclusion, the model of vulnerability for maladaptive behavior is only one illustration of the many potential applications of the person–environment interaction framework to the area of human development. Other possibilities offered by the interactional perspective have been discussed in other chapters in this book, as well as in the research and writings of many other investigators who have profitably used the model to formulate problems and interpret empirical results.

A Final Comment

Our purpose in this chapter has been to discuss the implications of an interactional perspective at a programmatic level rather than to present concrete solutions to specific problems. Each of the topics that we have discussed implies a series of methodological and strategical problems that must be solved when planning and carrying through research on well-defined, specific problems in development. In many cases this points to a need for new methods and techniques. The development of new methodologies is an important task for further research.

References

Allport, G. W. *Personality: A psychological interpretation.* New York: Holt, 1937.

Backteman, G., & Magnusson, D. Longitudinal stability of personality characteristics. *Journal of Personality,* 1981, *49,* 148–160.

Baltes, P. B., Reese, H. W., & Lipsitt, L. P. Life-span developmental psychology. *Annual Review of Psychology,* 1980, *31,* 65–110.

Bergman, L. R. Is intellectual development more vulnerable in boys than in girls? *The Journal of Genetic Psychology,* 1981, *138,* 175–181.

Bergman, L. R., & Magnusson, D. The development of patterns of maladjustment. I: Theoretical background and methodological considerations. In *Individual Development and Environment* (No. 50). Stockholm: Department of Psychology, University of Stockholm, 1983.

Block, J., & Block, J. H. Studying situational dimensions: A grand perspective and some limited empiricism. In D. Magnusson (Ed.), *Toward a psychology of situations: An interactional perspective.* Hillsdale, N.J.: Erlbaum, 1981. Pp. 85–102.

Boring, E. G. *A history of experimental psychology.* New York: Appleton, 1950.

Bronfenbrenner, U. Lewinian space and ecological substance. *Journal of Social Issues,* 1977, *33,* 199–213.

Bronfenbrenner, U. *The ecology of human development.* Cambridge, Mass.: Harvard University Press, 1979. (a)

Bronfenbrenner, U. Context of child rearing: Problems and prospects. *American Psychologist,* 1979, *34*(10), 844–850. (b)

Carlsson, R. Personality. *Annual Review of Psychology,* 1971, *26,* 393–414.

Dunér, A., & Magnusson, D. *Achievement, social adjustment and home background.* Reports from the Department of Psychology, the University of Stockholm, 1979, No. 547.

Emmerich, W. Continuity and stability in early social development. *Child Development,* 1968, *39,* 671–690.

Garmezy, N. *Vulnerable and invulnerable children: Theory, research and intervention.* Master lecture on developmental psychology. Washington, D. C.: American Psychological Association, 1976, No. 1337.

Garn, S. M. Continuities and change in maturational timing. In O. G. Brim and J. Kagan (Eds.), *Constancy and change in human development.* Cambridge, Mass.: Harvard University Press, 1980, pp. 113–162.

Kagan, J. *Change and continuity in infancy.* New York: Wiley, 1971.

Krauth, J., & Lienert, G. A. *Die Konfigurationsfrequenzanalyse und ihre Anwendung in Psychologie und Medicin.* München: Verlag Karl Alber, 1973.

Lamiell, J. T. The case for an idiothetic psychology of personality: A conceptual and empirical foundation. In B. A. Maher & W. B. Maher (Eds.), *Progress in experimental personality research* (Vol. II). New York: Academic Press, 1982.

Loevinger, J. Measurement in clinical research. In B. B. Wolman (Ed.), *Handbook of clinical psychology.* New York: McGraw-Hill, 1965.

Loevinger, J. Models and measures of developmental variation. *Annals from the New York Academy of Sciences,* 1966, *134:2,* pp. 585–590.

Magnusson, D. Some methodology and strategy problems in longitudinal research. In F. Schulzinger, S. A. Mednick, & J. Knop (Eds.), *Longitudinal research: Methods and uses in behavioral science.* Boston: Martinus Nijhoff, 1981. Pp. 192–215.

Magnusson, D. Situational determinants of stress. In L. Goldberger and S. Bresniz (Eds.), *Handbook of stress.* New York: The Free Press, 1982.

Magnusson, D. *Implications of an interactional paradigm for research on human development.* Invited address at the Seventh Biennial Meeting of ISSBD, Munich, August 1983.

Magnusson, D., & Stattin, H. *Biological age, environment, and behavior in interaction: A methodological problem.* Reports from the Department of Psychology, University of Stockholm, 1982, No. 587.

McCall, R. B. Challenges to a science of developmental psychology. *Child Development,* 1977, *48,* 333–344.

Moss, H. A., & Susman, E. J. Longitudinal study of personality development. In O. G. Brim, Jr., and J. Kagan (Eds.), *Constancy and change in human development.* Cambridge, Mass.: Harvard University Press, 1980.

Olweus, D. The stability of aggressive reaction patterns in males: A review. *Psychological Bulletin,* 1979, *86,* 852–875.

Pervin, L. A. The relations of situations to behavior. In D. Magnusson (Ed.), *Toward a psychology of situations: An interactional perspective.* Hillsdale, N. J.: Erlbaum, 1981. Pp. 343–362.

Pervin, L. Idiographic approaches to personality. In N. S. Endler & J. McV. Hunt (Eds.), *Personality and behavior disorders.* New York: Wiley, in press.

Rausch, H. L. Interaction sequences. *Journal of Personality and Social Psychology,* 1965, *2,* 487–499.

Rausch, H. L. Process and change—A model for interaction. *Family Process,* 1972, *11,* 275–298.

Tanner, J. M. *Foetus into man: Physical growth from conception to maturity.* London: Open Books, 1978.

Weiner, H. *Psychobiology and human disease.* New York: Elsevier, 1977.

Werner, E. E., & Smith, R. S. *Vulnerable but invincible: A study of resilient children.* New York: McGraw-Hill, 1982.

Wohlwill, J. F. The age variable in psychological research. *Psychological Review,* 1970, *77,* 49–64.

Zubin, J., & Spring, B. Vulnerability: A review of schizophrenia. *Journal of Abnormal Psychology,* 1977, *186,* 103–126.

Subject Index

A

Accommodation, 23, 142
Achievement
  motivation, 167, 177
  school, 353
Action, 21, 178
  additive, co-action, 296
  direct, 18
  of others, 80
Adaptation, social, 277, 288
Adolescence, 144, 160, 196, 321, 333
Adoption studies, 223, 227
Adulthood, 145, 321, 337
Affect, 64
Affordance, 80, 118
Aggression, 61, 355
Alcoholism, 225ff., 238
Analysis
  cross-fostering, 232
  of environments, 10, 381
  retrospective, 379
  of situations, 10
  systematic conceptual, 381
  units of, 371, 379
Anxiety, 37, 143, 145
Approach
  biological, 264
  cytological, 212

  environment-oriented, 5
  ideographic, 373
  interactionistic, 4, 167, 279
  nomothetic, 373
  parent–child interaction, 67, 367
  person, 372
  person-oriented, 4
  prospective, 378
  retrospective, 378
  variable, 372
Assimilation, 23, 142, 145
Attachment, 42, 50, 309
  ambivalent, 37
  anxious, 37, 137
  continuity, 44
  cross-cultural studies of, 50
  infant–mother, 35ff.
  patterns of, 35ff., 102, 137
  stability, 44
  theory, 42
Attention
  levels of, 288
  mechanisms, 154
  selective, 121

B

Behavior
  aberrant, 248

Behavior (cont'd.)
  across situations, 22
  aggressive, 353
  attachment, 63
  contemporaneous, 3
  criminal, 229ff.
  delinquent, 353
  developmental, 3
  disorder, 382
  disturbances, 246
  functional equivalence in, 373
  infant, 37
  manifest, 18, 21
  maternal, 38
  outcome contingency, 13
  patterns, 68
  person–situation, 187
  prediction of, 367, 374
  problem, 322
  self-control, 150
  study of, 149
  transition, 340, 372
  waiting, 159, 164
Biological factors, 5
  risk factors, 243
  subsystems, 21
  systems, 18
Brain injury, 296, 306

C

Central Nervous System, 263, 266
Change, 26, 138, 168ff., 188, 190, 321ff.,
    344
  of behavior, 190
  cognitive, 194
  differential, 322, 333
  environmental, 17, 49, 120
  interpersonal environment, 82
  physical, 145
  psychosocial, 324, 333
  social, 145
  in social conditions, 80
  stability of, 321
Childhood, 243, 343
Childrearing, 57ff.
  affects, 64
  direct behavioral interchanges, 61
  teaching, 64
Cognition, social, 80
Cognitive
  activity, 19

  appraisal, 190
  competence, 151
  distraction, 153
  processes, 131
  representations, 17
  styles, 196
  systems, 19
  transformations, 155
Coherence, 24
  child abuse, 67, 96
Competence, 167ff., 182
Conceptions
  of environment, 57
  self, 20
  world, 20
Conflict, 288
Consequences, outcome, 178
Consistency, 24
  of behavior, 24
  cross-situational, 25, 164
  temporal, 23, 367, 375, 377
Context
  environmental, 8, 9
  general, 12
Control, 62
  action, 14, 178
  of behavior, 142
  ego, 157
  personal, 179
  predictive, 14
  self, 150, 156
  stimulus, 150
Conventionality, 333
Coping, 19, 151, 159, 169, 187, 189, 196,
    343ff.
Cross-situational profile, 22, 24
Crowding, 117
Cyclicity, 216

D

Data collection and treatment, 375, 379, 380
Defense mechanisms, 343ff., 350
Delay of gratification, 151ff.
Denial, 344
Depression, 68, 299
Development, 172, 189
  cognitive, 116, 175, 309
  critical period of, 13, 376
  curves, 322
  emotional, 261ff.
  fetal, 214

genes and, 201ff.
  human, 3ff., 279
  individual, 3, 58, 377
  infant, 244
  life span, 5
  mental, 249
  ontogenetic, 168
  personality, 167, 272
  psychosocial, 322
Deviance, 330
  human, 221ff.
Differences
  cross-cultural, 23, 49
  cultural, 285
  individual, 149, 376
  neonatal, 47
  sex, 84, 204, 304, 384
Disorders
  behavioral, 382
  psychiatric, 297
Down's syndrome, 212, 221
Dyad
  daughter–mother, 288
  father–infant, 96
  mother–infant, 97, 269

E

Ego resiliency, 45
Emotional
  development, 261, 265
  elicitors, 263
  experiences, 263
  expression, 263
  receptors, 263
  states, 261, 263
Emotions, 17, 19, 65, 71, 141, 145, 265ff.,
    267
Endocrinology, 213
Enhancement, 12
Environment, 4, 7, 9, 23, 33, 62, 69, 75, 96,
    215, 309, 322, 391
  actual, 15, 79
  analysis of, 381
  behavior, 117
  characteristics of, 12, 117
  childhood, 343
  complexity of, 68
  components of, 9
  consistent, 14
  constraints, 150
  dimensions, 69

effective, 77
  foundations of, 12
  interpersonal, 75, 82
  macrolevel of, 9, 11, 17
  meaning of, 306
  micro-level of, 9, 11, 18
  optimal, 13
  patterned, 14
  perceived, 15, 16, 79, 190, 381
  physical, 14, 15, 111ff., 114
  psychological, 68
  rearing, 59
  selectors, 310
  social, 14, 15, 111ff., 194
  total, 10
Eugenics, 5

F

Factors
  biological, 5, 243, 253
  cognitive, 150, 187
  environmental, 6, 188, 376
  genetic, 5, 221
  hereditary, 6
  person, 7, 190
  psychological, 253
  psychosocial, 243
  situation, 7, 187, 190
Family studies, 222

G

Gaucher's disease, 204
Genes, 201ff., 213ff.
Goal, 19, 51
Goodness of fit model, 280ff.
  empirical support for, 282
Growth, 213
  curves, 376
  physical, 144

H

Helplessness, 175
Hereditary–environment issue, 5, 112
Hierarchy, 9, 370
History, developmental, 4
Holism, 372
Homeothetic process, 46
Hormones, 21
Huntington's disease, 205, 221
Hyperactivity, 89

I

Imprinting, 26, 215
Infant, 104, 119, 137
    theories of, 58
    premature, 93, 245
Inheritance, 221
Interaction, 167, 248, 255, 279, 310, 313
    additive, 299
    bidirectional, 7, 375
    child environment, 244
    concepts of, 60
    disordinal, 30
    distal, 86
    environment–development, 123
    gene–environment, 209, 221, 307
    interventions and, 189
    long term, 85
    multiplicative, 299
    ordinal, 30
    parents–infant, 60, 82, 99
    personal, 298, 309
    person–environment, 3, 7, 8, 19, 33, 50,
        57, 76, 167ff., 156, 369, 370, 374, 379
    person–situation, 12, 187
    proximal, 26
    stage–environment, 59
    statistical, 295ff., 298, 300
    synergistic, 297ff.
Interactional model of behavior, 14, 23, 37,
    382
Interactionism, 4, 7, 22, 149, 188
    conceptual and methodological, 367
    implications, 369, 370
    individual functioning and, 7
    interactional paradigm, 8
Intervention, 189, 195

L

Lawfulness, 15, 22, 52, 367, 373, 374
Learning theory
    classic, 13
    social, 13, 50, 112

M

Maladaptation, 368, 382
Maternal care, 35ff.
Model of man
    dynamic, 6
    mechanic, 6, 374

N

Nature–nurture debate, 5, 112
Neurotransmittors, 21
Niemann-Pick, 204
Nomothetic fallacy, 167

O

Observation
    direct, 61
    systematic, 367, 380
Obsessive-compulsive character, 41

R

Rank orders, stability, 367, 375
Reactions, 21
    mode of, 141
Readiness, 25, 376
    child's, 59, 77
Reciprocity, 7, 309
Reinforcement, 135, 262
Repetition compulsion, 135
Repression, 344
Research
    attachment, 50
    cross-cultural, 49, 284
    cross-sectional, 368, 378
    developmental, 3, 372, 377, 381
    longitudinal, 35, 57, 62, 123, 209, 244,
        282, 298, 322, 330, 350, 378, 385
Responsiveness, 39, 42
Rewards
    delayed, 152
    preferred, 153

S

Salience, 190
Sample heterogenity, 35
Schizophrenia, 222ff., 237
Self
    competent, 171
    esteem, 142, 146, 177
    instrumental, 171
    originating, 171
    regulation, 151, 291
    selection, 120
    unaware, 171
Situations
    actual, 11

delay, 156
  description of, 380
  face-to-face, 38
  as independent variables, 149
  momentary, 11
  new, 191, 193
  outcome-contingency, 13
  perceived, 11, 59, 188
  psychological, 163
  real life, 367, 380
  strange, 36, 66
  stressful, 196
Socialization rules, 268
Social support, 101ff.
Stability coefficient, 376, 377
States, 376
Stimulation, 26, 113, 140
  active, 13, 115
  ambient, 119
  optimal, 12, 376
  patterned, 16, 113
Stress, 13, 49, 94, 101, 143, 193, 298, 367,
    822
Support systems, 100, 103
System
  action—reaction, 8
  biological, 8, 22
  conceptual, 145

  interplay of, 22
  mediating, 8, 22
  person—environment interaction, 370
  person—situation—behavior, 187

T

TAT, 179
Tay-Sachs, 204
Temperament, 47, 60, 77, 81, 282
Theories of personality, 155ff.
Tones, affective, 19
Traits
  quantitative, 206
  threshold, 205
Transactional effects, 305
Twins
  dyzygotic, 210, 222
  monozygotic, 210, 227
  studies of, 226

V

Variables
  dependent, 7
  independent, 7, 149, 314
Vulnerability, 299, 368, 382, 383

DEVELOPMENTAL PSYCHOLOGY SERIES

Continued from page ii

GEORGE E. FORMAN. (Editor). *Action and Thought: From Sensorimotor Schemes to Symbolic Operations*

EUGENE S. GOLLIN. (Editor). *Developmental Plasticity: Behavioral and Biological Aspects of Variations in Development*

W. PATRICK DICKSON. (Editor). *Children's Oral Communication Skills*

LYNN S. LIBEN, ARTHUR H. PATTERSON, and NORA NEWCOMBE. (Editors). *Spatial Representation and Behavior across the Life Span: Theory and Application*

SARAH L. FRIEDMAN and MARIAN SIGMAN. (Editors). *Preterm Birth and Psychological Development*

HARBEN BOUTOURLINE YOUNG and LUCY RAU FERGUSON. *Puberty to Manhood in Italy and America*

RAINER H. KLUWE and HANS SPADA. (Editors). *Developmental Models of Thinking*

ROBERT L. SELMAN. *The Growth of Interpersonal Understanding: Developmental and Clinical Analyses*

BARRY GHOLSON. *The Cognitive-Developmental Basis of Human Learning: Studies in Hypothesis Testing*

TIFFANY MARTINI FIELD, SUSAN GOLDBERG, DANIEL STERN, and ANITA MILLER SOSTEK. (Editors). *High-Risk Infants and Children: Adult and Peer Interactions*

GILBERTE PIERAUT-LE BONNIEC. *The Development of Modal Reasoning: Genesis of Necessity and Possibility Notions*

JONAS LANGER. *The Origins of Logic: Six to Twelve Months*

LYNN S. LIBEN. *Deaf Children: Developmental Perspectives*